Trigonometric Functions

1. $\sin \theta = \dfrac{y}{r}$

2. $\cos \theta = \dfrac{x}{r}$

3. $\tan \theta = \dfrac{y}{x}$

4. $\cot \theta = \dfrac{x}{y}$

5. $\sec \theta = \dfrac{r}{x}$

6. $\csc \theta = \dfrac{r}{y}$

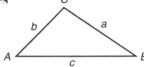

$r = \sqrt{x^2 + y^2}$

Geometric Formulas

Area

Triangle: $A = \dfrac{1}{2}bh$

Rectangle: $A = lw$

Parallelogram: $A = bh$

Trapezoid: $A = \dfrac{1}{2}h(a + b)$

Circle: $A = \pi r^2$ (Circumference: $C = \pi d = 2\pi r$)

Volume

Prism: $V = Bh$

Cylinder: $V = \pi r^2 h$

Pyramid: $V = \dfrac{1}{3}Bh$

Cone: $V = \dfrac{1}{3}\pi r^2 h$

Sphere: $V = \dfrac{4}{3}\pi r^3$

Oblique Triangles

Law of sines: $\dfrac{a}{\sin A} = \dfrac{b}{\sin B} = \dfrac{c}{\sin C}$

Law of cosines: $a^2 = b^2 + c^2 - 2bc \cos A$

$$b^2 = a^2 + c^2 - 2ac \cos B$$

$$c^2 = a^2 + b^2 - 2ab \cos C$$

Complex Numbers

$j = \sqrt{-1}, j^2 = -1, j^3 = -j, j^4 = 1, j^5 = j, \dots$

Rectangular form   *Trigonometric form*   *Exponential form*

$a + bj \quad = r(\cos \theta + j \sin \theta) = re^{j\theta}$

$r_1(\cos \theta_1 + j \sin \theta_1) \cdot r_2(\cos \theta_2 + j \sin \theta_2) = r_1 r_2[\cos (\theta_1 + \theta_2) + j \sin (\theta_1 + \theta_2)]$

$\dfrac{r_1(\cos \theta_1 + j \sin \theta_1)}{r_2(\cos \theta_2 + j \sin \theta_2)} = \dfrac{r_1}{r_2}[\cos (\theta_1 - \theta_2) + j \sin (\theta_1 - \theta_2)]$

DeMoivre's Theorem

$[r(\cos \theta + j \sin \theta)]^n = r^n(\cos n\theta + j \sin n\theta)$

TECHNICAL CALCULUS

Dale Ewen
Joan S. Gary
James E. Trefzger

Taken from:

Technical Calculus, Fifth Edition
by Dale Ewen, Joan S. Gary, and James E. Trefzger

PEARSON
Custom
Publishing

PEARSON
Prentice
Hall

Taken from:

Technical Calculus, Fifth Edition
by Dale Ewen, Joan S. Gary, and James E. Trefzger
Copyright © 2005, 2002, 1998, 1986, 1977 by Pearson Education, Inc.
Published by Prentice-Hall, Inc.
Upper Saddle River, New Jersey 07458

This special edition published in cooperation with Pearson Custom Publishing.

Printed in the United States of America

10 9 8 7 6 5 4 3 2 1

ISBN 0-536-91610-1

2005360184

EM

Please visit our web site at *www.pearsoncustom.com*

PEARSON CUSTOM PUBLISHING
75 Arlington Street, Suite 300, Boston, MA 02116
A Pearson Education Company

Contents

APPENDIX C

Using a Graphing Calculator 225

Answers to Odd-Numbered Exercises and Chapter Reviews 261

Index 273

1
Methods
of Integration

INTRODUCTION

We studied several applications of the integral of a function. We are now ready to learn more sophisticated methods of integration so that we may solve a wider variety of problems.

Objectives

- Integrate products and quotients of algebraic and exponential functions.
- Integrate expressions that are derivatives of logarithmic functions.
- Integrate trigonometric functions.
- Integrate expressions that are derivatives of inverse trigonometric functions.
- Use the partial fraction technique to express a fraction as the sum of two or more simpler fractions.
- Use the method of integration by parts.
- Use the method of integration by trigonometric substitution.
- Use tables to find integrals.
- Use the trapezoidal rule and Simpson's rule to approximate definite integrals.
- Find the area of a region defined with polar coordinates.
- Evaluate improper integrals.

1.1 THE GENERAL POWER FORMULA

In this chapter we develop techniques that can be used to integrate more complicated functions. The first technique is based on the use of the general power formula.

$$\int u^n \, du = \frac{u^{n+1}}{n+1} + C \qquad (n \neq -1)$$

This formula can be effectively used to integrate numerous functions involving either transcendental or algebraic functions. The effective use of this formula depends on the proper choice of u and du.

1

EXAMPLE 1

Integrate $\int \sin^5 2x \cos 2x \, dx$.

If we choose $u = \sin 2x$, then $du = 2 \cos 2x \, dx$. We can then apply the general power formula with $n = 5$.

$$\int \sin^5 2x \cos 2x \, dx = \int u^5 \frac{du}{2}$$

$$= \frac{1}{2} \int u^5 \, du$$

$$= \frac{1}{2} \cdot \frac{u^6}{6} + C$$

$$= \frac{1}{12} \sin^6 2x + C$$

$\boxed{\begin{aligned} u &= \sin 2x \\ du &= 2 \cos 2x \, dx \\ n &= 5 \end{aligned}}$

EXAMPLE 2

Integrate $\int e^{3x}(2 - e^{3x})^4 \, dx$.

$$\int e^{3x}(2 - e^{3x})^4 \, dx = \int u^4 \left(-\frac{du}{3} \right)$$

$$= -\frac{1}{3} \int u^4 \, du$$

$$= -\frac{1}{3} \cdot \frac{u^5}{5} + C$$

$$= -\frac{1}{15}(2 - e^{3x})^5 + C$$

$\boxed{\begin{aligned} u &= 2 - e^{3x} \\ du &= -3e^{3x} \, dx \\ n &= 4 \end{aligned}}$

EXAMPLE 3

Integrate $\int \dfrac{\sec^2 x \, dx}{\sqrt{4 + \tan x}}$.

$$\int \frac{\sec^2 x \, dx}{\sqrt{4 + \tan x}} = \int (4 + \tan x)^{-1/2} \sec^2 x \, dx$$

$$= \int u^{-1/2} \, du$$

$$= \frac{u^{1/2}}{\frac{1}{2}} + C$$

$$= 2\sqrt{4 + \tan x} + C$$

$\boxed{\begin{aligned} u &= 4 + \tan x \\ du &= \sec^2 x \, dx \\ n &= -\frac{1}{2} \end{aligned}}$

EXAMPLE 4

Evaluate $\int_1^e \dfrac{\ln x}{x} \, dx$.

$$\int \frac{\ln x}{x} \, dx = \int u \, du$$

$$= \frac{u^2}{2} + C$$

$$= \frac{1}{2} \ln^2 x + C$$

$\boxed{\begin{aligned} u &= \ln x \\ du &= \frac{1}{x} \, dx \\ n &= 1 \end{aligned}}$

So

$$\int_1^e \frac{\ln x}{x}\,dx = \frac{1}{2}\ln^2 x \,\Big|_1^e = \frac{1}{2}\ln^2 e - \frac{1}{2}\ln^2 1 = \frac{1}{2}(1)^2 - \frac{1}{2}(0)^2 = \frac{1}{2}$$

An appropriate change in the form of the integral is needed to integrate some functions. In Example 5 we need to multiply the function $\dfrac{\tan x}{\sec^3 x}$ by 1 in the form $\dfrac{\sec x}{\sec x}$.

EXAMPLE 5

Integrate $\displaystyle\int \frac{\tan x}{\sec^3 x}\,dx.$

$$\int \frac{\tan x}{\sec^3 x}\,dx = \int \left(\frac{\sec x}{\sec x}\right)\left(\frac{\tan x}{\sec^3 x}\right)\,dx$$

$$= \int \frac{\sec x \tan x}{\sec^4 x}\,dx$$

$$= \int \frac{du}{u^4} = \int u^{-4}\,du$$

$$= \frac{u^{-3}}{-3} + C$$

$$= -\frac{1}{3}\frac{1}{\sec^3 x} + C$$

$$= -\frac{1}{3}\cos^3 x + C$$

> $u = \sec x$
> $du = \sec x \tan x\,dx$
> $n = -4$

EXAMPLE 6

Evaluate $\displaystyle\int_{1/6}^{1/3} \frac{\arccos^2 3x}{\sqrt{1 - 9x^2}}\,dx.$

First, find the indefinite integral.

$$\int \frac{\arccos^2 3x}{\sqrt{1 - 9x^2}}\,dx = \int \frac{u^2}{-3}\,du$$

$$= -\frac{1}{3}\cdot\frac{u^3}{3} + C$$

$$= -\frac{1}{9}\arccos^3 3x + C$$

> $u = \arccos 3x$
> $du = \dfrac{-3}{\sqrt{1 - 9x^2}}\,dx$
> $n = 2$

Thus,

$$\int_{1/6}^{1/3} \frac{\arccos^2 3x}{\sqrt{1 - 9x^2}}\,dx = -\frac{1}{9}\arccos^3 3x \,\Big|_{1/6}^{1/3}$$

$$= -\frac{1}{9}\left[0 - \left(\frac{\pi}{3}\right)^3\right]$$

$$= \frac{\pi^3}{243}$$

Using a calculator, we have

```
fnInt(cos⁻¹(3X)²/
√(1-9X²),X,1/6,1
/3)
          .1275981268
π³/243
          .1275978464
■
```

```
          .1275981268
π³/243
          .1275978464
fnInt(cos⁻¹(3X)²/
√(1-9X²),X,1/6,1
/3,.000000001)
          .1275978464
■
```

MATH 9 2nd COS⁻¹ 3x) **x²/ 2nd** $\sqrt{}$ 1-9x **²**),x,1/6,1/3) **ENTER** Note that the numerical integrator (**fnInt**) of the TI-83 Plus originally calculated six significant digits. The last frame shows that greater accuracy can be obtained by specifying the optional error tolerance.

Exercises 1.1

Integrate.

1. $\int \sqrt{3x + 2}\, dx$ **2.** $\int \sqrt[3]{2x - 1}\, dx$ **3.** $\int \frac{dx}{\sqrt{4 + x}}$

4. $\int \frac{dx}{(2x + 1)^3}$ **5.** $\int (x + 2)(x^2 + 4x)^{3/4}\, dx$ **6.** $\int x\sqrt{x^2 + 4}\, dx$

7. $\int \cos^3 x \sin x\, dx$ **8.** $\int \frac{\cos 2x\, dx}{\sqrt{\sin 2x}}$ **9.** $\int \tan^3 4x \sec^2 4x\, dx$

10. $\int \cos x \sin x\, dx$ **11.** $\int \sin 4x\, (\cos 4x + 1)\, dx$

12. $\int \cos 2x\, (1 - \sin 2x)^2\, dx$ **13.** $\int \sqrt{9 + \sec x}\, \sec x \tan x\, dx$

14. $\int \frac{\csc^2 2x\, dx}{\sqrt{8 - \cot 2x}}$ **15.** $\int \sqrt{1 + e^{2x}}\, e^{2x}\, dx$ **16.** $\int (10 - e^{-2x})^3\, e^{-2x}\, dx$

17. $\int \frac{xe^{x^2}\, dx}{\sqrt{1 + e^{x^2}}}$ **18.** $\int \frac{e^{\tan x} \sec^2 x\, dx}{\sqrt{2 + e^{\tan x}}}$ **19.** $\int \frac{\ln (3x - 5)}{3x - 5}\, dx$

20. $\int \frac{\ln 4x}{x}\, dx$ **21.** $\int \frac{dx}{x \ln^2 x}$ **22.** $\int \frac{x \ln (x^2 + 1)\, dx}{x^2 + 1}$

23. $\int \frac{\arcsin 3x}{\sqrt{1 - 9x^2}}\, dx$ **24.** $\int \frac{\arctan 2x}{1 + 4x^2}\, dx$ **25.** $\int \frac{\cot x}{\csc^4 x}\, dx$

26. $\int \frac{x \sec^2 x^2\, dx}{\sqrt{9 + \tan x^2}}$ **27.** $\int \frac{\arctan^2 x}{1 + x^2}\, dx$ **28.** $\int \frac{\ln^2 4x}{2x}\, dx$

29. $\int_3^5 x\sqrt{x^2 - 9}\, dx$ **30.** $\int_0^6 3x\sqrt{x^2 + 1}\, dx$ **31.** $\int_0^1 \frac{e^{3x}\, dx}{\sqrt{1 + e^{3x}}}$

32. $\int_0^{\pi/12} \sin^3 6x \cos 6x\, dx$ **33.** $\int_1^2 \frac{\ln (2x - 1)}{2x - 1}\, dx$ **34.** $\int_0^{\sqrt{2}/4} \frac{\arcsin 2x}{\sqrt{1 - 4x^2}}\, dx$

35. Find the area bounded by $y = \sin^2 x \cos x$ from $x = 0$ to $x = \pi/2$ and $y = 0$.

36. Find the area bounded by $y = \frac{\ln^2 x}{x}$ from $x = 1$ to $x = e$ and $y = 0$.

1.2 LOGARITHMIC AND EXPONENTIAL FORMS

Since integration is the inverse of differentiation and $\dfrac{d}{du}(\ln u) = \dfrac{1}{u}$, we find

$$\int \frac{du}{u} = \ln|u| + C$$

The absolute value of u is necessary because logarithms are defined only for positive numbers. If $u > 0$, then $\int \dfrac{du}{u} = \ln u + C$ and if $u < 0$, then $\int \dfrac{du}{u} = \int \dfrac{-du}{-u} = \ln(-u) + C$, so that in both cases we obtain $\ln|u| + C$. *Note:* This form is the general power formula for $n = -1$.

EXAMPLE 1

Integrate $\displaystyle\int \frac{dx}{x-1}$.

$$\int \frac{dx}{x-1} = \int \frac{du}{u}$$
$$= \ln|u| + C$$
$$= \ln|x-1| + C$$

$$\boxed{\begin{array}{l} u = x - 1 \\ du = dx \end{array}}$$

EXAMPLE 2

Integrate $\displaystyle\int \frac{x\,dx}{x^2+6}$.

$$\int \frac{x\,dx}{x^2+6} = \int \frac{1}{u}\left(\frac{du}{2}\right)$$
$$= \frac{1}{2}\int \frac{du}{u}$$
$$= \frac{1}{2}\ln|u| + C$$
$$= \frac{1}{2}\ln|x^2+6| + C$$

$$\boxed{\begin{array}{l} u = x^2 + 6 \\ du = 2x\,dx \end{array}}$$

Use the integral formula $\displaystyle\int \frac{du}{u} = \ln|u| + C$ whenever the integrand is a quotient and the derivative of the denominator is a constant multiple of the numerator.

EXAMPLE 3

Integrate $\displaystyle\int \frac{\sec 3x \tan 3x\, dx}{2 + \sec 3x}$.

$$\int \frac{\sec 3x \tan 3x\, dx}{2 + \sec 3x} = \int \frac{1}{u}\left(\frac{du}{3}\right)$$
$$= \frac{1}{3}\int \frac{du}{u}$$
$$= \frac{1}{3}\ln|u| + C$$
$$= \frac{1}{3}\ln|2 + \sec 3x| + C$$

$$\boxed{\begin{array}{l} u = 2 + \sec 3x \\ du = 3 \sec 3x \tan 3x\, dx \end{array}}$$

EXAMPLE 4

Evaluate $\displaystyle\int_2^3 \frac{x^2\,dx}{1-x^3}$.

$$\int \frac{x^2\,dx}{1-x^3} = \int \frac{1}{u}\left(\frac{du}{-3}\right)$$

$$= -\frac{1}{3}\int \frac{du}{u}$$

$$= -\frac{1}{3}\ln|u| + C$$

$$= -\frac{1}{3}\ln|1-x^3| + C$$

$$\boxed{\begin{aligned} u &= 1-x^3 \\ du &= -3x^2\,dx \end{aligned}}$$

So

$$\int_2^3 \frac{x^2\,dx}{1-x^3} = -\frac{1}{3}\ln|1-x^3|\Big|_2^3$$

$$= -\frac{1}{3}\ln|-26| + \frac{1}{3}\ln|-7|$$

$$= \frac{1}{3}(\ln 7 - \ln 26)$$

$$= \frac{1}{3}\ln\left(\frac{7}{26}\right) = -0.437$$

From the derivative formula $\dfrac{d}{du}(e^u) = e^u$, we find

$$\int e^u\,du = e^u + C$$

EXAMPLE 5

Integrate $\displaystyle\int e^{5x}\,dx$.

$$\int e^{5x}\,dx = \int e^u\left(\frac{du}{5}\right)$$

$$= \frac{1}{5}\int e^u\,du$$

$$= \frac{1}{5}e^u + C$$

$$= \frac{1}{5}e^{5x} + C$$

$$\boxed{\begin{aligned} u &= 5x \\ du &= 5\,dx \end{aligned}}$$

EXAMPLE 6

Integrate $\displaystyle\int \frac{dx}{e^{2x}}$.

$$\int \frac{dx}{e^{2x}} = \int e^{-2x}\,dx = \int e^u\left(\frac{du}{-2}\right)$$

$$= -\frac{1}{2}\int e^u\,du$$

$$= -\frac{1}{2}e^u + C$$

$$= -\frac{1}{2}e^{-2x} + C$$

$$\boxed{\begin{aligned} u &= -2x \\ du &= -2\,dx \end{aligned}}$$

EXAMPLE 7

Evaluate $\displaystyle\int_0^1 x^2 e^{x^3+1} dx$.

First,

$$\int x^2 e^{x^3+1} dx = \int e^u \left(\frac{du}{3}\right)$$

$$= \frac{1}{3} \int e^u \, du$$

$$= \frac{1}{3} e^u + C$$

$$= \frac{1}{3} e^{x^3+1} + C$$

$$\boxed{\begin{aligned} u &= x^3 + 1 \\ du &= 3x^2 \, dx \end{aligned}}$$

So

$$\int_0^1 x^2 e^{x^3+1} dx = \frac{1}{3} e^{x^3+1} \bigg|_0^1$$

$$= \frac{1}{3} e^2 - \frac{1}{3} e$$

$$= \frac{1}{3} e(e-1)$$

For bases other than e, we have

$$\int a^u \, du = \frac{a^u}{\ln a} + C \qquad (a > 0, a \neq 1)$$

EXAMPLE 8

Find the area bounded by $xy = 1$, $x = 1$, $x = 2$, and $y = 0$.

This area is given by the definite integral (see Fig. 1.1).

$$\int_1^2 \frac{dx}{x} = \ln |x| \bigg|_1^2 = \ln 2 - \ln 1 = \ln 2 = 0.6931$$

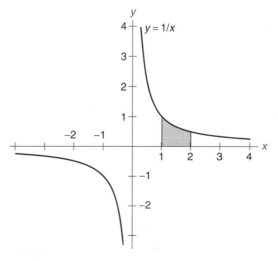

Figure 1.1

Exercises 1.2

Integrate.

1. $\displaystyle\int \frac{dx}{3x + 2}$ **2.** $\displaystyle\int \frac{dx}{x + 5}$ **3.** $\displaystyle\int \frac{dx}{1 - 4x}$

4. $\displaystyle\int \frac{dx}{4x + 2}$ **5.** $\displaystyle\int \frac{4x\,dx}{1 - x^2}$ **6.** $\displaystyle\int \frac{3x\,dx}{x^2 + 1}$

7. $\displaystyle\int \frac{x^3\,dx}{x^4 - 1}$ **8.** $\displaystyle\int \frac{(x + 1)\,dx}{x^2 + 2x - 3}$ **9.** $\displaystyle\int \frac{\csc^2 x\,dx}{\cot x}$

10. $\displaystyle\int \frac{\sin x\,dx}{\cos x}$ **11.** $\displaystyle\int \frac{\sec^2 3x\,dx}{1 + \tan 3x}$ **12.** $\displaystyle\int \frac{\cos 2x}{1 + \sin 2x}\,dx$

13. $\displaystyle\int \frac{\csc x \cot x}{1 + \csc x}\,dx$ **14.** $\displaystyle\int \frac{\csc^2 4x}{1 - \cot 4x}\,dx$ **15.** $\displaystyle\int \frac{\cos x}{1 + \sin x}\,dx$

16. $\displaystyle\int \frac{(x - \sin 2x)\,dx}{x^2 + \cos 2x}$ **17.** $\displaystyle\int \frac{dx}{x \ln x}$ **18.** $\displaystyle\int \frac{dx}{x(4 + \ln x)}$

19. $\displaystyle\int e^{2x}\,dx$ **20.** $\displaystyle\int e^{3x-1}\,dx$ **21.** $\displaystyle\int \frac{dx}{e^{4x}}$

22. $\displaystyle\int \frac{dx}{e^{2x+3}}$ **23.** $\displaystyle\int xe^{x^2}\,dx$ **24.** $\displaystyle\int x^3 e^{x^4 - 1}\,dx$

25. $\displaystyle\int \frac{x\,dx}{e^{x^2+9}}$ **26.** $\displaystyle\int xe^{-x^2}\,dx$ **27.** $\displaystyle\int (\sin x)\,e^{\cos x}\,dx$

28. $\displaystyle\int (\sec^2 x)\,e^{2\tan x}\,dx$ **29.** $\displaystyle\int_0^2 xe^{x^2+2}\,dx$ **30.** $\displaystyle\int_0^{\pi/2} (\cos x)\,e^{\sin x}\,dx$

31. $\displaystyle\int 4^x\,dx$ **32.** $\displaystyle\int 10^{2x}\,dx$ **33.** $\displaystyle\int \frac{2e^x}{e^x + 4}\,dx$

34. $\displaystyle\int \frac{e^{-x}}{1 - e^{-x}}\,dx$ **35.** $\displaystyle\int_0^1 \frac{x\,dx}{x^2 + 1}$ **36.** $\displaystyle\int_{\pi/4}^{\pi/2} \frac{\cos x\,dx}{\sin x}$

37. $\displaystyle\int_1^5 \frac{4\,dx}{2x - 1}$ **38.** $\displaystyle\int_0^6 \frac{dx}{5x + 4}$ **39.** $\displaystyle\int_0^2 e^{x/2}\,dx$

40. $\displaystyle\int_{-2}^0 e^{-4x}\,dx$ **41.** $\displaystyle\int_0^1 x^2 e^{x^3}\,dx$ **42.** $\displaystyle\int_1^2 xe^{x^2}\,dx$

43. $\displaystyle\int_0^{\pi/6} \frac{\cos x\,dx}{1 - \sin x}$ **44.** $\displaystyle\int_{\pi/3}^{\pi/2} \frac{\sin x}{1 + \cos x}\,dx$

45. Find the area bounded by $y = 1/(1 + 2x)$, $x = 0$, $x = 1$, and $y = 0$.

46. Find the area bounded by $xy = 1$, $x = 1$, $x = 3$, and $y = 0$.

47. Find the area bounded by $y = e^{2x}$, $x = 0$, $x = 4$, and $y = 0$.

48. Find the area bounded by $y = e^{-x}$, $x = 0$, $x = 5$, and $y = 0$.

1.3 BASIC TRIGONOMETRIC FORMS

We have found that

$$\frac{d}{du}(\sin u) = \cos u \quad \text{and} \quad \frac{d}{du}(\cos u) = -\sin u$$

Now, since integration is the inverse of differentiation, we have

$$\int \cos u \, du = \sin u + C$$

$$\int \sin u \, du = -\cos u + C$$

EXAMPLE 1

Integrate $\displaystyle\int \cos 3x \, dx$.

$$\int \cos 3x \, dx = \int (\cos u)\left(\frac{du}{3}\right)$$

$$= \frac{1}{3} \int \cos u \, du$$

$$= \frac{1}{3} \sin u + C$$

$$= \frac{1}{3} \sin 3x + C$$

$$u = 3x$$
$$du = 3 \, dx$$

EXAMPLE 2

Integrate $\displaystyle\int \sin(4x + 3) \, dx$.

$$\int \sin(4x + 3) \, dx = \int (\sin u)\left(\frac{du}{4}\right)$$

$$= \frac{1}{4} \int \sin u \, du$$

$$= \frac{1}{4}(-\cos u) + C$$

$$= -\frac{1}{4} \cos(4x + 3) + C$$

$$u = 4x + 3$$
$$du = 4 \, dx$$

EXAMPLE 3

Integrate $\displaystyle\int x^2 \sin(x^3 + 2) \, dx$.

$$\int x^2 \sin(x^3 + 2) \, dx = \int (\sin u)\left(\frac{du}{3}\right)$$

$$= \frac{1}{3} \int \sin u \, du$$

$$= \frac{1}{3}(-\cos u) + C$$

$$= -\frac{1}{3} \cos(x^3 + 2) + C$$

$$u = x^3 + 2$$
$$du = 3x^2 \, dx$$

EXAMPLE 4

Find $\displaystyle\int_0^{\pi/4} \cos 2x \, dx$.

$$\int \cos 2x \, dx = \int \cos u \left(\frac{du}{2}\right)$$

$$u = 2x$$
$$du = 2 \, dx$$

$$= \frac{1}{2} \int \cos u \, du$$

$$= \frac{1}{2} \sin u + C$$

$$= \frac{1}{2} \sin 2x + C$$

So

$$\int_0^{\pi/4} \cos 2x \, dx = \frac{1}{2} \sin 2x \Big|_0^{\pi/4} = \frac{1}{2} \sin \frac{\pi}{2} - \frac{1}{2} \sin 0$$

$$= \frac{1}{2}(1) - \frac{1}{2}(0) = \frac{1}{2}$$

From the derivatives of $\tan u$, $\cot u$, $\sec u$, and $\csc u$ and noting that integration is the inverse of differentiation, we have

$$\int \sec^2 u \, du = \tan u + C$$

$$\int \csc^2 u \, du = -\cot u + C$$

$$\int \sec u \tan u \, du = \sec u + C$$

$$\int \csc u \cot u \, du = -\csc u + C$$

EXAMPLE 5

Integrate $\displaystyle\int \sec^2 3x \, dx$

$$\int \sec^2 3x \, dx = \int (\sec^2 u)\left(\frac{du}{3}\right)$$

$$u = 3x$$
$$du = 3 \, dx$$

$$= \frac{1}{3} \int \sec^2 u \, du$$

$$= \frac{1}{3} \tan u + C$$

$$= \frac{1}{3} \tan 3x + C$$

EXAMPLE 6

Integrate $\int \sec(2x + 5) \tan(2x + 5)\, dx.$

$$\int \sec(2x + 5) \tan(2x + 5)\, dx = \int (\sec u \tan u)\left(\frac{du}{2}\right)$$

$$\begin{array}{|c|}\hline u = 2x + 5 \\ du = 2\, dx \\ \hline \end{array}$$

$$= \frac{1}{2} \int \sec u \tan u\, du$$

$$= \frac{1}{2} \sec u + C$$

$$= \frac{1}{2} \sec(2x + 5) + C$$

We determine $\int \tan u\, du$ as follows:

$$\int \tan u\, du = \int \frac{\sin u}{\cos u}\, du$$

$$\begin{array}{|c|}\hline w = \cos u \\ dw = -\sin u\, du \\ \hline \end{array}$$

$$= \int \frac{1}{w}(-dw)$$

$$= -\int \frac{dw}{w}$$

$$= -\ln|w| + C$$

$$= -\ln|\cos u| + C$$

In a similar manner,

$$\int \cot u\, du = \int \frac{\cos u}{\sin u}\, du$$

$$\begin{array}{|c|}\hline w = \sin u \\ dw = \cos u\, du \\ \hline \end{array}$$

$$= \int \frac{1}{w}\, dw$$

$$= \ln|w| + C$$

$$= \ln|\sin u| + C$$

To find $\int \sec u\, du$, first multiply $\sec u$ by 1 in the form

$$\frac{\sec u + \tan u}{\sec u + \tan u}$$

That is,

$$\int \sec u\, du = \int \sec u \left(\frac{\sec u + \tan u}{\sec u + \tan u}\right) du$$

$$= \int \frac{\sec^2 u + \sec u \tan u}{\sec u + \tan u}\, du$$

$$= \int \frac{dw}{w}$$

$$\begin{array}{|c|}\hline w = \sec u + \tan u \\ dw = (\sec u \tan u + \sec^2 u)\, du \\ \hline \end{array}$$

$$= \ln|w| + C$$

$$= \ln|\sec u + \tan u| + C$$

In a similar manner, we find that

$$\int \csc u\, du = \ln|\csc u - \cot u| + C$$

We now can integrate all six basic trigonometric functions:

$$\int \sin u \, du = -\cos u + C$$

$$\int \cos u \, du = \sin u + C$$

$$\int \tan u \, du = -\ln |\cos u| + C$$

$$\int \cot u \, du = \ln |\sin u| + C$$

$$\int \sec u \, du = \ln |\sec u + \tan u| + C$$

$$\int \csc u \, du = \ln |\csc u - \cot u| + C$$

EXAMPLE 7

Integrate $\int \tan 3x \, dx$.

$$\int \tan 3x \, dx = \int \tan u \left(\frac{du}{3} \right) \qquad \boxed{\begin{array}{l} u = 3x \\ du = 3\, dx \end{array}}$$

$$= \frac{1}{3} \int \tan u \, du$$

$$= \frac{1}{3} (-\ln |\cos u|) + C$$

$$= -\frac{1}{3} \ln |\cos 3x| + C$$

EXAMPLE 8

Integrate $\int x \sec 3x^2 \, dx$.

$$\int x \sec 3x^2 \, dx = \int \sec u \left(\frac{du}{6} \right) \qquad \boxed{\begin{array}{l} u = 3x^2 \\ du = 6x\, dx \end{array}}$$

$$= \frac{1}{6} \int \sec u \, du$$

$$= \frac{1}{6} \ln |\sec u + \tan u| + C$$

$$= \frac{1}{6} \ln |\sec 3x^2 + \tan 3x^2| + C$$

EXAMPLE 9

Evaluate $\int_{\pi/8}^{\pi/4} \cot 2x \, dx$.

$$\int \cot 2x \, dx = \int \cot u \left(\frac{du}{2} \right) \qquad \boxed{\begin{array}{l} u = 2x \\ du = 2\, dx \end{array}}$$

$$= \frac{1}{2} \int \cot u \, du$$

$$= \frac{1}{2} \ln |\sin u| + C$$

$$= \frac{1}{2} \ln |\sin 2x| + C$$

So,

$$\int_{\pi/8}^{\pi/4} \cot 2x \, dx = \frac{1}{2} \ln |\sin 2x| \Big|_{\pi/8}^{\pi/4} = \frac{1}{2} \ln \left| \sin \frac{\pi}{2} \right| - \frac{1}{2} \ln \left| \sin \frac{\pi}{4} \right|$$

$$= \frac{1}{2} \ln 1 - \frac{1}{2} \ln \frac{1}{\sqrt{2}}$$

$$= 0 - \frac{1}{2} \ln 2^{-1/2} = \frac{1}{4} \ln 2 = 0.173$$

Algebraic simplifications often lead to less complicated integrals as shown in Example 10.

EXAMPLE 10

Integrate $\int \dfrac{2 - \cos x}{\sin x} \, dx$.

$$\int \frac{2 - \cos x}{\sin x} \, dx = \int \frac{2 \, dx}{\sin x} - \int \frac{\cos x}{\sin x} \, dx$$

$$= 2 \int \csc x \, dx - \int \cot x \, dx$$

$$= 2 \ln |\csc x - \cot x| - \ln |\sin x| + C$$

Exercises 1.3

Integrate.

1. $\displaystyle\int \sin 5x \, dx$ **2.** $\displaystyle\int \cos 6x \, dx$ **3.** $\displaystyle\int \cos (3x - 1) \, dx$

4. $\displaystyle\int \sin (2x + 7) \, dx$ **5.** $\displaystyle\int x \sin (x^2 + 5) \, dx$ **6.** $\displaystyle\int x^3 \cos x^4 \, dx$

7. $\displaystyle\int (3x^2 - 2x) \cos (x^3 - x^2) \, dx$ **8.** $\displaystyle\int (x - 1) \sin (x^2 - 2x + 3) \, dx$

9. $\displaystyle\int \csc^2 5x \, dx$ **10.** $\displaystyle\int \sec^2 2x \, dx$ **11.** $\displaystyle\int \sec 3x \tan 3x \, dx$

12. $\displaystyle\int \csc 7x \cot 7x \, dx$ **13.** $\displaystyle\int \sec^2 (4x + 3) \, dx$ **14.** $\displaystyle\int \csc^2 (3x - 2) \, dx$

15. $\displaystyle\int \csc (2x - 3) \cot (2x - 3) \, dx$ **16.** $\displaystyle\int \sec \frac{x}{2} \tan \frac{x}{2} \, dx$

17. $\displaystyle\int x \sec^2 (x^2 + 3) \, dx$ **18.** $\displaystyle\int x^2 \csc^2 x^3 \, dx$

19. $\displaystyle\int x^2 \csc (x^3 - 1) \cot (x^3 - 1) \, dx$ **20.** $\displaystyle\int x \sec 3x^2 \tan 3x^2 \, dx$

21. $\displaystyle\int \tan 4x \, dx$ **22.** $\displaystyle\int x \cot x^2 \, dx$ **23.** $\displaystyle\int \sec 5x \, dx$

24. $\displaystyle\int x^2 \csc x^3 \, dx$ **25.** $\displaystyle\int e^x \cot e^x \, dx$ **26.** $\displaystyle\int \frac{\sec (\ln x)}{x} \, dx$

27. $\displaystyle\int (1 + \sec x)^2 \, dx$ **28.** $\displaystyle\int (1 + \tan 3x)^2 \, dx$ **29.** $\displaystyle\int \frac{5 + \sin x}{\cos x} \, dx$

30. $\displaystyle\int \frac{\tan x - \cos x}{\sin x} \, dx$ **31.** $\displaystyle\int_0^{\pi/4} \sin 2x \, dx$ **32.** $\displaystyle\int_0^{\pi/6} 2 \cos 3x \, dx$

33. $\displaystyle\int_0^{\pi/2} 3 \cos\left(x - \frac{\pi}{2}\right) dx$ **34.** $\displaystyle\int_0^{\pi/2} \sin\left(x - \frac{\pi}{4}\right) dx$ **35.** $\displaystyle\int_0^{\pi/4} \sec^2 x \, dx$

36. $\displaystyle\int_{\pi/4}^{\pi/2} \csc^2 x \, dx$ **37.** $\displaystyle\int_0^{\pi/8} \sec 2x \tan 2x \, dx$ **38.** $\displaystyle\int_{1/4}^{1/2} \csc \pi x \cot \pi x \, dx$

Find the area of each region bounded by the given curves.

39. $y = \sin x$ from $x = 0$ to $x = \pi$ and $y = 0$.

40. $y = 2 \cos x$ from $x = 0$ to $x = \pi/2$ and $y = 0$.

41. $y = \sec^2 x$, $x = 0$, $x = \pi/4$, and $y = 0$.

42. $y = \sec x \tan x$, $x = 0$, $x = \pi/4$, and $y = 0$.

43. $y = \tan x$, $x = 0$, $x = \pi/4$, and $y = 0$.

44. $y = \sin x + \cos x$, $x = 0$, and $y = 0$.

45. Find the volume of the solid formed by revolving the region bounded by $y = \sec x$ from $x = 0$ to $x = \pi/4$ and $y = 0$ about the x-axis.

1.4   OTHER TRIGONOMETRIC FORMS

To integrate powers of trigonometric functions, use trigonometric identities as shown in the following methods.

Odd Powers of Sines or Cosines

Various forms of the trigonometric identity $\sin^2 x + \cos^2 x = 1$ are needed for this case.

EXAMPLE 1

Integrate $\displaystyle\int \sin^5 x \, dx$.

$$\int \sin^5 x \, dx = \int \sin^4 x \sin x \, dx = \int (\sin^2 x)^2 \sin x \, dx$$

$$= \int (1 - \cos^2 x)^2 \sin x \, dx \qquad (\sin^2 x = 1 - \cos^2 x)$$

$$= \int (1 - 2 \cos^2 x + \cos^4 x) \sin x \, dx$$

$$= \int (1 - 2u^2 + u^4)(-du) \qquad \boxed{\begin{array}{l} u = \cos x \\ du = -\sin x \, dx \end{array}}$$

$$= -u + 2\frac{u^3}{3} - \frac{u^5}{5} + C$$

$$= -\cos x + \frac{2}{3} \cos^3 x - \frac{1}{5} \cos^5 x + C$$

EXAMPLE 2

Integrate $\displaystyle\int \sin^2 x \cos^3 x \, dx$.

$$\int \sin^7 x \cos^3 x \, dx - \int \sin^7 x \cos^2 x \cos x \, dx$$

$$= \int \sin^2 x (1 - \sin^2 x) \cos x \, dx \qquad (\cos^2 x = 1 - \sin^2 x)$$

$$= \int u^2 (1 - u^2) \, du$$

$$= \int (u^2 - u^4) \, du$$

$$\boxed{\begin{aligned} u &= \sin x \\ du &= \cos x \, dx \end{aligned}}$$

$$= \frac{u^3}{3} - \frac{u^5}{5} + C$$

$$= \frac{1}{3} \sin^3 x - \frac{1}{5} \sin^5 x + C$$

In each of the two previous examples the method used involved making a substitution so that the function to be integrated becomes a product of a power of sine (or cosine) and the first power only of cosine (or sine).

Even Powers of Sines and Cosines

For this case we use the identities

$$\sin^2 x = \frac{1}{2}(1 - \cos 2x)$$

$$\cos^2 x = \frac{1}{2}(1 + \cos 2x)$$

EXAMPLE 3

Integrate $\int \cos^2 x \, dx$.

$$\int \cos^2 x \, dx = \int \frac{1}{2}(1 + \cos 2x) \, dx \qquad \left[\cos^2 x = \frac{1}{2}(1 + \cos 2x)\right]$$

$$-\frac{1}{2}\int dx + \frac{1}{2}\int \cos 2x \, dx$$

$$= \frac{1}{2}x + \frac{1}{4}\sin 2x + C \qquad \left[\int \cos nx \, dx = \frac{1}{n}\sin nx + C\right]$$

EXAMPLE 4

Integrate $\int \sin^4 x \, dx$.

$$\int \sin^4 x \, dx = \int (\sin^2 x)^2 \, dx$$

$$= \int \left[\frac{1}{2}(1 - \cos 2x)\right]^2 dx \qquad \left[\sin^2 x = \frac{1}{2}(1 - \cos 2x)\right]$$

$$= \int \left(\frac{1}{4} - \frac{1}{2}\cos 2x + \frac{1}{4}\cos^2 2x\right) dx$$

$$= \frac{1}{4}\int dx - \frac{1}{2}\int \cos 2x \, dx + \frac{1}{4}\int \cos^2 2x \, dx$$

$$= \frac{1}{4}x - \frac{1}{4}\sin 2x + \frac{1}{4}\int \cos^2 2x \, dx.$$

Now, find

$$\int \cos^2 2x \, dx = \int \frac{1}{2}(1 + \cos 4x) \, dx \qquad \left[\cos^2 2x = \frac{1}{2}(1 + \cos 4x)\right]$$

$$= \frac{1}{2} \int dx + \frac{1}{2} \int \cos 4x \, dx$$

$$= \frac{1}{2}x + \frac{1}{8} \sin 4x + C_1$$

So,

$$\int \sin^4 x \, dx = \frac{1}{4}x - \frac{1}{4} \sin 2x + \frac{1}{4}\left(\frac{1}{2}x + \frac{1}{8} \sin 4x + C_1\right)$$

$$= \frac{1}{4}x - \frac{1}{4} \sin 2x + \frac{1}{8}x + \frac{1}{32} \sin 4x + \frac{1}{4}C_1$$

$$= \frac{3}{8}x - \frac{1}{4} \sin 2x + \frac{1}{32} \sin 4x + C$$

Powers of Other Trigonometric Functions

The identities $1 + \tan^2 x = \sec^2 x$ and $1 + \cot^2 x = \csc^2 x$ are used to integrate even powers of $\sec x$ and $\csc x$ and powers of $\tan x$ and $\cot x$.

EXAMPLE 5

Integrate $\int \sec^4 x \, dx$.

$$\int \sec^4 x \, dx = \int (1 + \tan^2 x) \sec^2 x \, dx$$

$$= \int \sec^2 x \, dx + \int \tan^2 x \sec^2 x \, dx$$

$$= \tan x + \frac{1}{3} \tan^3 x + C$$

EXAMPLE 6

Integrate $\int \tan^5 x \, dx$.

$$\int \tan^5 x \, dx = \int \tan^3 x \tan^2 x \, dx$$

$$= \int \tan^3 x \, (\sec^2 x - 1) \, dx \qquad (\tan^2 x = \sec^2 x - 1)$$

$$= \int \tan^3 x \sec^2 x \, dx - \int \tan^3 x \, dx$$

$$= \frac{1}{4} \tan^4 x - \int \tan x \tan^2 x \, dx$$

$$= \frac{1}{4} \tan^4 x - \int \tan x \, (\sec^2 x - 1) \, dx$$

$$= \frac{1}{4} \tan^4 x - \int \tan x \sec^2 x \, dx + \int \tan x \, dx$$

$$= \frac{1}{4} \tan^4 x - \frac{1}{2} \tan^2 x - \ln |\cos x| + C$$

EXAMPLE 7

Integrate $\int \csc^6 5x \, dx$.

$$\int \csc^6 5x \, dx = \int \csc^4 5x \csc^2 5x \, dx$$

$$= \int (1 + \cot^2 5x)^2 \csc^2 5x \, dx \qquad (\csc^2 5x = 1 + \cot^2 5x)$$

$$= \int (1 + u^2)^2 \left(\frac{du}{-5} \right)$$

$$\boxed{\begin{aligned} \text{let } u &= \cot 5x \\ du &= (-\csc^2 5x) \, 5 \, dx \end{aligned}}$$

$$= -\frac{1}{5} \int (1 + 2u^2 + u^4) \, du$$

$$= -\frac{1}{5} \left(u + \frac{2}{3} u^3 + \frac{1}{5} u^5 \right) + C$$

$$= -\frac{1}{5} \cot 5x - \frac{2}{15} \cot^3 5x - \frac{1}{25} \cot^5 5x + C$$

Exercises 1.4

Integrate.

1. $\displaystyle\int \sin^3 x \, dx$ **2.** $\displaystyle\int \cos^3 x \, dx$ **3.** $\displaystyle\int \cos^5 x \, dx$

4. $\displaystyle\int \sin^7 x \, dx$ **5.** $\displaystyle\int \sin^2 x \cos x \, dx$ **6.** $\displaystyle\int \cos^2 x \sin x \, dx$

7. $\displaystyle\int \frac{\sin x \, dx}{\cos^3 x}$ **8.** $\displaystyle\int \sin^3 x \cos x \, dx$ **9.** $\displaystyle\int \sin^3 x \cos^2 x \, dx$

10. $\displaystyle\int \sin^2 3x \cos^3 3x \, dx$ **11.** $\displaystyle\int \sin^2 x \, dx$ **12.** $\displaystyle\int \cos^2 4x \, dx$

13. $\displaystyle\int \cos^4 3x \, dx$ **14.** $\displaystyle\int \sin^4 7x \, dx$ **15.** $\displaystyle\int \sin^2 x \cos^2 x \, dx$

16. $\displaystyle\int \sin^4 x \cos^2 x \, dx$ **17.** $\displaystyle\int \sin^2 x \cos^4 x \, dx$ **18.** $\displaystyle\int \sin^4 2x \cos^4 2x \, dx$

19. $\displaystyle\int \tan^3 x \, dx$ **20.** $\displaystyle\int \cot^5 4x \, dx$ **21.** $\displaystyle\int \cot^4 2x \, dx$

22. $\displaystyle\int \sec^4 7x \, dx$ **23.** $\displaystyle\int \sec^6 x \, dx$ **24.** $\displaystyle\int \csc^4 3x \, dx$

25. $\displaystyle\int \tan^4 2x \, dx$ **26.** $\displaystyle\int \cot^6 x \, dx$

27. Find the area of the region bounded by $y = \sin^2 x$, $x = 0$, $x = \pi$, and $y = 0$.

28. Find the volume of the solid formed by revolving the region bounded by $y = \cos^3 x$ from $x = 0$ to $x = \pi/2$ and $y = 0$ about the x-axis.

1.5   INVERSE TRIGONOMETRIC FORMS

A major use of the inverse trigonometric functions is to integrate certain algebraic functions. Two important integral formulas are based on the derivatives of the inverse sine and inverse tangent functions:

$$\int \frac{du}{\sqrt{a^2 - u^2}} = \arcsin \frac{u}{a} + C$$

since

$$\frac{d}{du}\left(\arcsin\frac{u}{a}\right) = \frac{1}{\sqrt{1 - \left(\frac{u}{a}\right)^2}} \cdot \frac{1}{a} = \frac{a}{\sqrt{a^2 - u^2}} \cdot \frac{1}{a} = \frac{1}{\sqrt{a^2 - u^2}}$$

$$\int \frac{du}{a^2 + u^2} = \frac{1}{a}\arctan\frac{u}{a} + C$$

since

$$\frac{d}{du}\left(\arctan\frac{u}{a}\right) = \frac{1}{1 + \left(\frac{u}{a}\right)^2} \cdot \frac{1}{a} = \frac{a^2}{a^2 + u^2} \cdot \frac{1}{a} = \frac{a}{a^2 + u^2}$$

so that

$$\frac{d}{du}\left(\frac{1}{a}\arctan\frac{u}{a}\right) = \frac{1}{a} \cdot \frac{d}{du}\left(\arctan\frac{u}{a}\right) = \frac{1}{a^2 + u^2}$$

EXAMPLE 1

Integrate $\displaystyle\int \frac{dx}{\sqrt{16 - x^2}}$.

$$\int \frac{dx}{\sqrt{16 - x^2}} = \int \frac{du}{\sqrt{a^2 - u^2}} \qquad \boxed{\begin{array}{l} u = x \\ du = dx \\ a = 4 \end{array}}$$

$$= \arcsin\frac{u}{a} + C$$

$$= \arcsin\frac{x}{4} + C$$

EXAMPLE 2

Evaluate $\displaystyle\int_0^2 \frac{dx}{x^2 + 4}$.

$$\int \frac{dx}{x^2 + 4} = \int \frac{du}{a^2 + u^2} \qquad \boxed{\begin{array}{l} u = x \\ du = dx \\ a = 2 \end{array}}$$

$$= \frac{1}{a}\arctan\frac{u}{a} + C$$

$$= \frac{1}{2}\arctan\frac{x}{2} + C$$

So,

$$\int_0^2 \frac{dx}{x^2 + 4} = \frac{1}{2}\arctan\frac{x}{2}\Big|_0^2$$

$$= \frac{1}{2}\arctan 1 - \frac{1}{2}\arctan 0$$

$$= \frac{1}{2}\left(\frac{\pi}{4}\right) - 0 = \frac{\pi}{8}.$$

EXAMPLE 3

Integrate $\int \dfrac{dx}{4x^2 + 9}$.

$$\int \frac{dx}{4x^2 + 9} = \int \frac{1}{a^2 + u^2} \cdot \frac{du}{2} = \frac{1}{2} \int \frac{du}{a^2 + u^2}$$

$$= \frac{1}{2}\left(\frac{1}{a}\arctan\frac{u}{a}\right) + C$$

$$= \frac{1}{2}\left(\frac{1}{3}\arctan\frac{2x}{3}\right) + C$$

$$= \frac{1}{6}\arctan\frac{2x}{3} + C$$

$$u = 2x$$
$$du = 2\,dx$$
$$a = 3$$

EXAMPLE 4

Integrate $\int \dfrac{dx}{x^2 + 2x + 5}$.

Here, we must complete the square in the denominator:

$$x^2 + 2x + 5 = (x + 1)^2 + 4 = (x + 1)^2 + (2)^2$$

Then, let $u = x + 1$ and $a = 2$.

$$\int \frac{dx}{x^2 + 2x + 5} = \int \frac{dx}{(x + 1)^2 + (2)^2} = \int \frac{du}{u^2 + a^2}$$

$$= \frac{1}{a}\arctan\frac{u}{a} + C$$

$$= \frac{1}{2}\arctan\left(\frac{x + 1}{2}\right) + C$$

$$u = x + 1$$
$$du = dx$$
$$a = 2$$

EXAMPLE 5

Evaluate $\int_{1}^{2} \dfrac{dx}{\sqrt{25 - 4x^2}}$.

$$\int \frac{dx}{\sqrt{25 - 4x^2}} = \int \frac{1}{\sqrt{a^2 - u^2}} \cdot \frac{du}{2}$$

$$= \frac{1}{2} \int \frac{du}{\sqrt{a^2 - u^2}}$$

$$= \frac{1}{2}\arcsin\frac{u}{a} + C$$

$$= \frac{1}{2}\arcsin\frac{2x}{5} + C$$

$$u = 2x$$
$$du = 2\,dx$$
$$a = 5$$

So,

$$\int_{1}^{2} \frac{dx}{\sqrt{25 - 4x^2}} = \frac{1}{2}\arcsin\frac{2x}{5}\Big|_{1}^{2} = \frac{1}{2}\left(\arcsin\frac{4}{5} - \arcsin\frac{2}{5}\right)$$

$$= \frac{1}{2}(0.93 - 0.41) = 0.26 \quad \text{(radian measure)}$$

Exercises 1.5

Integrate.

1. $\displaystyle\int \frac{dx}{\sqrt{1 - 9x^2}}$

2. $\displaystyle\int \frac{dx}{\sqrt{1 - x^2}}$

3. $\displaystyle\int \frac{dx}{\sqrt{9 - x^2}}$

4. $\displaystyle\int \frac{dx}{\sqrt{144 - 25x^2}}$

5. $\displaystyle\int \frac{dx}{x^2 + 25}$

6. $\displaystyle\int \frac{dx}{x^2 + 4}$

7. $\displaystyle\int \frac{dx}{9x^2 + 4}$

8. $\displaystyle\int \frac{dx}{16 + 25x^2}$

9. $\displaystyle\int \frac{dx}{\sqrt{36 - 25x^2}}$

10. $\displaystyle\int \frac{dx}{\sqrt{5 - 6x^2}}$

11. $\displaystyle\int \frac{dx}{\sqrt{3 - 12x^2}}$

12. $\displaystyle\int \frac{dx}{\sqrt{3 - 4x^2}}$

13. $\displaystyle\int \frac{dx}{4 + (x - 1)^2}$

14. $\displaystyle\int \frac{dx}{16 + (x - 3)^2}$

15. $\displaystyle\int \frac{dx}{x^2 + 6x + 25}$

16. $\displaystyle\int \frac{dx}{x^2 + 4x + 13}$

17. $\displaystyle\int \frac{e^x \, dx}{\sqrt{1 - e^{2x}}}$

18. $\displaystyle\int \frac{\sec x \tan x \, dx}{1 + \sec^2 x}$

19. $\displaystyle\int \frac{\sin x \, dx}{1 + \cos^2 x}$

20. $\displaystyle\int \frac{\cos x \, dx}{\sqrt{4 - \sin^2 x}}$

21. $\displaystyle\int_0^1 \frac{dx}{1 + x^2}$

22. $\displaystyle\int_0^2 \frac{dx}{\sqrt{4 - x^2}}$

23. $\displaystyle\int_0^1 \frac{dx}{\sqrt{25 - 9x^2}}$

24. $\displaystyle\int_0^1 \frac{dx}{25x^2 + 9}$

25. A force is acting on an object according to the equation

$$F = \frac{100}{1 + 4x^2}$$

where x is measured in metres and F is measured in newtons. Find the work done in moving the object from $x = 1$ m to $x = 2$ m.

26. Find an equation for the distance traveled by an object moving along a straight line if the velocity at time t is given by

$$v = \frac{1}{\sqrt{9 - t^2}}$$

The object was 10 m from the point of reference at $t = 0$ s.

1.6 PARTIAL FRACTIONS

The following is an example of finding the sum of two algebraic fractions:

$$\frac{5}{x + 1} + \frac{6}{x - 2} = \frac{5(x - 2)}{(x + 1)(x - 2)} + \frac{6(x + 1)}{(x + 1)(x - 2)}$$

$$= \frac{5x - 10 + 6x + 6}{(x + 1)(x - 2)}$$

$$= \frac{11x - 4}{(x + 1)(x - 2)}$$

At times, we need to express a fraction as the sum of two or more fractions that are each simpler than the original, that is, we reverse the operation. Such simpler fractions whose numerators are of lower degree than their denominators are called **partial fractions.**

We separate our study of partial fractions into four cases. In each case we assume that the given fraction is expressed in lowest terms and the degree of each numerator is less than the degree of its denominator.

For every nonrepeated factor $ax + b$ of the denominator of a given fraction, there corresponds the partial fraction $\dfrac{A}{ax + b}$, where A is a constant.

EXAMPLE 1

Find the partial fractions of $\dfrac{11x - 4}{(x + 1)(x - 2)}$.

The possible partial fractions are

$$\frac{A}{x + 1} \quad \text{and} \quad \frac{B}{x - 2}$$

So, we have

$$\frac{11x - 4}{(x + 1)(x - 2)} = \frac{A}{x + 1} + \frac{B}{x - 2}$$

Multiply each side of this equation by the L.C.D.: $(x + 1)(x - 2)$.

$$11x - 4 = A(x - 2) + B(x + 1)$$

Removing parentheses and rearranging terms, we have

$$11x - 4 = Ax - 2A + Bx + B$$
$$11x - 4 = Ax + Bx - 2A + B$$
$$11x - 4 = (A + B)x - 2A + B$$

Next, the coefficients of x must be equal and the constant terms must be equal. This gives the following system of linear equations:

$$A + B = 11$$
$$-2A + B = -4$$

Subtracting the two equations gives

$$3A = 15$$
$$A = 5$$

Substituting $A = 5$ into either of the preceding equations gives

$$B = 6$$

Then,

$$\frac{11x - 4}{(x + 1)(x - 2)} = \frac{5}{x + 1} + \frac{6}{x - 2}$$

EXAMPLE 2

Find the partial fractions of $\dfrac{3x^2 - 27x - 12}{x(2x + 1)(x - 4)}$.

The possible partial fractions are

$$\frac{A}{x} \quad \frac{B}{2x + 1} \quad \text{and} \quad \frac{C}{x - 4}$$

So, we have

$$\frac{3x^2 - 27x - 12}{x(2x + 1)(x - 4)} = \frac{A}{x} + \frac{B}{2x + 1} + \frac{C}{x - 4}$$

Now multiply each side of this equation by the L.C.D.: $x(2x + 1)(x - 4)$.

$$3x^2 - 27x - 12 = A(2x + 1)(x - 4) + Bx(x - 4) + Cx(2x + 1)$$

Removing parentheses and rearranging terms, we have

$$3x^2 - 27x - 12 = 2Ax^2 - 7Ax - 4A + Bx^2 - 4Bx + 2Cx^2 + Cx$$
$$3x^2 - 27x - 12 = (2A + B + 2C)x^2 + (-7A - 4B + C)x - 4A$$

Then, the coefficients of x^2 must be equal, the coefficients of x must be equal, and the constant terms must be equal. This gives the following system of linear equations:

$$2A + B + 2C = 3$$
$$-7A - 4B + C = -27$$
$$-4A = -12$$

Note that $A = 3$ from the third equation. Substituting $A = 3$ into the first two equations gives

$$6 + B + 2C = 3$$
$$-21 - 4B + C = -27$$

or

$$B + 2C = -3$$
$$-4B + C = -6$$

Multiplying the second equation by 2 gives

$$B + 2C = -3$$
$$-8B + 2C = -12$$

Subtracting these two equations gives

$$9B = 9$$
$$B = 1$$

Then, $C = -2$ and

$$\frac{3x^2 - 27x - 12}{x(2x + 1)(x - 4)} = \frac{3}{x} + \frac{1}{2x + 1} - \frac{2}{x - 4}$$

CASE 2: REPEATED LINEAR DENOMINATOR FACTORS

For every factor $(ax + b)^k$ of the denominator of a given fraction, there correspond the possible partial fractions

$$\frac{A_1}{ax + b}, \frac{A_2}{(ax + b)^2}, \frac{A_3}{(ax + b)^3}, \cdots, \frac{A_k}{(ax + b)^k}$$

where $A_1, A_2, A_3, \ldots, A_k$ are constants.

EXAMPLE 3

Find the partial fractions of $\dfrac{-x^2 - 8x + 27}{x(x - 3)^2}$.

The possible partial fractions are

$$\frac{A}{x} \quad \frac{B}{x - 3} \quad \text{and} \quad \frac{C}{(x - 3)^2}$$

So, we have

$$\frac{-x^2 - 8x + 27}{x(x - 3)^2} = \frac{A}{x} + \frac{B}{x - 3} + \frac{C}{(x - 3)^2}$$

Then multiply each side of this equation by the L.C.D.: $x(x - 3)^2$.

$$-x^2 - 8x + 27 = A(x - 3)^2 + Bx(x - 3) + Cx$$

Removing parentheses and rearranging terms, we have

$$-x^2 - 8x + 27 = Ax^2 - 6Ax + 9A + Bx^2 - 3Bx + Cx$$
$$-x^2 - 8x + 27 = (A + B)x^2 + (-6A - 3B + C)x + 9A$$

Equating coefficients, we have

$$A + B = -1$$
$$-6A - 3B + C = -8$$
$$9A = 27$$

From the third equation, we have $A = 3$. Substituting $A = 3$ into the first equation gives $B = -4$. Then substituting $A = 3$ and $B = -4$ into the second equation gives $C = -2$. Thus,

$$\frac{-x^2 - 8x + 27}{x(x - 3)^2} = \frac{3}{x} - \frac{4}{x - 3} - \frac{2}{(x - 3)^2}$$

EXAMPLE 4

Find the partial fractions of $\dfrac{3x^2 - 12x + 17}{(x - 2)^3}$.

Since $x - 2$ is repeated as a linear factor three times, the possible partial fractions are

$$\frac{A}{x - 2} \qquad \frac{B}{(x - 2)^2} \quad \text{and} \quad \frac{C}{(x - 2)^3}$$

So, we have

$$\frac{3x^2 - 12x + 17}{(x - 2)^3} = \frac{A}{x - 2} + \frac{B}{(x - 2)^2} + \frac{C}{(x - 2)^3}$$

Then multiply each side of this equation by the L.C.D.: $(x - 2)^3$.

$$3x^2 - 12x + 17 = A(x - 2)^2 + B(x - 2) + C$$

Removing parentheses and rearranging terms, we have

$$3x^2 - 12x + 17 = Ax^2 - 4Ax + 4A + Bx - 2B + C$$
$$3x^2 - 12x + 17 = Ax^2 + (-4A + B)x + 4A - 2B + C$$

Equating coefficients, we have the system

$$A = 3$$
$$-4A + B = -12$$
$$4A - 2B + C = 17$$

Substituting $A = 3$ into the second equation, we have $B = 0$. Then substituting $A = 3$ and $B = 0$ into the third equation, we have $C = 5$. Thus,

$$\frac{3x^2 - 12x + 17}{(x - 2)^3} = \frac{3}{x - 2} + \frac{5}{(x - 2)^3}$$

CASE 3: NONREPEATED QUADRATIC DENOMINATOR FACTORS

For every nonrepeated factor $ax^2 + bx + c$ of the denominator of a given fraction, there corresponds the partial fraction

$$\frac{Ax + B}{ax^2 + bx + c}$$

where A and B are constants.

EXAMPLE 5

Find the partial fractions of $\dfrac{11x^2 + 8x - 12}{(2x^2 + x + 2)(x + 1)}$.

The possible partial fractions are

$$\frac{Ax + B}{2x^2 + x + 2} \quad \text{and} \quad \frac{C}{x + 1}$$

So, we have

$$\frac{11x^2 + 8x - 12}{(2x^2 + x + 2)(x + 1)} = \frac{Ax + B}{2x^2 + x + 2} + \frac{C}{x + 1}$$

Then, multiply each side of this equation by the L.C.D.: $(2x^2 + x + 2)(x + 1)$.

$$11x^2 + 8x - 12 = (Ax + B)(x + 1) + C(2x^2 + x + 2)$$

Removing parentheses and rearranging terms, we have

$$11x^2 + 8x - 12 = Ax^2 + Ax + Bx + B + 2Cx^2 + Cx + 2C$$
$$11x^2 + 8x - 12 = (A + 2C)x^2 + (A + B + C)x + B + 2C$$

Equating coefficients, we have

$$A + 2C = 11$$
$$A + B + C = 8$$
$$B + 2C = -12$$

The solution of this system of linear equations is $A = 17, B = -6, C = -3$. Then

$$\frac{11x^2 + 8x - 12}{(2x^2 + x + 2)(x + 1)} = \frac{17x - 6}{2x^2 + x + 2} - \frac{3}{x + 1}$$

EXAMPLE 6

Find the partial fractions of $\dfrac{2x^3 - 2x^2 + 8x + 7}{(x^2 + 1)(x^2 + 4)}$.

The possible partial fractions are

$$\frac{Ax + B}{x^2 + 1} \quad \text{and} \quad \frac{Cx + D}{x^2 + 4}$$

So, we have

$$\frac{2x^3 - 2x^2 + 8x + 7}{(x^2 + 1)(x^2 + 4)} = \frac{Ax + B}{x^2 + 1} + \frac{Cx + D}{x^2 + 4}$$

Then, multiply each side of this equation by the L.C.D.: $(x^2 + 1)(x^2 + 4)$.

$$2x^3 - 2x^2 + 8x + 7 = (Ax + B)(x^2 + 4) + (Cx + D)(x^2 + 1)$$

Removing parentheses and rearranging terms, we have

$$2x^3 - 2x^2 + 8x + 7 = Ax^3 + Bx^2 + 4Ax + 4B + Cx^3 + Dx^2 + Cx + D$$
$$2x^3 - 2x^2 + 8x + 7 = (A + C)x^3 + (B + D)x^2 + (4A + C)x + 4B + D$$

Equating coefficients, we have

$$A + C = 2$$
$$B + D = -2$$
$$4A + C = 8$$
$$4B + D = 7$$

The solution of this system of linear equations is $A = 2, B = 3, C = 0, D = -5$. Then

$$\frac{2x^3 - 2x^2 + 8x + 7}{(x^2 + 1)(x^2 + 4)} = \frac{2x + 3}{x^2 + 1} - \frac{5}{x^2 + 4}$$

CASE 4: REPEATED QUADRATIC DENOMINATOR FACTORS

For every factor $(ax^2 + bx + c)^k$ of the denominator of a given fraction, there correspond the possible partial fractions

$$\frac{A_1x + B_1}{ax^2 + bx + c}, \frac{A_2x + B_2}{(ax^2 + bx + c)^2}, \frac{A_3x + B_3}{(ax^2 + bx + c)^3}, \ldots, \frac{A_kx + B_k}{(ax^2 + bx + c)^k}$$

where $A_1, A_2, A_3, \ldots, A_k, B_1, B_2, B_3, \ldots, B_k$ are constants.

EXAMPLE 7

Find the partial fractions of $\dfrac{5x^4 - x^3 + 44x^2 - 5x + 75}{x(x^2 + 5)^2}$.

The possible partial fractions are

$$\frac{A}{x} \quad \frac{Bx + C}{x^2 + 5} \quad \text{and} \quad \frac{Dx + E}{(x^2 + 5)^2}$$

So, we have

$$\frac{5x^4 - x^3 + 44x^2 - 5x + 75}{x(x^2 + 5)^2} = \frac{A}{x} + \frac{Bx + C}{x^2 + 5} + \frac{Dx + E}{(x^2 + 5)^2}$$

Then, multiply each side of this equation by the L.C.D.: $x(x^2 + 5)^2$.

$$5x^4 - x^3 + 44x^2 - 5x + 75 = A(x^2 + 5)^2 + (Bx + C)(x^2 + 5)(x) + (Dx + E)x$$

Removing parentheses and rearranging terms, we have

$$5x^4 - x^3 + 44x^2 - 5x + 75 = Ax^4 + 10Ax^2 + 25A + Bx^4 + Cx^3$$
$$+ 5Bx^2 + 5Cx + Dx^2 + Ex$$
$$5x^4 - x^3 + 44x^2 - 5x + 75 = (A + B)x^4 + Cx^3 + (10A + 5B + D)x^2$$
$$+ (5C + E)x + 25A$$

Equating coefficients, we have

$$A + B = 5$$
$$C = -1$$
$$10A + 5B + D = 44$$

$$5C + E = -5$$

$$25A = 75$$

The solution of this system of linear equations is $A = 3, B = 2, C = -1, D = 4, E = 0$. Then

$$\frac{5x^4 - x^3 + 44x^2 - 5x + 75}{x(x^2 + 5)^2} = \frac{3}{x} + \frac{2x - 1}{x^2 + 5} + \frac{4x}{(x^2 + 5)^2}$$

If the degree of the numerator is greater than or equal to the degree of the denominator of the original fraction, you must first divide the numerator by the denominator using long division. Then find the partial fractions of the resulting remainder term.

EXAMPLE 8

Find the partial fractions of $\dfrac{x^3 + 3x^2 + 7x + 4}{x^2 + 2x}$.

Since the degree of the numerator is greater than the degree of the denominator, divide as follows:

$$
\begin{array}{r}
x + 1 \\
x^2 + 2x \overline{)x^3 + 3x^2 + 7x + 4} \\
\underline{x^3 + 2x^2} \\
x^2 + 7x \\
\underline{x^2 + 2x} \\
5x + 4
\end{array}
$$

or

$$\frac{x^3 + 3x^2 + 7x + 4}{x^2 + 2x} = x + 1 + \frac{5x + 4}{x^2 + 2x}$$

Now factor the denominator and find the partial fractions of the remainder term.

$$\frac{5x + 4}{x(x + 2)} = \frac{A}{x} + \frac{B}{x + 2}$$

$$5x + 4 = A(x + 2) + Bx$$

$$5x + 4 = Ax + 2A + Bx$$

$$5x + 4 = (A + B)x + 2A$$

Then,

$$A + B = 5$$

$$2A = 4$$

So, $A = 2$ and $B = 3$ and

$$\frac{x^3 + 3x^2 + 7x + 4}{x^2 + 2x} = x + 1 + \frac{2}{x} + \frac{3}{x + 2}$$

Exercises 1.6

Find the partial fractions of each expression.

1. $\dfrac{8x - 29}{(x + 2)(x - 7)}$

2. $\dfrac{10x - 34}{(x - 4)(x - 2)}$

3. $\dfrac{-x - 18}{2x^2 - 5x - 12}$

4. $\dfrac{17x - 18}{3x^2 + x - 2}$

5. $\dfrac{61x^2 - 53x - 28}{x(3x - 4)(2x + 1)}$

6. $\dfrac{11x^2 - 7x - 42}{(2x + 3)(x^2 - 2x - 3)}$

7. $\dfrac{x^2 + 7x + 10}{(x + 1)(x + 3)^2}$

8. $\dfrac{3x^2 - 18x + 9}{(2x - 1)(x - 1)^2}$

9. $\dfrac{48x^2 - 20x - 5}{(4x - 1)^3}$

10. $\dfrac{x^2 + 8x}{(x + 4)^3}$

11. $\dfrac{11x^2 - 18x + 3}{x(x - 1)^2}$

12. $\dfrac{6x^2 + 4x + 4}{x^3 + 2x^2}$

13. $\dfrac{-x^2 - 4x + 3}{(x^2 + 1)(x^2 - 3)}$

14. $\dfrac{-6x^3 + 2x^2 - 3x + 10}{(2x^2 + 1)(x^2 + 5)}$

15. $\dfrac{4x^3 - 21x - 6}{(x^2 + x + 1)(x^2 - 5)}$

16. $\dfrac{x^3 + 6x^2 + 2x - 2}{(3x^2 - x - 1)(x^2 + 4)}$

17. $\dfrac{4x^3 - 16x^2 - 93x - 9}{(x^2 + 5x + 3)(x^2 - 9)}$

18. $\dfrac{12x^2 + 8x - 72}{(x^2 + x - 1)(x^2 - 16)}$

19. $\dfrac{8x^4 - x^3 + 13x^2 - 6x + 5}{x(x^2 + 1)^2}$

20. $\dfrac{-4x^4 + 6x^3 + 8x^2 - 19x + 17}{(x - 1)(x^2 - 3)^2}$

21. $\dfrac{x^5 - 2x^4 - 8x^2 + 4x - 8}{x^2(x^2 + 2)^2}$

22. $\dfrac{3x^5 + x^4 + 24x^3 + 10x^2 + 48x + 16}{x^2(x^2 + 4)^2}$

23. $\dfrac{6x^2 + 108x + 54}{x^4 - 81}$

24. $\dfrac{x^6 + 2x^4 + 3x^2 + 1}{x^2(x^2 + 1)^3}$

25. $\dfrac{x^3}{x^2 - 1}$

26. $\dfrac{x^4 + x^2}{(x + 1)(x - 2)}$

27. $\dfrac{x^3 - x^2 + 8}{x^2 - 4}$

28. $\dfrac{2x^3 - 2x^2 + 8x - 3}{x(x - 1)}$

29. $\dfrac{3x^4 - 2x^3 - 2x + 5}{x(x^2 + 1)}$

30. $\dfrac{x^5 - x^4 - 3x^3 + 7x^2 + 3x + 20}{(x + 2)(x^2 + 2)}$

1.7 INTEGRATION USING PARTIAL FRACTIONS

Integrals of the form $\displaystyle\int \dfrac{P(x)}{Q(x)}\,dx$, where $P(x)$ and $Q(x)$ are polynomials, may be integrated by first writing the rational expression as a sum of partial fractions (see Section 1.6), then integrating each term.

EXAMPLE 1

Integrate $\displaystyle\int \dfrac{3x + 1}{x^2 - x - 6}\,dx.$

First, write $\dfrac{3x + 1}{x^2 - x - 6}$ as a sum of partial fractions.

$$\frac{3x + 1}{(x - 3)(x + 2)} = \frac{A}{x - 3} + \frac{B}{x + 2}$$

Multiply each side of this equation by the L.C.D.: $(x - 3)(x + 2)$.

$$3x + 1 = A(x + 2) + B(x - 3)$$

Removing parentheses and rearranging terms, we have

$$3x + 1 = Ax + 2A + Bx - 3B$$
$$3x + 1 = Ax + Bx + 2A - 3B$$
$$3x + 1 = (A + B)x + 2A - 3B$$

Next, equate the coefficients of x and the constant terms, which gives the following system of linear equations:

$$3 = A + B$$
$$1 = 2A - 3B$$

Solving this system, we have

$$A = 2 \qquad B = 1$$

So, we write

$$\frac{3x + 1}{x^2 - x - 6} = \frac{2}{x - 3} + \frac{1}{x + 2}$$

So,

$$\int \frac{3x + 1}{x^2 - x - 6} dx = \int \left(\frac{2}{x - 3} + \frac{1}{x + 2} \right) dx$$
$$= 2 \int \frac{dx}{x - 3} + \int \frac{dx}{x + 2}$$
$$= 2 \ln|x - 3| + \ln|x + 2| + C$$

Using the properties of logarithms, we can write the result above as

$$\int \frac{3x + 1}{x^2 - x - 6} dx = \ln|(x - 3)^2(x + 2)| + C$$

We thus see how a complicated integral can be written as a sum of less complicated integrals by using partial fractions.

EXAMPLE 2

Integrate $\displaystyle\int \frac{x^3 + 3x^2 + 7x + 4}{x^2 + 2x} dx$.

This rational expression was written as a sum of partial fractions in Example 8 in Section 1.6.

$$\int \frac{x^3 + 3x^2 + 7x + 4}{x^2 + 2x} dx = \int \left(x + 1 + \frac{2}{x} + \frac{3}{x + 2} \right) dx$$
$$= \int x \, dx + \int dx + 2 \int \frac{dx}{x} + 3 \int \frac{dx}{x + 2}$$
$$= \frac{x^2}{2} + x + 2 \ln|x| + 3 \ln|x + 2| + C$$
$$= \frac{x^2}{2} + x + \ln|x^2(x + 2)^3| + C$$

Since the method of writing a rational expression as a sum of partial fractions was presented in detail in Section 1.6, the next examples will concentrate on the integration. The process of finding the partial fractions is left to the student.

EXAMPLE 3

Integrate $\int \dfrac{x^2 - x + 2}{x^3 - 2x^2 + x}\,dx.$

$$\int \dfrac{x^2 - x + 2}{x^3 - 2x^2 + x}\,dx = \int \left[\dfrac{2}{x} - \dfrac{1}{x - 1} + \dfrac{2}{(x - 1)^2}\right] dx$$

$$= 2\int \dfrac{dx}{x} - \int \dfrac{dx}{x - 1} + 2\int (x - 1)^{-2}\,dx$$

$$= 2\ln|x| - \ln|x - 1| - \dfrac{2}{x - 1} + C$$

$$= \ln\left|\dfrac{x^2}{x - 1}\right| - \dfrac{2}{x - 1} + C$$

EXAMPLE 4

Integrate $\int \dfrac{x^2 + x - 1}{x^3 + x}\,dx.$

$$\int \dfrac{x^2 + x - 1}{x^3 + x}\,dx = \int \left(\dfrac{2x + 1}{x^2 + 1} - \dfrac{1}{x}\right) dx$$

$$= \int \dfrac{2x + 1}{x^2 + 1}\,dx - \int \dfrac{dx}{x}$$

$$= \int \dfrac{2x}{x^2 + 1}\,dx + \int \dfrac{dx}{x^2 + 1} - \int \dfrac{dx}{x}$$

$$= \ln|x^2 + 1| + \arctan x - \ln|x| + C$$

$$= \ln\left|\dfrac{x^2 + 1}{x}\right| + \arctan x + C$$

EXAMPLE 5

Integrate $\int \dfrac{4x^2 - 3x + 2}{x^3 - x^2 - 2x}\,dx.$

$$\int \dfrac{4x^2 - 3x + 2}{x^3 - x^2 - 2x}\,dx = \int \left(-\dfrac{1}{x} + \dfrac{2}{x - 2} + \dfrac{3}{x + 1}\right) dx$$

$$= -\int \dfrac{dx}{x} + 2\int \dfrac{dx}{x - 2} + 3\int \dfrac{dx}{x + 1}$$

$$= -\ln|x| + 2\ln|x - 2| + 3\ln|x + 1| + C$$

$$= \ln\left|\dfrac{(x - 2)^2(x + 1)^3}{x}\right| + C$$

Exercises 1.7

Integrate.

1. $\displaystyle\int \dfrac{dx}{1 - x^2}$

2. $\displaystyle\int \dfrac{dx}{x^2 - 5x + 6}$

3. $\displaystyle\int \dfrac{dx}{x^2 + 2x - 8}$ $\displaystyle\int \dfrac{dx}{(x+4)(x-2)}$

4. $\displaystyle\int \dfrac{dx}{x^2 + x}$

5. $\displaystyle\int \dfrac{x\,dx}{x^2 - 3x + 2}$

6. $\displaystyle\int \dfrac{x\,dx}{x^3 - 3x^2 + 2x}$

7. $\displaystyle\int \dfrac{x + 1}{x^2 + 4x - 5}\,dx$

8. $\displaystyle\int \dfrac{3x - 4}{2 - x - x^2}\,dx$

9. $\displaystyle\int \dfrac{dx}{x(x + 1)^2}$ $\dfrac{A}{x} + \dfrac{B}{(x+1)} + \dfrac{C}{(x+1)}$

10. $\displaystyle\int \frac{7x - 4}{(x - 1)^2(x + 2)}\,dx$ **11.** $\displaystyle\int \frac{2x^2 + x + 3}{x^2(x + 3)}\,dx$ **12.** $\displaystyle\int \frac{x^2 - x + 2}{x^2(x + 2)}\,dx$

13. $\displaystyle\int \frac{x^3\,dx}{x^2 + 3x + 2}$ **14.** $\displaystyle\int \frac{x^2\,dx}{x^2 + 2x + 1}$ **15.** $\displaystyle\int \frac{x^2 - 2}{(x^2 + 1)x}\,dx$

16. $\displaystyle\int \frac{5x^2 - x + 11}{(x^2 + 4)(x - 1)}\,dx$ **17.** $\displaystyle\int \frac{x^3 + 2x^2 - 9}{x^2(x^2 + 9)}\,dx$ **18.** $\displaystyle\int \frac{2x^3 + 3x}{(x^2 + 1)(x^2 + 2)}\,dx$

19. $\displaystyle\int \frac{x^3\,dx}{(x^2 + 1)^2}$ **20.** $\displaystyle\int \frac{x^2 - 2x + 1}{(x^2 + 1)^2}\,dx$ **21.** $\displaystyle\int_2^3 \frac{3\,dx}{1 - x^2}$

22. $\displaystyle\int_2^3 \frac{5x + 1}{x^2 + x - 2}\,dx$ **23.** $\displaystyle\int_2^4 \frac{x\,dx}{x^2 + 4x - 5}$ **24.** $\displaystyle\int_1^3 \frac{x - 2}{x^3 + x^2}\,dx$

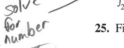 *solve for number*

x solve from F

25. Find the area of the region bounded by $y = \dfrac{4x}{x^2 + 2x - 3}$, $x = 2$, $x = 4$, and $y = 0$.

26. Find the area of the region bounded by $y = \dfrac{x + 1}{(x + 2)^2}$, $x = 0$, $x = 1$, and $y = 0$.

1.8   INTEGRATION BY PARTS

Integration by parts is another method of transforming integrals into a form that can be integrated by using familiar integration formulas. This method is based on the formula for differentiating the product of two functions u and v:

$$\frac{d}{dx}(u \cdot v) = u\frac{dv}{dx} + v\frac{du}{dx}$$

The differential form is then

$$d(u \cdot v) = u\,dv + v\,du$$

Integrating each side, we have

$$\int d(u \cdot v) = \int (u\,dv + v\,du)$$

$$u \cdot v = \int u\,dv + \int v\,du$$

Solving for $\displaystyle\int u\,dv$, we can write this equation as follows:

> **INTEGRATION BY PARTS**
>
> $$\int u\,dv = u \cdot v - \int v\,du$$

We now demonstrate the method of integration by parts.

EXAMPLE 1

Integrate $\displaystyle\int xe^{2x}\,dx$.

   Let $u = x$ and $dv = e^{2x}\,dx$; then

$$\int (x)(e^{2x}\,dx) = \int u\,dv$$

which is the left-hand side of the formula for integration by parts. Note that what we choose to call dv must contain the factor dx.

If $u = x$, then $du = dx$ and if $dv = e^{2x}\,dx$, then $v = \displaystyle\int dv = \int e^{2x}\,dx = \tfrac{1}{2}e^{2x} + C_1$.

Since

$$\int u\,dv = \quad uv \quad - \int v\,du$$

we have

$$\int (x)(e^{2x}\,dx) = (x)\left(\frac{1}{2}e^{2x} + C_1\right) - \int \left(\frac{1}{2}e^{2x} + C_1\right)dx$$

$$= \frac{1}{2}xe^{2x} + C_1x \quad - \int \frac{1}{2}e^{2x}\,dx - C_1\int dx$$

$$= \frac{1}{2}xe^{2x} + C_1x \quad - \frac{1}{4}e^{2x} - C_1x + C$$

$$= \frac{1}{2}xe^{2x} - \frac{1}{4}e^{2x} + C$$

Note: The constant of integration C_1 that arose from integrating dv disappears in the final result. This will *always* occur when using the method of integration by parts. Because of this, we will omit C_1 when integrating dv.

The decision on what to choose for u and dv is not always clear. A trial-and-error approach may be necessary. For example, we could have chosen $u = e^{2x}$ and $dv = x\,dx$ in Example 1. We would then have had $du = 2e^{2x}\,dx$ and $v = \tfrac{1}{2}x^2$. So,

$$\int e^{2x}(x\,dx) = \frac{1}{2}x^2e^{2x} - \int x^2e^{2x}\,dx$$

and the right-hand integral is more complicated than the original integral. When this occurs, you should try another choice for u and dv.

EXAMPLE 2

Integrate $\displaystyle\int x \sin x\,dx$.

$$\int u\,dv \qquad\qquad \int v\,du$$

$$\boxed{\begin{array}{l} u = x \\ dv = \sin x\,dx \end{array}} \quad\longrightarrow\quad \boxed{\begin{array}{l} du = dx \\ v = -\cos x \end{array}}$$

$$\int u\,dv = \quad uv \quad - \int v\,du$$

$$\int x \sin x\,dx = -x \cos x - \int (-\cos x)\,dx$$

$$= -x \cos x + \int \cos x\,dx$$

$$= -x \cos x + \sin x + C$$

EXAMPLE 3

Integrate $\int x^3 \ln x \, dx$.

$$\int u \, dv \qquad\qquad \int v \, du$$

$$\boxed{\begin{array}{l} u = \ln x \\ dv = x^3 \, dx \end{array}} \longrightarrow \boxed{\begin{array}{l} du = \dfrac{1}{x} dx \\ v = \dfrac{x^4}{4} \end{array}}$$

$$\int u \, dv = \quad uv \quad - \int v \, du$$

$$\int (\ln x)(x^3 \, dx) = (\ln x)\left(\frac{x^4}{4}\right) - \int \left(\frac{x^4}{4}\right)\left(\frac{1}{x} dx\right)$$

$$= \frac{1}{4} x^4 \ln x \quad - \frac{1}{4} \int x^3 \, dx$$

$$= \frac{1}{4} x^4 \ln x \quad - \frac{1}{16} x^4 + C$$

EXAMPLE 4

Integrate $\int \arcsin x \, dx$.

$$\int u \, dv \qquad\qquad \int v \, du$$

$$\boxed{\begin{array}{l} u = \arcsin x \\ dv = dx \end{array}} \longrightarrow \boxed{\begin{array}{l} du = \dfrac{dx}{\sqrt{1 - x^2}} \\ v = x \end{array}}$$

$$\int u \, dv = \quad uv \quad - \int v \, du$$

$$\int (\arcsin x)(dx) = (\arcsin x)(x) - \int (x)\left(\frac{dx}{\sqrt{1 - x^2}}\right)$$

$$= x \arcsin x \quad - \int (1 - x^2)^{-1/2} x \, dx$$

$$= x \arcsin x \quad + \sqrt{1 - x^2} + C$$

EXAMPLE 5

Integrate $\int \sec^3 x \, dx$.

$$\int u \, dv \qquad\qquad \int v \, du$$

$$\boxed{\begin{array}{l} u = \sec x \\ dv = \sec^2 x \, dx \end{array}} \longrightarrow \boxed{\begin{array}{l} du = \sec x \tan x \, dx \\ v = \tan x \end{array}}$$

$$\int u \, dv = \quad uv \quad - \int v \, du$$

$$\int (\sec x)(\sec^2 x \, dx) = (\sec x)(\tan x) - \int (\tan x)(\sec x \tan x \, dx)$$

$$= \sec x \tan x \quad - \int \sec x \tan^2 x \, dx$$

$$= \sec x \tan x \quad - \int (\sec x)(\sec^2 x - 1) \, dx$$

$$= \sec x \tan x \quad - \int \sec^3 x \, dx + \int \sec x \, dx$$

or

$$\int \sec^3 x \, dx = \sec x \tan x - \int \sec^3 x \, dx + \ln|\sec x + \tan x| + C_1$$

$$2 \int \sec^3 x \, dx = \sec x \tan x + \ln|\sec x + \tan x| + C_1 \quad \text{(Add } \int \sec^3 x \, dx \text{ to each side.)}$$

$$\int \sec^3 x \, dx = \frac{1}{2}[\sec x \tan x + \ln|\sec x + \tan x|] + C$$

Note: Whenever a multiple (not equal to 1) of the original integral appears on the right-hand side, it may be combined with the left-hand integral to complete the integration process.

EXAMPLE 6

Evaluate $\int_0^{\pi/2} e^{2x} \sin x \, dx$.

$$\int u \, dv \qquad\qquad \int v \, du$$

$$\boxed{\begin{array}{l} u = e^{2x} \\ dv = \sin x \, dx \end{array}} \qquad \longrightarrow \qquad \boxed{\begin{array}{l} du = 2e^{2x} \, dx \\ v = -\cos x \end{array}}$$

$$\int u \, dv = \quad uv \quad - \int v \, du$$

$$\int (e^{2x})(\sin x \, dx) = (e^{2x})(-\cos x) - \int (-\cos x)(2e^{2x} \, dx)$$

$$= -e^{2x} \cos x \quad + 2 \int e^{2x} \cos x \, dx \qquad\qquad \textbf{(1)}$$

In this example, we need to repeat the integration by parts process for the integral $\int e^{2x} \cos x \, dx$.

$$\int u' \, dv' \qquad\qquad \int v' \, du'$$

$$\boxed{\begin{array}{l} u' = e^{2x} \\ dv' = \cos x \, dx \end{array}} \qquad \longrightarrow \qquad \boxed{\begin{array}{l} du' = 2e^{2x} \, dx \\ v' = \sin x \end{array}}$$

$$\int u' \, dv' = \quad u'v' \quad - \int v' \, du'$$

$$\int (e^{2x})(\cos x \, dx) = (e^{2x})(\sin x) - \int (\sin x)(2e^{2x} \, dx)$$

$$= e^{2x} \sin x - 2 \int e^{2x} \sin x \, dx$$

So, substituting this result in Equation (1), we have

$$\int e^{2x} \sin x \, dx = -e^{2x} \cos x + 2\left(e^{2x} \sin x - 2 \int e^{2x} \sin x \, dx \right)$$

$$\int e^{2x} \sin x \, dx = -e^{2x} \cos x + 2e^{2x} \sin x - 4 \int e^{2x} \sin x \, dx$$

Adding $4 \int e^{2x} \sin x \, dx$ to each side and including a constant of integration, we have

$$5 \int e^{2x} \sin x \, dx = -e^{2x} \cos x + 2e^{2x} \sin x + C_1$$

$$\int e^{2x} \sin x \, dx = \frac{e^{2x}}{5}(2 \sin x - \cos x) + C$$

$$\int_0^{\pi/2} e^{2x} \sin x \, dx = \frac{e^{2x}}{5}(2 \sin x - \cos x) \Big|_0^{\pi/2}$$

$$= \frac{e^\pi}{5}(2 - 0) - \frac{1}{5}(0 - 1)$$

$$= \frac{1}{5}(2e^\pi + 1)$$

Exercises 1.8

Integrate.

1. $\displaystyle\int \ln x \, dx$ 2. $\displaystyle\int x \cos x \, dx$ 3. $\displaystyle\int xe^x \, dx$ 4. $\displaystyle\int xe^{-x} \, dx$

5. $\displaystyle\int \sqrt{x} \ln x \, dx$ 6. $\displaystyle\int x^2 \ln x \, dx$ 7. $\displaystyle\int \ln x^2 \, dx$ 8. $\displaystyle\int \frac{\ln x}{\sqrt{x}} \, dx$

9. $\displaystyle\int \arccos x \, dx$ 10. $\displaystyle\int \arctan x \, dx$ 11. $\displaystyle\int e^x \cos x \, dx$ 12. $\displaystyle\int x^2 \sin x \, dx$

13. $\displaystyle\int x^2 \cos x \, dx$ 14. $\displaystyle\int x^3 \ln x \, dx$ 15. $\displaystyle\int x \sec^2 x \, dx$ 16. $\displaystyle\int x^2 e^{2x} \, dx$

17. $\displaystyle\int (\ln x)^2 \, dx$ 18. $\displaystyle\int x \arctan x \, dx$ 19. $\displaystyle\int x \sec x \tan x \, dx$ 20. $\displaystyle\int x^3 e^{3x} \, dx$

21. $\displaystyle\int_0^1 xe^{3x} \, dx$ 22. $\displaystyle\int_0^1 \arcsin x \, dx$ 23. $\displaystyle\int_1^2 x\sqrt{x-1} \, dx$ 24. $\displaystyle\int_0^3 x\sqrt{x+1} \, dx$

25. $\displaystyle\int_1^2 \ln(x+1) \, dx$ 26. $\displaystyle\int_0^{\pi/2} x^2 \cos x \, dx$

27. Find the area of the region bounded by $y = \ln 2x$, $x = \frac{1}{2}$, $x = 1$, and $y = 0$.

28. Find the area of the region bounded by $y = x^2 e^x$, $x = 0$, $x = 2$, and $y = 0$.

29. Find the volume of the solid generated by revolving the region bounded by $y = e^x$, $y = 0$, $x = 0$, and $x = 1$ about the y-axis.

30. Find the volume of the solid generated by revolving the region bounded by $y = \sin x$, $y = 0$, $x = 0$, and $x = \pi$ about the y-axis.

1.9 INTEGRATION BY TRIGONOMETRIC SUBSTITUTION

Certain algebraic functions cannot be integrated by the methods presented so far. Appropriate trigonometric substitutions often lead to an integration solution. Algebraic functions involving the expressions $\sqrt{a^2 - u^2}$, $\sqrt{u^2 - a^2}$, or $\sqrt{u^2 + a^2}$ can often be integrated by substitutions based on the diagrams in Fig. 1.2.

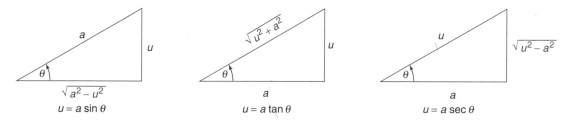

Figure 1.2 Reference triangles used for integrating expressions in the form $\sqrt{a^2 - u^2}$, $\sqrt{u^2 + a^2}$, and $\sqrt{u^2 - a^2}$, respectively.

The following examples illustrate the use of these substitutions.

EXAMPLE 1

Integrate $\displaystyle\int \frac{x^2\, dx}{\sqrt{9 - x^2}}$ (see Fig. 1.3).

Since $\sqrt{9 - x^2}$ appears in the integral, we will use the substitution

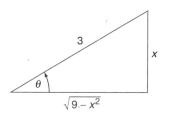

Figure 1.3

$$u = a \sin \theta \qquad (u = x, a = 3)$$
$$x = 3 \sin \theta$$
$$dx = 3 \cos \theta\, d\theta$$
$$9 - x^2 = 9 - (3 \sin \theta)^2$$
$$= 9 - 9 \sin^2 \theta$$
$$= 9(1 - \sin^2 \theta)$$
$$= 9 \cos^2 \theta$$

So,

$$\sqrt{9 - x^2} = 3 \cos \theta$$

Then,

$$\int \frac{x^2\, dx}{\sqrt{9 - x^2}} = \int \frac{(3 \sin \theta)^2 (3 \cos \theta\, d\theta)}{3 \cos \theta}$$

$$= 9 \int \sin^2 \theta\, d\theta$$

$$= 9 \int \frac{1}{2}(1 - \cos 2\theta)\, d\theta \qquad \left[\sin^2 \theta = \frac{1}{2}(1 - \cos 2\theta)\right]$$

$$= \frac{9}{2} \int d\theta - \frac{9}{2} \int \cos 2\theta\, d\theta$$

$$= \frac{9}{2}\theta - \frac{9}{4}\sin 2\theta + C$$

$$= \frac{9}{2}\theta - \frac{9}{2}\sin \theta \cos \theta + C \qquad (\sin 2\theta = 2 \sin \theta \cos \theta)$$

From Fig. 1.3

$$\sin \theta = \frac{x}{3}, \qquad \text{so} \qquad \theta = \arcsin \frac{x}{3}$$

$$\cos \theta = \frac{\sqrt{9 - x^2}}{3}$$

Making these substitutions, we have

$$\int \frac{x^2 \, dx}{\sqrt{9 - x^2}} = \frac{9}{2}\arcsin \frac{x}{3} - \frac{9}{2} \cdot \frac{x}{3} \cdot \frac{\sqrt{9 - x^2}}{3} + C = \frac{9}{2}\arcsin \frac{x}{3} - \frac{x\sqrt{9 - x^2}}{2} + C$$

EXAMPLE 2

Integrate $\displaystyle\int \frac{dx}{\sqrt{x^2 + 4}}$ (see Fig. 1.4).

Since $\sqrt{x^2 + 4}$ appears in the integral, we use the substitutions

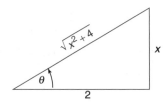

$$u = a \tan \theta \qquad (u = x, a = 2)$$

$$x = 2 \tan \theta$$

$$dx = 2 \sec^2 \theta \, d\theta$$

$$x^2 + 4 = (2 \tan \theta)^2 + 4$$

$$= 4 \tan^2 \theta + 4$$

$$= 4(\tan^2 \theta + 1)$$

$$= 4 \sec^2 \theta$$

Figure 1.4

So,

$$\sqrt{x^2 + 4} = 2 \sec \theta$$

Then,

$$\int \frac{dx}{\sqrt{x^2 + 4}} = \int \frac{2 \sec^2 \theta \, d\theta}{2 \sec \theta}$$

$$= \int \sec \theta \, d\theta$$

$$= \ln |\sec \theta + \tan \theta| + C$$

From Fig 1 4 we have

$$\sec \theta = \frac{\sqrt{x^2 + 4}}{2}$$

$$\tan \theta = \frac{x}{2}$$

Making these substitutions, we have

$$\int \frac{dx}{\sqrt{x^2 + 4}} = \ln \left| \frac{\sqrt{x^2 + 4}}{2} + \frac{x}{2} \right| + C$$

$$= \ln \left| \frac{\sqrt{x^2 + 4} + x}{2} \right| + C$$

$$= \ln \left| \sqrt{x^2 + 4} + x \right| - \ln 2 + C$$

$$= \ln \left| \sqrt{x^2 + 4} + x \right| + C' \qquad \text{(since } -\ln 2 \text{ is also a } constant\text{)}$$

EXAMPLE 3

Integrate $\displaystyle\int \frac{dx}{\sqrt{(4x^2 - 25)^3}}$ (see Fig. 1.5).

The denominator can be written as $\sqrt{(4x^2 - 25)^3} = (4x^2 - 25)\sqrt{4x^2 - 25}$. This suggests the substitutions:

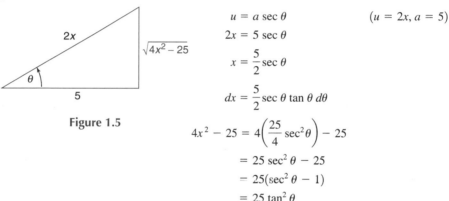

Figure 1.5

$$u = a \sec \theta \qquad\qquad (u = 2x, a = 5)$$

$$2x = 5 \sec \theta$$

$$x = \frac{5}{2} \sec \theta$$

$$dx = \frac{5}{2} \sec \theta \tan \theta \, d\theta$$

$$4x^2 - 25 = 4\left(\frac{25}{4} \sec^2\theta\right) - 25$$

$$= 25 \sec^2 \theta - 25$$

$$= 25(\sec^2 \theta - 1)$$

$$= 25 \tan^2 \theta$$

So,

$$\sqrt{4x^2 - 25} = 5 \tan \theta$$

Then,

$$\int \frac{dx}{\sqrt{(4x^2 - 25)^3}} = \int \frac{\frac{5}{2} \sec \theta \tan \theta \, d\theta}{(5 \tan \theta)^3}$$

$$= \frac{1}{50} \int \frac{\sec \theta \tan \theta \, d\theta}{\tan^3 \theta}$$

$$= \frac{1}{50} \int \frac{\sec \theta}{\tan^2 \theta} \, d\theta$$

$$= \frac{1}{50} \int \frac{\dfrac{1}{\cos \theta}}{\dfrac{\sin^2 \theta}{\cos^2 \theta}} \, d\theta$$

$$= \frac{1}{50} \int \frac{\cos \theta}{\sin^2 \theta} \, d\theta$$

$$= \frac{1}{50}\left(-\frac{1}{\sin\theta}\right) + C$$

$$= -\frac{1}{50}\csc\theta + C \qquad \left(\csc\theta = \frac{2x}{\sqrt{4x^2 - 25}} \text{ from Fig. 7.5}\right)$$

$$= \frac{-x}{25\sqrt{4x^2 - 25}} + C$$

EXAMPLE 4

Evaluate $\displaystyle\int_0^4 \frac{dx}{(\sqrt{x^2 + 9})^3}$ (see Fig. 1.6).

$$\begin{array}{|c|}\hline x = 3\tan\theta \\ dx = 3\sec^2\theta\, d\theta \\\hline\end{array}$$

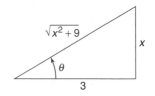

Figure 1.6

$$\int \frac{dx}{(\sqrt{x^2 + 9})^3} = \int \frac{3\sec^2\theta\, d\theta}{(\sqrt{9\tan^2\theta + 9})^3}$$

$$= \int \frac{3\sec^2\theta\, d\theta}{(\sqrt{9\sec^2\theta})^3}$$

$$= \int \frac{3\sec^2\theta\, d\theta}{27\sec^3\theta}$$

$$= \frac{1}{9}\int \frac{1}{\sec\theta}\, d\theta$$

$$= \frac{1}{9}\int \cos\theta\, d\theta$$

$$= \frac{1}{9}\sin\theta + C$$

$$= \frac{1}{9}\cdot\frac{x}{\sqrt{x^2 + 9}} + C$$

$$= \frac{x}{9\sqrt{x^2 + 9}} + C$$

So,

$$\int_0^4 \frac{dx}{(\sqrt{x^2 + 9})^3} = \frac{x}{9\sqrt{x^2 + 9}}\Bigg|_0^4 = \frac{4}{9\sqrt{25}} - 0 = \frac{4}{45}$$

Using a calculator, we have

2nd 7 1/ **2nd** $\sqrt{}$ x^2+9)^3,x,0,4) **ENTER**

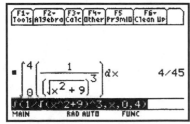

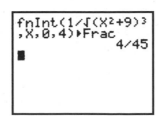

Math 9 1/ **2nd** $\sqrt{}$ x x^2 +9) **MATH 3** ,x,0,4) **MATH 1 ENTER**

Exercises 1.9

Integrate.

1. $\displaystyle\int \frac{dx}{\sqrt{9 + 4x^2}}$

2. $\displaystyle\int \frac{dx}{\sqrt{9 - 16x^2}}$

3. $\displaystyle\int \frac{x^2}{\sqrt{4 - 9x^2}}\,dx$

4. $\displaystyle\int \frac{x^2}{\sqrt{1 - 16x^2}}\,dx$

5. $\displaystyle\int_0^1 \frac{dx}{\sqrt{9 - x^2}}$

6. $\displaystyle\int_0^2 \frac{dx}{\sqrt{16 + x^2}}$

7. $\displaystyle\int_0^1 \frac{dx}{\sqrt{(4 - x^2)^3}}$

8. $\displaystyle\int_2^3 \frac{dx}{\sqrt{4x^2 - 9}}$

9. $\displaystyle\int \frac{dx}{x\sqrt{x^2 + 4}}$

10. $\displaystyle\int \frac{dx}{x\sqrt{9 - x^2}}$

11. $\displaystyle\int \frac{\sqrt{x^2 - 9}}{x^2}\,dx$

12. $\displaystyle\int \frac{dx}{\sqrt{(x^2 + 4)^3}}$

13. $\displaystyle\int \frac{dx}{x^2\sqrt{16 - x^2}}$

14. $\displaystyle\int \frac{dx}{x\sqrt{x^2 + 9}}$

15. $\displaystyle\int \frac{\sqrt{9 + x^2}}{x}\,dx$

16. $\displaystyle\int \frac{\sqrt{4 + 9x^2}}{x}\,dx$

17. $\displaystyle\int \frac{dx}{(25 - x^2)^{3/2}}$

18. $\displaystyle\int \frac{dx}{(x^2 - 5)^{3/2}}$

19. $\displaystyle\int \frac{dx}{\sqrt{x^2 - 9}}$

20. $\displaystyle\int \frac{dx}{x\sqrt{1 - x^2}}$

21. $\displaystyle\int \frac{x^3\,dx}{\sqrt{9x^2 + 4}}$

22. $\displaystyle\int \frac{x^2\,dx}{(4 + x^2)^2}$

23. $\displaystyle\int \frac{dx}{\sqrt{x^2 - 6x + 8}}$

(*Hint:* Complete the square under the radical.)

24. $\displaystyle\int \frac{dx}{\sqrt{-9x^2 + 18x - 5}}$

25. $\displaystyle\int \frac{dx}{(x^2 + 8x + 15)^{3/2}}$

26. $\displaystyle\int \frac{dx}{\sqrt{9x^2 + 36x + 52}}$

27. Find the area of the region bounded by $y = \dfrac{1}{\sqrt{x^2 + 4}}$, $x = 0$, $x = 2$, and $y = 0$.

28. Find the area of the region bounded by $y = \sqrt{4 - x^2}$, $x = 0$, $x = 2$, and $y = 0$.

1.10 INTEGRATION USING TABLES

The Table of Integrals in Appendix B lists some standard integration formulas for integrating selected functions. These formulas have been developed using the techniques of this chapter and other methods of integrating various complicated functions. A more extensive list of integration formulas (usually more than 400) can be found in most standard handbooks of mathematical tables.

We now illustrate how to use these tables. In the Table of Integrals in Appendix B, u represents a function of x.

EXAMPLE 1

Integrate $\displaystyle\int x\sqrt{3 + 4x}\,dx$.

If we let $u = x$, $a = 3$, and $b = 4$, this integral is in the form of Formula 11 in Appendix B. Substituting these values of u, a, and b in this formula, we have

$$\int x\sqrt{3 + 4x}\,dx = \frac{-2[2(3) - 3(4)(x)][(3) + (4)(x)]^{3/2}}{15(4)^2} + C$$

$$= \frac{(2x - 1)(3 + 4x)^{3/2}}{20} + C$$

EXAMPLE 2

Integrate $\displaystyle\int \frac{dx}{x\sqrt{9 + 5x}}$.

If we let $u = x$, $a = 9$, and $b = 5$, then the integral is in the form of Formula 15. Substituting these values of u, a, and b in this formula, we have

$$\int \frac{dx}{x\sqrt{9 + 5x}} = \frac{1}{3}\ln\left|\frac{\sqrt{9 + 5x} - 3}{\sqrt{9 + 5x} + 3}\right| + C$$

EXAMPLE 3

Integrate $\displaystyle\int x^{100}\ln x\,dx$.

If we let $u = x$ and $n = 100$, then this integral is in the form of Formula 57.

$$\int x^{100}\ln x\,dx = \frac{x^{101}\ln x}{101} - \frac{x^{101}}{(101)^2} + C$$

EXAMPLE 4

Integrate $\displaystyle\int 2^{\sin x}\cos x\,dx$.

If we let $u = \sin x$ and $a = 2$, then since $du = \cos x\,dx$, this integral is in the form of Formula 52.

$$\int 2^{\sin x}\cos x\,dx = \int 2^u\,du$$
$$= \frac{2^u}{\ln 2} + C$$
$$= \frac{2^{\sin x}}{\ln 2} + C$$

$$\boxed{\begin{array}{l} u = \sin x \\ du = \cos x\,dx \end{array}}$$

EXAMPLE 5

Integrate $\displaystyle\int \sin^5 3x\,dx$.

If we let $u = 3x$ and $n = 5$, then the integral is in the form of Formula 83.

$$\int \sin^5 3x\,dx = \int \sin^5 u\,\frac{du}{3}$$
$$= \frac{1}{3}\int \sin^5 u\,du$$
$$= \frac{1}{3}\left(-\frac{1}{5}\sin^{5-1}u\cos u + \frac{4}{5}\int \sin^3 u\,du\right)$$
$$= -\frac{1}{15}\sin^4 u\cos u + \frac{4}{15}\int \sin^3 u\,du$$

$$\boxed{\begin{array}{l} u = 3x \\ du = 3\,dx \end{array}}$$

The solution is not complete. We still need to integrate $\int \sin^3 u \, du$, which can be integrated by using Formula 83 again.

$$\int \sin^3 u \, du = -\frac{1}{3} \sin^2 u \cos u + \frac{2}{3} \int \sin u \, du$$

$$= -\frac{1}{3} \sin^2 u \cos u - \frac{2}{3} \cos u$$

So,

$$\int \sin^5 3x \, dx = -\frac{1}{15} \sin^4 u \cos u + \frac{4}{15}\left(-\frac{1}{3} \sin^2 u \cos u - \frac{2}{3} \cos u\right) + C$$

$$= -\frac{1}{15} \sin^4 3x \cos 3x - \frac{4}{45} \sin^2 3x \cos 3x - \frac{8}{45} \cos 3x + C$$

Exercises 1.10

Integrate using the Table of Integrals in Appendix B. Give the number of the formula used.

1. $\displaystyle\int \frac{dx}{x\sqrt{x + 5}}$

2. $\displaystyle\int \frac{x \, dx}{2 + 7x}$

3. $\displaystyle\int \frac{dx}{\sqrt{x^2 - 4}}$

4. $\displaystyle\int \frac{dx}{\sqrt{6 + x^2}}$

5. $\displaystyle\int \frac{x \, dx}{\sqrt{2x + 3}}$

6. $\displaystyle\int x\sqrt{4x + 7} \, dx$

7. $\displaystyle\int \sin 7x \sin 3x \, dx$

8. $\displaystyle\int \cos 5x \cos 2x \, dx$

9. $\displaystyle\int \frac{x^2 \, dx}{\sqrt{9 - x^2}}$

10. $\displaystyle\int \frac{dx}{x\sqrt{16 - x^2}}$

11. $\displaystyle\int \frac{dx}{x(1 + 9x)^2}$

12. $\displaystyle\int x^2 e^{4x} \, dx$

13. $\displaystyle\int \frac{dx}{x^2 - 25}$

14. $\displaystyle\int \frac{dx}{x\sqrt{9 - 16x^2}}$

15. $\displaystyle\int \sqrt{x^2 + 4} \, dx$

16. $\displaystyle\int \frac{dx}{x(2 + 5x)^2}$

17. $\displaystyle\int \frac{x \, dx}{(3 + 4x)^2}$

18. $\displaystyle\int \frac{5x \, dx}{\sqrt{2 + 4x}}$

19. $\displaystyle\int \frac{dx}{x\sqrt{9x^2 - 16}}$

20. $\displaystyle\int xe^{5x} \, dx$

21. $\displaystyle\int e^{3x} \sin 4x \, dx$

22. $\displaystyle\int e^{2x} \cos 5x \, dx$

23. $\displaystyle\int (2x - 3)\sin(2x - 3) \, dx$

24. $\displaystyle\int x^2 \cos x^2 \, dx$

25. $\displaystyle\int \sin^4 x \, dx$

26. $\displaystyle\int \cos^5 x \, dx$

27. $\displaystyle\int \frac{\sqrt{9x^2 - 16}}{x} \, dx$

28. $\displaystyle\int \frac{dx}{(25 - 4x^2)^{3/2}}$

1.11 NUMERICAL METHODS OF INTEGRATION

Despite the numerous integration techniques and formulas available, there are still many functions that are difficult to integrate. In fact, the value of some integrals cannot be exactly determined by any known method of integration. However, several numerical techniques have been developed for approximating the value of an integral. These numerical methods can easily be used with the help of a calculator or a computer.

The *trapezoidal rule* can be demonstrated by considering $\int_a^b f(x) \, dx$ as representing the area bounded by the curves $y = f(x)$, $x = a$, $x = b$, and the x-axis. The trapezoidal rule is based on approximating this area by the sum of the areas of selected trapezoids.

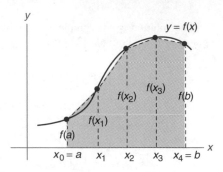

Figure 1.7 The area under a curve may be estimated by adding the areas of the trapezoids.

The line segment from a to b is divided into n intervals, each of width $\Delta x = \dfrac{b-a}{n}$ as shown in Fig. 1.7. $\left(\text{Here, } n = 4, \text{ so } \Delta x = \dfrac{b-a}{4}.\right)$ This process determines $(n+1)$ numbers on the x-axis: $x_0 = a,\, x_1 = a + \Delta x,\, x_2 = a + 2\,\Delta x,\, x_3 = a + 3\,\Delta x, \ldots,$ $x_n = a + n\,\Delta x = b$. Then, forming the $n = 4$ trapezoids as shown in Fig. 1.7, we have

$$\frac{1}{2}[f(a) + f(x_1)]\Delta x \qquad \text{as the area of the first trapezoid}$$

$$\frac{1}{2}[f(x_1) + f(x_2)]\Delta x \qquad \text{as the area of the second trapezoid}$$

$$\frac{1}{2}[f(x_2) + f(x_3)]\Delta x \qquad \text{as the area of the third trapezoid}$$

$$\frac{1}{2}[f(x_3) + f(b)]\Delta x \qquad \text{as the area of the fourth trapezoid}$$

The sum of these four areas is then used as an approximation for the area $\int_a^b f(x)\, dx$. In summing these four areas, we have

$$\frac{\Delta x}{2}[f(a) + 2f(x_1) + 2f(x_2) + 2f(x_3) + f(b)]$$

In general, we have the following rule:

TRAPEZOIDAL RULE

$$\int_a^b f(x)\, dx \cong \frac{\Delta x}{2}[f(a) + 2f(x_1) + 2f(x_2) + 2f(x_3) + \cdots + 2f(x_{n-1}) + f(b)]$$

The symbol $\cong$ means "approximately equals."
Note: The pattern of coefficients is $1, 2, 2, 2, \ldots, 2, 2, 1$.

EXAMPLE 1

Use the trapezoidal rule with $n = 4$ to find the approximate value of $\int_1^2 \dfrac{dx}{x}$ (see Fig. 1.8).

Since $n = 4$, $\Delta x = \dfrac{b-a}{n} = \dfrac{2-1}{4} = \dfrac{1}{4}$ and

$$x_0 = a = 1 \qquad\qquad f(a) = \frac{1}{1} = 1$$

$$x_1 = 1 + \frac{1}{4} = \frac{5}{4} \qquad f(x_1) = \frac{1}{\frac{5}{4}} = \frac{4}{5}$$

$$x_2 = 1 + 2\left(\frac{1}{4}\right) = \frac{3}{2} \qquad f(x_2) = \frac{1}{\frac{3}{2}} = \frac{2}{3}$$

$$x_3 = 1 + 3\left(\frac{1}{4}\right) = \frac{7}{4} \qquad f(x_3) = \frac{1}{\frac{7}{4}} = \frac{4}{7}$$

$$x_4 = b = 1 + 4\left(\frac{1}{4}\right) = 2 \qquad f(b) = \frac{1}{2}$$

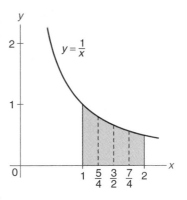

Figure 1.8

$$\int_1^2 \frac{dx}{x} \cong \frac{\Delta x}{2}[f(a) + 2f(x_1) + 2f(x_2) + 2f(x_3) + f(b)]$$

$$= \frac{\frac{1}{4}}{2}\left[1 + 2\left(\frac{4}{5}\right) + 2\left(\frac{2}{3}\right) + 2\left(\frac{4}{7}\right) + \frac{1}{2}\right]$$

$$= \frac{1}{8}\left(1 + \frac{8}{5} + \frac{4}{3} + \frac{8}{7} + \frac{1}{2}\right) = 0.6970$$

For comparison, in Section 1.2, Example 8, we found the exact value to be

$$\int_1^2 \frac{dx}{x} = \ln x\Big|_1^2 = \ln 2 - \ln 1 = \ln 2 - 0 = \ln 2 = 0.6931.$$

EXAMPLE 2

Use the trapezoidal rule with $n = 8$ to find the approximate value of $\int_1^5 x\sqrt{x-1}\, dx$

(see Fig. 1.9). First, $\Delta x = \dfrac{b-a}{n} = \dfrac{5-1}{8} = \dfrac{4}{8} = \dfrac{1}{2} = 0.5$. We have

$$x_0 = a = 1 \qquad f(a) = f(1) = 0$$
$$x_1 = 1.5 \qquad f(x_1) = f(1.5) = 1.061$$
$$x_2 = 2 \qquad f(x_2) = f(2) = 2$$
$$x_3 = 2.5 \qquad f(x_3) = f(2.5) = 3.062$$
$$x_4 = 3 \qquad f(x_4) = f(3) = 4.243$$
$$x_5 = 3.5 \qquad f(x_5) = f(3.5) = 5.534$$
$$x_6 = 4 \qquad f(x_6) = f(4) = 6.928$$
$$x_7 = 4.5 \qquad f(x_7) = f(4.5) = 8.419$$
$$x_8 = b = 5 \qquad f(b) = f(5) = 10$$

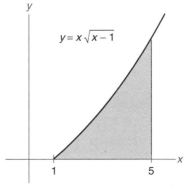

Figure 1.9

So,

$$\int_1^5 x\sqrt{x-1}\, dx \cong \frac{\Delta x}{2}[f(a) + 2f(x_1) + 2f(x_2) + 2f(x_3) + 2f(x_4) + 2f(x_5)$$

$$+ 2f(x_6) + 2f(x_7) + f(b)]$$

$$= \frac{0.5}{2}[0 + 2(1.061) + 2(2) + 2(3.062) + 2(4.243) + 2(5.534)$$

$$+ 2(6.928) + 2(8.419) + 10]$$

$$= 18.12$$

Note: Slight variations in the results may occur due to rounding.

Numerical methods of integration are especially helpful when the function to be integrated is not completely known.

EXAMPLE 3

Find the work done in moving an object along a straight line for 10 ft if the following measurements were made:

Distance moved (ft)	0	2	4	6	8	10
Force (lb)	12	9	7	5	4	2

The formula for work W done in moving an object from a to b is $W = \int_a^b f(x)\,dx$, where $f(x)$ is the force exerted on the object at x.

In this example we do not know what the function $f(x)$ looks like, but we do know its values at 2-ft intervals $(\Delta x = 2)$. Here, $x_0 = a = 0$, $x_1 = 2$, $x_2 = 4$, $x_3 = 6$, $x_4 = 8$, and $x_5 = b = 10$. So,

$$W = \int_0^{10} f(x)\,dx \cong \frac{\Delta x}{2}[f(a) + 2f(x_1) + 2f(x_2) + 2f(x_3) + 2f(x_4) + f(b)]$$

$$= \frac{2}{2}[12 + 2(9) + 2(7) + 2(5) + 2(4) + 2]$$

$$= 64 \text{ foot-pounds (ft-lb)}$$

A second method of approximating the value of an integral is called *Simpson's rule*, which uses parabolic areas instead of trapezoidal areas and is usually more accurate. As before, divide the line segment from a to b into n intervals, each of width $\Delta x = \dfrac{b-a}{n}$ (n must be even here). Then fit parabolas to adjacent triples of points as shown in Fig. 1.10.

The areas under the parabolic segments are then summed. The development of this formula is rather difficult and can be found in more advanced texts.

SIMPSON'S RULE

$$\int_a^b f(x)\,dx \cong \frac{\Delta x}{3}[f(a) + 4f(x_1) + 2f(x_2) + 4f(x_3) + 2f(x_4)$$

$$+ \cdots + 4f(x_{n-1}) + f(b)]$$

(n must be an even integer.)

Note: The pattern of coefficients is 1, 4, 2, 4, 2, 4, ... , 2, 4, 1.

We now use Simpson's rule to obtain another approximation for $\displaystyle\int_1^2 \frac{dx}{x}$ (see Example 1).

$$\int_1^2 \frac{dx}{x} \cong \frac{\frac{1}{4}}{3}\left[1 + 4\left(\frac{4}{5}\right) + 2\left(\frac{2}{3}\right) + 4\left(\frac{4}{7}\right) + \frac{1}{2}\right]$$

$$= \frac{1}{12}\left(1 + \frac{16}{5} + \frac{4}{3} + \frac{16}{7} + \frac{1}{2}\right) = 0.6933$$

Note that the exact answer is ln 2, which is approximately 0.693147.

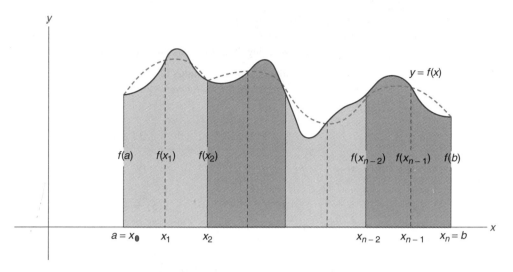

Figure 1.10 The area under a curve may be estimated by adding the areas under parabolic segments instead of trapezoidal strips.

EXAMPLE 4

Use Simpson's rule with $n = 6$ to find the approximate value of $\displaystyle\int_1^4 \frac{dx}{x+2}$.

First, $\Delta x = \dfrac{b-a}{n} = \dfrac{4-1}{6} = \dfrac{3}{6} = \dfrac{1}{2} = 0.5$. We have

$$x_0 = a = 1 \qquad f(a) = f(1) = \frac{1}{3}$$

$$x_1 = 1.5 \qquad f(x_1) = f(1.5) = \frac{1}{3.5}$$

$$x_2 = 2 \qquad f(x_2) = f(2) = \frac{1}{4}$$

$$x_3 = 2.5 \qquad f(x_3) = f(2.5) = \frac{1}{4.5}$$

$$x_4 = 3 \qquad f(x_4) = f(3) = \frac{1}{5}$$

$$x_5 = 3.5 \qquad f(x_5) = f(3.5) = \frac{1}{5.5}$$

$$x_6 = b = 4 \qquad f(b) = f(4) = \frac{1}{6}$$

Then,

$$\int_1^4 \frac{dx}{x+2} \cong \frac{\Delta x}{3}[f(a) + 4f(x_1) + 2f(x_2) + 4f(x_3) + 2f(x_4) + 4f(x_5) + f(b)]$$

$$= \frac{0.5}{3}\left[\frac{1}{3} + 4\left(\frac{1}{3.5}\right) + 2\left(\frac{1}{4}\right) + 4\left(\frac{1}{4.5}\right) + 2\left(\frac{1}{5}\right) + 4\left(\frac{1}{5.5}\right) + \frac{1}{6}\right]$$

$$= 0.6932$$

EXAMPLE 5

Estimate $\int_{2}^{5} f(x)\,dx$ using Simpson's rule and the following table of values of $f(x)$ (note that since Simpson's rule requires the number of intervals to be *even*, the number of function values must be *odd*; for example, these seven equally spaced x-values have six spaces between them):

x	2	2.5	3	3.5	4	4.5	5
$f(x)$	3	6	5	4	7	8	9

$$\int_{2}^{5} f(x)\,dx \cong \frac{0.5}{3}[(3) + 4(6) + 2(5) + 4(4) + 2(7) + 4(8) + (9)] = 18$$

Calculator Programs: Trapezoidal Rule, Simpson's Rule

The following programs are written for a Texas Instruments TI-83 or TI-83 Plus Graphing Calculator. Sample output is shown in Figs. 1.11a and 1.11b.

Exercises 1.11

Use the trapezoidal rule to approximate the value of each integral.

1. $\int_{1}^{3} \frac{dx}{x}, n = 4$ **2.** $\int_{1}^{2} \frac{dx}{x}, n = 10$ **3.** $\int_{0}^{1} \frac{dx}{1 + x^2}, n = 4$

4. $\int_{0}^{2} \frac{dx}{4 + x}, n = 6$ **5.** $\int_{0}^{1} \sqrt{4 - x^2}\,dx, n = 10$ **6.** $\int_{0}^{2} 2^x\,dx, n = 4$

7. $\int_{0}^{3} \sqrt{1 + x^3}\,dx, n = 6$ **8.** $\int_{0}^{2} \frac{dx}{\sqrt{1 + x^3}}, n = 4$ **9.** $\int_{0}^{\pi/3} \cos x^2\,dx, n = 8$

10. $\int_{0}^{\pi/4} \tan x^2\,dx, n = 4$

11. Use the trapezoidal rule to find the work done in moving an object along a straight line for 14 ft if the following measurements were made:

Distance moved (ft)	0	2	4	6	8	10	12	14
Force (lb)	24	21	18	17	15	12	10	9

12. Use the trapezoidal rule to find the distance traveled in 6 s by an object moving along a straight line if the following data were recorded:

Time (s)	0	1	2	3	4	5	6
Velocity (m/s)	20	30	50	60	40	30	10

Use the trapezoidal rule to find the approximate area under the curve through each set of points.

13.

x	3	6	9	12	15	18	21
y	12	11	18	25	19	6	10

Program: TRAPZOID

```
:ClrHome
:Output(1,4,"NUMERICAL")
:Output(2,3,"INTEGRATION")
:Output(4,1,"TRAPEZOIDAL RULE")
:Output(8,1,"* PRESS  ENTER *")
:Pause
:Radian
:ClrHome
:Menu("INTEGRATING:","THE CURRENT Y₀",1,"WRITE A NEW Y₀",A)
:Lbl A
:ClrHome
:Disp "ENTER YOUR NEW","FUNCTION.",""
:Input "Y₀=",Str0
:String▶Equ(Str0,Y₀)
:FnOff 0
:Lbl 1
:ClrHome
:Disp "LIMITS OF","INTEGRATION:",""
:Input "LOWER=",A
:Input "UPPER=",B
:Disp "","N SUBINTERVALS:"
:Input "N=",N
:Output(1,1,"PLEASE WAIT ...")
:0→S
:0→K
:B-A→D
:For(J,1,N)
:Y₀(A+KD/N)+S→S
:Y₀(A+(K+1)D/N)+S→S
:K+1→K
:End
:SD/(2N)→I
:Disp "TRAPEZ. INTEGRAL",I
:Output(3,1,"Y₀=")
:Equ▶String(Y₀,Str0)
:Output(3,4,Str0)
```

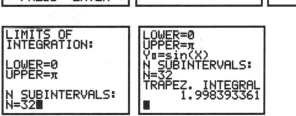

Figure 1.11a

14.

x	−4	0	4	8	12	16	20
y	11	9	3	10	21	30	40

Use Simpson's rule to approximate the value of each integral.

15. $\displaystyle\int_0^2 \frac{dx}{\sqrt{1+x^2}}, n = 4$

16. $\displaystyle\int_0^2 \sqrt[3]{8-x^2}\,dx, n = 4$

```
Program:    SIMPSON
------------------------------
:ClrHome
:Output(1,4,"NUMERICAL")
:Output(2,3,"INTEGRATION")
:Output(4,2,"SIMPSON'S RULE")
:Output(8,1,"* PRESS  ENTER *")
:Pause
:Radian
:ClrHome
:Menu("INTEGRATING:","THE CURRENT Y₀",1,"WRITE A NEW Y₀",A)
:Lbl A
:ClrHome
:Disp "ENTER YOUR NEW","FUNCTION.",""
:Input "Y₀=",Str0
:String▶Equ(Str0,Y₀)
:FnOff 0
:Lbl 1
:ClrHome
:Disp "LIMITS OF","INTEGRATION:",""
:Input "LOWER=",A
:Input "UPPER=",B
:Lbl 2
:Disp "","N SUBINTERVALS:"
:Input "N=",N
:If N-2int(N/2)≠0:Then
:Disp "N MUST BE EVEN,","TRY AGAIN.","",""
:Goto 2
:End
:Output(1,1,"PLEASE WAIT ...")
:0→S
:0→K
:B-A→D
:For(J,1,N/2)
:Y₀(A+KD/N)+S→S
:4Y₀(A+(K+1)D/N)+S→S
:Y₀(A+(K+2)D/N)+S→S
:K+2→K
:End
:SD/(3N)→I
:Disp "SIMPSON INTEGRAL",I
:Output(3,1,"Y₀=")
:Equ▶String(Y₀,Str0)
:Output(3,4,Str0)
```

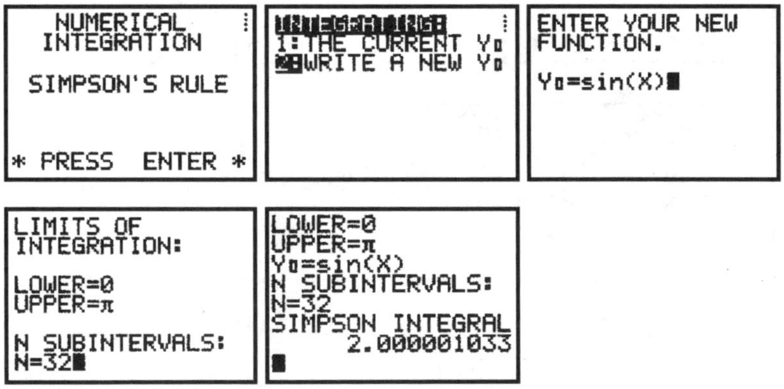

```
   NUMERICAL
   INTEGRATION

  SIMPSON'S RULE


* PRESS  ENTER *
```

```
INTEGRATING:
1:THE CURRENT Y₀
2:WRITE A NEW Y₀
```

```
ENTER YOUR NEW
FUNCTION.

Y₀=sin(X)■
```

```
LIMITS OF
INTEGRATION:

LOWER=0
UPPER=π

N SUBINTERVALS:
N=32■
```

```
LOWER=0
UPPER=π
Y₀=sin(X)
N SUBINTERVALS:
N=32
SIMPSON INTEGRAL
      2.000001033
■
```

Figure 1.11b

17. $\displaystyle\int_2^6 \frac{dx}{1+x^3}, n = 8$ **18.** $\displaystyle\int_1^3 x^x \, dx, n = 8$

19. $\displaystyle\int_0^1 e^{x^2} \, dx, n = 4$ **20.** $\displaystyle\int_0^1 e^{-x^2} \, dx, n = 4$

21. $\int_0^{\pi/4} x \tan x \, dx, \, n = 4$

22. $\int_1^2 \sqrt{x} \sin x \, dx, \, n = 4$

23. $\int_0^{\pi/2} \sqrt{1 + \cos^2 x} \, dx, \, n = 6$

24. $\int_{\pi/6}^{\pi/3} \csc x \, dx, \, n = 4$

Approximate the value of each integral by (a) using the trapezoidal rule and (b) using Simpson's rule.

25. $\int_0^3 \sqrt{9 - x^2} \, dx, \, n = 6$

26. $\int_0^\pi \frac{\sin x}{1 + x} \, dx, \, n = 6$

27. $\int_0^1 x e^x \, dx, \, n = 4$

28. $\int_0^1 x e^{x^2} \, dx, \, n = 4$

29. $\int_0^{\pi/2} \cos \sqrt{x} \, dx, \, n = 6$

30. $\int_0^{\pi/2} \cos^2 x \, dx, \, n = 6$

31. Find the approximate area of the field in Fig. 1.12 **(a)** using the trapezoidal rule and **(b)** using Simpson's rule.

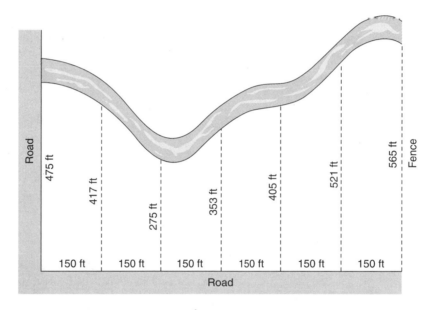

Figure 1.12

1.12 AREAS IN POLAR COORDINATES

Finding areas in polar coordinates is similar to finding the area of a region in rectangular coordinates. Suppose that we have a region bounded by $r = f(\theta)$ and the terminal sides of angles α and β in standard position, where $\alpha < \beta$ (see Fig. 1.13a). Instead of rectangles as in rectangular coordinates, let's subdivide the angular region into n subintervals of circular sectors as follows:

$$\alpha = \theta_0, \theta_1, \theta_2, \dots, \theta_n = \beta$$

Let r_i be any ray within the ith sector. Then, $\Delta\theta_i$ is the central angle of the ith sector and $r_i = f(\theta_i)$ is the radius of the ith sector.

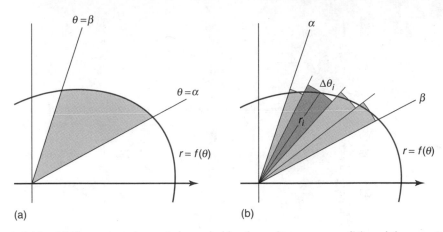

Figure 1.13 (a) The region shown is bounded by the polar curve $r = f(\theta)$ and the rays $\theta = \alpha$ and $\theta = \beta$. (b) The area of the region shown can be estimated by adding the areas of the small circular sectors.

Recall that the area of a sector of a circle whose central angle is θ (in radians) with radius r is

$$A = \frac{1}{2} r^2 \theta$$

The area of the ith sector in Fig. 1.13(b) is

$$\frac{1}{2} r_i^2 \, \Delta\theta_i = \frac{1}{2} [f(\theta_i)]^2 \, \Delta\theta_i$$

The total area is

$$\frac{1}{2} r_1^2 \, \Delta\theta_1 + \frac{1}{2} r_2^2 \, \Delta\theta_2 + \frac{1}{2} r_3^2 \, \Delta\theta_3 + \cdots + \frac{1}{2} r_n^2 \, \Delta\theta_n$$

which can be represented by the integral

AREA OF A REGION IN POLAR COORDINATES

$$A = \frac{1}{2} \int_\alpha^\beta r^2 \, d\theta = \frac{1}{2} \int_\alpha^\beta [f(\theta)]^2 \, d\theta$$

Due to the squaring of r, you should review Section 1.4 and the integration of even powers of sine and cosine functions. Recall that the identities used are

$$\sin^2 x = \frac{1}{2} (1 - \cos 2x)$$

$$\cos^2 x = \frac{1}{2} (1 + \cos 2x)$$

EXAMPLE 1

Find the area of the region inside $r^2 = 4 \sin 2\theta$.

First, graph $r^2 = 4 \sin 2\theta$ (see Fig. 1.14).

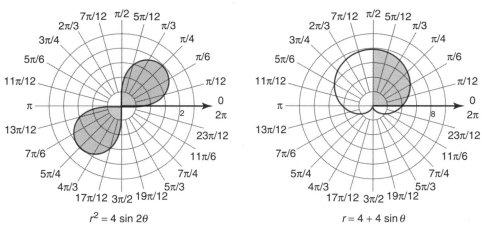

$r^2 = 4 \sin 2\theta$

Figure 1.14

$r = 4 + 4 \sin \theta$

Figure 1.15

Due to symmetry, the area may be expressed by

$$A = 2\left[\frac{1}{2} \int_0^{\pi/2} r^2 \, d\theta\right]$$

$$= \int_0^{\pi/2} 4 \sin 2\theta \, d\theta$$

$$= 4\left(-\frac{1}{2} \cos 2\theta\right)\Big|_0^{\pi/2}$$

$$= -2[-1 - 1] = 4$$

EXAMPLE 2

Find the area of the region in the first quadrant within $r = 4 + 4 \sin \theta$.

First, graph $r = 4 + 4 \sin \theta$ (see Fig. 1.15).

$$A = \frac{1}{2} \int_\alpha^\beta r^2 \, d\theta$$

$$= \frac{1}{2} \int_0^{\pi/2} (4 + 4 \sin \theta)^2 \, d\theta$$

$$= 8 \int_0^{\pi/2} (1 + \sin \theta)^2 \, d\theta$$

$$= 8 \int_0^{\pi/2} (1 + 2 \sin \theta + \sin^2 \theta) \, d\theta$$

$$= 8 \int_0^{\pi/2} \left[1 + 2 \sin \theta + \frac{1}{2}(1 - \cos 2\theta)\right] d\theta$$

$$= 8 \int_0^{\pi/2} \left[\frac{3}{2} + 2 \sin \theta - \frac{1}{2} \cos 2\theta\right] d\theta$$

$$= 8\left(\frac{3\theta}{2} - 2 \cos \theta - \frac{1}{4} \sin 2\theta\right)\Big|_0^{\pi/2}$$

$$= 8\left[\left(\frac{3}{2}\cdot\frac{\pi}{2} - 2\cdot 0 - \frac{1}{4}\cdot 0\right) - \left(\frac{3}{2}\cdot 0 - 2\cdot 1 - \frac{1}{4}\cdot 0\right)\right]$$

$$= 8\left(\frac{3\pi}{4} + 2\right) = 6\pi + 16$$

Using a calculator, we have

```
1/2*fnInt((4+4si
n(θ))²,θ,0,π/2)
        34.84955592
6π+16
        34.84955592
■
```

1/2* **MATH 9** (4+4 **SIN ALPHA 3**)) **x²**, **ALPHA 3** ,0, **2nd** π /2) **ENTER**

EXAMPLE 3

Find the area within the inner loop of $r = 2 + 4\cos\theta$.

First, graph $r = 2 + 4\cos\theta$ (see Fig. 1.16). The endpoints of the inner loop are found by noting that $r = 0$ at the endpoints.

$$r = 2 + 4\cos\theta$$
$$0 = 2 + 4\cos\theta$$
$$\cos\theta = -\frac{1}{2}$$
$$\theta = \frac{2\pi}{3}, \frac{4\pi}{3}$$

The inner loop is determined by $\frac{2\pi}{3} \leq \theta \leq \frac{4\pi}{3}$.

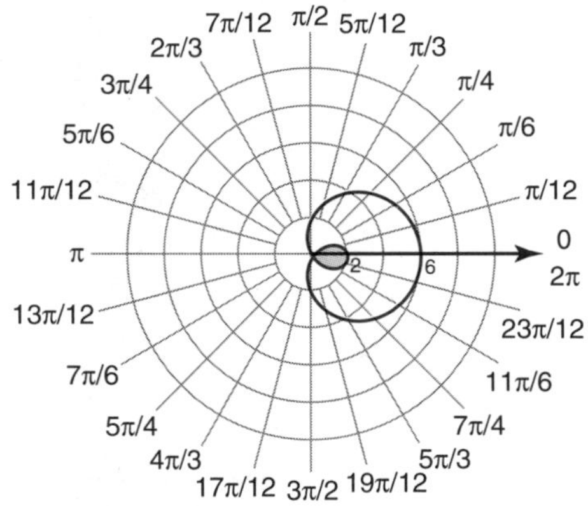

$r = 2 + 4\cos\theta$

Figure 1.16

$$A = \frac{1}{2}\int_{2\pi/3}^{4\pi/3} r^2\,d\theta$$

$$= \frac{1}{2}\int_{2\pi/3}^{4\pi/3} (2 + 4\cos\theta)^2\,d\theta$$

$$= 2\int_{2\pi/3}^{4\pi/3} (1 + 4\cos\theta + 4\cos^2\theta)\,d\theta$$

$$= 2\int_{2\pi/3}^{4\pi/3} \left[1 + 4\cos\theta + 4\cdot\frac{1}{2}(1 + \cos 2\theta)\right]\,d\theta$$

$$= 2\int_{2\pi/3}^{4\pi/3} (3 + 4\cos\theta + 2\cos 2\theta)\,d\theta$$

$$= 2[3\theta + 4\sin\theta + \sin 2\theta]\,\Big|_{2\pi/3}^{4\pi/3}$$

$$= 2\left\{\left[3\cdot\frac{4\pi}{3} + 4\left(\frac{-\sqrt{3}}{2}\right) + \frac{\sqrt{3}}{2}\right] - \left[3\cdot\frac{2\pi}{3} + 4\cdot\frac{\sqrt{3}}{2} + \left(\frac{\sqrt{3}}{2}\right)\right]\right\}$$

$$= 2\left(4\pi - 2\sqrt{3} + \frac{\sqrt{3}}{2} - 2\pi - 2\sqrt{3} + \frac{\sqrt{3}}{2}\right)$$

$$= 2(2\pi - 3\sqrt{3})$$

$$= 4\pi - 6\sqrt{3}$$

The area between two polar curves may be expressed by

$$A = \frac{1}{2} \int_{\alpha}^{\beta} \left\{ [f(\theta)]^2 - [g(\theta)]^2 \right\} d\theta$$

EXAMPLE 4

Find the area of the region inside $r = 1$ and outside $r = 1 + \sin \theta$.

First, graph the two equations (see Fig. 1.17).

Use the substitution method of solving equations simultaneously to find the points of intersection.

$$1 + \sin \theta = 1$$

$$\sin \theta = 0$$

$$\theta = 0, \pi, 2\pi$$

Due to symmetry with respect to the y-axis, the area may be expressed by

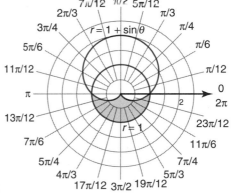

Figure 1.17

$$A = 2\left[\frac{1}{2} \int_{\pi}^{3\pi/2} [1^2 - (1 + \sin \theta)^2] \, d\theta\right]$$

$$= \int_{\pi}^{3\pi/2} (1 - 1 - 2\sin \theta - \sin^2 \theta) \, d\theta$$

$$= \int_{\pi}^{3\pi/2} \left(-2\sin \theta - \frac{1}{2}(1 - \cos 2\theta)\right) d\theta$$

$$= \int_{\pi}^{3\pi/2} \left(-2\sin \theta - \frac{1}{2} + \frac{1}{2}\cos 2\theta\right) d\theta$$

$$= \left(2\cos \theta - \frac{\theta}{2} + \frac{1}{4}\sin 2\theta\right)\Big|_{\pi}^{3\pi/2}$$

$$= \left(2 \cdot 0 - \frac{3\pi/2}{2} + \frac{1}{4} \cdot 0\right) - \left(2(-1) - \frac{\pi}{2} + \frac{1}{4} \cdot 0\right)$$

$$= -\frac{3\pi}{4} + 2 + \frac{\pi}{2}$$

$$= 2 - \frac{\pi}{4}$$

EXAMPLE 5

A microphone with a cardioid pickup pattern is often the choice of sound engineers recording live performances. The cardioid pattern offers good frontal sensitivity, while suppressing audience noise in back of the microphone. In Fig. 1.18, find the area on the stage that lies within the optimal pickup range of the microphone if the boundaries of this region are given by the cardioid $r = 20 + 20 \cos \theta$ and the vertical line $x = 15$ (the microphone has been placed 15 ft from the edge of the stage).

First, rewrite $x = 15$ in polar coordinates.

$$x = 15$$

$$r \cos \theta = 15 \qquad \text{(Recall that in polar form, } x = r \cos \theta.\text{)}$$

$$r = \frac{15}{\cos \theta}$$

$$r = 15 \sec \theta$$

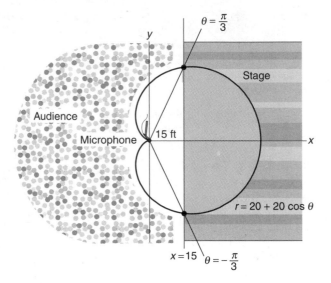

Figure 1.18

Next, find the θ-values of the points of intersection by equating the two expressions for r.

$$20 + 20 \cos \theta = \frac{15}{\cos \theta}$$

$$20 \cos \theta + 20 \cos^2 \theta = 15 \qquad \text{(multiplying both sides by } \cos \theta\text{)}$$

$$20 \cos^2 \theta + 20 \cos \theta - 15 = 0$$

$$4 \cos^2 \theta + 4 \cos \theta - 3 = 0 \qquad \text{(dividing both sides by 5)}$$

$$(2 \cos \theta + 3)(2 \cos \theta - 1) = 0$$

$$\cos \theta = -\frac{3}{2} \quad \text{or} \quad \cos \theta = \frac{1}{2}$$

$$\theta = \pm \frac{\pi}{3}$$

Note: $\cos \theta = -\dfrac{3}{2}$ is impossible since $-1 \leq \cos \theta \leq 1$.

The integral for the area of the region is

$$\frac{1}{2} \int_{-\pi/3}^{\pi/3} \left[(20 + 20 \cos \theta)^2 - (15 \sec \theta)^2 \right] d\theta$$

$$= 2 \cdot \frac{1}{2} \int_{0}^{\pi/3} \left[(20 + 20 \cos \theta)^2 - (15 \sec \theta)^2 \right] d\theta \qquad \text{(using } x\text{-axis symmetry)}$$

$$= \int_{0}^{\pi/3} \left[400 + 800 \cos \theta + 400 \cos^2 \theta - 225 \sec^2 \theta \right] d\theta$$

$$= \int_0^{\pi/3} \left[400 + 800 \cos\theta + 400\left(\frac{1 + \cos 2\theta}{2}\right) - 225 \sec^2\theta \right] d\theta$$

$$= \int_0^{\pi/3} \left[600 + 800 \cos\theta + 200 \cos 2\theta - 225 \sec^2\theta \right] d\theta$$

$$= (600\theta + 800 \sin\theta + 100 \sin 2\theta - 225 \tan\theta) \Big|_0^{\pi/3}$$

$$= 600\left(\frac{\pi}{3}\right) + 800\left(\frac{\sqrt{3}}{2}\right) + 100\left(\frac{\sqrt{3}}{2}\right) - 225\sqrt{3} - 0$$

$$= 200\pi + 225\sqrt{3}$$

$$= 1018 \text{ ft}^2$$

Using a calculator (which must be set in *radians*), we have

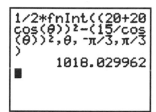
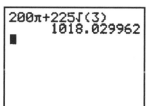

1/2* **MATH 9** (20+20 **COS ALPHA 3**)) x² -(15/ **COS ALPHA 3**)) x², **ALPHA 3**, -π/3, π/3) **ENTER**

Exercises 1.12

Find the area of each region.

1. $r = 2, 0 \le \theta \le \frac{2\pi}{3}$
2. $r = 4, \frac{\pi}{3} \le \theta \le \frac{7\pi}{6}$
3. Inside $r = 3 \cos\theta$

4. Inside $r = 6 \sin\theta$
5. Inside $r^2 = 9 \sin 2\theta$
6. Inside $r^2 = \cos 2\theta$

7. Inside $r = 1 + \cos\theta$
8. Inside $r = 2 - \sin\theta$
9. Inside $r = 4 \sin 2\theta$

10. Inside $r = 2 \sin 3\theta$
11. Inside $r^2 = 16 \cos^2\theta$
12. Inside $r^2 = 4 \sin^2\theta$

13. Inside $r = 4 + 3 \cos\theta$
14. Inside $r = 3 + 3 \sin\theta$

15. $r = e^\theta, 0 \le \theta \le \pi$
16. $r = 2^\theta, 0 \le \theta \le \pi$

17. Inside the inner loop of $r = 1 - 2 \cos\theta$

18. Inside the outer loop and outside the inner loop of $r = 2 - 4 \sin\theta$

19. Inside $r = 2 \sin\theta + 2 \cos\theta$
20. Inside $r = 2 \sin\theta - 2 \cos\theta$

21. Inside $r = \sin\theta$ and $r = \sin 2\theta$
22. Inside $r = \sin\theta$ and $r = \cos\theta$

23. Inside $r = 2 \cos 2\theta$ and outside $r = 1$

24. Inside $r^2 = 8 \cos 2\theta$ and outside $r = 2$

25. Inside $r = 2 + \sin \theta$ and outside $r = 5 \sin \theta$

26. Inside $r = -6 \cos \theta$ and outside $r = 2 - 2 \cos \theta$

27. Inside $r = 3 + 3 \cos \theta$ and outside $r = 3 + 3 \sin \theta$

28. Inside the resulting inner loops of $r = 3 + 3 \sin \theta$ and $r = 3 - 3 \sin \theta$

1.13 IMPROPER INTEGRALS

Integrals which have an upper limit of ∞ or a lower limit of $-\infty$ are commonly encountered in applied mathematics and statistics. Within the scope of this text, they will provide an important convergence test for infinite series and the background necessary to study Laplace transforms. In general, an *improper integral* is any integral which represents the area of a region that is infinite in extent. The question to be answered is whether that area might still comprise only a finite number of square units, and to find that finite value when it exists. What all improper integrals have in common is that the Fundamental Theorem of Calculus does *not* directly apply to them (thus the name "improper"). The secret to evaluating an improper integral is to express it as a *limit*. In particular, it must be expressed as the limit of a definite integral to which the Fundamental Theorem of Calculus *does* apply.

EXAMPLE 1

Discuss the meaning of $\displaystyle\int_1^\infty \frac{3}{x^2}\, dx$ and evaluate it.

$\displaystyle\int_1^\infty \frac{3}{x^2}\, dx$ represents the area under the curve $f(x) = \dfrac{3}{x^2}$, starting at $x = 1$ and continuing (infinitely) to the right. We are about to show that this region, while infinite in extent, has an area of only 3 square units! First, express the improper integral as the *limit* of a definite integral with a variable upper limit of integration t.

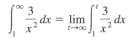

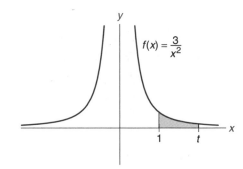

Figure 1.19

The Fundamental Theorem of Calculus applies to this definite integral since $f(x) = \dfrac{3}{x^2}$ is a continuous function for $1 \le x \le t$, where t is any finite value greater than one (see Fig. 1.19). So, the next step is to evaluate this definite integral in terms of t, finding a formula for the area under the curve from $x = 1$ to $x = t$ which would work even for extremely large finite values of t. The *final* step is to evaluate the limit, showing us where this area formula is headed as $t \to \infty$.

$$\int_1^\infty \frac{3}{x^2}\, dx = \lim_{t \to \infty} \int_1^t \frac{3}{x^2}\, dx$$

$$= \lim_{t \to \infty} \int_1^t 3x^{-2}\, dx$$

$$= \lim_{t \to \infty} \frac{3x^{-1}}{-1} \bigg|_1^t$$

$$= \lim_{t \to \infty} -\frac{3}{x} \bigg|_1^t$$

$$= \lim_{t \to \infty} \left[-\frac{3}{t} - \left(-\frac{3}{1} \right) \right]$$

$$= \lim_{t \to \infty} \left(-\frac{3}{t} + 3 \right)$$

$$= 0 + 3$$

$$= 3$$

The area is exactly 3 square units.

EXAMPLE 2

Evaluate and interpret $\displaystyle\int_{-\infty}^{0} e^{2x} \, dx$.

$$\int_{-\infty}^{0} e^{2x} \, dx = \lim_{t \to -\infty} \int_{t}^{0} e^{2x} \, dx$$

$$= \lim_{t \to -\infty} \frac{e^{2x}}{2} \bigg|_t^0$$

$$= \lim_{t \to -\infty} \left(\frac{e^0}{2} - \frac{e^{2t}}{2} \right)$$

$$= \frac{1}{2} - 0$$

$$= \frac{1}{2}$$

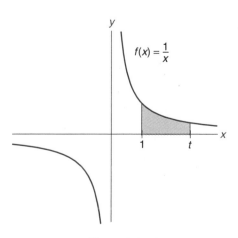

Figure 1.20

This result means that there is exactly $\dfrac{1}{2}$ square unit of area to the left of the y-axis under the curve $f(x) = e^{2x}$ (see Fig. 1.20).

In the first two examples, regions that were infinite in extent had *finite* areas. Not surprisingly, some regions that are infinite in extent have *infinite* areas.

EXAMPLE 3

Evaluate and interpret $\displaystyle\int_{1}^{\infty} \frac{1}{x} \, dx$.

$$\int_{1}^{\infty} \frac{1}{x} \, dx = \lim_{t \to \infty} \int_{1}^{t} \frac{1}{x} \, dx$$

$$= \lim_{t \to \infty} \ln x \bigg|_1^t$$

$$= \lim_{t \to \infty} (\ln t - \ln 1)$$

$$= \lim_{t \to \infty} (\ln t - 0)$$

$$= \lim_{t \to \infty} \ln t$$

$$= \infty$$

Figure 1.21

Since there is no "biggest" natural logarithm, the area to the right of $x = 1$ under $f(x) = \dfrac{1}{x}$ consists of an infinite number of square units (see Fig. 1.21). When the final answer is ∞ or $-\infty$, we say that the improper integral *diverges*.

A two-dimensional region can be infinite in extent without having any infinite limits of integration on the x-axis. Such cases typically involve a function with one or more vertical asymptotes.

EXAMPLE 4

Evaluate $\displaystyle\int_0^9 \dfrac{1}{\sqrt{x}}\,dx$.

This region under the curve $f(x) = \dfrac{1}{\sqrt{x}}$ from $x = 0$ to $x = 9$ is bounded on the left-hand side by the vertical asymptote $x = 0$ (note that the function has a zero denominator when $x = 0$). Of course, the integrand's discontinuity at $x = 0$ means that this is an improper integral. The limit we will use to make things "proper" is called a right-hand limit, and is notated "$\lim\limits_{x \to 0^+}$," which means "the limit as x approaches zero from the *right*." The reason for this one-sided limit is that our definite integral must represent the area from t to 9, where t is a number a little to the *right* of zero (since we don't wish to straddle the discontinuity; see Fig. 1.22). Evaluating a one-sided limit is usually no more difficult than evaluating an ordinary limit. In this case, just think of t going to zero, but only through *positive* values. This distinction is quite important, especially when technology is used to evaluate limits, since an ordinary (two-sided) limit might fail to exist when the desired one-sided limit has a value.

$$
\begin{aligned}
\int_0^9 \frac{1}{\sqrt{x}}\,dx &= \lim_{t \to 0^+} \int_t^9 \frac{1}{\sqrt{x}}\,dx \\[2mm]
&= \lim_{t \to 0^+} \int_t^9 x^{-1/2}\,dx \\[2mm]
&= \lim_{t \to 0^+} \frac{x^{1/2}}{\frac{1}{2}}\Bigg|_t^9 \\[2mm]
&= \lim_{t \to 0^+} 2\sqrt{x}\,\Bigg|_t^9 \\[2mm]
&= \lim_{t \to 0^+} (2\sqrt{9} - 2\sqrt{t}) \\[2mm]
&= 6 - 0 \\[2mm]
&= 6
\end{aligned}
$$

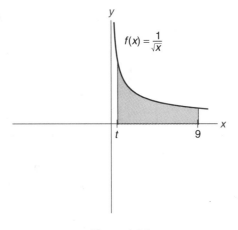

Figure 1.22

EXAMPLE 5

Evaluate $\displaystyle\int_0^2 \frac{1}{(x-2)^4}\,dx.$

   This time, it's the upper limit of integration, $x = 2$, that corresponds to a vertical asymptote and a point of discontinuity of the integrand (see Fig. 1.23). To keep from straddling the discontinuity, our values of t must stay to the *left* of 2 (be between zero and 2). Thus, we will use a left-hand limit, notated as "$\lim_{t\to 2^-}$" and pronounced "the limit as t approaches 2 from the left." The small, raised negative sign placed immediately after the 2 indicates that only values of t to the *left* of 2 will be considered, for example, $t = 1.99$, $t = 1.9999$, and so on (it does *not* imply that negative values of t are being used).

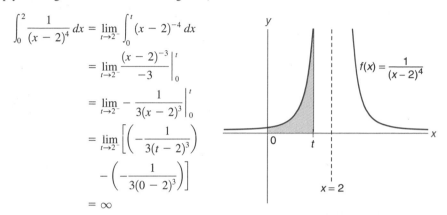

$$\int_0^2 \frac{1}{(x-2)^4}\,dx = \lim_{t\to 2^-}\int_0^t (x-2)^{-4}\,dx$$

$$= \lim_{t\to 2^-}\frac{(x-2)^{-3}}{-3}\bigg|_0^t$$

$$= \lim_{t\to 2^-} -\frac{1}{3(x-2)^3}\bigg|_0^t$$

$$= \lim_{t\to 2^-}\left[\left(-\frac{1}{3(t-2)^3}\right)\right.$$

$$\left.-\left(-\frac{1}{3(0-2)^3}\right)\right]$$

$$= \infty$$

Figure 1.23

   This improper integral *diverges*. Thus, the area under the curve $f(x) = \dfrac{1}{(x-2)^4}$ from $x = 0$ to its vertical asymptote $x = 2$ consists of an infinite number of square units.

   Sometimes, the evaluation of an improper integral is complicated enough to require integration by parts (to find the antiderivative) or l'Hospital's rule (to evaluate the limit). The following example illustrates both techniques.

EXAMPLE 6

Evaluate $\displaystyle\int_0^\infty xe^{-2x}\,dx$.

Recall, using integration by parts, that

$$\int xe^{-2x}\,dx = uv - \int v\,du$$

$$= -\frac{xe^{-2x}}{2} - \int -\frac{1}{2}e^{-2x}\,dx$$

$$= -\frac{xe^{-2x}}{2} + \frac{1}{2}\cdot\frac{e^{-2x}}{-2} + C$$

$$= -\frac{xe^{-2x}}{2} - \frac{1}{4}e^{-2x} + C$$

$u = x$	$dv = e^{-2x}\,dx$
$du = dx$	$v = \dfrac{e^{-2x}}{-2}$

Therefore,

$$\int_0^\infty xe^{-2x}\,dx = \lim_{t\to\infty}\int_0^t xe^{-2x}\,dx$$

$$= \lim_{t\to\infty}\left(-\frac{xe^{-2x}}{2} - \frac{1}{4}e^{-2x}\right)\Big|_0^t$$

$$= \lim_{t\to\infty}\left[\left(-\frac{te^{-2t}}{2} - \frac{1}{4}e^{-2t}\right) - \left(-\frac{0e^0}{2} - \frac{1}{4}e^0\right)\right]$$

$$= \lim_{t\to\infty}\left(-\frac{te^{-2t}}{2} - \frac{1}{4}e^{-2t} + \frac{1}{4}\right)$$

$$= \lim_{t\to\infty}\frac{-t}{2e^{2t}} - \lim_{t\to\infty}\frac{1}{4e^{2t}} + \lim_{t\to\infty}\frac{1}{4}$$

$$= \lim_{t\to\infty}\frac{-1}{4e^{2t}} - 0 + \frac{1}{4} \qquad \text{(using l'Hospital's rule } \frac{\infty}{\infty}$$
$$\text{in the first limit)}$$

$$= 0 - 0 + \frac{1}{4}$$

$$= \frac{1}{4}$$

Exercises 1.13

Evaluate the following improper integrals.

1. $\displaystyle\int_1^\infty \frac{2}{x^3}\,dx$
2. $\displaystyle\int_2^\infty \frac{1}{x^4}\,dx$
3. $\displaystyle\int_0^\infty e^{-3x}\,dx$

4. $\int_0^\infty e^{-x}\,dx$

5. $\int_1^\infty \frac{1}{\sqrt{x}}\,dx$

6. $\int_1^\infty x^{-2/3}\,dx$

7. $\int_{-\infty}^0 e^{5x}\,dx$

8. $\int_{-\infty}^{-1} \frac{1}{x^2}\,dx$

9. $\int_0^1 x^{-2/3}\,dx$

10. $\int_0^1 \frac{1}{x^2}\,dx$

11. $\int_0^5 \frac{1}{(x-5)^2}\,dx$

12. $\int_0^3 \frac{1}{x-3}\,dx$ — $see\ 1.2,\ pg5$

13. $\int_0^\infty x e^{-x^2}\,dx$

14. $\int_0^\infty \frac{3x^2}{(x^3+1)^2}\,dx$

15. $\int_{-\infty}^0 -2x e^x\,dx$

16. $\int_0^\infty x^2 e^{-x}\,dx$

17. $\int_0^1 -x \ln x\,dx$

18. $\int_0^1 -\ln x\,dx$

19. $\int_1^\infty \frac{4}{x^2+1}\,dx$

20. $\int_{-\infty}^0 \frac{1}{x^2+1}\,dx$

CHAPTER 1 SUMMARY

1. *Basic integration formulas:*

(a) $\displaystyle\int u^n\,du = \frac{u^{n+1}}{n+1} + C \qquad (n \neq -1)$

(b) $\displaystyle\int \frac{du}{u} = \ln|u| + C$

(c) $\displaystyle\int e^u\,du = e^u + C$

(d) $\displaystyle\int a^u\,du = \frac{a^u}{\ln a} + C$

(e) $\displaystyle\int \ln u\,du = u \ln u - u + C$

(f) $\displaystyle\int \sin u\,du = -\cos u + C$

(g) $\displaystyle\int \cos u\,du = \sin u + C$

(h) $\displaystyle\int \tan u\,du = -\ln|\cos u| + C$

(i) $\displaystyle\int \cot u\,du = \ln|\sin u| + C$

(j) $\displaystyle\int \sec u\,du = \ln|\sec u + \tan u| + C$

(k) $\displaystyle\int \csc u\,du = \ln|\csc u - \cot u| + C$

(l) $\displaystyle\int \sec^2 u\,du = \tan u + C$

(m) $\displaystyle\int \csc^2 u\,du = -\cot u + C$

(n) $\displaystyle\int \sec u \tan u \; du = \sec u + C$

(o) $\displaystyle\int \csc u \cot u \; du = -\csc u + C$

(p) $\displaystyle\int \frac{du}{\sqrt{a^2 - u^2}} = \arcsin \frac{u}{a} + C$

(q) $\displaystyle\int \frac{du}{a^2 + u^2} = \frac{1}{a}\arctan \frac{u}{a} + C$

(r) $\displaystyle\int u \; dv = uv - \int v \; du$ (integration by parts)

Other integrals can often be written in terms of these basic integrals by using the methods of partial fractions and trigonometric substitution.

2. *Partial fractions:*
   (a) *Case 1: Nonrepeated linear denominator factors.* For every nonrepeated factor $ax + b$ of the denominator of a given fraction, there corresponds the partial fraction $\dfrac{A}{ax + b}$, where A is a constant.

   (b) *Case 2: Repeated linear denominator factors.* For every factor $(ax + b)^k$ of the denominator of the given fraction, there correspond the possible partial fractions

$$\frac{A_1}{ax + b}, \frac{A_2}{(ax + b)^2}, \frac{A_3}{(ax + b)^3}, \dots, \frac{A_k}{(ax + b)^k}$$

   where $A_1, A_2, A_3, \dots, A_k$ are constants.

   (c) *Case 3: Nonrepeated quadratic denominator factors.* For every nonrepeated factor $ax^2 + bx + c$ of the denominator of the given fraction, there corresponds the partial fraction

$$\frac{Ax + B}{ax^2 + bx + c}$$

   where A and B are constants.

   (d) *Case 4: Repeated quadratic denominator factors.* For every factor $(ax^2 + bx + c)^k$ of the denominator of the given fraction, there correspond the possible partial fractions

$$\frac{A_1 x + B_1}{ax^2 + bx + c}, \frac{A_2 x + B_2}{(ax^2 + bx + c)^2}, \frac{A_3 x + B_3}{(ax^2 + bx + c)^3}, \dots, \frac{A_k x + B_k}{(ax^2 + bx + c)^k}$$

   where $A_1, A_2, A_3, \dots, A_k, B_1, B_2, B_3, \dots, B_k$ are constants.

3. *Trigonometric substitutions* (see Fig. 1.24):

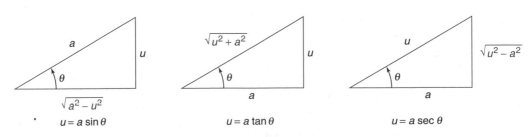

Figure 1.24

4. *Trapezoidal rule for approximating the value of an integral:*

$$\int_a^b f(x)\,dx \cong \frac{\Delta x}{2}\left[f(a) + 2\,f(x_1) + 2\,f(x_2) + 2\,f(x_3) + \cdots + 2\,f(x_{n-1}) + f(b)\right]$$

5. *Simpson's rule for approximating the value of an integral:*

$$\int_a^b f(x)\,dx \cong \frac{\Delta x}{3}\left[f(a) + 4\,f(x_1) + 2\,f(x_2) + 4\,f(x_3) + 2\,f(x_4) + \cdots\right.$$
$$\left. + 4\,f(x_{n-1}) + f(b)\right] \qquad n \text{ must be an even integer}$$

6. *Area of a region in polar coordinates:*

$$A = \frac{1}{2}\int_\alpha^\beta r^2\,d\theta = \frac{1}{2}\int_\alpha^\beta [f(\theta)]^2\,d\theta$$

7. *Area between polar curves:*

$$A = \frac{1}{2}\int_\alpha^\beta \{[f(\theta)]^2 - [g(\theta)]^2\}\,d\theta$$

8. *Improper integrals:*

$$\int_a^\infty f(x)\,dx = \lim_{t\to\infty}\int_a^t f(x)\,dx$$

$$\int_{-\infty}^b f(x)\,dx = \lim_{t\to-\infty}\int_t^b f(x)\,dx$$

If $x = c$ is a vertical asymptote of the graph of $y = f(x)$ and $a < c < b$,

$$\int_a^c f(x)\,dx = \lim_{t\to c^-}\int_a^t f(x)\,dx$$

$$\int_c^b f(x)\,dx = \lim_{t\to c^+}\int_t^b f(x)\,dx$$

CHAPTER 1 REVIEW

Integrate without using a table of integrals.

1. $\displaystyle\int \frac{\cos 3x\,dx}{\sqrt{2 + \sin 3x}}$

2. $\displaystyle\int (5 + \tan 2x)^3 \sec^2 2x\,dx$

3. $\displaystyle\int \cos 3x\,dx$

4. $\displaystyle\int \frac{x\,dx}{x^2 - 5}$

5. $\displaystyle\int xe^{3x^2}\,dx$

6. $\displaystyle\int \frac{dx}{9 + 4x^2}$

7. $\displaystyle\int \frac{dx}{\sqrt{16 - x^2}}$

8. $\displaystyle\int \sec^2 (7x + 2)\,dx$

9. $\displaystyle\int \frac{\sec^2 x\,dx}{3 + 5\tan x}$

10. $\displaystyle\int x^2 \sin (x^3 + 4)\,dx$

11. $\displaystyle\int_0^1 \frac{dx}{16 + 9x^2}$

12. $\displaystyle\int_0^{1/2} \sin \pi x\,dx$

13. $\displaystyle\int_0^{\pi/4} \frac{\sin x\,dx}{\cos x}$

14. $\displaystyle\int_0^1 \frac{dx}{\sqrt{9 - 4x^2}}$

15. $\displaystyle\int \frac{dx}{x\sqrt{16x^2 - 9}}$

16. $\displaystyle\int \frac{\tan 3x}{\sec^4 3x}\,dx$

17. $\displaystyle\int \frac{\arctan 3x}{1 + 9x^2}\,dx$

18. $\int \sec 5x \, dx$

19. $\int x \tan x^2 \, dx$

20. $\int \sin^5 2x \cos^2 2x \, dx$

21. $\int \cos^4 3x \sin^2 3x \, dx$

22. $\int \dfrac{dx}{x^2 + 2x - 3}$

23. $\int e^{3x} \cos 4x \, dx$

24. $\int \sin x \ln (\cos x) \, dx$

25. $\int \tan^4 x \, dx$

26. $\int \cos^2 5x \, dx$

27. $\int \dfrac{x - 3}{6x^2 - x - 1} \, dx$

28. $\int \sqrt{x} \ln x \, dx$

29. $\int e^{-x}(\cos^2 e^{-x})(\sin e^{-x}) \, dx$

30. $\int \dfrac{4 \, dx}{x^2 - 4}$

31. $\int x^2 \sin x \, dx$

32. $\int \dfrac{\arcsin 5x}{\sqrt{1 - 25x^2}} \, dx$

33. $\int_2^3 \dfrac{dx}{x\sqrt{x^2 - 1}}$

34. $\int_0^1 xe^{4x} \, dx$

35. $\int_0^{\pi/8} 4 \tan 2x \, dx$

36. $\int_0^1 \dfrac{8 \, dx}{4 - x^2}$

37. $\int \dfrac{3x^2 - 11x + 12}{x^3 - 4x^2 + 4x} \, dx$

38. $\int \dfrac{dx}{x\sqrt{16 - 9x^2}}$

Find the area bounded by the given curves.

39. $y(x - 1) = 1, x = 2, x = 4,$ and $y = 0$.

40. $y = e^{x+2}, x = 1, x = 3,$ and $y = 0$.

41. $y = e^{2x}, x = 0, x = 1,$ and $y = 0$.

42. $y(1 + x^2) = 1, x = 0, x = 1,$ and $y = 0$.

43. $y^2(4 - x^2) = 1, x = 0, x = 1,$ and $y = 0$.

44. $xy = 1, y = x, y = 0,$ and $x = 2$.

45. $y = \sec^2 x, y = 0, x = 0,$ and $x = \pi/4$.

46. $y(4 + x^2) = 1, x = 0, x = 2,$ and $y = 0$.

47. $y = \tan x, x = 0, x = \pi/4,$ and $y = 0$.

48. Find the volume of the solid formed by revolving the region bounded by $y = \ln x, x = 1,$ $x = 2,$ and $y = 0$ about the *x*-axis.

49. Find the volume of the solid formed by revolving the region bounded by $y = e^x, x = 0, x = 1,$ and $y = 0$ about the *x*-axis.

50. The current i in an electric circuit varies according to the equation $i = 4t \sin 3t$ amperes. Find an equation for the charge q in coulombs transferred as a function of time $(q = \int i \, dt)$.

51. The current i in an electric circuit varies according to the equation $i = \dfrac{5t + 1}{t^2 + t - 2}$ amperes.

Find an equation for the charge q in coulombs transferred as a function of time.

52. A force is acting on an object according to the equation $F = xe^{x^2}$, where x is measured in metres and F is measured in newtons. Find the work done in moving the object from $x = 1$ m to $x = 2$ m.

Integrate using the Table of Integrals in Appendix B. Give the number of the formula used.

53. $\int \dfrac{dx}{x(5 + 3x)}$

54. $\int \dfrac{\sqrt{16 - x^2}}{x^2} \, dx$

55. $\int \dfrac{dx}{\sqrt{3 + 6x + x^2}}$

56. $\int e^x \sin 2x \, dx$

57. $\int \dfrac{\sqrt{4x^2 - 9}}{x} \, dx$

58. $\int \cos^4 3x \sin 3x \, dx$

59. $\int \dfrac{\sqrt{9 + 4x}}{x} \, dx$

60. $\int \tan^6 x \, dx$

Use the trapezoidal rule to approximate the value of each integral.

61. $\int_1^4 \dfrac{dx}{2x - 1}, n = 6$

62. $\int_1^3 \dfrac{dx}{9 + x^2}, n = 4$

63. $\int_0^4 \sqrt{16 - x^2}\, dx, \ n = 8$ **64.** $\int_1^4 \sqrt[3]{18 - x^2}\, dx, \ n = 6$

Use the trapezoidal rule to find the approximate area under the curve through each set of points.

65.

x	1	3	5	7	9
y	2.3	2.8	3.4	2.7	2.1

66.

x	1.6	1.8	2.0	2.2	2.4	2.6
y	0.9	0.7	0.8	1.1	1.3	0.9

Use Simpson's rule to approximate the value of each integral.

67. $\int_0^4 \sqrt{16 + x^2}\, dx, \ n = 8$ **68.** $\int_0^{12} \dfrac{4}{1 + x^2}\, dx, \ n = 6$

69. $\int_0^{\pi/2} \dfrac{dx}{2 + \sin x}, \ n = 4$ **70.** $\int_0^8 \dfrac{x^3}{\sqrt{1 + x^3}}\, dx, \ n = 8$

Find the area of each region.

71. Inside $r^2 = 4 \cos 2\theta$ **72.** Inside $r = 1 - \sin \theta$

73. Inside $r = 3 - 2 \sin \theta$ **74.** Inside $r = \frac{1}{2} \cos 3\theta$

75. Inside $r = \frac{1}{2}(\theta + \pi)$ and outside $r = \theta$ for $0 \le \theta \le \pi$

76. Inside $r = 2 \cos \theta$ and outside $r = 1$ **77.** Inside the inner loop of $r = 2 - 4 \cos \theta$

78. Inside $r = 1$ and outside $r = 1 + \sin \theta$ **79.** Inside $r^2 = 8 \sin 2\theta$ and outside $r = 2$

80. Inside both $r^2 = \cos 2\theta$ and $r^2 = \sin 2\theta$

Evaluate the improper integrals.

81. $\int_1^\infty \dfrac{1}{x^{4/3}}\, dx$ **82.** $\int_1^\infty \dfrac{1}{x^{2/3}}\, dx$

83. $\int_{-\infty}^0 e^{\frac{1}{2}x}\, dx$ **84.** $\int_{-\infty}^0 xe^x\, dx$

85. $\int_3^4 \dfrac{1}{\sqrt{x - 3}}\, dx$ **86.** $\int_1^2 \dfrac{1}{x \ln x}\, dx$

2

Three-Space
Partial Derivatives and Double Integrals

INTRODUCTION

We have been discussing functions of only one variable whose graphs lie in a plane, which is often called the Euclidian plane or two-space. Now, we need to extend our discussion to functions of two variables whose graphs require three dimensions, sometimes called three-space.

Objectives

- Sketch graphs in three-space.
- Find the equation of a surface given appropriate information.
- Find first and second partial derivatives.
- Given a surface, find the slope of the tangent lines parallel to the xz- and yz-planes through a given point.
- Find the total differential of a function of two variables.
- Find relative maximum and minimum points of a function of two variables.
- Evaluate double integrals.

2.1 FUNCTIONS IN THREE-SPACE

Consider three mutually perpendicular number lines (x-, y-, and z-axes) with their zero points intersecting at point O, called the origin. Although these axes may be oriented in any way, we will use the orientation as shown in Fig. 2.1(a), which is often called the *right-handed system*.

Think of the y- and z-axes lying in the plane of the paper with the positive y-direction to the right and the positive z-direction upward. The x-axis is perpendicular to the paper, and its positive direction is toward us. This is called a right-handed system because if the fingers on the right hand are cupped so they curve from the positive x-axis to the positive y-axis, the thumb points along the positive z-axis as shown in Fig. 2.1(b).

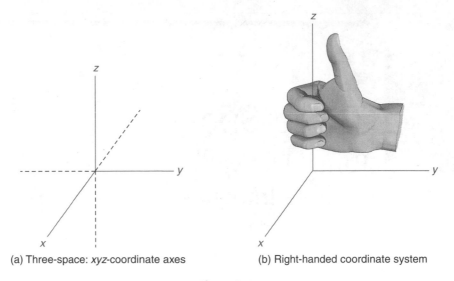

(a) Three-space: *xyz*-coordinate axes   (b) Right-handed coordinate system

Figure 2.1

The three axes determine three planes (*xy*-, *xz*-, and *yz*-planes), which divide three-space into octants as shown in Fig. 2.2.

Each point in three-space is represented by an ordered triple of numbers in the form (*x*, *y*, *z*), which indicate the directed distances from the three planes as shown in Fig. 2.3.

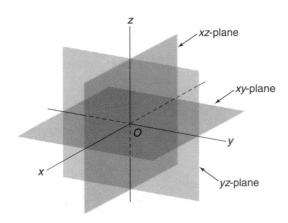

Figure 2.2   Coordinate planes.

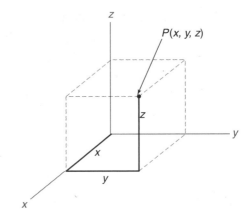

Figure 2.3   An ordered triple of numbers in the form *P*(*x*, *y*, *z*) represents a point in three-space.

EXAMPLE 1

Plot the points $(2, -4, 5)$ and $(-3, 5, -4)$ (see Fig. 2.4).

The graph of an equation expressed in three variables is normally a surface. We shall now discuss the graphs of some surfaces on a case-by-case basis.

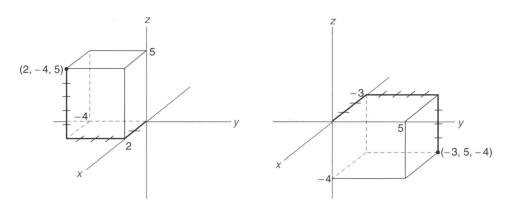

Figure 2.4   Plotting points in three-space.

> **PLANE**
>
> The graph of an equation in the form
> $$Ax + By + Cz + D = 0$$
> is a plane.

EXAMPLE 2

Sketch $3x + 6y + 2z = 12$.

If the plane does not pass through the origin, its sketch may be found by graphing the intercepts. To find the x-intercept, set y and z equal to zero and solve for x: $x = 4$, which corresponds to the point $(4, 0, 0)$. Similarly, the y- and z-intercepts are $(0, 2, 0)$ and $(0, 0, 6)$, respectively. These three points determine the plane. The lines through pairs of these points are in the coordinate planes and are called *traces,* as shown in Fig. 2.5.

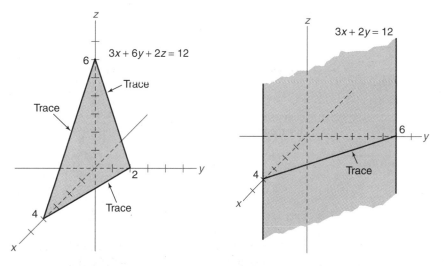

Figure 2.5   **Figure 2.6**

EXAMPLE 3

Sketch $3x + 2y = 12$ in three-space.

The x- and y-intercepts are $(4, 0, 0)$ and $(0, 6, 0)$, respectively, which determine the trace in the xy-plane. Note that the plane never crosses the z-axis because x and y cannot both be zero. Thus the plane is parallel to the z-axis, as shown in Fig. 2.6.

EXAMPLE 4

Sketch $x = 3$ in three-space.

Its x-intercept is $(3, 0, 0)$. The plane is parallel to both the y- and z-axes, as shown in Fig. 2.7.

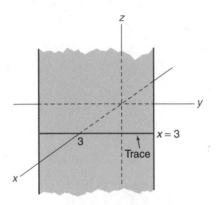

Figure 2.7

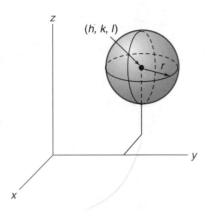

Figure 2.8 Graph of sphere with center at (h, k, l) and radius r.

The formula for the distance between two points in three-space is given in Exercise 41. Using this formula, we obtain the following equation of a sphere:

SPHERE

A sphere with center at (h, k, l) and radius r (see Fig. 2.8) is given by the equation

$$(x - h)^2 + (y - k)^2 + (z - l)^2 = r^2$$

EXAMPLE 5

Find the center and the radius of the sphere whose equation is

$$x^2 + y^2 + z^2 - 6x + 10y - 16z + 82 = 0$$

and sketch its graph.

First, complete the square on each variable.

$$(x^2 - 6x \quad) + (y^2 + 10y \quad) + (z^2 - 16z \quad) = -82$$
$$(x^2 - 6x + 9) + (y^2 + 10y + 25) + (z^2 - 16z + 64) = -82 + 9 + 25 + 64$$
$$(x - 3)^2 + (y + 5)^2 + (z - 8)^2 = 16$$

The center is at $(3, -5, 8)$ and the radius is 4 (see Fig. 2.9).

In general, graphing more complex surfaces can be quite complicated. One helpful technique involves graphing the intersections of the surface with the coordinate planes. Such intersections of the surfaces and the coordinate planes are called *traces*.

CYLINDRICAL SURFACE

The graph in three-space of an equation expressed in only two variables is a cylindrical surface. The surface is parallel to the coordinate axis of the missing variable.

EXAMPLE 6

Sketch the graph of $y^2 = 4x$ in three-space.

First, graph the trace $y^2 = 4x$ in the xy-plane. Then extend the cylindrical surface parallel to the z-axis as in Fig. 2.10.

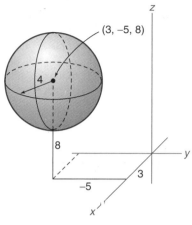

$x^2 + y^2 + z^2 - 6x + 10y - 16z + 82 = 0$

Figure 2.9

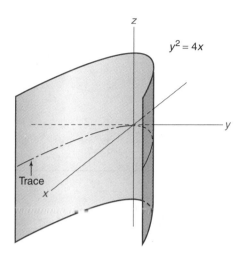

Figure 2.10

EXAMPLE 7

Sketch the graph of $z = \sin y$ in three-space.

First, graph the trace $z = \sin y$ in the yz-plane. Then extend the cylindrical surface parallel to the x-axis as in Fig. 2.11.

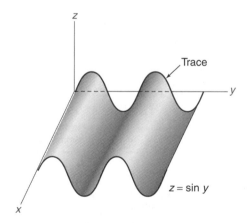

Figure 2.11

QUADRIC SURFACE

The graph in three-space of a second-degree equation is a quadric surface. Plane sections, intersections, or slices of the given surface with planes are conics.

Surface	Equation	Traces
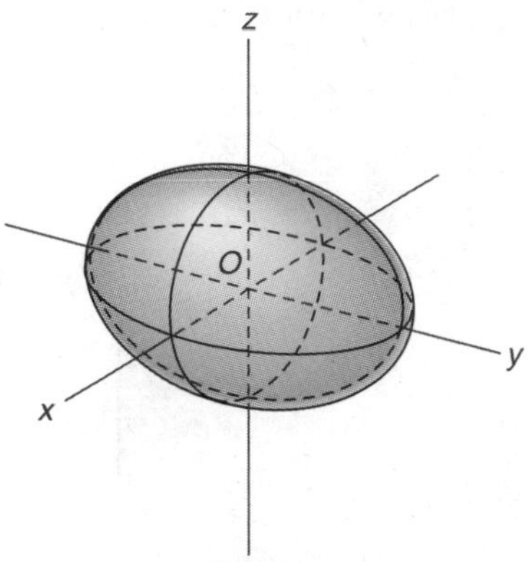 Ellipsoid	$\dfrac{x^2}{a^2} + \dfrac{y^2}{b^2} + \dfrac{z^2}{c^2} = 1$ *Note:* If $a = b = c$, the surface is a sphere.	xy-plane: ellipse xz-plane: ellipse yz-plane: ellipse All traces in planes parallel to the coordinate planes are ellipses.
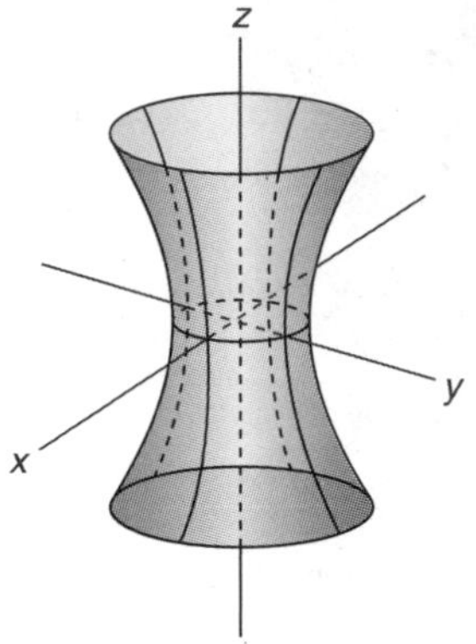 Hyperboloid of one sheet	$\dfrac{x^2}{a^2} + \dfrac{y^2}{b^2} - \dfrac{z^2}{c^2} = 1$ *Note:* If $a = b$, the surface may be generated by rotating a hyperbola about its conjugate axis.	xy-plane: ellipse xz-plane: hyperbola yz-plane: hyperbola All traces parallel to the xy-plane are ellipses.
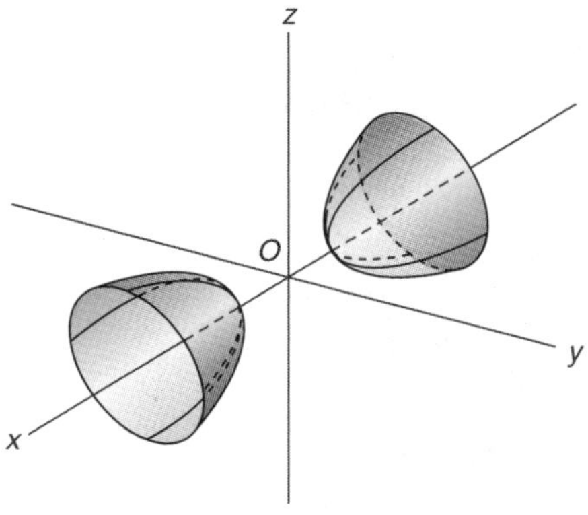 Hyperboloid of two sheets	$\dfrac{x^2}{a^2} - \dfrac{y^2}{b^2} - \dfrac{z^2}{c^2} = 1$ *Note:* If $b = c$, the surface may be generated by rotating a hyperbola about its transverse axis.	xy-plane: hyperbola xz-plane: hyperbola yz-plane: no trace All traces parallel to the yz-plane that intersect the surface are ellipses.

Figure 2.12   Six basic types of quadric surfaces.

Surface	Equation	Traces
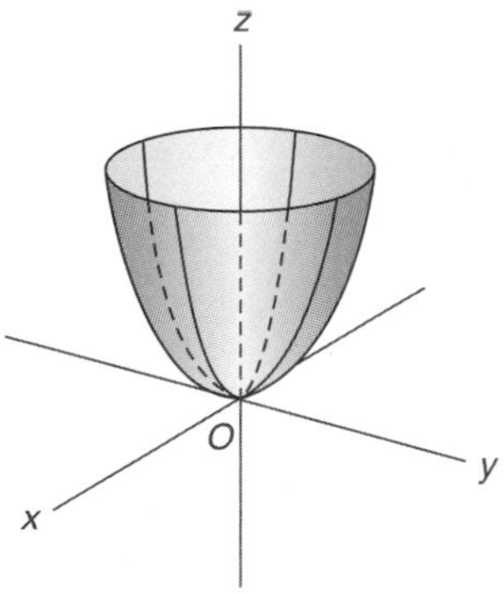 Elliptic paraboloid	$\dfrac{x^2}{a^2} + \dfrac{y^2}{b^2} = \dfrac{z}{c}$ *Note:* If $a = b$, the surface may be generated by rotating a parabola about its axis.	*xy*-plane: point *xz*-plane: parabola *yz*-plane: parabola If $c > 0$, all traces parallel to and above the *xy*-plane are ellipses; below the *xy*-plane, there is no intersection. If $c < 0$, the situation is reversed.
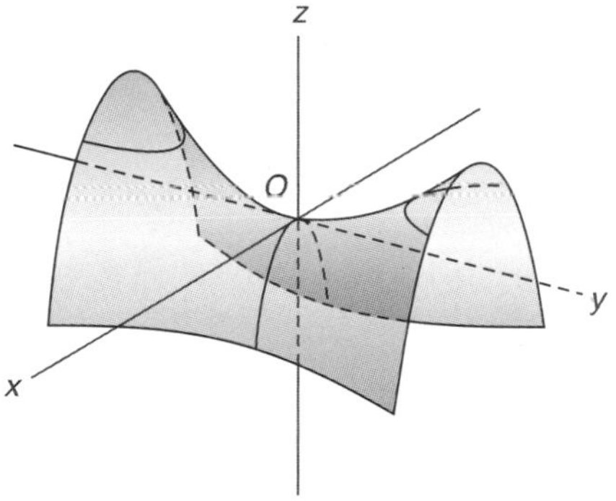 Hyperbolic paraboloid	$\dfrac{x^2}{a^2} - \dfrac{y^2}{b^2} = \dfrac{z}{c}$ *Note:* The origin is called a saddle point because this surface looks like a saddle.	*xy*-plane: pair of intersecting lines *xz*-plane: parabola ⎫ one opens up, *yz*-plane: parabola ⎭ one opens down Traces parallel to the *xy*-plane are hyperbolas.
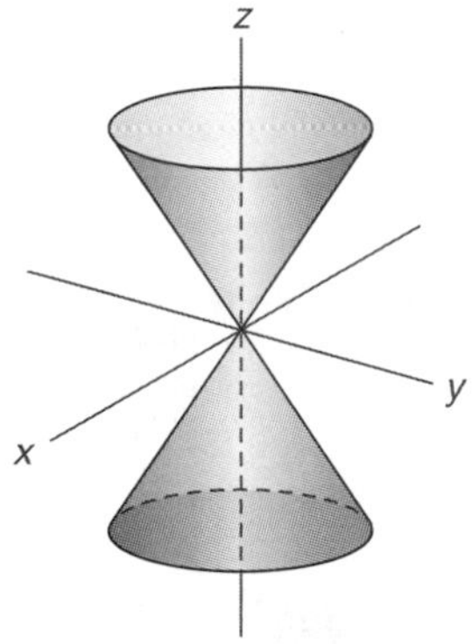 Elliptic cone	$\dfrac{x^2}{a^2} + \dfrac{y^2}{b^2} - \dfrac{z^2}{c^2} = 0$	*xy*-plane: point *xz*-plane: pair of intersecting lines *yz*-plane: pair of intersecting lines Traces parallel to the *xy*-plane are ellipses. Traces parallel to the *xz*- and *yz*-planes are hyperbolas.

Figure 2.12   *(continued)*

The second-degree equation in three-space has the form

$$Ax^2 + By^2 + Cz^2 + Dxy + Exz + Fyz + Gx + Hy + Iz + J = 0$$

The equations of the basic or central quadrics after translations and/or rotations can be expressed in one of the two general forms

$$Ax^2 + By^2 + Cz^2 + J = 0$$

and

$$Ax^2 + By^2 + Iz = 0$$

Figure 2.12 shows six basic types of quadric surfaces.

EXAMPLE 8

Name and sketch the graph of $\dfrac{x^2}{16} + \dfrac{y^2}{9} - \dfrac{z^2}{36} = 1$.

First, find the traces in the three coordinate planes:

xy-plane: Set $z = 0$, $\dfrac{x^2}{16} + \dfrac{y^2}{9} = 1$, an ellipse.

xz-plane: Set $y = 0$, $\dfrac{x^2}{16} - \dfrac{z^2}{36} = 1$, a hyperbola.

yz-plane: Set $x = 0$, $\dfrac{y^2}{9} - \dfrac{z^2}{36} = 1$, a hyperbola.

This is a hyperboloid of one sheet (see Fig. 2.13).

EXAMPLE 9

Name and sketch the graph of $2x^2 + 2y^2 = 8z$.

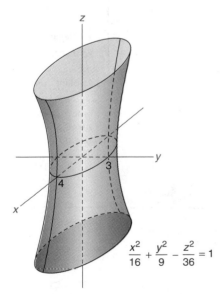

$$\frac{x^2}{16} + \frac{y^2}{9} - \frac{z^2}{36} = 1$$

Figure 2.13

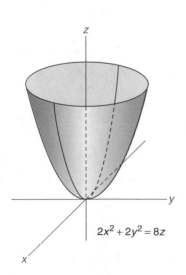

$$2x^2 + 2y^2 = 8z$$

Figure 2.14

First, divide both sides by 2.

$$x^2 + y^2 = 4z$$

Then, find the traces in the three coordinate planes:

xy-plane: Set $z = 0$, $x^2 + y^2 = 0$, the origin (degenerate circle).

xz-plane: Set $y = 0$, $x^2 = 4z$, a parabola.

yz-plane: Set $x = 0$, $y^2 = 4z$, a parabola.

(See Fig. 2.14.) This is an elliptic paraboloid.

Exercises 2.1

Plot each point.

1. $(2, 4, 5)$ **2.** $(3, 5, 2)$ **3.** $(3, -2, 4)$

4. $(-2, 0, 3)$ **5.** $(-1, 4, -3)$ **6.** $(3, -2, -4)$

Name and sketch the graph of each equation in three-space. Sketch the traces in the coordinate planes when appropriate.

7. $2x + 3y + 8z = 24$ **8.** $6x - 3y + 9z = 18$ **9.** $x + 3y - z = 9$

10. $-4x + 8y + 3z = 12$ **11.** $2x + 5y = 20$ **12.** $4x - 3y - 12$

13. $y = 4$ **14.** $z = -5$

15. $x^2 + y^2 + z^2 = 25$ **16.** $(x - 3)^2 + y^2 + (z - 2)^2 = 36$

17. $x^2 + y^2 + z^2 - 8x + 6y - 4z + 4 = 0$

18. $x^2 + y^2 + z^2 + 6x - 6y + 9 = 0$

19. $z^2 = 8y$ **20.** $x^2 + z^2 = 16$ **21.** $9x^2 + 4y^2 = 36$

22. $y^2 - z^2 = 4$ **23.** $4x^2 + 9y^2 + z^2 = 36$ **24.** $x^2 - y^2 = 16z$

25. $x^2 + y^2 - 4z = 0$ **26.** $y = e^x$

27. $9x^2 - 36y^2 - 4z^2 = 36$ **28.** $16x^2 + 9y^2 - 36z^2 = 144$

29. $y = \cos x$ **30.** $4x^2 + 9y^2 + 9z^2 = 36$

31. $y^2 - z^2 = 8x$ **32.** $y^2 + z^2 = 4x$

33. $4x^2 + 9y^2 - 9z^2 = 0$ **34.** $9x^2 - 16y^2 - 16z^2 = 144$

35. $81y^2 + 36z^2 - 4x^2 = 324$ **36.** $x^2 + y^2 - z^2 = 0$

37. Find the equation of the sphere with center at $(3, -2, 4)$ and radius 6. reverse it

38. Find the equation of the sphere with center at $(3, -2, 4)$ and tangent to the *xz*-plane.

39. Find the equation of the sphere with center at $(3, -2, 4)$ and tangent to the *xy*-plane.

40. Find the equation of the sphere of radius 4 that is tangent to the three coordinate planes and whose center is in the first octant.

41. Given two points $P_1(x_1, y_1, z_1)$ and $P_2(x_2, y_2, z_2)$, show that the distance between them is given by

$$d = P_1 P_2 = \sqrt{(x_2 - x_1)^2 + (y_2 - y_1)^2 + (z_2 - z_1)^2}$$

Find the distance between each pair of points.

42. $(3, 6, 8)$ and $(7, -2, 7)$ **43.** $(5, -3, 2)$ and $(3, 1, -2)$ **44.** $(-4, 0, 6)$ and $(2, 5, -2)$

45. Show that $(5, 6, 3)$, $(2, 8, 4)$, and $(3, 5, 6)$ are vertices of an equilateral triangle.

46. Show that $(1, 1, 2)$, $(3, 1, 0)$, and $(5, 3, 2)$ are vertices of a right triangle. (*Hint:* Use the Pythagorean theorem.)

2.2 PARTIAL DERIVATIVES

Let $z = f(x, y)$ represent a function z with independent variables x and y. That is, there exists a unique value of z for every pair of x- and y-values.

PARTIAL DERIVATIVES

If $z = f(x, y)$ is a function of two variables, the partial derivative of z with respect to x (y is treated as a constant) is defined by

$$\frac{\partial z}{\partial x} = \lim_{\Delta x \to 0} \frac{f(x + \Delta x, y) - f(x, y)}{\Delta x}$$

y con

provided that this limit exists.

If $z = f(x, y)$ is a function of two variables, the partial derivative of z with respect to y (x is treated as a constant) is defined by

$$\frac{\partial z}{\partial y} = \lim_{\Delta y \to 0} \frac{f(x, y + \Delta y) - f(x, y)}{\Delta y}$$

x con

provided that this limit exists.

Other common notations for partial derivatives include

$$\frac{\partial z}{\partial x} \qquad \frac{\partial f}{\partial x} \qquad f_x \qquad f_x(x, y)$$

$$\frac{\partial z}{\partial y} \qquad \frac{\partial f}{\partial y} \qquad f_y \qquad f_y(x, y)$$

Note that in the definition of $\dfrac{\partial z}{\partial x}$, y is treated as a constant (held fixed) and only x is allowed to vary. Think of z as a function of only one variable x and find the usual derivative with respect to x, treating y as a constant. For $\dfrac{\partial z}{\partial y}$, find the usual derivative with respect to y, treating x as a constant.

EXAMPLE 1

If $z = 5x^2 - 4x^2 y + y^3$, find $\dfrac{\partial z}{\partial x}$ and $\dfrac{\partial z}{\partial y}$.

$$\frac{\partial z}{\partial x} = 10x - 8xy$$

$$\frac{\partial z}{\partial y} = -4x^2 + 3y^2$$

EXAMPLE 2

If $z = x^2 \ln y - e^{xy}$, find $\dfrac{\partial z}{\partial x}$ and $\dfrac{\partial z}{\partial y}$.

$$\frac{\partial z}{\partial x} = 2x \ln y - ye^{xy}$$

$$\frac{\partial z}{\partial y} = \frac{x^2}{y} - xe^{xy}$$

EXAMPLE 3

If $z = e^{-x} \sin y + \ln (x^2 + y^2)$, find $\frac{\partial z}{\partial x}$ and $\frac{\partial z}{\partial y}$.

$$\frac{\partial z}{\partial x} = -e^{-x} \sin y + \frac{2x}{x^2 + y^2}$$

$$\frac{\partial z}{\partial y} = e^{-x} \cos y + \frac{2y}{x^2 + y^2}$$

Now, let's consider a graphical interpretation of partial derivatives. Let $z = f(x, y)$ be a function of x and y. Suppose that we are considering the partial derivative of z with respect to x at the point (x_0, y_0, z_0). We treat y as a constant and take the usual derivative with respect to x; this is graphically equivalent to finding the slope at $x = x_0$ of the curve, which is determined by the intersection of the plane $y = y_0$ and the surface $z = f(x, y)$ (see Fig. 2.15a).

Likewise for the partial derivative of z with respect to y; this is graphically equivalent to finding the slope at $y = y_0$ of the curve which is determined by the intersection of the plane $x = x_0$ and the surface $z = f(x, y)$ (see Fig. 2.15b).

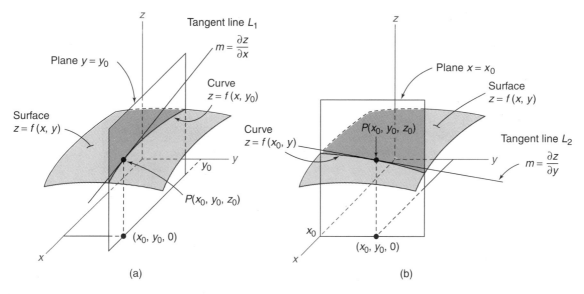

(a)   (b)

Figure 2.15 (a) The partial derivative of z with respect to x at the point $P(x_0, y_0, z_0)$ is graphically equivalent to the slope of L_1, the tangent line to the surface through P and parallel to the xz-plane. (b) The partial derivative of z with respect to y at the point $P(x_0, y_0, z_0)$ is graphically equivalent to the slope of L_2, the tangent line to the surface through P and parallel to the yz-plane.

EXAMPLE 4

Given the surface $z = 4x^2 + y^2$, find the slope of the tangent lines parallel to the xz- and yz-planes and through the point $(2, -1, 9)$.

First,

$$\frac{\partial z}{\partial x} = 8x \quad \text{and} \quad \frac{\partial z}{\partial y} = 2y$$

The slope of each tangent line is the value of each partial derivative evaluated at the point $(2, -1, 9)$. Thus,

$$\left.\frac{\partial z}{\partial x}\right|_{(2,-1,9)} = 16 \quad \text{and} \quad \left.\frac{\partial z}{\partial y}\right|_{(2,-1,9)} = -2$$

So, the slope of the tangent line parallel to the xz-plane is 16 and the slope of the tangent line parallel to the yz-plane is -2.

EXAMPLE 5

In an RC-circuit, the current I is given by

$$I = \frac{E}{R}e^{-t/(RC)}$$

Assume that all quantities are constant except I and R. Find $\dfrac{\partial I}{\partial R}$.

$$\frac{\partial I}{\partial R} = \frac{E}{R}e^{-t/(RC)}\left(\frac{-t}{C}\cdot\frac{-1}{R^2}\right) + e^{-t/(RC)}\left(\frac{-E}{R^2}\right)$$

$$= \frac{tE}{CR^3}e^{-t/(RC)} - \frac{E}{R^2}e^{-t/(RC)}$$

$$= \frac{E}{R^2}e^{-t/(RC)}\left(\frac{t}{RC} - 1\right)$$

Exercises 2.2

Find (a) $\dfrac{\partial z}{\partial x}$ *and (b)* $\dfrac{\partial z}{\partial y}$ *for each function.*

1. $z = 4x^3y^2$ **2.** $z = 8\pi x^2\sqrt{y}$ **3.** $z = 6x^2y^4 + 2xy^2$

4. $z = 3xy^5 - 4x^2y^2$ **5.** $z = \sqrt{x^2 + y^2}$ **6.** $z = \ln\sqrt{x^2 + y^2}$

7. $z = \dfrac{x^2 - y^2}{2xy}$ **8.** $z = \dfrac{1}{3}\pi x^2 y$ **9.** $z = axy$

10. $z = e^{xy} - e^{-x}$ **11.** $z = \ln\dfrac{x}{y}$ **12.** $z = (x^2 - y^2)^{-3}$

13. $z = \tan(x - y)$ **14.** $z = \sin(x - y)$ **15.** $z = e^{3x}\sin xy$

16. $z = \tan\dfrac{x}{y}$ **17.** $z = \dfrac{e^{xy}}{x\sin y}$ **18.** $z = ye^{\sin x}$

19. $z = 2\sin y\cos x$ **20.** $z = x^2\cos 2y$ **21.** $z = xy\tan xy$

22. $z = x^2y\cos y$

The following formulas are used in electronics and physics. Find the indicated partial derivative.

23. $P = I^2R;\ \dfrac{\partial P}{\partial I}$ **24.** $P = \dfrac{V^2}{R};\ \dfrac{\partial P}{\partial R}$

25. $I = \dfrac{E}{R + r}; \dfrac{\partial I}{\partial R}$

26. $R = \dfrac{R_1 R_2}{R_1 + R_2}; \dfrac{\partial R}{\partial R_1}$

27. $Z = \sqrt{R^2 + X_L^2}; \dfrac{\partial Z}{\partial R}$

28. $Z = \sqrt{R^2 + (X_L - X_C)^2}; \dfrac{\partial Z}{\partial X_L}$

29. $e = E \sin 2\pi f t; \dfrac{\partial e}{\partial t}$

30. $E = I_2 R_2 + I_3 R_3; \dfrac{\partial E}{\partial I_2}$

31. $E = I_2 R_2 + I_2 R_3; \dfrac{\partial E}{\partial I_2}$

32. $I = \dfrac{E_2 R_1 + E_2 R_3 - E_1 R_3}{R_1 R_2 + R_1 R_3 + R_2 R_3}; \dfrac{\partial I}{\partial R_1}$

33. $I = \dfrac{E}{R} e^{-t/(RC)}; \dfrac{\partial I}{\partial t}$

34. $I = \dfrac{E}{R} e^{-t/(RC)}; \dfrac{\partial I}{\partial C}$

35. $q = CE e^{-t/(RC)}; \dfrac{\partial q}{\partial C}$

36. $q = CE(1 - e^{-t/(RC)}); \dfrac{\partial q}{\partial C}$

37. $\tan \phi = \dfrac{X_L}{R}; \dfrac{\partial \phi}{\partial R}$

38. $\tan \phi = \dfrac{X_L - X_C}{R}; \dfrac{\partial \phi}{\partial X_L}$

For each surface, find the slope of the tangent lines parallel to (a) the xz-plane and (b) the yz-plane and through the given point.

39. $z = 9x^2 + 4y^2; (1, -2, 25)$

40. $z = 8y^2 - x^2; (-2, 1, 4)$ slope $xz = 4$ $yz = 16$

41. $z = \sqrt{25x^2 + 36y^2 + 164}; (1, -1, 15)$

42. $z = 6x^2 + 2xy + 4y^2 - 6x + 8y - 2; (1, -2, -6)$

43. The ideal gas law is $PV = nRT$, where P is the pressure, V is the volume, T is the absolute temperature, n is the number of moles of gas, and R is a constant. Show that

$$\frac{\partial P}{\partial V} \cdot \frac{\partial V}{\partial T} \cdot \frac{\partial T}{\partial P} = -1$$

44. Find the only point on the surface $z = x^2 + 3xy + 4y^2 - 10x - 8y + 4 = 0$ at which its tangent plane is horizontal.

45. The volume of a right circular cylinder is given by $V = \pi r^2 h$. If the height h is fixed at 8 cm, find the rate of change of the volume V with respect to the radius r when $r = 6$ cm.

46. Given that $z = \dfrac{e^{x+y}}{e^x + e^y}$, show that $\dfrac{\partial z}{\partial x} + \dfrac{\partial z}{\partial y} = z$.

47. Given $w = t^2 + \tan t e^{1/s}$, show that $s^2 \dfrac{\partial w}{\partial s} + t \dfrac{\partial w}{\partial t} = 2t^2$.

2.3 APPLICATIONS OF PARTIAL DERIVATIVES

Earlier applications of the derivative of a function of one variable may be extended to functions of two variables by using partial derivatives. We define the differential of a function of one variable as

$$dy = f'(x)\, dx$$

Similarly, we define the total differential of a function of two variables as

---

TOTAL DIFFERENTIAL OF $z = f(x, y)$

$$dz = \frac{\partial f}{\partial x}\, dx + \frac{\partial f}{\partial y}\, dy$$

The same type of definition may be extended to functions of three or more variables.

EXAMPLE 1

Find dz for $z = x^3 + 5x^2y - 4xy^2$.

$$dz = \frac{\partial z}{\partial x}\,dx + \frac{\partial z}{\partial y}\,dy$$

$$= (3x^2 + 10xy - 4y^2)\,dx + (5x^2 - 8xy)\,dy$$

We use differential approximations to find changes in the function as small changes are made in the independent variable. Now we can use the total differential to find changes in a function of two variables as small changes are made in one or both variables.

EXAMPLE 2

The height of a right circular cylinder measures 20.00 cm with a maximum possible error of 0.10 cm, while its radius measures 8.00 cm with a maximum possible error of 0.05 cm. Find the maximum possible error in its volume.

$$V = \pi r^2 h$$

$$dV = \frac{\partial V}{\partial r}\,dr + \frac{\partial V}{\partial h}\,dh$$

$$= 2\pi rh\,dr + \pi r^2\,dh$$

$$= 2\pi(8.00 \text{ cm})(20.00 \text{ cm})(0.05 \text{ cm}) + \pi(8.00 \text{ cm})^2(0.10 \text{ cm})$$

$$= 70.4 \text{ cm}^3$$

EXAMPLE 3

The angle of elevation to the top of a monument when measured 150 ft ($\pm$ 0.5 ft) from its base is 31.00° with a maximum possible error of 0.05°. Find the maximum possible error in measuring its height (see Fig. 2.16).

$$\tan\theta = \frac{y}{x}$$

$$y = x\tan\theta$$

$$dy = \frac{\partial y}{\partial x}\,dx + \frac{\partial y}{\partial \theta}\,d\theta$$

$$= \tan\theta\,dx + x\sec^2\theta\,d\theta$$

$$= (\tan 31.00°)(0.5 \text{ ft}) + (150 \text{ ft})(\sec 31.00°)^2\left(0.05° \times \frac{\pi \text{ rad}}{180°}\right)$$

$$= 0.479 \text{ ft}$$

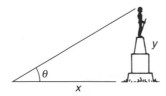

Figure 2.16

The second partial derivatives of a function of two variables are calculated by taking partial derivatives of the first partials. There are four possibilities. The second partial derivative with respect to x is notated $f_{xx}(x, y)$ or $\dfrac{\partial^2 f}{\partial x^2}$, the second partial with respect to y is notated $f_{yy}(x, y)$ or $\dfrac{\partial^2 f}{\partial y^2}$, and the mixed partials $f_{xy}(x, y)$ and $f_{yx}(x, y)$ can also be notated as

$\dfrac{\partial^2 f}{\partial y \partial x}$ and $\dfrac{\partial^2 f}{\partial x \partial y}$, respectively. While the order of differentiation in the mixed partials may look significant, a theorem of advanced calculus guarantees that $f_{xy}(x, y) = f_{yx}(x, y)$ if the original function, its first partials, and these mixed partials are all continuous functions of two variables (note the equality of the mixed partials in the following example).

EXAMPLE 4

Find the second partial derivatives of $f(x, y) = x^3 y^5 + x \cos y$.
The first partials are

$$f_x(x, y) = \frac{\partial f}{\partial x} = 3x^2 y^5 + \cos y$$

$$f_y(x, y) = \frac{\partial f}{\partial y} = 5x^3 y^4 - x \sin y$$

so the second partials are

$$f_{xx}(x, y) = 6xy^5 \qquad \text{[the partial with respect to } x \text{ of } f_x(x, y)]$$
$$f_{yy}(x, y) = 20x^3 y^3 - x \cos y \qquad \text{[the partial with respect to } y \text{ of } f_y(x, y)]$$
$$f_{xy}(x, y) = 15x^2 y^4 - \sin y \qquad \text{[the partial with respect to } y \text{ of } f_x(x, y)]$$
$$f_{yx}(x, y) = 15x^2 y^4 - \sin y \qquad \text{[the partial with respect to } x \text{ of } f_y(x, y)]$$

One principal application of the derivative of a function in one variable is finding relative maximums and minimums. This application may also be extended to functions of two variables by using partial derivatives. Geometrically, let's start this discussion with a surface $z = f(x, y)$ as shown in Fig. 2.17. If point P is a relative maximum (or minimum), then every tangent line through P must be parallel to the xy-plane. That is, $\dfrac{\partial z}{\partial x} = 0$ and $\dfrac{\partial z}{\partial y} = 0$.

Note: Both partial derivatives must equal zero. However, this result gives only critical points, that is, only possible relative maximum or minimum values. A saddle point is a

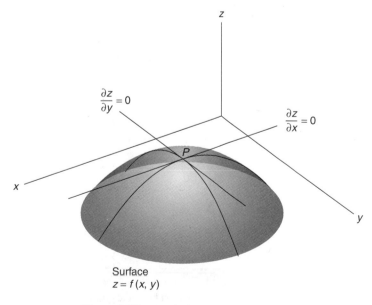

Figure 2.17 A relative maximum point.

critical point that is neither a maximum nor a minimum. The name "saddle point" refers to the center point on a horse's saddle, which has this property. For a drawing of a saddle point, see the hyperbolic paraboloid in Fig. 2.12.

DISCRIMINANT

Let $f(x, y)$ be a function that has continuous second partial derivatives; then its discriminant $D(x, y)$ is given by $D(x, y) = f_{xx}(x, y)f_{yy}(x, y) - [f_{xy}(x, y)]^2$.

The Second Partials Test

Let $f(x, y)$ be a function that has continuous second partial derivatives and a critical point $(a, b, f(a, b))$:

1. If $D(a, b) < 0$, then the point $(a, b, f(a, b))$ is a saddle point (it's neither a maximum nor a minimum).

2. If $D(a, b) > 0$ and $f_{xx}(a, b) < 0$, then $(a, b, f(a, b))$ is a relative maximum point.

3. If $D(a, b) > 0$ and $f_{xx}(a, b) > 0$, then $(a, b, f(a, b))$ is a relative minimum point.

4. Nothing can be concluded if $D(a, b) = 0$.

Though this is a rather advanced theorem, just think of the discriminant's job as telling us whether or not our critical point corresponds to an extreme point on the surface. A *negative* discriminant means *no,* it's not a relative extreme (our critical point is a saddle point). A *positive* discriminant means *yes,* our critical point is either a relative maximum or minimum. To distinguish a maximum from a minimum, $f_{xx}(a, b)$ is evaluated to measure the concavity of the surface (using a trace parallel to the xz-plane). If $f_{xx}(a, b)$ is negative, the surface is opening downward, so our critical point is a relative maximum. Similarly, if $f_{xx}(a, b)$ is positive, the surface is opening upward, so our critical point is a relative minimum. As noted in Part 4, a zero discriminant does not allow any conclusion to be made. An interested student with access to a computer graphics utility may wish to investigate $f(x, y) = 1 + x^4 - y^4$, $g(x, y) = 1 - x^4 - y^4$, and $h(x, y) = 1 + x^4 + y^4$, which all have zero discriminants at the critical point $(0, 0, 1)$. This critical point turns out to be a saddle point of f, a relative maximum of g, and a relative minimum of h, so any of the three cases are possible with a zero discriminant.

EXAMPLE 5

Find any relative maximum or minimum points for $z = f(x, y) = 3x - x^2 - xy - y^2 - 2$.
    The first partial derivatives are

$$\frac{\partial z}{\partial x} = f_x(x, y) = 3 - 2x - y$$

$$\frac{\partial z}{\partial y} = f_y(x, y) = -x - 2y$$

Set each expression equal to zero and solve the resulting system of equations.

$$3 - 2x - y = 0$$
$$-x - 2y = 0$$

Multiply the second equation by 2 and add.

$$2x + y = 3$$
$$\underline{-2x - 4y = 0}$$
$$-3y = 3$$
$$y = -1 \quad \text{and} \quad x = 2$$

Then,

$$z = f(2, -1) = 3(2) - (2)^2 - (2)(-1) - (-1)^2 - 2 = 1$$

Next, we need to determine if the point $(2, -1, 1)$ is a maximum or a minimum.

$$f_{xx}(x, y) = -2$$
$$f_{yy}(x, y) = -2$$
$$f_{xy}(x, y) = -1 \qquad \text{(note that quadric surfaces yield } \textit{constant} \text{ second partials)}$$
$$D(x, y) = f_{xx}(x, y) f_{yy}(x, y) - [f_{xy}(x, y)]^2$$
$$D(x, y) = \quad (-2)(-2) \quad - [-1]^2 = 3$$

$D(2, -1) = 3 > 0$ and $f_{xx}(2, -1) = -2 < 0$, so $(2, -1, 1)$ is a relative maximum point.

A professionally drawn sketch is shown in Fig. 2.18.

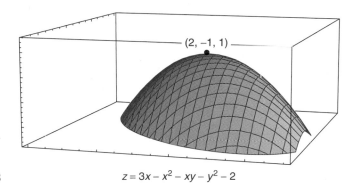

Figure 2.18 $z = 3x - x^2 - xy - y^2 - 2$

EXAMPLE 6

Find any relative maximum or minimum points for $z = f(x, y) = x^3 + y^3 - 3xy + 4$.

The first partial derivatives are

$$\frac{\partial z}{\partial x} = f_x(x, y) = 3x^2 - 3y$$

$$\frac{\partial z}{\partial y} = f_y(x, y) = 3y^2 - 3x$$

Set each expression equal to zero and solve the resulting system of equations.

$$3x^2 - 3y = 0$$
$$3y^2 - 3x = 0$$

The first equation implies that $y = x^2$. Substitute this into the second equation.

$$3(x^2)^2 - 3x = 0$$
$$3x^4 - 3x = 0$$
$$3x(x^3 - 1) = 0$$
$$3x = 0 \quad \text{or} \quad x^3 = 1$$
$$x = 0 \quad \text{or} \quad x = 1$$

If $x = 0$, then $y = 0^2 = 0$ and $z = f(0, 0) = (0)^3 + (0)^3 - 3(0)(0) + 4 = 4$
If $x = 1$, then $y = 1^2 = 1$ and $z = f(1, 1) = (1)^3 + (1)^3 - 3(1)(1) + 4 = 3$
So $(0, 0, 4)$ and $(1, 1, 3)$ are critical points.

The second partials are

$$f_{xx}(x, y) = 6x$$
$$f_{yy}(x, y) = 6y$$
$$f_{xy}(x, y) = -3$$
$$D(x, y) = f_{xx}(x, y) f_{yy}(x, y) - [f_{xy}(x, y)]^2$$
$$D(x, y) = (6x)(6y) - [-3]^2 = 36xy - 9$$

$D(0, 0) = 36(0)(0) - 9 = -9 < 0$, so $(0, 0, 4)$ is a saddle point.
$D(1, 1) = 36(1)(1) - 9 = 27 > 0$ and $f_{xx}(1, 1) = 6(1) = 6 > 0$, so $(1, 1, 3)$ is a relative minimum point.

Two different views of professionally drawn sketches are shown in Fig. 2.19.

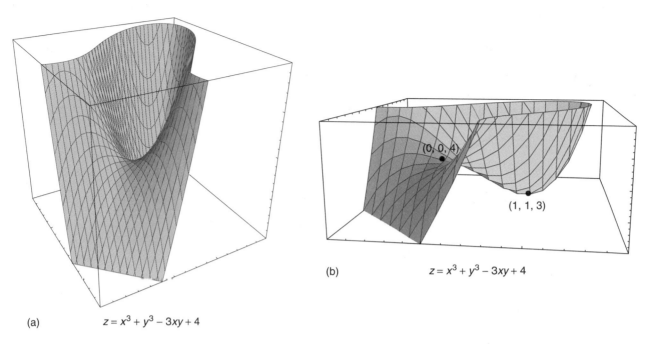

(a) $z = x^3 + y^3 - 3xy + 4$

(b) $z = x^3 + y^3 - 3xy + 4$

Figure 2.19

EXAMPLE 7

Find the dimensions of a rectangular box, with no top, having a volume of 32 m^3 and using the least amount of material.

The area or amount of the material is $A = lw + 2wh + 2lh$. The volume of the box is $V = lwh = 32$ (see Fig. 2.20). Next, solve this volume equation for h, $h = \dfrac{32}{lw}$, and substitute into the area equation.

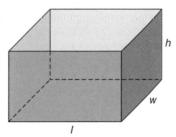

Figure 2.20

$$A = lw + 2w\left(\frac{32}{lw}\right) + 2l\left(\frac{32}{lw}\right)$$

$$A = lw + \frac{64}{l} + \frac{64}{w}$$

which expresses A as a function of two variables. Now find the partial derivatives.

$$\frac{\partial A}{\partial l} = w - \frac{64}{l^2} \quad \text{and} \quad \frac{\partial A}{\partial w} = l - \frac{64}{w^2}$$

Setting each partial derivative equal to zero, we have

$$w - \frac{64}{l^2} = 0 \quad \text{and} \quad l - \frac{64}{w^2} = 0$$

$$w = \frac{64}{l^2}$$

Substitute $w = 64/l^2$ into the second equation.

$$l - \frac{64}{w^2} = 0$$

$$l - \frac{64}{(64/l^2)^2} = 0$$

$$l - \frac{l^4}{64} = 0$$

$$l\left(1 - \frac{l^3}{64}\right) = 0$$

Then $l = 0$ or $l = 4$. (*Note:* $l = 0$ is impossible.) When $l = 4$,

$$w = \frac{64}{l^2} = \frac{64}{16} = 4$$

and

$$h = \frac{32}{lw} = \frac{32}{4 \cdot 4} = 2$$

So the dimensions of the box are 4 m $\times$ 4 m $\times$ 2 m.

Exercises 2.3

Find the total differential for each function.

1. $z = 3x^2 + 4xy + y^3$ **2.** $z = x^2y + 4x^2y^2 - 5x^3y^3$

3. $z = x^2 \cos y$ **4.** $z = \dfrac{y}{x} + \ln x$ **5.** $z = \dfrac{x - y}{xy}$

6. $z = \arctan xy$ **7.** $z = \ln \sqrt{1 + xy}$ **8.** $z = e^{xy} + \sin xy$

9. The sides of a box measure 26.00 cm $\times$ 26.00 cm $\times$ 12.00 cm with a maximum possible error of 0.15 cm on each side. Use a differential to approximate the change in volume.

10. A 6.00-in.-radius cylindrical rod is 2 ft long. Use a differential to approximate how much nickel (in in^3) is needed to coat the entire rod with a thickness of 0.12 in.

11. The total resistance R of two resistors R_1 and R_2 connected in parallel is $R = \dfrac{R_1 R_2}{R_1 + R_2}$. Resistance R_1 measures 400 Ω with a maximum possible error of 25 Ω. Resistance R_2 measures 600 Ω with a maximum possible error of 50 Ω. Use a differential to approximate the change in R.

12. The angle of elevation to the top of a hill is 18.00°. The distance to the top of the hill is 450 $\pm$ 15 ft. If the maximum possible error in measuring the angle is 0.5°, find the maximum possible error in calculating the height of the hill.

$R_1 = 400\,\Omega$

$dR_1 = 25\,\Omega$

$R_2 = 600\,\Omega$

$dR_2 = 50\,\Omega$

$dR = \dfrac{\partial R}{\partial R_1}\, dR_1 + \dfrac{\partial R}{\partial R_2}\, dR_2$ $\dfrac{\partial R}{\partial R_1} =$

$$V = \frac{\pi r^2 h}{3}$$

13. The height of a right circular cone increases from 21.00 cm to 21.10 cm while the radius decreases from 12.00 cm to 11.85 cm. Use a total differential to approximate the change in volume.

14. The electric current in a circuit containing a variable resistor R is given by $i = 25(1 - e^{-Rt/25})$. Use a total differential to approximate the change in current as R changes from 8.00 Ω to 8.25 Ω and t changes from 4.0 s to 4.1 s.

Find any relative maximum or minimum points or saddle points for each function.

15. $z = 9 + 6x - 8y - 3x^2 - 2y^2$ **16.** $z = 4x^2 + 3y^2 - 16x - 24y + 5$

17. $z = \dfrac{1}{x} + \dfrac{1}{y} + xy$ **18.** $z = 60x + 60y - xy - x^2 - y^2$

19. $z = x^2 - y^2 - 2x - 4y - 4$ **20.** $z = x^2 + y^2 + 2x + 3y + 3$

21. $z = x^2 - y^2 - 6x + 4y$ **22.** $z = x^3 + y^3 + 3xy + 4$

23. $z = 4x^3 + y^2 - 12x^2 - 36x - 2y$ **24.** $z = x^3 + y^3 - 3x^2 - 9y^2 - 24x$

25. Find the dimensions of a rectangular box, with no top, having a volume of 500 cm³ and using the least amount of material.

26. A rectangular box with no top and a volume of 6 ft³ needs to be built from material that costs $6/ft² for the bottom, $2/ft² for the front and back, and $1/ft² for the sides. Find the dimensions of the box in order to minimize the cost.

27. Find three positive numbers whose sum is 30 and whose product is a maximum.

28. Find three positive numbers whose sum is 30 and whose sum of squares is a minimum.

2.4   DOUBLE INTEGRALS

In Section 2.2, partial differentiation with respect to y turned out to be like ordinary differentiation with respect to y, expect that x was held *constant*. In a similar fashion, we wish to explore an *antidifferentiation* with respect to y that holds x constant. This will usually be the first of two integrations, the second being an ordinary integration with respect to x. Of course, the order might be reversed, meaning an integration with respect to x in which y is held constant, followed by an ordinary integration with respect to y. Either sequence of integrations is called *double integration* using an iterated double integral.

> **DOUBLE INTEGRAL**
>
> $$\int_a^b \left[\int_{g(x)}^{G(x)} f(x, y)\, dy \right] dx = \int_a^b \int_{g(x)}^{G(x)} f(x, y)\, dy\, dx$$
>
> $$\int_c^d \left[\int_{h(y)}^{H(y)} f(x, y)\, dx \right] dy = \int_c^d \int_{h(y)}^{H(y)} f(x, y)\, dx\, dy$$

Note: The brackets are normally not included when writing a double integral.

To integrate the double integral $\displaystyle\int_a^b \int_{g(x)}^{G(x)} f(x, y)\, dy\, dx$:

1. Integrate $f(x, y)$ with respect to y, holding x constant.

2. Evaluate this integral by substituting the limits on the inner or right integral. These limits are either numbers or functions of x.

3. Integrate the result from Step 2 with respect to x.

4. Evaluate this integral by substituting the remaining limits (those on the outer or left integral), which are numerical values.

EXAMPLE 1

Evaluate $\displaystyle\int_0^1 \int_x^{3x^2} (6xy - x)\, dy\, dx.$

First, integrate with respect to y, holding x constant.

$$\int_0^1 \int_x^{3x^2} (6xy - x)\, dy\, dx = \int_0^1 (3xy^2 - xy)\Big|_x^{3x^2} dx$$

$$= \int_0^1 \{[3x(3x^2)^2 - x(3x^2)] - [3x(x)^2 - x(x)]\}\, dx$$

$$= \int_0^1 (27x^5 - 3x^3 - 3x^3 + x^2)\, dx$$

$$= \int_0^1 (27x^5 - 6x^3 + x^2)\, dx$$

$$= \left(\frac{9x^6}{2} - \frac{3x^4}{2} + \frac{x^3}{3}\right)\Big|_0^1$$

$$= \left(\frac{9}{2} - \frac{3}{2} + \frac{1}{3}\right) - (0)$$

$$= \frac{10}{3}$$

EXAMPLE 2

Evaluate $\displaystyle\int_0^4 \int_{-y}^{3y} \sqrt{x + y}\, dx\, dy.$

First, integrate with respect to x, holding y constant.

$$\int_0^4 \int_{-y}^{3y} \sqrt{x + y}\, dx\, dy = \int_0^4 \frac{2}{3}(x + y)^{3/2}\Big|_{-y}^{3y} dy$$

$$= \int_0^4 \left[\frac{2}{3}(3y + y)^{3/2} - \frac{2}{3}(-y + y)^{3/2}\right] dy$$

$$= \int_0^4 \frac{2}{3}(4y)^{3/2}\, dy$$

$$= \int_0^4 \frac{16}{3} y^{3/2}\, dy \qquad (4^{3/2} = 8)$$

$$= \frac{16}{3} \cdot \frac{y^{5/2}}{5/2}\Big|_0^4$$

$$= \frac{16}{3} \cdot \frac{2}{5}(4^{5/2} - 0)$$

$$= \frac{16}{3} \cdot \frac{2}{5} \cdot 32$$

$$= \frac{1024}{15}$$

Geometrically, a double integral may be interpreted as the volume under a surface. Let $z = f(x, y)$ be a continuous function whose surface is shown in Fig. 2.21. Let R be a region in the xy-plane bounded by $x = a$, $x = b$, $y = g(x)$, and $y = G(x)$.

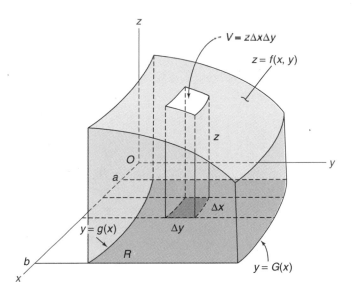

Figure 2.21 The volume of the solid is approximated by summing rectangular solids.

First, divide region R into n rectangles, each of which has dimensions Δx and Δy or dx and dy. Note that we have chosen to draw a typical rectangle. Next, construct a box with the rectangle as the base and z or $f(x, y)$ as its height. The volume of this typical volume element can be approximated by

$$z\,\Delta x\,\Delta y$$

Now let $n \to \infty$, where n is the number of such rectangles and the number of volume elements. Then we have

$$V = \int_a^b \int_{g(x)}^{G(x)} f(x, y)\, dy\, dx$$

VOLUME OF A SOLID

Let R be a region in the xy-plane bounded by $x = a$, $x = b$, $y = g(x)$, and $y = G(x)$. The volume of the solid between R and the surface $z = f(x, y)$ is

$$\int_a^b \int_{g(x)}^{G(x)} f(x, y)\, dy\, dx$$

Similarly, let R be a region in the xy-plane bounded by $y = c$, $y = d$, $x = h(y)$, and $x = H(y)$. The volume of the solid between R and the surface $z = f(x, y)$ is

$$\int_c^d \int_{h(y)}^{H(y)} f(x, y)\, dx\, dy$$

EXAMPLE 3

Find the volume of the solid bounded by the plane $2x + 3y + z = 6$ and the coordinate planes.
    First, make a sketch as in Fig. 2.22.

The region R is bounded in the xy-plane by $x = 0$, $y = 0$, and $2x + 3y = 6$ or $y = \dfrac{6 - 2x}{3}$.

    Next, determine the variable and constant limits for the double integral.

    Constant limits for x: $0 \le x \le 3$

    Variable limits for y: $0 \le y \le \dfrac{6 - 2x}{3}$

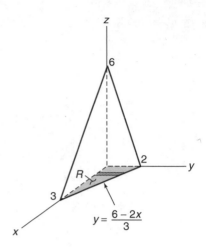

Figure 2.22

The volume is then

$$V = \int_0^3 \int_0^{(6-2x)/3} (6 - 2x - 3y) \, dy \, dx$$

$$= \int_0^3 \left(6y - 2xy - \frac{3y^2}{2} \right)\Bigg|_0^{(6-2x)/3} dx$$

$$= \int_0^3 \left\{ \left[6\left(\frac{6-2x}{3}\right) - 2x\left(\frac{6-2x}{3}\right) - \frac{3}{2}\left(\frac{6-2x}{3}\right)^2 \right] - (0) \right\} dx$$

$$= \int_0^3 \left(12 - 4x - 4x + \frac{4}{3}x^2 - 6 + 4x - \frac{2}{3}x^2 \right) dx$$

$$= \int_0^3 \left(6 - 4x + \frac{2}{3}x^2 \right) dx$$

$$= \left(6x - 2x^2 + \frac{2}{9}x^3 \right)\Bigg|_0^3$$

$$= (18 - 18 + 6) - (0)$$

$$= 6$$

Note: Since we have a pyramid, we can check this result using the formula

$V = \dfrac{1}{3}Bh$, where B is the area of the base and h is the height of the pyramid.

$B = \dfrac{1}{2}(3)(2) = 3 \qquad$ (area of triangular base)

$V = \dfrac{1}{3}(3)(6) = 6$

What happens if you reverse the order of the integration in Example 3?

Constant limits for y: $\quad 0 \le y \le 2$

Variable limits for x: $\quad 0 \le x \le \dfrac{6 - 3y}{2}$

Then the double integral is

$$V = \int_0^2 \int_0^{(6-3y)/2} (6 - 2x - 3y) \, dx \, dy$$

Show that this double integral also gives 6 as the result.

EXAMPLE 4

Find the volume of the solid inside the cylinder $x^2 + y^2 = 4$, below the plane $y = z$, and above the xy-plane.

Region R in Fig. 2.23 is bounded in the xy-plane by $x^2 + y^2 = 4$ and $y = 0$.

Constant limits for x: $\quad -2 \leq x \leq 2$

Variable limits for y: $\quad 0 \leq y \leq \sqrt{4 - x^2}$

Note that the height of a typical volume element is $z = y$.

The volume is then

$$
\begin{aligned}
V &= \int_{-2}^{2} \int_0^{\sqrt{4-x^2}} y \, dy \, dx \\
&= \int_{-2}^{2} \frac{y^2}{2} \bigg|_0^{\sqrt{4-x^2}} dx \\
&= \int_{-2}^{2} \left(\frac{4 - x^2}{2} \right) dx \\
&= \frac{1}{2} \left(4x - \frac{x^3}{3} \right) \bigg|_{-2}^{2} \\
&= \frac{1}{2} \left(8 - \frac{8}{3} \right) - \frac{1}{2} \left(-8 + \frac{8}{3} \right) \\
&= \frac{8}{3} + \frac{8}{3} = \frac{16}{3}
\end{aligned}
$$

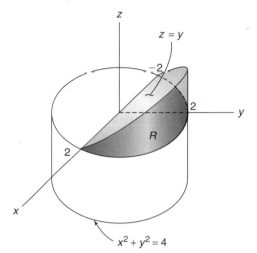

Figure 2.23

Exercises 2.4

Evaluate each double integral.

1. $\displaystyle\int_0^2 \int_0^{3x} (x + y)\, dy\, dx$

2. $\displaystyle\int_0^3 \int_0^{1-y} (x + y)\, dx\, dy$

3. $\displaystyle\int_0^1 \int_y^{2y} (3x^2 + xy)\, dx\, dy$

4. $\displaystyle\int_0^2 \int_0^x (4x^2 - 3xy^2 + 8y^3)\, dy\, dx$

5. $\displaystyle\int_{-1}^1 \int_x^{x^2} (4xy + 9x^2 + 6y)\, dy\, dx$

6. $\displaystyle\int_0^1 \int_{x^2}^{3x+1} x\, dy\, dx$

7. $\displaystyle\int_0^1 \int_0^{\sqrt{1-y^2}} (x + y)\, dx\, dy$

8. $\displaystyle\int_0^2 \int_0^{\sqrt{4-y^2}} \frac{2}{\sqrt{4 - y^2}}\, dx\, dy$

9. $\displaystyle\int_0^1 \int_0^x e^{x+y}\, dy\, dx$

10. $\displaystyle\int_0^1 \int_0^{x^3} e^{y/x}\, dy\, dx$

11. $\displaystyle\int_0^3 \int_0^{4y} \sqrt{y^2 + 16}\, dx\, dy$

12. $\displaystyle\int_0^1 \int_0^{4x} \frac{1}{x^2 + 1}\, dy\, dx$

13. $\displaystyle\int_0^{\pi/2} \int_0^x \cos x \sin y\, dy\, dx$

14. $\displaystyle\int_0^{\pi} \int_0^x x \sin y\, dy\, dx$

Find the volume of each solid bounded by the given surfaces.

15. $3x + y + 6z = 12$ and the coordinate planes
16. $3x + 4y + 2z = 12$ and the coordinate planes
17. $z = xy$, $y = x$, $x = 2$ (first octant)
18. $x^2 + y^2 = 4$, $z = x + y$ (first octant)
19. $x^2 + y^2 = 4$, $z = 2x + 3y$, and above the xy-plane
20. $x^2 + y^2 = 1$ and $x^2 + z^2 = 1$

CHAPTER 2 SUMMARY

1. *Surface:* The graph of an equation expressed in three variables or in the form $z = f(x, y)$.

2. *Plane:* The graph of an equation in the form
$$Ax + By + Cz + D = 0$$

3. A *sphere* with center at (h, k, l) and radius r is given by the equation
$$(x - h)^2 + (y - k)^2 + (z - l)^2 = r^2$$

4. *Cylindrical surface:* The graph in three-space of an equation expressed in only two variables. The surface is parallel to the coordinate axis of the missing variable.

5. The graph in three-space of a second-degree equation is a *quadric surface*. Plane sections, intersections, or slices of the given surface with planes are conics. The graphs, equations, and trace information of six basic quadric surfaces are given in Fig. 2.12.

6. *Distance between two points* $P_1(x_1, y_1, z_1)$ *and* $P_2(x_2, y_2, z_2)$:
$$d = P_1P_2 = \sqrt{(x_2 - x_1)^2 + (y_2 - y_1)^2 + (z_2 - z_1)^2}$$

7. *Partial derivatives:* If $z = f(x, y)$ is a function of two variables, the partial derivative of z with respect to x (y is treated as a constant) is defined by

$$\frac{\partial z}{\partial x} = \lim_{\Delta x \to 0} \frac{f(x + \Delta x, y) - f(x, y)}{\Delta x}$$

provided that this limit exists.

If $z = f(x, y)$ is a function of two variables, the partial derivative of z with respect to y (x is treated as a constant) is defined by

$$\frac{\partial z}{\partial y} = \lim_{\Delta y \to 0} \frac{f(x, y + \Delta y) - f(x, y)}{\Delta y}$$

provided that this limit exists.

8. *Total differential of $z = f(x, y)$:*

$$dz = \frac{\partial f}{\partial x} \, dx + \frac{\partial f}{\partial y} \, dy$$

9. *To find a relative maximum or minimum of a function of two variables* in the form $z = f(x, y)$, set both

$$\frac{\partial f}{\partial x} = 0 \quad \text{and} \quad \frac{\partial f}{\partial y} = 0$$

which will determine the critical points. Using the discriminant

$$D(x, y) = f_{xx}(x, y)f_{yy}(x, y) - [f_{xy}(x, y)]^2$$

and the Second Partials Test, check each critical point $(a, b, f(a, b))$ as follows:
(a) If $D(a, b) < 0$, then the point $(a, b, f(a, b))$ is a saddle point (it's neither a maximum nor a minimum).
(b) If $D(a, b) > 0$ and $f_{xx}(a, b) < 0$, then $(a, b, f(a, b))$ is a relative maximum point.
(c) If $D(a, b) > 0$ and $f_{xx}(a, b) > 0$, then $(a, b, f(a, b))$ is a relative minimum point.
(d) Nothing can be concluded if $D(a, b) = 0$.

10. To integrate the *double integral* $\displaystyle\int_a^b \int_{g(x)}^{G(x)} f(x, y) \, dy \, dx$:

(a) Integrate $f(x, y)$, with respect to y, holding x constant.
(b) Evaluate this integral by substituting the limits on the inner or right integral. These limits are either numbers or functions of x.
(c) Integrate the result from Step (b) with respect to x.
(d) Evaluate this integral by substituting the remaining limits (those on the outer or left integral), which are numerical values.

11. *Volume of a solid:* Let R be a region in the xy-plane bounded by $x = a$, $x = b$, $y = g(x)$, and $y = G(x)$. The volume of the solid between R and the surface $z = f(x, y)$ is

$$\int_a^b \int_{g(x)}^{G(x)} f(x, y) \, dy \, dx$$

Similarly, let R be a region in the xy-plane bounded by $y = c$, $y = d$, $x = h(y)$, and $x = H(y)$. The volume of the solid between R and the surface $z = f(x, y)$ is

$$\int_c^d \int_{h(y)}^{H(y)} f(x, y) \, dx \, dy$$

CHAPTER 2 REVIEW

Name and sketch the graph of each equation in three-space. Sketch the traces in the coordinate planes when appropriate.

1. $3x + 6y + 4z = 36$

2. $9x^2 + 9y^2 = 3z$

3. $36y^2 + 9z^2 - 16x^2 = 144$

4. $16x^2 + 9y^2 + 36z^2 = 144$

5. $x^2 = -12y$

6. $9x^2 - 9y^2 = 3z$

7. $9y^2 - 36x^2 - 16z^2 = 144$

8. $9x^2 + 36y^2 - 16z^2 = 0$

9. Find the equation of the sphere with the center at $(-3, 2, 1)$ and tangent to the yz-plane.

10. Find the distance between the points $(1, 2, 9)$ and $(4, -2, 4)$.

Find (a) $\dfrac{\partial z}{\partial x}$ and (b) $\dfrac{\partial z}{\partial y}$ for each function.

11. $z = x^3 + 3x^2y + 2y^2$

12. $z = 3x^2 e^{2y}$

13. $z = \ln(3x^2 y)$

14. $z = \sin 3x \sin 3y$

15. $z = \dfrac{y\, e^{x^2}}{x \ln y}$

16. $z = \dfrac{e^x \sin y}{y \sin x}$

Find the indicated partial derivative.

17. $v = \sqrt{\dfrac{P}{w}}; \dfrac{\partial v}{\partial w}$

18. $U = \dfrac{1}{2} LI^2; \dfrac{\partial U}{\partial I}$

19. $Z = \sqrt{R^2 + X_C^2}; \dfrac{\partial Z}{\partial X_C}$

20. $V = \dfrac{RE}{R + r}; \dfrac{\partial V}{\partial R}$

21. Find the slope of the tangent lines to $z = y^2 + xy + 3x^2 - 4x$ parallel to (a) the xz-plane and (b) the yz-plane and through the point $(2, 0, 4)$.

Find the total differential for each function.

22. $z = \ln \sqrt{x^2 + xy}$

23. $z = \dfrac{x - y}{x + y}$

24. A cylindrical tank has a radius of 2.000 m and a length of 10.000 m. Use a total differential to approximate the amount of paint (in litres) needed to paint one coat a thickness of 3 mm over its total exterior.

25. An electric current varies according to $i = 50(1 - e^{-t/(50R)})$. Use a total differential to approximate the change in current as R changes from 150 Ω to 160 Ω and t changes from 6.0 s to 6.5 s.

Find any relative maximum or minimum points or saddle points for each function.

26. $z = x^2 + 2xy - y^2 - 14x - 6y + 8$

27. $z = y^2 - xy - x^2 + 4x - 3y - 6$

28. $z = -x^2 + xy - y^2 + 4x - 8y + 9$

29. A rectangular box with no top needs to be built to hold 8 m³. The material for the bottom costs twice as much as the material for the sides. Find the dimensions of the box in order to minimize the cost.

Evaluate each double integral.

30. $\displaystyle\int_0^1 \int_0^{x^2} (x - 2y)\, dy\, dx$

31. $\displaystyle\int_0^2 \int_y^{4y} (4xy + 6x^2 - 9y^2)\, dx\, dy$

32. $\displaystyle\int_1^3 \int_0^{\ln y} ye^x\, dx\, dy$

33. $\displaystyle\int_0^{\pi/4} \int_0^x \sec^2 y\, dy\, dx$

Find the volume of each solid bounded by the given surfaces.

34. $ax + by + cz = d, a > 0, b > 0, c > 0$, and the coordinate planes.

35. $x^2 + y^2 = 1, z = 2x$ (first octant)

36. $z = 1 - y - x^2$ (first octant)

3
Progressions and the Binomial Theorem

INTRODUCTION

The fact that the sum of an infinite number of numbers could be finite is somewhat startling, yet we use this concept when we consider a rational number written as a repeating decimal. For example,

$$\frac{2}{3} = 0.666\ldots$$

$$= \frac{6}{10} + \frac{6}{100} + \frac{6}{1000} + \cdots$$

The numbers $\frac{6}{10}, \frac{6}{100}, \frac{6}{1000}, \ldots$ form a progression or sequence, and their sum is called a series. In this chapter we study progressions and series as well as the binomial theorem.

Objectives

- Find the nth term of an arithmetic progression.
- Find the sum of the first n terms of an arithmetic series.
- Find the nth term of a geometric progression.
- Find the sum of the first n terms of a geometric series.
- Use the binomial theorem to expand a binomial raised to the nth power.
- Find a specified term of a binomial expansion.

3.1 ARITHMETIC PROGRESSIONS

Many technical applications make use of infinite series. One in particular, the Fourier series, is very useful in the field of electronics. An *infinite series* is the summation of an infinite sequence of numbers. We will first look, however, at sums of finite sequences.

A *finite sequence* consists of a succession of quantities $a_1, a_2, a_3, \ldots, a_n$, where the three dots represent the quantities or terms between a_3 and a_n. The term a_n is called the

nth term or last term. An *infinite sequence* is a succession of quantities which continues indefinitely and may be written

$$a_1, a_2, a_3, \ldots, a_n, \ldots \quad \text{or} \quad a_1, a_2, a_3, \ldots$$

A basic example of an infinite sequence is an arithmetic progression. An *arithmetic progression* is a sequence of terms where each term differs from the immediately preceding term by a fixed number d, which is called the *common difference* of the progression. For example, the sequence 5, 10, 15, 20, 25, 30, . . . is an arithmetic progression with a common difference of 5. The sequence $1, \frac{1}{3}, -\frac{1}{3}, -1, -\frac{5}{3}, \ldots$ is an arithmetic progression with a common difference of $-\frac{2}{3}$.

In any arithmetic progression if a is the first term and d is the common difference, then the second term is $a + d$. Likewise, the third term is $a + 2d$ and the fourth term is $a + 3d$. Continuing in this manner, we can express the arithmetic progression as follows:

$$a, a + d, a + 2d, a + 3d, \ldots$$

Note that the first n terms of an arithmetic progression, an example of a finite sequence, can be written as

$$a, a + d, a + 2d, a + 3d, \ldots, a + (n - 1)d$$

The nth or last term l of such a finite arithmetic progression is then given by

$$an \quad l = a + (n - 1)\, d$$

EXAMPLE 1

Find the sixth term of the arithmetic progression 5, 9, 13, ...

The common difference is the difference between *any* term and the preceding term, that is,

$$d = 9 - 5 = 13 - 9 = 4, \qquad a = 5 \quad \text{and} \quad n = 6$$

We then have

$$
\begin{aligned}
l &= a + (n - 1)\, d \\
&= 5 + (6 - 1)(4) \\
&= 25
\end{aligned}
$$

EXAMPLE 2

Find the 22nd term of the arithmetic progression $1, \frac{1}{3}, -\frac{1}{3}, \ldots$.

Since $d = \frac{1}{3} - 1 = -\frac{2}{3}$, $a = 1$, and $n = 22$, we have

$$
\begin{aligned}
l &= a + (n - 1)d \\
&= 1 + (22 - 1)(-\tfrac{2}{3}) \\
&= -13
\end{aligned}
$$

To find the sum S_n of the first n terms of an arithmetic progression, note that the first n terms can be written as an expression involving l instead of a:

$$a, \ldots, l - 2d, l - d, l$$

In fact, we can indicate the sum S_n of these terms by

$$S_n = a + (a + d) + (a + 2d) + \cdots + (l - 2d) + (l - d) + l$$

or

$$S_n = l + (l - d) + (l - 2d) + \cdots + (a + 2d) + (a + d) + a$$

where the terms of the last equation are written in reverse order.

If we add these two equations for S_n, we have

$$2S_n = (a + l) + (a + l) + (a + l) + \cdots + (a + l) + (a + l) + (a + l)$$

since, term by term, the multiples of d add to zero. Note that we obtain a sum of n terms of the form $(a + l)$. That is,

$$2S_n = n(a + l)$$

or

$$S_n = \frac{n}{2}(a + l)$$

EXAMPLE 3

Find the sum of the first 12 terms of the arithmetic progression 6, 11, 16, ...
Since $d = 11 - 6 = 5, a = 6$, and $n = 12$, we have

$$l = a + (n - 1)d$$
$$l = 6 + (12 - 1)(5)$$
$$= 61$$

$$S_n = \frac{n}{2}(a + l)$$
$$= \frac{12}{2}(6 + 61)$$
$$= 402$$

EXAMPLE 4

Find the sum of the first 500 positive integers.
Since $a = 1, d = 1, n = 500$, and $l = 500$, we have

$$S_n = \frac{n}{2}(a + l)$$
$$= \frac{500}{2}(1 + 500)$$
$$= 125{,}250$$

Exercises 3.1

Find the nth term of each arithmetic progression.

1. $2, 5, 8, \ldots, n = 6$ **2.** $-3, -7, -11, \ldots, n = 7$ **3.** $3, 4\frac{1}{2}, 6, \ldots, n = 15$

4. $-2, \frac{1}{5}, 2\frac{2}{5}, \ldots, n = 8$ **5.** $4, -5, -14, \ldots, n = 12$ **6.** $10, 50, 90, \ldots, n = 9$

7–12. Find the sum of the first n terms of the progressions in Exercises 1 through 6.

Write the first five terms of each arithmetic progression whose first term is a and whose common difference is d.

13. $a = 2, d = -3$ **14.** $a = -4, d = 2$ **15.** $a = 5, d = \frac{2}{3}$ **16.** $a = 3, d = -\frac{1}{2}$

17. Find the first term of an arithmetic progression whose tenth term is 12 and whose sum of the first 10 terms is 80.

18. Find the common difference of an arithmetic progression whose first term is 7 and whose eighth term is 16.

19. Find the sum of the first 1000 odd positive integers.

20. Find the sum of the first 500 even positive integers.

21. A man is employed at an initial salary of $36,000. If he receives an annual raise of $1400, what is his salary for the tenth year?

22. Equipment purchased at an original value of $13,600 is depreciated $1200 per year for 10 years. Find the depreciated value after 4 years. Find the scrap value (depreciated value after 10 years).

3.2 GEOMETRIC PROGRESSIONS

A geometric progression is another example of a sequence. A *geometric progression* is a sequence of terms where each term can be obtained by multiplying the preceding term by a fixed number r, which is called the *common ratio*. For example, $1, \frac{1}{2}, \frac{1}{4}, \frac{1}{8}, \ldots$ is a geometric progression with a common ratio of $\frac{1}{2}$, and $-6, -18, -54, -162, \ldots$ is a geometric progression with a common ratio of 3.

For any geometric progression if a is the first term and r is the common ratio, then ar is the second term. Likewise, $(ar)r = ar^2$ is the third term and $(ar^2)r = ar^3$ is the fourth term. Continuing in this manner, we can express a geometric progression as follows:

$$a, ar, ar^2, ar^3, \ldots, ar^{n-1}$$

where ar^{n-1} is the nth or last term l of the progression. That is,

$$l = ar^{n-1}$$

EXAMPLE 1

Find the eighth term of the geometric progression $1, \frac{1}{2}, \frac{1}{4}, \frac{1}{8}, \ldots$.

The common ratio is found by dividing *any* term by the preceding term. So

$$r = \frac{\frac{1}{2}}{1} = \frac{\frac{1}{4}}{\frac{1}{2}} = \frac{\frac{1}{8}}{\frac{1}{4}} = \frac{1}{2}$$

Since $a = 1$ and $n = 8$, we have

$$l = ar^{n-1}$$
$$= (1)(\tfrac{1}{2})^{8-1}$$
$$= \frac{1}{128}$$

EXAMPLE 2

Find the 10th term of the geometric progression $3, -6, 12, -24, \ldots$.

In this example $a = 3$, $r = -\dfrac{6}{3} = -2$, and $n = 10$.

$$l = ar^{n-1}$$
$$= (3)(-2)^{10-1}$$
$$= -1536$$

To find the sum S_n of the first n terms of the geometric progression

$$S_n = a + ar + ar^2 + ar^3 + \cdots + ar^{n-2} + ar^{n-1}$$

multiply each side of this equation by r and subtract as follows:

$$S_n = a + ar + ar^2 + ar^3 + \cdots + ar^{n-2} + ar^{n-1}$$
$$rS_n = \quad\quad ar + ar^2 + ar^3 + ar^4 + \cdots \quad\quad + ar^{n-1} + ar^n$$
$$\overline{S_n - rS_n = a \quad\quad\quad\quad\quad\quad\quad\quad\quad\quad\quad\quad\quad\quad\quad - ar^n}$$

Solving for S_n, we have

$$S_n(1 - r) = a(1 - r^n)$$

or

$$S_n = \frac{a(1 - r^n)}{1 - r}$$

EXAMPLE 3

Find the sum of the first eight terms of the geometric progression $1, \frac{1}{2}, \frac{1}{4}, \frac{1}{8}, \ldots$.
Since $r = \frac{1}{2}$, $a = 1$, and $n = 8$, we have

$$S_n = \frac{a(1 - r^n)}{1 - r}$$
$$= \frac{(1)[1 - (\frac{1}{2})^8]}{1 - \frac{1}{2}}$$
$$= \frac{1 - \frac{1}{256}}{\frac{1}{2}} = \frac{255}{128}$$

EXAMPLE 4

Find the sum of the first five terms of the geometric progression $2, -\frac{2}{3}, \frac{2}{9}, -\frac{2}{27}, \ldots$.
In this example $a = 2$, $r = -\frac{1}{3}$, and $n = 5$.

$$S_n = \frac{a(1 - r^n)}{1 - r}$$
$$= \frac{(2)[1 - (-\frac{1}{3})^5]}{1 - (-\frac{1}{3})}$$
$$= \frac{(2)(1 + \frac{1}{243})}{\frac{4}{3}} = \frac{122}{81}$$

EXAMPLE 5

If \$3000 is deposited annually in a savings account at 8% interest compounded annually, find the total amount in this account after 4 years.

The total amount in the account is the sum of a geometric progression

$$(3000)(1.08) + (3000)(1.08)^2 + (3000)(1.08)^3 + (3000)(1.08)^4$$

since the value of each dollar in the account increases by 8% each year. Note that the first term $(3000)(1.08) = \$3240$ represents the amount in the account after 1 year. Thus $a = 3240$, $r = 1.08$, and $n = 4$.

$$S_n = \frac{a(1 - r^n)}{1 - r}$$
$$= \frac{(3240)(1 - 1.08^4)}{1 - 1.08}$$
$$= \$14,600$$

The term *series* is used to denote the sum of a sequence of terms. Each S_n is thus a finite series. The methods of computing the sums S_n of finite arithmetic and geometric series have already been shown.

An infinite series is the indicated sum of an infinite sequence of terms. For example, $1 + \frac{1}{2} + \frac{1}{4} + \frac{1}{8} + \cdots$ is an infinite series. Since it is the infinite summation of the terms of a geometric sequence, it is called an *infinite geometric series*.

In Example 3 we found that the sum of the first eight terms of the geometric progression $1, \frac{1}{2}, \frac{1}{4}, \frac{1}{8}, \ldots$ is $\frac{255}{128}$. The sum of the first nine terms can be shown to be $\frac{511}{256}$ and the sum of the first ten terms is $\frac{1023}{512}$. This last sum is close to the value 2. In fact, the sum of the first 50 terms is given by

$$S_n = \frac{(1)[1 - (\frac{1}{2})^{50}]}{1 - \frac{1}{2}} = \frac{1 - (\frac{1}{2})^{50}}{\frac{1}{2}} = 2[1 - (\frac{1}{2})^{50}]$$

But since $\left(\frac{1}{2}\right)^{50} = \dfrac{1}{1,125,899,906,842,624}$, which is practically zero, we conclude that the sum S_n is very close to the value 2. The sum S_n gets closer and closer to 2 as n is given a larger and larger value.

If we denote the sum of the first n terms of a geometric progression by S_n and S as the sum of the terms of an infinite geometric progression, then

$$S = 1 + \frac{1}{2} + \frac{1}{4} + \frac{1}{8} + \cdots = 2$$

Not every infinite series has a finite sum. For example, $3 + 6 + 12 + 24 + \cdots$ has no finite sum. When the sum exists, the series is said to *converge*. When the limit or sum does not exist, the series is said to *diverge*.

In general, if $|r| < 1$, the infinite geometric series

$$a + ar + ar^2 + \cdots + ar^{n-1} + \cdots$$

has the sum

$$S = \frac{a}{1 - r}$$

If $|r| \geq 1$, the infinite geometric series has no sum (it diverges).

EXAMPLE 6

Find the sum of the infinite geometric series $3 + \frac{3}{5} + \frac{3}{25} + \cdots + 3(\frac{1}{5})^{n-1} + \cdots$
Since $r = \frac{1}{5}$ and $a = 3$, we have

$$S = \frac{a}{1 - r}$$

$$= \frac{3}{1 - \frac{1}{5}} = \frac{15}{4}$$

EXAMPLE 7

Find, if possible, the sum of the infinite geometric series

$$1 + 2 + (2)^2 + (2)^3 + \cdots + (2)^{n-1} + \cdots$$

Since $r = 2 \geq 1$, this infinite geometric series diverges.

EXAMPLE 8

Find a fraction that is equivalent to the decimal $0.232323 \ldots$.

We can write this decimal as the infinite series

$$0.23 + 0.0023 + 0.000023 + \cdots$$

Then $a = 0.23$ and $r = 0.01$. Thus,

$$S = \frac{a}{1 - r} = \frac{0.23}{1 - 0.01} = \frac{0.23}{0.99} = \frac{23}{99}$$

Note that any repeating decimal can be expressed as a fraction. The fractional form can be found by using the method shown in Example 8.

EXAMPLE 9

A tank contains 1000 gal of alcohol. Then 100 gal are drained out and the tank refilled with water. Then 100 gal of the mixture are drained out and the tank refilled with water. Assuming this process continues, how much alcohol remains in the tank after eight 100-gal units are drained out?

Draining the first 100 gal of alcohol leaves 900 gal or 9/10 of the alcohol in the tank. The amount of alcohol left after eight drainings is the ninth term in a geometric progression where $a = 1000$ gal and $r = 9/10$.

Term	Gallons of alcohol	Drain number
1	1000	0
2	1000 (9/10)	1
3	1000 (9/10)(9/10)	2
.	.	.
.	.	.
.	.	.
9	$1000 (9/10)^8$	8

The formula $l = ar^{n-1}$ gives

$$l = 1000 \text{ gal} \cdot (9/10)^8 = 430 \text{ gal}$$

Exercises 3.2

Find the nth term of each geometric progression.

1. $20, \frac{20}{3}, \frac{20}{9}, \ldots, n = 8$ **2.** $\frac{1}{8}, -\frac{1}{4}, \frac{1}{2}, \ldots, n = 7$

3. $\sqrt{2}, 2, 2\sqrt{2}, \ldots, n = 6$ **4.** $6, 3, \frac{3}{2}, \ldots, n = 8$

5. $8, -4, 2, \ldots, n = 10$ **6.** $3, 12, 48, \ldots, n = 5$

7–12. Find the sum of the first n terms of the progressions in Exercises 1 through 6.

Write the first five terms of each geometric progression whose first term is a and whose common ratio is r.

13. $a = 3, r = \frac{1}{2}$ **14.** $a = -6, r = \frac{1}{3}$ **15.** $a = 5, r = -\frac{1}{4}$

16. $a = 2, r = -\frac{3}{2}$ **17.** $a = -4, r = 3$ **18.** $a = -5, r = -2$

19. Find the common ratio of a geometric progression whose first term is 6 and whose fourth term is $\frac{3}{4}$.

20. Find the first term of a geometric progression with common ratio $\frac{1}{3}$ if the sum of the first three terms is 13.

21. If \$1000 is deposited annually in an account at 5.75% interest compounded annually, find the total amount in the account after 10 years.

22. If \$200 is deposited quarterly in an account at 4% annual interest compounded quarterly, find the total amount in the account after 10 years.

23. A ball is dropped from a height of 12 ft. After each bounce, it rebounds to $\frac{1}{2}$ the height of the previous height from which it fell. Find the distance the ball rises after the fifth bounce.

24. The half-life of a chlorine isotope, ^{38}Cl, used in radioisotope therapy is 37 min. This means that half of a given amount will disintegrate in 37 min. This means also that three-fourths will have disintegrated after 74 min. Find how much will have disintegrated in 148 min.

25. A salt solution is being cooled so that the temperature decreases 20% each minute. Find the temperature of the solution after 8 min if the original temperature was 90°C.

26. A tank contains 400 gal of acid. Then 100 gal is drained out and refilled with water. Then 100 gal of the mixture is drained out and refilled with water. Assuming that this process continues, how much acid remains in the tank after five 100-gal units are drained out?

Find the sum, when possible, for each infinite geometric series.

27. $4 + \frac{4}{7} + \frac{4}{49} + \cdots + 4(\frac{1}{7})^{n-1} + \cdots$

28. $6 + \frac{6}{11} + \frac{6}{121} + \cdots + 6(\frac{1}{11})^{n-1} + \cdots$

29. $3 - \frac{3}{8} + \frac{3}{64} - \cdots + 3(-\frac{1}{8})^{n-1} + \cdots$

30. $1 - \frac{1}{9} + \frac{1}{81} - \cdots + (-\frac{1}{9})^{n-1} + \cdots$

31. $4 + 12 + 36 + \cdots + 4(3)^{n-1} + \cdots$

32. $-5 - \frac{5}{2} - \frac{5}{4} - \cdots - 5(\frac{1}{2})^{n-1} - \cdots$

33. $5 + 1 + 0.2 + 0.04 + \cdots + 5(0.2)^{n-1} + \cdots$

34. $2 + 2 + 2 + \cdots + 2(1)^{n-1} + \cdots$

Find the fraction that is equivalent to each decimal.

35. $0.3333\ldots$

36. $0.135135135\ldots$

37. $0.0121212\ldots$

38. $0.6252525\ldots$

39. $0.86666\ldots$

40. $0.365365365\ldots$

3.3 THE BINOMIAL THEOREM

The *binomial theorem* provides us with a convenient means of expressing any power of a binomial as a sum of terms.

For small nonnegative integers n, we can find $(a + b)^n$ by actual multiplication.

$$n = 0: \quad (a + b)^0 = \qquad\qquad 1$$
$$n = 1: \quad (a + b)^1 = \qquad\qquad a + b$$
$$n = 2: \quad (a + b)^2 = \qquad\qquad a^2 + 2ab + b^2$$
$$n = 3: \quad (a + b)^3 = \qquad\quad a^3 + 3a^2b + 3ab^2 + b^3$$
$$n = 4: \quad (a + b)^4 = \quad\; a^4 + 4a^3b + 6a^2b^2 + 4ab^3 + b^4$$
$$n = 5: \quad (a + b)^5 = a^5 + 5a^4b + 10a^3b^2 + 10a^2b^3 + 5ab^4 + b^5$$

We could continue this process, but the multiplications become more complicated for larger values of n.

No matter what positive integral value of n is chosen, we obtain the following results:

1. $(a + b)^n$ has $n + 1$ terms.

2. The first term is a^n.

3. The second term is $na^{n-1}b$.

4. The exponent of a decreases by 1 and the exponent of b increases by 1 for each successive term.

5. In each term, the sum of the exponents of a and b is n.

6. The last term is b^n.

The kth term is given by the formula

$$\frac{n(n-1)(n-2)\cdots(n-k+2)}{(k-1)!}a^{n-k+1}b^{k-1}$$

where $k!$ (k factorial) indicates the product of the first k positive integers. (For example, $3! = 3 \cdot 2 \cdot 1 = 6$; $5! = 5 \cdot 4 \cdot 3 \cdot 2 \cdot 1 = 120$; and $6! = 6 \cdot 5 \cdot 4 \cdot 3 \cdot 2 \cdot 1 = 720$.) The three dots in the numerator indicate that the multiplication of decreasing numbers is to continue until the number $n - k + 2$ is reached. For example, if $n = 8$ and $k = 4$, then the formula gives

$$\frac{8 \cdot 7 \cdot 6}{3 \cdot 2 \cdot 1} = 56$$

BINOMIAL THEOREM

$$(a+b)^n = a^n + na^{n-1}b + \frac{n(n-1)}{2!}a^{n-2}b^2 + \frac{n(n-1)(n-2)}{3!}a^{n-3}b^3 + \cdots$$

$$+ \frac{n(n-1)(n-2)\cdots(n-k+2)}{(k-1)!}a^{n-k+1}b^{k-1} + \cdots + b^n$$

where the three dots indicate that you are to complete the process of calculating the terms. The expression for the kth term is also given.

EXAMPLE 1

Expand $(x + 4y)^5$ by using the binomial theorem.
Let $a = x$, $b = 4y$, and $n = 5$.

$$(x+4y)^5 = x^5 + 5x^{5-1}(4y) + \frac{5(5-1)}{2!}x^{5-2}(4y)^2 + \frac{5(5-1)(5-2)}{3!}x^{5-3}(4y)^3$$

$$+ \frac{5(5-1)(5-2)(5-3)}{4!}x^{5-4}(4y)^4 + (4y)^5$$

$$= x^5 + 20x^4y + 160x^3y^2 + 640x^2y^3 + 1280xy^4 + 1024y^5$$

For small values of n, it is possible to determine the coefficients of each term of the expansion by the use of *Pascal's triangle* as shown below:

$$
\begin{array}{ccccccccccc}
n = 0: & & & & & & 1 & & & & \\
n = 1: & & & & & 1 & & 1 & & & \\
n = 2: & & & & 1 & & 2 & & 1 & & \\
n = 3: & & & 1 & & 3 & & 3 & & 1 & \\
n = 4: & & 1 & & 4 & & 6 & & 4 & & 1 \\
n = 5: & 1 & & 5 & & 10 & & 10 & & 5 & & 1 \\
\end{array}
$$

Observe the similarity of this triangle to the triangular format shown earlier when expanding $(a + b)^n$ for $n = 0, 1, 2, 3, 4,$ and 5. Each row gives the coefficients for all terms of the binomial expansion for a given integer n. Each successive row provides the coefficients for the next integer n. Each row is read from left to right. The first and last coefficients are always 1 as observed in the triangle. Beginning with the third row ($n = 2$), coefficients of terms other than the first and last are found by adding together the two nearest coefficients found in the row above. For example, the coefficient of the fourth term for the expansion with $n = 5$ is 10, which is the sum of 6 and 4. The numbers 6 and 4 appear just above 10 in Pascal's triangle.

We can enlarge Pascal's triangle to obtain a row for any desired integer n. However, this is not practical for large values of n.

EXAMPLE 2

Using Pascal's triangle, find the coefficients of the terms of the binomial expansion for $n = 7$.
We need two more rows of the triangle:

$$n = 6: \quad 1 \quad 6 \quad 15 \quad 20 \quad 15 \quad 6 \quad 1$$
$$n = 7: \quad 1 \quad 7 \quad 21 \quad 35 \quad 35 \quad 21 \quad 7 \quad 1$$

The last row provides the desired coefficients.

Using a calculator, we can show that the entries in the row of Pascal's triangle for $n = 7$ match the decimal digits of $(1.01)^7$. To understand this, think of $(1.01)^7$ as $(1 + 0.01)^7$ and apply the binomial theorem. Note that we can also produce the first several rows of Pascal's triangle by entering the number 1 and multiplying it by 1.01 *repeatedly*. Unfortunately, three-digit numbers appear in the rows of Pascal's triangle for $n \geq 9$, so powers of 1.01 cannot be used beyond the row for $n = 8$.

1.01^7 **ENTER** up arrow **ENTER F1 8** 1 **ENTER** × 1.01 **ENTER ENTER ENTER,** *etc.*

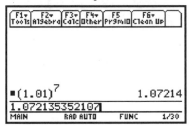 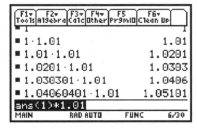 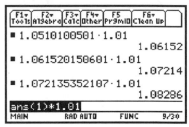

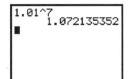 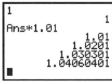 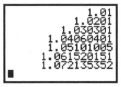

1.01^7 **ENTER**   1 **ENTER** × 1.01 **ENTER ENTER ENTER,** *etc.*

EXAMPLE 3

Expand $(2m + k)^7$ using the binomial theorem.
Let $a = 2m$, $b = k$, and $n = 7$.

$$(2m + k)^7 = 1(2m)^7 + 7(2m)^{7-1}k^1 + 21(2m)^{7-2}k^2 + 35(2m)^{7-3}k^3$$
$$+ 35(2m)^{7-4}k^4 + 21(2m)^{7-5}k^5 + 7(2m)^{7-6}k^6 + (1)k^7$$
$$= 128m^7 + 448m^6k + 672m^5k^2 + 560m^4k^3$$
$$+ 280m^3k^4 + 84m^2k^5 + 14mk^6 + k^7$$

EXAMPLE 4

Find the seventh term of $(x^3 - 2y)^{10}$.
First, note that $k = 7$, $n = 10$, $a = x^2$, and $b = -2y$.

$$k\text{th term} = \frac{n(n - 1)(n - 2)\cdots(n - k + 2)}{(k - 1)!}a^{n-k+1}b^{k-1}$$

$$\text{seventh term} = \frac{10 \cdot 9 \cdot 8 \cdot 7 \cdot 6 \cdot 5}{6!}(x^3)^4(-2y)^6$$
$$= 210(x^{12})(64y^6)$$
$$= 13{,}440x^{12}y^6$$

Graphing calculators are programmed to calculate the kth binomial coefficient. The notation is $_nC_{r-1}$, where r is used instead of k. For $(a + b)^n$ the rth term is $_nC_{r-1}(a)^{n-(r-1)}(b)^{r-1}$. Doing Example 4 with a calculator, we have $r = 7, n = 10, a = x^2$, and $b = -2y$.

$$\text{seventh term} = {}_{10}C_{7-1}(x^2)^{10-(7-1)}(-2y)^{7-1}$$
$$\text{seventh term} = {}_{10}C_6(x^2)^4(-2y)^6$$

Use your calculator to find $_{10}C_6$ as follows:

2nd MATH 7 3

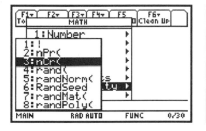 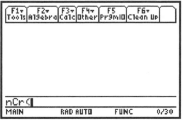

10,6) ENTER

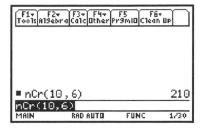

10   **MATH** left arrow **3**   **6 ENTER**

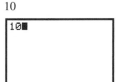  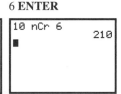

$$\text{seventh term} = 210x^8(-2)^6y^6$$
$$\text{seventh term} = 210x^8(64)y^6 = 13{,}400x^8y^6$$

Exercises 3.3

Expand each binomial using the binomial theorem.

1. $(3x + y)^3$ **2.** $(2x - 3y)^4$ **3.** $(a - 2)^5$ **4.** $(5x + 1)^4$

5. $(2x - 1)^4$ **6.** $(1 + x)^7$ **7.** $(2a + 3b)^6$ **8.** $(a - 2b)^8$

9. $(\frac{2}{3}x - 2)^5$ **10.** $(\frac{3}{4}m + \frac{2}{3}k)^5$ **11.** $(a^{1/2} + 3b^2)^4$ **12.** $(x^{1/2} - y^{1/2})^4$

13. $\left(\dfrac{x}{y} - \dfrac{2}{z}\right)^4$ **14.** $\left(\dfrac{2x}{y} + \dfrac{3}{z}\right)^6$

Find the indicated term of each binomial expansion.

15. $(x - y)^9$; 6th term   **16.** $(4x + 2y)^5$; 3rd term

17. $(2x - y)^{13}$; 9th term   **18.** $(x^{1/2} + 2)^{10}$; 8th term

19. $(2x + y^2)^7$; 5th term   **20.** $(x^2 - y^3)^8$; middle term 5th Term

21. $(3x + 2y)^6$; middle term **22.** $(x - 2y)^{10}$; middle term
23. $(2x - 1)^{10}$; term containing x^5 **24.** $(x^2 + 1)^8$; term containing x^6

CHAPTER 3 SUMMARY

1. *Arithmetic progression:* a sequence of terms where each term differs from the immediately preceding term by a fixed number d, which is called the common difference. The general form of an arithmetic progression is written

$$a, a + d, a + 2d, a + 3d, \ldots, a + (n - 1)d$$

(a) The nth or last term l of such a finite arithmetic progression is given by

$$l = a + (n - 1)d$$

(b) The sum of the first n terms of a finite arithmetic progression is given by

$$S_n = \frac{n}{2}(a + l)$$

2. *Geometric progression:* a sequence of terms each of which can be obtained by multiplying the preceding term by a fixed number r, which is called the common ratio. The general form of a geometric progression is given by

$$a, ar, ar^2, ar^3, \ldots, ar^{n-1}$$

(a) The nth or last term l of such a finite geometric progression is given by

$$l = ar^{n-1}$$

(b) The sum of the first n terms of a finite geometric progression is given by

$$S_n = \frac{a(1 - r^n)}{1 - r}$$

(c) The sum of the infinite geometric series, where $|r| < 1$, is

$$S = \frac{a}{1 - r}$$

3. $k!$ (k factorial) $= k(k - 1)(k - 2) \cdots 4 \cdot 3 \cdot 2 \cdot 1$. For example,

$$5! = 5 \cdot 4 \cdot 3 \cdot 2 \cdot 1$$
$$10! = 10 \cdot 9 \cdot 8 \cdot 7 \cdot 6 \cdot 5 \cdot 4 \cdot 3 \cdot 2 \cdot 1$$

4. *Binomial theorem:*

$$(a + b)^n = a^n + na^{n-1}b + \frac{n(n - 1)}{2!}a^{n-2}b^2 + \frac{n(n - 1)(n - 2)}{3!}a^{n-3}b^3 + \cdots$$

$$+ \frac{n(n - 1)(n - 2) \cdots (n - k + 2)}{(k - 1)!}a^{n-k+1}b^{k-1} + \cdots + b^n$$

5. The *kth term of a binomial expansion* is given by the formula

$$\frac{n(n - 1)(n - 2) \cdots (n - k + 2)}{(k - 1)!}a^{n-k+1}b^{k-1}$$

$$\text{or} \quad {}_nC_{k-1}\, a^{n-k+1}\, b^{k-1}$$

CHAPTER 3 REVIEW

Find the nth term of each progression.

1. $3, 7, 11, 15, \ldots, n = 12$ **2.** $4, 2, 1, \frac{1}{2}, \ldots, n = 7$

3. $\sqrt{3}, -3, 3\sqrt{3}, -9, \ldots, n = 8$ **4.** $4, -2, -8, -14, \ldots, n = 12$

5. $6, 2, \frac{2}{3}, \frac{2}{9}, \ldots, n = 6$ **6.** $5, 15, 25, 35, \ldots, n = 10$

7–12. Find the sum of the first n terms of the progressions in Exercises 1 through 6.

13. Find the sum of the first 1000 even positive integers.

14. If \$500 is deposited annually in a savings account at 6% interest compounded annually, find the total amount in the account after 5 years.

Find the sum, when possible, for each infinite geometric series.

15. $3 + 6 + 12 + \cdots$ **16.** $5 + \frac{5}{7} + \frac{5}{49} + \cdots$

17. $2 - \frac{2}{3} + \frac{2}{9} - \cdots$ **18.** $3 + \frac{9}{2} + \frac{27}{4} + \cdots$

19. Find the fraction equivalent to $0.454545\ldots$.

20. Find the fraction equivalent to $0.9212121\ldots$.

Expand each binomial using the binomial theorem.

21. $(a - b)^6$ **22.** $(2x^2 - 1)^5$ **23.** $(2x + 3y)^4$ **24.** $(1 + x)^8$

Find the indicated term of each binomial expansion.

25. $(1 - 3x)^5$; 3rd term   **26.** $(a + 4b)^6$; 4th term

27. $(x + 2b^2)^{10}$; middle term   **28.** $(3x^2 - 1)^{12}$; term containing x^{16}

4
Series

INTRODUCTION

The functions e^x, sin x, cos x, ln x, and many others may be written as polynomials with an infinite number of terms called *power series*. When you use your calculator to evaluate one of these functions, the calculator is evaluating a polynomial with a finite number of terms to give an approximation of the functional value you have indicated. In this chapter we study the conditions needed for writing a power series.

Objectives

- Use the Σ notation.
- Know the convergence conditions for a *p*-series.
- Use the comparison test for convergence.
- Use the limit comparison test for convergence.
- Use the ratio test for convergence.
- Use the integral test for convergence.
- Use the alternating series test for convergence.
- Know the definitions for absolute and conditional convergence.
- Find the interval of convergence of a series.
- Find a Maclaurin series expansion for a given function.
- Find a Taylor series expansion for a given function for a given value of *a*.
- Find a Fourier series that represents a given wave function.

4.1   SERIES AND CONVERGENCE

We now begin a more general study of series. *Sigma notation* is used for writing series. The Greek letter Σ (sigma) is used to indicate that the given expression is a sum. The term following Σ represents the general form of each term. For example,

$$\sum_{n=1}^{6} n^2 = 1^2 + 2^2 + 3^2 + 4^2 + 5^2 + 6^2$$

where the general form of each term is n^2. The numbers below and above Σ must be integers and indicate the values of *n* to be used for the first and last terms, respectively, of the series. The other terms are found by replacing n by the consecutive integers between 1 and 6. The finite sum

$$1 + 2 + 3 + \cdots + n$$

can be represented by $\displaystyle\sum_{k=1}^{n} k$, while the infinite sum

$$\frac{2}{3} + \frac{2}{9} + \frac{2}{27} + \cdots$$

can be represented by $\displaystyle\sum_{n=1}^{\infty} 2\left(\frac{1}{3}\right)^{n}$.

The following example illustrates the use of sigma notation.

EXAMPLE 1

Σ notation	Expanded form of sum
(a) $\displaystyle\sum_{k=1}^{6} (2k)$	$2 + 4 + 6 + 8 + 10 + 12$
(b) $\displaystyle\sum_{k=5}^{9} (3k - 4)$	$11 + 14 + 17 + 20 + 23$
(c) $\displaystyle\sum_{k=1}^{n} (k - 2)$	$-1 + 0 + 1 + 2 + 3 + \cdots + (n - 2)$
(d) $\displaystyle\sum_{k=0}^{n} 2^{k}$	$1 + 2 + 2^2 + 2^3 + \cdots + 2^n$
(e) $\displaystyle\sum_{k=1}^{n} A_k$	$A_1 + A_2 + A_3 + \cdots + A_n$

EXAMPLE 2

Write the expanded form of $\displaystyle\sum_{n=1}^{5} \frac{4}{2n + 1}$.

$$\sum_{n=1}^{5} \frac{4}{2n + 1} = \frac{4}{2 \cdot 1 + 1} + \frac{4}{2 \cdot 2 + 1} + \frac{4}{2 \cdot 3 + 1} + \frac{4}{2 \cdot 4 + 1} + \frac{4}{2 \cdot 5 + 1}$$

$$= \frac{4}{3} + \frac{4}{5} + \frac{4}{7} + \frac{4}{9} + \frac{4}{11}$$

For calculator examples using the TI-83 Plus, see Appendix C, Section C.12.

EXAMPLE 3

Write the sum $\dfrac{6}{9} + \dfrac{6}{16} + \dfrac{6}{25} + \cdots + \dfrac{6}{121}$ using sigma notation.

Build the general form of each term. Note that 6 appears in the numerator of each term while the denominator changes in a pattern of perfect squares beginning with 3^2. Do you see that this series has nine terms?

$$\sum_{n=3}^{11} \frac{6}{n^2} \quad \text{or} \quad \sum_{n=1}^{9} \frac{6}{(n+2)^2}$$

are acceptable forms.

Next, we need to study convergence and divergence of infinite series. To begin this process, consider the following series:

DEFINITION OF CONVERGENCE AND DIVERGENCE

$$\sum_{n=1}^{\infty} a_n = a_1 + a_2 + a_3 + \cdots$$

Then

$$S_1 = a_1$$
$$S_2 = a_1 + a_2$$
$$S_3 = a_1 + a_2 + a_3$$
$$\vdots$$
$$S_n = a_1 + a_2 + a_3 + \cdots + a_n$$
$$\vdots$$

where S_1 is the sum of the first term, S_2 is the sum of the first two terms, S_3 is the sum of the first three terms, . . . , S_n is the sum of the first n terms (sometimes called the nth partial sum), ...

(a) If $\lim\limits_{n\to\infty} S_n = S$ (where S is finite), the series $\sum\limits_{n=1}^{\infty} a_n$ *converges,* and S is the *sum of the infinite series.*

(b) If $\lim\limits_{n\to\infty} S_n$ does not exist, the series $\sum\limits_{n=1}^{\infty} a_n$ *diverges.*

The geometric series $1 + \dfrac{1}{2} + \dfrac{1}{4} + \dfrac{1}{8} + \cdots$ from Section 3.2 converges because $\lim\limits_{n\to\infty} S_n = 2$. The arithmetic series $1 + 2 + 3 + 4 + \cdots$ diverges because $\lim\limits_{n\to\infty} S_n = \infty$.

In the remainder of this section and Sections 4.2 to 4.4, we seek answers to the following two questions regarding infinite series:

1. Does a given series converge or diverge?

2. If the series converges, to what value does it converge?

The answers to these questions are not always easy, especially the second one. There is no general method for finding the sum of a convergent infinite series. We will begin the study of these two questions with a simple test for divergence.

---

nTH-TERM TEST FOR DIVERGENCE OF A SERIES

If $\lim\limits_{n\to\infty} a_n \neq 0$, then the series $\sum\limits_{n=1}^{\infty} a_n$ *diverges.*

In other words, it is impossible for an infinite series to converge if the terms you are adding fail to get extremely small in absolute values as $n \to \infty$. Note that this test will help you to identify some, but not all, divergent series (many infinite series diverge for a completely different reason).

EXAMPLE 4

Show that each series diverges by using the nth-term test for divergence.

(a) $\sum\limits_{n=1}^{\infty} 2^n$ (b) $\sum\limits_{n=1}^{\infty} \dfrac{n}{n+1}$ (c) $1 - 1 + 1 - 1 + 1 - 1 + \cdots$

The series in Parts (a) and (b) diverge because

(a) $\lim\limits_{n\to\infty} 2^n = \infty$ and (b) $\lim\limits_{n\to\infty} \dfrac{n}{n+1} = \lim\limits_{n\to\infty} \dfrac{1}{1 + \dfrac{1}{n}} = 1.$

The series in Part (c) also diverges because $\lim\limits_{n\to\infty} a_n$ clearly is not zero.

Note of warning: If $\lim\limits_{n\to\infty} a_n = 0$, there is no guarantee that the series converges. For example, the series

$$\sum_{n=1}^{\infty} \frac{1}{n} = 1 + \frac{1}{2} + \frac{1}{3} + \frac{1}{4} + \cdots \qquad \text{(called the harmonic series)}$$

diverges even though $\lim\limits_{n\to\infty} \dfrac{1}{n} = 0.$

We now present some tests to determine whether a given series of positive terms converges or diverges. The next special series that we need to consider is the p-series. We will show in Section 4.2 that the conditions for convergence and divergence of the p-series are the following:

CONVERGENCE AND DIVERGENCE OF A p-SERIES

Any series in the form

$$\sum_{n=1}^{\infty} \frac{1}{n^p} = \frac{1}{1^p} + \frac{1}{2^p} + \frac{1}{3^p} + \cdots$$

where p is a real number, is called a p-series. The p-series

(a) converges for $p > 1$ and

(b) diverges for $p \leq 1$.

EXAMPLE 5

Determine whether each *p*-series converges or diverges.

(a) $1 + \dfrac{1}{2^3} + \dfrac{1}{3^3} + \dfrac{1}{4^3} + \cdots$ (b) $1 + \dfrac{1}{2} + \dfrac{1}{3} + \dfrac{1}{4} + \cdots$

(c) $1 + \dfrac{1}{\sqrt{2}} + \dfrac{1}{\sqrt{3}} + \cdots$

(a) This *p*-series ($p = 3$) converges.
(b) This *p*-series ($p = 1$) diverges. Recall that this series is called the *harmonic series*.
(c) This *p*-series ($p = 1/2$) diverges.

The next test for convergence is called the *comparison test*.

COMPARISON TEST FOR CONVERGENCE AND DIVERGENCE

Let N be a positive integer, $\displaystyle\sum_{n=1}^{\infty} a_n$ and $\displaystyle\sum_{n=1}^{\infty} b_n$ be series of positive terms, and $0 \le a_n \le b_n$ for all $n > N$; then

1. If $\displaystyle\sum_{n=1}^{\infty} b_n$ converges, then $\displaystyle\sum_{n=1}^{\infty} a_n$ also converges.

2. If $\displaystyle\sum_{n=1}^{\infty} a_n$ diverges, then $\displaystyle\sum_{n=1}^{\infty} b_n$ also diverges.

In other words, the comparison test says

1. A series of positive terms that is term by term smaller than a known convergent series must also converge.

2. A series of positive terms that is term by term larger than a known divergent series must also diverge.

EXAMPLE 6

Use the comparison test to determine whether each series converges or diverges.

(a) $\displaystyle\sum_{n=1}^{\infty} \dfrac{1}{2^n + 1}$ (b) $\displaystyle\sum_{n=2}^{\infty} \dfrac{1}{\sqrt{n} - 1}$

(a) We know that the geometric series $\displaystyle\sum_{n=1}^{\infty} \dfrac{1}{2^n}$ converges, and

$$\frac{1}{2^n + 1} \le \frac{1}{2^n} \quad \text{for} \quad n \ge 1$$

Then, by the comparison test, $\displaystyle\sum_{n=1}^{\infty} \dfrac{1}{2^n + 1}$ also converges.

(b) We know that the *p*-series $\displaystyle\sum_{n=2}^{\infty} \dfrac{1}{\sqrt{n}}$ ($p = \tfrac{1}{2}$) diverges, and

$$\frac{1}{\sqrt{n} - 1} \ge \frac{1}{\sqrt{n}} \quad \text{for } n \ge 2$$

Then, by the comparison test, $\displaystyle\sum_{n=2}^{\infty} \dfrac{1}{\sqrt{n} - 1}$ also diverges.

A test that is often easier to apply than the comparison test is the *limit comparison test*.

First, a definition:

Let $\sum_{n=1}^{\infty} a_n$ and $\sum_{n=1}^{\infty} b_n$ be two series of positive terms.

(a) Then $\sum_{n=1}^{\infty} a_n$ and $\sum_{n=1}^{\infty} b_n$ have the *same order of magnitude* if $\lim_{n\to\infty} \dfrac{a_n}{b_n} = L$, where L is a real number and $L \neq 0$.

(b) The series $\sum_{n=1}^{\infty} a_n$ has a *lesser order of magnitude* than $\sum_{n=1}^{\infty} b_n$ if $\lim_{n\to\infty} \dfrac{a_n}{b_n} = 0$.

(c) The series $\sum_{n=1}^{\infty} a_n$ has a *greater order of magnitude* than $\sum_{n=1}^{\infty} b_n$ if $\lim_{n\to\infty} \dfrac{a_n}{b_n} = \infty$.

EXAMPLE 7

Compare the orders of magnitude of each pair of series.

(a) $\sum_{n=1}^{\infty} (2n)$ and $\sum_{n=1}^{\infty} (n-4)$

(b) $\sum_{n=1}^{\infty} (3n)$ and $\sum_{n=1}^{\infty} (n^2 + 1)$

(c) $\sum_{n=1}^{\infty} \left(\dfrac{1}{n}\right)$ and $\sum_{n=1}^{\infty} \dfrac{1}{n^2 + 1}$

(a) $\lim_{n\to\infty} \dfrac{2n}{n-4} = \lim_{n\to\infty} \dfrac{2}{1 - \dfrac{4}{n}} = 2$. These two series have the same order of magnitude.

(b) $\lim_{n\to\infty} \dfrac{3n}{n^2 + 1} = \lim_{n\to\infty} \dfrac{3}{n + \dfrac{1}{n}} = 0$. So $\sum_{n=1}^{\infty} (3n)$ has a lesser order of magnitude than

$\sum_{n=1}^{\infty} (n^2 + 1)$.

(c) $\lim_{n\to\infty} \dfrac{\dfrac{1}{n}}{\dfrac{1}{n^2 + 1}} = \lim_{n\to\infty} \dfrac{n^2 + 1}{n} = \lim_{n\to\infty} \left(n + \dfrac{1}{n}\right) = \infty$. So $\sum_{n=1}^{\infty} \left(\dfrac{1}{n}\right)$ has a greater order of

magnitude than $\sum_{n=1}^{\infty} \dfrac{1}{n^2 + 1}$.

We can now give the limit comparison test:

LIMIT COMPARISON TEST

Let $\sum_{n=1}^{\infty} a_n$ and $\sum_{n=1}^{\infty} b_n$ be series of positive terms.

(a) If these series have the same order of magnitude, then either both series converge or both series diverge.

(b) If the series $\sum_{n=1}^{\infty} a_n$ has a lesser order of magnitude than $\sum_{n=1}^{\infty} b_n$ and $\sum_{n=1}^{\infty} b_n$ is known to converge, then $\sum_{n=1}^{\infty} a_n$ also converges.

(c) If $\sum_{n=1}^{\infty} a_n$ has a greater order of magnitude than $\sum_{n=1}^{\infty} b_n$ and $\sum_{n=1}^{\infty} b_n$ is known to diverge, then $\sum_{n=1}^{\infty} a_n$ also diverges.

EXAMPLE 8

Use the limit comparison test to determine whether each series converges or diverges.

(a) $\displaystyle\sum_{n=1}^{\infty} \frac{1}{n(3n+1)}$ (b) $\displaystyle\sum_{n=1}^{\infty} \frac{\ln n}{n}$

(a) Let's compare with $\displaystyle\sum_{n=1}^{\infty} \frac{1}{n^2}$ (p-series, $p=2$), which converges.

$$\lim_{n\to\infty} \frac{\dfrac{1}{n(3n+1)}}{\dfrac{1}{n^2}} = \lim_{n\to\infty} \frac{n^2}{3n^2+n} = \lim_{n\to\infty} \frac{1}{3+\dfrac{1}{n}} = \frac{1}{3}$$

Since $\displaystyle\sum_{n=1}^{\infty} \frac{1}{n^2}$ converges and both series have the same order of magnitude, the series $\displaystyle\sum_{n=1}^{\infty} \frac{1}{n(3n+1)}$ also converges.

(b) Let's compare with $\displaystyle\sum_{n=1}^{\infty} \frac{1}{n}$ (harmonic series), which diverges.

$$\lim_{n\to\infty} \frac{\dfrac{\ln n}{n}}{\dfrac{1}{n}} = \lim_{n\to\infty} \ln n = \infty$$

Since $\displaystyle\sum_{n=1}^{\infty} \frac{1}{n}$ diverges and the series $\displaystyle\sum_{n=1}^{\infty} \frac{\ln n}{n}$ has a greater order of magnitude, the series $\displaystyle\sum_{n=1}^{\infty} \frac{\ln n}{n}$ also diverges.

Exercises 4.1

Write the expanded form of each series.

1. $\displaystyle\sum_{n=1}^{6} (4n+1)$ **2.** $\displaystyle\sum_{n=1}^{5} (1-n^2)$ **3.** $\displaystyle\sum_{n=3}^{8} (n^2+1)$

4. $\displaystyle\sum_{n=1}^{6} (n^2-4n)$ **5.** $\displaystyle\sum_{k=1}^{n} \frac{k^2}{k+1}$ **6.** $\displaystyle\sum_{k=1}^{n} \frac{4}{k(k+1)}$

7. $\displaystyle\sum_{n=1}^{\infty} (-1)^n \frac{1}{n^2}$ **8.** $\displaystyle\sum_{n=1}^{\infty} (-1)^{n+1} \frac{n}{n+1}$

Write each sum using sigma notation.

9. $1 + 2 + 3 + \cdots + 12$ **10.** $1 + 3 + 5 + \cdots + 43$

11. $2 + 4 + 6 + \cdots + 100$ **12.** $1^3 + 2^3 + 3^3 + \cdots + (n-1)^3$

13. $1 + 3 + 5 + \cdots + (2n-1)$ **14.** $\dfrac{1}{2} + \dfrac{1}{4} + \dfrac{1}{8} + \cdots + \dfrac{1}{2^n}$

15. $10 + 17 + 26 + 37 + \cdots + (n^2+1)$ **16.** $\dfrac{1}{2} + \dfrac{2}{3} + \dfrac{3}{4} + \cdots + \dfrac{n+1}{n+2}$

Determine whether each series converges or diverges.

17. $3 + 9 + 27 + \cdots + 3^n + \cdots$ **18.** $1 + 2 + 3 + \cdots + n + \cdots$

19. $\displaystyle\sum_{n=2}^{\infty} \frac{2n}{n-1}$ **20.** $\displaystyle\sum_{n=1}^{\infty} \frac{3n+1}{2n-1}$

21. $1 + \dfrac{1}{\sqrt[4]{2}} + \dfrac{1}{\sqrt[4]{3}} + \dfrac{1}{\sqrt[4]{4}} + \cdots + \dfrac{1}{\sqrt[4]{n}} + \cdots$

22. $1 + \dfrac{1}{2^4} + \dfrac{1}{3^4} + \dfrac{1}{4^4} + \cdots + \dfrac{1}{n^4} + \cdots$

23. $\displaystyle\sum_{n=1}^{\infty} \dfrac{1}{n^2}$ **24.** $\displaystyle\sum_{n=1}^{\infty} \dfrac{1}{\sqrt[3]{n}}$ **25.** $\displaystyle\sum_{n=1}^{\infty} \dfrac{1}{(n+1)^2}$ **26.** $\displaystyle\sum_{n=4}^{\infty} \dfrac{1}{n-3}$

27. $\dfrac{1}{1 \cdot 2} + \dfrac{1}{2 \cdot 3} + \dfrac{1}{3 \cdot 4} + \cdots + \dfrac{1}{n(n+1)} + \cdots$

28. $1 + \dfrac{1}{3} + \dfrac{1}{5} + \cdots + \dfrac{1}{2n-1} + \cdots$ **29.** $\dfrac{1}{2} + \dfrac{1}{4} + \dfrac{1}{6} + \dfrac{1}{8} + \cdots + \dfrac{1}{2n} + \cdots$

30. $\displaystyle\sum_{n=1}^{\infty} \dfrac{1}{n^2 + 3n}$ **31.** $\displaystyle\sum_{n=1}^{\infty} \dfrac{1}{(2n-1)^2}$ **32.** $\displaystyle\sum_{n=1}^{\infty} \dfrac{1}{n^2 + 1}$

33. $\displaystyle\sum_{n=1}^{\infty} \dfrac{1}{\sqrt{n^2 + 1}}$ **34.** $\displaystyle\sum_{n=2}^{\infty} \dfrac{1}{n\sqrt{n^2 - 1}}$ **35.** $\displaystyle\sum_{n=1}^{\infty} \dfrac{1}{\sqrt{n}(n+1)}$

36. $\displaystyle\sum_{n=1}^{\infty} \dfrac{1}{\sqrt[3]{n^2 + 1}}$ **37.** $\displaystyle\sum_{n=1}^{\infty} \dfrac{1}{2^n + 2n}$ **38.** $\displaystyle\sum_{n=3}^{\infty} \dfrac{1}{n^2 - 4}$

39. $\displaystyle\sum_{n=2}^{\infty} \dfrac{1}{\ln n}$ **40.** $\displaystyle\sum_{n=3}^{\infty} \dfrac{n^2}{n^2 - 4}$ **41.** $\displaystyle\sum_{n=1}^{\infty} \dfrac{1 + \sin n\pi}{n^2}$

42. $\displaystyle\sum_{n=1}^{\infty} \dfrac{3n}{(n+1)(n+2)}$ **43.** $\displaystyle\sum_{n=1}^{\infty} \dfrac{1}{\sqrt{n(n+1)}}$ **44.** $\displaystyle\sum_{n=1}^{\infty} \dfrac{1}{n^n}$

4.2 RATIO AND INTEGRAL TESTS

The tests for convergence and divergence in Section 4.1 work for some series but not others. As a result, we show two additional tests in this section.

RATIO TEST FOR CONVERGENCE AND DIVERGENCE

Let $\displaystyle\sum_{n=1}^{\infty} a_n$ be a series of positive terms and

$$r = \lim_{n \to \infty} \dfrac{a_{n+1}}{a_n}$$

(a) If $r < 1$, the series converges.

(b) If $r > 1$ (including $r = \infty$), the series diverges.

(c) If $r = 1$, the test fails. Some other test must be used.

EXAMPLE 1

Determine whether the series $\displaystyle\sum_{n=1}^{\infty} \dfrac{2n}{3^n}$ converges or diverges.

$$r = \lim_{n \to \infty} \dfrac{a_{n+1}}{a_n} = \lim_{n \to \infty} \dfrac{\dfrac{2(n+1)}{3^{n+1}}}{\dfrac{2n}{3^n}} = \lim_{n \to \infty} \dfrac{3^n \, 2(n+1)}{3^{n+1}\,(2n)} = \lim_{n \to \infty} \dfrac{n+1}{3n}$$

$$= \lim_{n \to \infty} \dfrac{1}{3}\left(1 + \dfrac{1}{n}\right) = \dfrac{1}{3} < 1.$$

Since $r < 1$, the given series converges.

The ratio test is especially helpful in testing expressions involving factorials. Recall that

$$5! = 5 \cdot 4 \cdot 3 \cdot 2 \cdot 1$$
$$10! = 10 \cdot 9 \cdot 8 \cdot 7 \cdot 6 \cdot 5 \cdot 4 \cdot 3 \cdot 2 \cdot 1$$
$$n! = n(n-1)(n-2) \cdots 4 \cdot 3 \cdot 2 \cdot 1 \qquad (n \text{ must be a positive integer.})$$

EXAMPLE 2

Determine whether the series $\displaystyle\sum_{n=1}^{\infty} \frac{2^n}{n!}$ converges or diverges.

$$r = \lim_{n \to \infty} \frac{a_{n+1}}{a_n} = \lim_{n \to \infty} \frac{\dfrac{2^{n+1}}{(n+1)!}}{\dfrac{2^n}{n!}} = \lim_{n \to \infty} \frac{n! \, 2^{n+1}}{(n+1)! \, 2^n}$$

$$= \lim_{n \to \infty} \frac{2}{n+1} = 0 < 1$$

Since $r < 1$, the given series converges.

EXAMPLE 3

Determine whether the series $\displaystyle\sum_{n=1}^{\infty} \frac{2^n}{n^2}$ converges or diverges.

$$r = \lim_{n \to \infty} \frac{a_{n+1}}{a_n} = \lim_{n \to \infty} \frac{\dfrac{2^{n+1}}{(n+1)^2}}{\dfrac{2^n}{n^2}} = \lim_{n \to \infty} \frac{n^2 \, 2^{n+1}}{(n+1)^2 \, 2^n}$$

$$= \lim_{n \to \infty} \frac{1(2)}{\left(1 + \dfrac{1}{n}\right)^2} = 2 > 1$$

Since $r > 1$, the given series diverges.

INTEGRAL TEST FOR CONVERGENCE AND DIVERGENCE

Let $\displaystyle\sum_{n=1}^{\infty} a_n$ be a series of positive terms and $f(x)$ be a continuous, decreasing function for $x \geq 1$ such that $f(n) = a_n$ for all positive integers n. Then $\displaystyle\sum_{n=1}^{\infty} a_n$ and $\displaystyle\int_{1}^{\infty} f(x)\,dx$ both converge or they both diverge.

Note: Before using the integral test, you must be certain that the function $f(x)$ is decreasing and continuous.

EXAMPLE 4

Determine whether the series $\displaystyle\sum_{n=2}^{\infty} \frac{1}{n \ln n}$ converges or diverges.

    Note: This series begins with $n = 2$ because $\ln 1 = 0$.

Let $f(x) = \dfrac{1}{x \ln x}$ for $x \geq 2$; $f(x)$ is continuous and decreasing for $x \geq 2$.

$$\int_2^{\infty} f(x)\,dx = \int_2^{\infty} \frac{dx}{x \ln x} = \lim_{b \to \infty} \int_2^b \frac{dx}{x \ln x}$$

First, integrate $\displaystyle\int \frac{dx}{x \ln x}$.

$$\int \frac{dx}{x \ln x} = \int \frac{du}{u}$$

$$= \ln u$$

$$= \ln \ln x \quad \text{or} \quad \ln(\ln x)$$

$$\boxed{\begin{aligned} u &= \ln x \\ du &= \frac{1}{x}\,dx \end{aligned}}$$

Then

$$\lim_{b \to \infty} \int_2^b \frac{dx}{x \ln x} = \lim_{b \to \infty} \ln \ln x \,\Big|_2^b = \lim_{b \to \infty} (\ln \ln b - \ln \ln 2) = \infty$$

Since $\displaystyle\int_2^{\infty} f(x)\,dx$ diverges, the given series also diverges.

EXAMPLE 5

Determine whether the series $\displaystyle\sum_{n=1}^{\infty} \frac{n}{e^n}$ converges or diverges.

    Let $f(x) = xe^{-x}$ for $x \geq 1$; $f(x)$ is continuous and decreasing for $x \geq 1$.

$$\int_1^{\infty} f(x)\,dx = \int_1^{\infty} xe^{-x}\,dx = \lim_{b \to \infty} \int_1^b xe^{-x}\,dx$$

Integrate $\displaystyle\int xe^{-x}\,dx$ using integration by parts.

$$\int u\,dv \qquad\qquad \int v\,du$$

$$\boxed{\begin{aligned} u &= x \\ dv &= e^{-x}\,dx \end{aligned}} \quad\longrightarrow\quad \boxed{\begin{aligned} du &= dx \\ v &= -e^{-x} \end{aligned}}$$

$$\int u\,dv = uv - \int v\,du$$

$$\int xe^{-x}\,dx = -xe^{-x} - \int (-e^{-x})\,dx$$

$$= -xe^{-x} - e^{-x}$$

$$= e^{-x}(-x - 1)$$

Then

$$\lim_{b \to \infty} \int_1^b xe^{-x}\,dx = \lim_{b \to \infty} \left[e^{-x}(-x - 1) \right] \Big|_1^b$$

$$= \lim_{b \to \infty} \left[e^{-b}(-b - 1) - e^{-1}(-1 - 1) \right]$$

$$= \lim_{b \to \infty} \left[\frac{-b - 1}{e^b} + \frac{2}{e} \right] = 0 + \frac{2}{e} = \frac{2}{e}$$

Since $\int_1^\infty f(x)\, dx$ converges (has a finite value), the given series also converges.

The integral test can be used to find the values of p for which the p-series converges. Let's begin by considering the p-series

$$\sum_{n=1}^\infty \frac{1}{n^p} \qquad \text{for } p > 0$$

Note: For $p \le 0$, $\displaystyle\lim_{n \to \infty} \frac{1}{n^p} \ne 0$, so the p-series diverges for $p \le 0$.

Let $f(x) = \dfrac{1}{x^p}$ for $p > 0$; $f(x)$ is continuous and decreasing for $x > 0$. We need two cases: For $p \ne 1$,

$$\int_1^\infty \frac{dx}{x^p} = \lim_{b \to \infty} \int_1^b x^{-p}\, dx$$

$$= \lim_{b \to \infty} \left. \frac{x^{1-p}}{1 - p} \right|_1^b$$

$$= \lim_{b \to \infty} \left(\frac{b^{1-p}}{1 - p} - \frac{1}{1 - p} \right) = \begin{cases} \dfrac{1}{p - 1} & \text{if } p > 1 \\ \infty & \text{if } p < 1 \end{cases}$$

For $p = 1$,

$$\int_1^\infty \frac{dx}{x} = \lim_{b \to \infty} \int_1^b \frac{dx}{x} = \lim_{b \to \infty} \left. \ln x \right|_1^b = \lim_{b \to \infty} (\ln b - \ln 1) = \infty$$

So, the p-series converges for $p > 1$ and diverges for $p \le 1$.

Exercises 4.2

Use either the ratio test or the integral test to determine whether each series converges or diverges.

1. $\displaystyle\sum_{n=1}^\infty \frac{n + 1}{n \cdot 3^n}$

2. $\displaystyle\sum_{n=1}^\infty \frac{2^{n+1}}{3^{n-1}}$

3. $\displaystyle\sum_{n=1}^\infty \frac{1}{n!}$

4. $\displaystyle\sum_{n=1}^\infty \frac{n + 2}{n!}$

5. $\displaystyle\sum_{n=1}^\infty \frac{n^2}{n!}$

6. $\displaystyle\sum_{n=1}^\infty \frac{n^2}{2^n}$

7. $\displaystyle\sum_{n=1}^\infty \frac{3^n}{n \cdot 2^n}$

8. $\displaystyle\sum_{n=1}^\infty \frac{n!}{10^n}$

9. $\displaystyle\sum_{n=1}^{\infty} \frac{2n+3}{2^n}$ 10. $\displaystyle\sum_{n=1}^{\infty} \frac{2^n}{n^3+1}$ 11. $\displaystyle\sum_{n=1}^{\infty} \frac{1}{2n+1}$ 12. $\displaystyle\sum_{n=1}^{\infty} \frac{1}{n\sqrt{n}}$

13. $\displaystyle\sum_{n=2}^{\infty} \frac{1}{n\sqrt{\ln n}}$ 14. $\displaystyle\sum_{n=1}^{\infty} \frac{1}{\sqrt[3]{n}}$

15. $1 + \dfrac{1}{3} + \dfrac{1}{5} + \dfrac{1}{7} + \cdots$ 16. $\dfrac{1}{2} + \dfrac{1}{4} + \dfrac{1}{6} + \dfrac{1}{8} + \cdots$

17. $\displaystyle\sum_{n=1}^{\infty} \frac{n}{n^2+1}$ 18. $\displaystyle\sum_{n=2}^{\infty} \frac{\ln n}{n}$ 19. $\displaystyle\sum_{n=1}^{\infty} \frac{n^2}{e^n}$ 20. $\displaystyle\sum_{n=1}^{\infty} \frac{n}{\sqrt{n^2+1}}$

4.3 ALTERNATING SERIES AND CONDITIONAL CONVERGENCE

Up to now we have considered only series with all positive terms. An *alternating series* is a series whose terms are alternately positive and negative. Examples of alternating series are

$$\sum_{n=1}^{\infty} (-1)^{n+1} 2^n = 2 - 4 + 8 - 16 + \cdots$$

$$\sum_{n=1}^{\infty} (-1)^n \frac{3}{n} = -3 + \frac{3}{2} - \frac{3}{3} + \frac{3}{4} - \frac{3}{5} + \cdots$$

$$\sum_{n=1}^{\infty} (-1)^{n+1} a_n = a_1 - a_2 + a_3 - a_4 + \cdots \qquad (a_n > 0 \text{ for each } n)$$

We have a relatively simple test for convergence of alternating series.

ALTERNATING SERIES TEST

The alternating series

$$\sum_{n=1}^{\infty} (-1)^{n+1} a_n = a_1 - a_2 + a_3 - a_4 + \cdots \qquad (a_n > 0 \text{ for each } n)$$

converges provided that both of the following conditions are fulfilled:

(a) $0 < a_{n+1} \le a_n$ for $n \ge 1$ and

(b) $\displaystyle\lim_{n\to\infty} a_n = 0$

In addition, if S is the sum of the infinite series and S_n is the nth partial sum, then

$$|S - S_n| \le a_{n+1}$$

Note: Condition (a) guarantees that the terms decrease in absolute value as n increases.

EXAMPLE 1

Determine whether the alternating series $\displaystyle\sum_{n=1}^{\infty} \frac{(-1)^{n+1}}{n} = 1 - \frac{1}{2} + \frac{1}{3} - \frac{1}{4} + \cdots$ converges or diverges.

Since $a_{n+1} = \dfrac{1}{n+1} < \dfrac{1}{n} = a_n$ and $\displaystyle\lim_{n\to\infty} \frac{1}{n} = 0$, this alternating series converges.

We have already shown that the harmonic series

$$\sum_{n=1}^{\infty} \frac{1}{n} = 1 + \frac{1}{2} + \frac{1}{3} + \frac{1}{4} + \cdots$$

diverges, even though $a_{n+1} < a_n$ and $\lim_{n \to \infty} a_n = 0$. The alternating series in Example 1 is sometimes called the *alternating harmonic series*.

EXAMPLE 2

Determine whether the series $\sum_{n=2}^{\infty} \frac{(-1)^{n+1}}{n \ln n}$ converges or diverges.

Since

$$a_{n+1} = \frac{1}{(n+1) \ln (n+1)} < \frac{1}{n \ln n} = a_n \quad \text{and} \quad \lim_{n \to \infty} \frac{1}{n \ln n} = 0$$

this alternating series converges.

We have shown that the series of positive terms $\sum_{n=2}^{\infty} \frac{1}{n \ln n}$ diverges in Example 4 of Section 4.2.

ABSOLUTE AND CONDITIONAL CONVERGENCE

Suppose that $\sum_{n=1}^{\infty} a_n$ converges.

1. If $\sum_{n=1}^{\infty} |a_n|$ converges, then $\sum_{n=1}^{\infty} a_n$ *converges absolutely.*

2. If $\sum_{n=1}^{\infty} |a_n|$ diverges, then $\sum_{n=1}^{\infty} a_n$ *converges conditionally.*

For example, the series $\sum_{n=1}^{\infty} (-1)^{n+1} \frac{1}{n^2}$ converges absolutely because $\sum_{n=1}^{\infty} \frac{1}{n^2}$ converges and the series $\sum_{n=1}^{\infty} (-1)^{n+1} \frac{1}{n}$ converges conditionally because $\sum_{n=1}^{\infty} \frac{1}{n}$ diverges.

Absolute convergence is a subtlety that plays an important role in analyzing the quality of a series representation. The names even seem to imply that *absolute* convergence is of higher quality than *conditional* convergence. An absolutely convergent alternating series converges because of the rapidly decreasing size of its terms (remember, it would still converge even if you changed all of its signs to positive). By contrast, a conditionally convergent alternating series only converges because of the "gimmick"of alternating signs (remember, it would *diverge* if all of its signs were made positive). Absolutely convergent alternating series tend to converge rapidly and often need only a few terms to give very good approximations (see Section 4.8). On the other hand, conditionally convergent series are notorious for slow convergence, sometimes requiring thousands or even millions of terms to yield three or four decimal place accuracy. Worse yet, advanced calculus has revealed that an infinite rearrangement of the terms of a conditionally convergent series can literally add up to any sum imaginable (or might even diverge). By contrast, an absolutely convergent series will always add up to the same sum, no matter how its terms might be rearranged.

Exercises 4.3

Determine whether each alternating series converges or diverges. If it converges, find whether it converges absolutely or converges conditionally.

1. $\displaystyle\sum_{n=1}^{\infty} (-1)^{n+1} \frac{1}{2n+1}$

2. $\displaystyle\sum_{n=1}^{\infty} (-1)^{n+1} \frac{1}{2^n}$

3. $\displaystyle\sum_{n=1}^{\infty} (-1)^{n} \frac{1}{(2n)^2}$

4. $\displaystyle\sum_{n=1}^{\infty} (-1)^{n} \frac{n}{2n-1}$

5. $\displaystyle\sum_{n=1}^{\infty} (-1)^{n+1} \frac{2n}{2n-1}$

6. $\displaystyle\sum_{n=1}^{\infty} (-1)^{n-1} \frac{1}{n^2}$

7. $\displaystyle\sum_{n=2}^{\infty} \frac{(-1)^{n-1}}{\ln n}$

8. $\displaystyle\sum_{n=1}^{\infty} (-1)^{n+1} \frac{1}{\sqrt{n}}$

9. $\displaystyle\sum_{n=1}^{\infty} (-1)^{n} \frac{n^2}{2^n}$

10. $\displaystyle\sum_{n=1}^{\infty} (-1)^{n} \frac{1}{n!}$

11. $\displaystyle\sum_{n=1}^{\infty} (-1)^{n+1} \frac{n^2}{n^2+1}$

12. $\displaystyle\sum_{n=1}^{\infty} (-1)^{n+1} \frac{n}{e^n}$

13. $\displaystyle\sum_{n=1}^{\infty} (-1)^{n+1} \frac{n!}{3^n}$

14. $\displaystyle\sum_{n=1}^{\infty} (-1)^{n+1} \frac{n}{2^n}$

15. $\displaystyle\sum_{n=1}^{\infty} (-1)^{n} \frac{2n+1}{n^2}$

16. $\displaystyle\sum_{n=1}^{\infty} (-1)^{n} \frac{1}{\sqrt{n^2+1}}$

17. $\displaystyle\sum_{n=2}^{\infty} (-1)^{n+1} \frac{n}{\ln n}$

18. $\displaystyle\sum_{n=1}^{\infty} (-1)^{n+1} \frac{\sin \pi n}{n}$

19. $\displaystyle\sum_{n=1}^{\infty} (-1)^{n} \frac{\cos n}{n^2}$

20. $\displaystyle\sum_{n=1}^{\infty} (-1)^{n} \frac{n+1}{n\sqrt{n}}$

4.4   POWER SERIES

A more general example of an infinite series is the power series. A *power series* is an infinite series in the form

$$\sum_{n=0}^{\infty} a_n x^n = a_0 + a_1 x + a_2 x^2 + \cdots + a_n x^n + \cdots$$

Certain functions can be written as a power series. For example, the function $f(x) = \dfrac{1}{1+x}$ can be expressed as a power series as follows:

$$
\begin{array}{r}
1 - x + x^2 - x^3 + \cdots \\
1 + x\,)\overline{1 \cdot \qquad\qquad\qquad\qquad} \\
\underline{1 + x} \\
-x \\
\underline{-x - x^2} \\
x^2 \\
\underline{x^2 + x^3} \\
-x^3 \\
\vdots
\end{array}
$$

Thus

$$f(x) = \frac{1}{1+x} = 1 - x + x^2 - x^3 + \cdots$$

Note, however, that the infinite division process as indicated is valid only for $|x| < 1$ because the right-hand side is a geometric series (Section 3.2) with $a = 1$ and $r = -x$, which has the sum $\dfrac{1}{1 - (-x)}$ only for $|x| < 1$. Thus, the equality is not valid for $|x| \geq 1$.

A more general series in the form

$$\sum_{n=0}^{\infty} a_n(x - a)^n = a_0 + a_1(x - a) + a_2(x - a)^2 + a_3(x - a)^3 + \cdots + a_n(x - a)^n + \cdots$$

is called a *power series centered at a.*

For each particular value of x (x is the variable in the power series), we have an infinite series of constants, which either converges or diverges. In many power series, the series converges for some values of x and diverges for other values of x. The ratio test is usually the simplest initial test to use on a power series.

Let

$$\lim_{n \to \infty} \left| \frac{u_{n+1}}{u_n} \right| = r(x)$$

where u_{n+1} is the $(n + 1)$st term and u_n is the nth term of a power series. This ratio is most often a function of x, namely $r(x)$. Then the series will

1. converge absolutely for $r(x) < 1$ and

2. diverge for $r(x) > 1$.

Recall that the ratio test is not valid for $r = 1$ or $r(x) = 1$. These values of x must be checked individually using other tests.

A power series always converges on an interval, which may vary from a single value of x to all real numbers x—the entire number line. This interval is called the *interval of convergence.* The interval of convergence may include both endpoints, only one endpoint, or neither endpoint. The interval of convergence of the power series

$$\sum_{n=0}^{\infty} a_n(x - a)^n$$

is always centered at $x = a$. The *radius of convergence* is the distance from the point $x = a$ to either endpoint of the interval. Thus the radius of convergence is one-half the length of the interval of convergence.

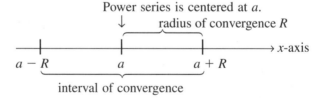

Power series is centered at a.

EXAMPLE 1

For what values of x does the series $\displaystyle\sum_{n=0}^{\infty} 5(x - 3)^n$ converge? That is, find the interval of convergence.

$$r(x) = \lim_{n \to \infty} \left| \frac{u_{n+1}}{u_n} \right| = \lim_{n \to \infty} \left| \frac{5(x - 3)^{n+1}}{5(x - 3)^n} \right| = \lim_{n \to \infty} |x - 3| = |x - 3|$$

This series converges for

$$|x - 3| < 1$$
$$-1 < x - 3 < 1$$
$$2 < x < 4$$

Next, check the endpoints. For $x = 2$, the series is

$$\sum_{n=0}^{\infty} (-1)^n (5), \qquad \text{which diverges.}$$

For $x = 4$, the series is

$$\sum_{n=0}^{\infty} 1^n (5), \qquad \text{which also diverges.}$$

Thus, the interval of convergence is $2 < x < 4$, whose graph is

Note: The interval of convergence is centered at $x = 3$ and the radius of convergence is 1.

EXAMPLE 2

Find the interval of convergence of the series $\displaystyle\sum_{n=0}^{\infty} \frac{x^n}{n!}$.

$$r(x) = \lim_{n\to\infty} \left| \frac{u_{n+1}}{u_n} \right| = \lim_{n\to\infty} \left| \frac{\dfrac{x^{n+1}}{(n+1)!}}{\dfrac{x^n}{n!}} \right| = \lim_{n\to\infty} \left| \frac{x}{n+1} \right| = 0$$

Since $r(x) < 1$ for all values of x, this series converges for all real numbers or for all values of x, which may also be written

$$-\infty < x < \infty$$

EXAMPLE 3

Find the interval of convergence of the series $\displaystyle\sum_{n=0}^{\infty} n! \, x^n$.

$$r(x) = \lim_{n\to\infty} \left| \frac{u_{n+1}}{u_n} \right| = \lim_{n\to\infty} \left| \frac{(n+1)! \, x^{n+1}}{n! \, x^n} \right|$$

$$= \lim_{n\to\infty} |(n+1)x| = \begin{cases} 0 & \text{if } x = 0 \\ \infty & \text{if } x \neq 0 \end{cases}$$

This series converges only for $x = 0$. This interval of convergence consists of one point.

EXAMPLE 4

Find the interval of convergence of the series $\displaystyle\sum_{n=0}^{\infty} \frac{n^2}{2^n} (x-1)^n$.

$$r(x) = \lim_{n\to\infty} \left| \frac{u_{n+1}}{u_n} \right| = \lim_{n\to\infty} \left| \frac{\dfrac{(n+1)^2}{2^{n+1}} (x-1)^{n+1}}{\dfrac{n^2}{2^n} (x-1)^n} \right| = \lim_{n\to\infty} \left| \frac{(n+1)^2 (x-1)}{2n^2} \right|$$

$$= \lim_{n\to\infty} \left| \frac{1}{2} \left(1 + \frac{1}{n} \right)^2 (x-1) \right| = \left| \frac{x-1}{2} \right|$$

This series converges for

$$\left| \frac{x-1}{2} \right| < 1$$

$$-1 < \frac{x-1}{2} < 1$$

$$-2 < x - 1 < 2$$

$$-1 < x < 3$$

Check the endpoints. For $x = -1$, the series is

$$\sum_{n=0}^{\infty} \frac{n^2(-2)^n}{2^n} = \sum_{n=0}^{\infty} (-1)^n n^2, \qquad \text{which diverges.}$$

For $x = 3$, the series is

$$\sum_{n=0}^{\infty} \frac{n^2 \, 2^n}{2^n} = \sum_{n=0}^{\infty} n^2, \qquad \text{which also diverges.}$$

Thus, the interval of convergence is $-1 < x < 3$.

EXAMPLE 5

Find the interval of convergence of the series $\displaystyle\sum_{n=0}^{\infty} \frac{nx^n}{(n+1)^2}$.

$$r(x) = \lim_{n \to \infty} \left| \frac{u_{n+1}}{u_n} \right| = \lim_{n \to \infty} \left| \frac{\dfrac{(n+1)x^{n+1}}{(n+2)^2}}{\dfrac{nx^n}{(n+1)^2}} \right| = \lim_{n \to \infty} \left| \frac{(n+1)^3 \, x}{n(n+2)^2} \right| = |x|$$

This series converges for $|x| < 1$ or $-1 < x < 1$.

Check the endpoints. For $x = -1$, the series is

$$\sum_{n=0}^{\infty} \frac{n(-1)^n}{(n+1)^2} \qquad \text{which converges conditionally}$$

For $x = 1$, the series is

$$\sum_{n=0}^{\infty} \frac{n \, 1^n}{(n+1)^2} \qquad \text{which diverges}$$

Thus the interval of convergence is $-1 \le x < 1$.

Exercises 4.4

Find the interval of convergence of each series.

1. $\displaystyle\sum_{n=0}^{\infty} \left(\frac{x}{2}\right)^n$

2. $\displaystyle\sum_{n=1}^{\infty} \frac{(-1)^n x^n}{n}$

3. $\displaystyle\sum_{n=0}^{\infty} (4n)! \left(\frac{x}{2}\right)^n$

4. $\displaystyle\sum_{n=0}^{\infty} nx^n$

5. $\displaystyle\sum_{n=1}^{\infty} \frac{(4x)^n}{(2n)!}$

6. $\displaystyle\sum_{n=1}^{\infty} \frac{x^n}{n}$

7. $\displaystyle\sum_{n=1}^{\infty} \frac{(-1)^{n+1} x^n}{(n+1)(n+2)}$

8. $\displaystyle\sum_{n=0}^{\infty} \frac{(-1)^{n+1} x^n}{4^n}$

9. $\displaystyle\sum_{n=0}^{\infty} \frac{nx^n}{(n+1)^2}$

10. $\displaystyle\sum_{n=0}^{\infty} 3^n x^n$

11. $\displaystyle\sum_{n=0}^{\infty} \frac{2^n x^n}{3^n}$

12. $\displaystyle\sum_{n=1}^{\infty} \frac{(-1)^{n+1}(x-1)^{n+1}}{n \cdot 1}$

13. $\displaystyle\sum_{n=1}^{\infty} \frac{(-1)^{n+1} x^n}{n \cdot 2^n}$

14. $\displaystyle\sum_{n=1}^{\infty} (-2)^n (x+1)^n$

15. $\displaystyle\sum_{n=1}^{\infty} \frac{(-1)^n (x-2)^n}{\sqrt{n}}$

16. $\displaystyle\sum_{n=1}^{\infty} \frac{(x+3)^n}{n^2 \cdot 2^n}$

17. $\displaystyle\sum_{n=1}^{\infty} \frac{x^n}{n^2}$

18. $\displaystyle\sum_{n=1}^{\infty} \frac{x^n}{\sqrt{n} \, 3^n}$

19. $\displaystyle\sum_{n=1}^{\infty} \frac{(-1)^n x^{2n}}{n!}$

20. $\displaystyle\sum_{n=1}^{\infty} \frac{n! \, x^n}{(2n)!}$

21. $\displaystyle\sum_{n=1}^{\infty} \frac{2^n x^{n+1}}{n(3^{n+1})}$

22. $\displaystyle\sum_{n=1}^{\infty} \frac{(-1)^n x^n}{n^n}$

23. $\displaystyle\sum_{n=1}^{\infty} \frac{(2x-5)^n}{n^2}$

24. $\displaystyle\sum_{n=1}^{\infty} \frac{\sin^n x}{n!}$

4.5 MACLAURIN SERIES

The Maclaurin series expansion of a function is a power series developed by differentiation. If a function can be differentiated repeatedly at $x = 0$, then it will have a Maclaurin series expansion. Thus we can write

$$f(x) = a_0 + a_1 x + a_2 x^2 + a_3 x^3 + a_4 x^4 + \cdots + a_n x^n + \cdots$$
$$f'(x) = a_1 + 2a_2 x + 3a_3 x^2 + 4a_4 x^3 + \cdots + na_n x^{n-1} + \cdots$$
$$f''(x) = 2a_2 + 2 \cdot 3a_3 x + 3 \cdot 4a_4 x^2 + \cdots + (n-1)(n)a_n x^{n-2} + \cdots$$
$$f'''(x) = 2 \cdot 3a_3 + 2 \cdot 3 \cdot 4a_4 x + \cdots + (n-2)(n-1)(n)a_n x^{n-3} + \cdots$$

$$\vdots \qquad \vdots$$

If we let $x = 0$, then

$$f(0) = a_0, \qquad f'(0) = a_1, \qquad f''(0) = 2a_2, \quad \text{and} \quad f'''(0) = 2 \cdot 3a_3$$

If we continue differentiating, the *n*th derivative at $x = 0$ is

$$f^{(n)}(0) = 1 \cdot 2 \cdot 3 \cdots (n-2)(n-1)(n)a_n = n!a_n$$

Rewriting, we have

$$a_0 = f(0)$$

$$a_1 = f'(0)$$

$$a_2 = \frac{f''(0)}{2!}$$

$$a_3 = \frac{f'''(0)}{3!}$$

$$\cdot$$
$$\cdot$$
$$\cdot$$

$$a_n = \frac{f^{(n)}(0)}{n!}$$

Replace the coefficients of the powers of x in the power series

$$f(x) = a_0 + a_1x + a_2x^2 + a_3x^3 + \cdots + a_nx^n + \cdots$$

by the preceding equivalent expressions to obtain the following result:

MACLAURIN SERIES EXPANSION

$$f(x) = f(0) + f'(0)x + \frac{f''(0)}{2!}x^2 + \frac{f'''(0)}{3!}x^3 + \cdots + \frac{f^{(n)}(0)}{n!}x^n + \cdots$$

The expansion is valid for all values of x for which the power series converges and for which the function $f(x)$ is repeatedly differentiable.

EXAMPLE 1

Find the first four terms of the Maclaurin expansion for $f(x) = \dfrac{1}{1 + x}$.

$$f(x) = \frac{1}{1 + x} \qquad f(0) = 1$$

$$f'(x) = \frac{-1}{(1 + x)^2} \qquad f'(0) = -1$$

$$f''(x) = \frac{2}{(1 + x)^3} \qquad f''(0) = 2$$

$$f'''(x) = \frac{-6}{(1 + x)^4} \qquad f'''(0) = -6$$

So

$$f(x) = 1 - x + \frac{2}{2!}x^2 + \frac{-6}{3!}x^3 + \cdots$$

$$= 1 - x + x^2 - x^3 + \cdots$$

which is the same power series we obtained earlier by division.

EXAMPLE 2

Find the first five terms of the Maclaurin series expansion for $f(x) = \cos 3x$.

$$f(x) = \cos 3x \qquad f(0) = 1$$
$$f'(x) = -3 \sin 3x \qquad f'(0) = 0$$
$$f''(x) = -9 \cos 3x \qquad f''(0) = -9$$
$$f'''(x) = 27 \sin 3x \qquad f'''(0) = 0$$
$$f^{(4)}(x) = 81 \cos 3x \qquad f^{(4)}(0) = 81$$

Thus,

$$f(x) = \cos 3x = 1 + 0x + \frac{-9}{2!}x^2 + 0x^3 + \frac{81}{4!}x^4 + \cdots$$

$$= 1 - \frac{9}{2}x^2 + \frac{27}{8}x^4 - \cdots$$

EXAMPLE 3

Find the Maclaurin series expansion for $f(x) = e^x$.

Since $\dfrac{d}{dx}(e^x) = e^x$, we have $f^{(n)}(x) = e^x$ for all n. Thus,

$$f(0) = f'(0) = f''(0) = f'''(0) = \cdots = f^{(n)}(0) = e^0 = 1$$

Thus,

$$f(x) = e^x = 1 + x + \frac{1}{2!}x^2 + \frac{1}{3!}x^3 + \frac{1}{4!}x^4 + \cdots + \frac{1}{n!}x^n + \cdots$$

$$= 1 + x + \frac{x^2}{2!} + \frac{x^3}{3!} + \frac{x^4}{4!} + \cdots + \frac{x^n}{n!} + \cdots$$

Note: This series converges (has a sum) and is a valid representation for $f(x) = e^x$ for all values of x (see Example 2, Section 4.4).

EXAMPLE 4

Find the first four nonzero terms of the Maclaurin expansion for $f(x) = e^x \cos x$.

$$f(x) = e^x \cos x \qquad\qquad\qquad f(0) = 1$$
$$f'(x) = e^x(-\sin x) + e^x \cos x$$
$$\quad = e^x(\cos x - \sin x) \qquad\qquad f'(0) = 1$$
$$f''(x) = e^x(-\sin x - \cos x) + e^x(\cos x - \sin x)$$
$$\quad = -2e^x \sin x \qquad\qquad\qquad f''(0) = 0$$
$$f'''(x) = -2e^x \cos x - 2e^x \sin x$$
$$\quad = -2e^x(\cos x + \sin x) \qquad\quad f'''(0) = -2$$
$$f^{(4)}(x) = -2e^x(-\sin x + \cos x) - 2e^x(\cos x + \sin x)$$
$$\quad = -4e^x \cos x \qquad\qquad\qquad f^{(4)}(0) = -4$$

Thus,

$$f(x) = 1 + x + \frac{0x^2}{2!} - \frac{2}{3!}x^3 - \frac{4}{4!}x^4$$

$$= 1 + x - \frac{1}{3}x^3 - \frac{1}{6}x^4$$

Exercises 4.5

Find a Maclaurin series expansion for each function.

1. $f(x) = \sin x$ **2.** $f(x) = \cos x$ **3.** $f(x) = e^{-x}$

4. $f(x) = \dfrac{1}{1-x}$ **5.** $f(x) = \ln(1+x)$ **6.** $f(x) = e^{3x}$

7. $f(x) = \cos 2x$ **8.** $f(x) = \sin 4x$ **9.** $f(x) = xe^x$

10. $f(x) = x \sin x$ **11.** $f(x) = \sqrt{4-x}$ **12.** $f(x) = \dfrac{1}{\sqrt{9+x}}$

13. $f(x) = \sin\left(x - \dfrac{\pi}{2}\right)$ **14.** $f(x) = \dfrac{1}{(1+x)^2}$ **15.** $f(x) = \dfrac{1}{(1-x)^2}$

16. $f(x) = (1+x)^{3/2}$ **17.** $f(x) = (1+x)^5$ **18.** $f(x) = (2x-1)^4$

19. $f(x) = e^{-x} \sin x$

20. Show that $(1+x)^n = 1 + nx + \dfrac{n(n-1)}{2!}x^2 + \dfrac{n(n-1)(n-2)}{3!}x^3 + \cdots$ by using the Maclaurin expansion. This series is called the *binomial series,* which is valid for all real numbers n for $|x| < 1$

4.6 OPERATIONS WITH SERIES

We now summarize four important series that were developed previously as exercises.

$$e^x = 1 + x + \frac{x^2}{2!} + \frac{x^3}{3!} + \frac{x^4}{4!} + \cdots + \frac{x^n}{n!} + \cdots \quad \text{(1)}$$

$$\sin x = x - \frac{x^3}{3!} + \frac{x^5}{5!} - \cdots \quad \text{(2)}$$

$$\cos x = 1 - \frac{x^2}{2!} + \frac{x^4}{4!} - \cdots \quad \text{(3)}$$

$$\ln(1+x) = x - \frac{x^2}{2} + \frac{x^3}{3} - \frac{x^4}{4} + \cdots \quad \text{(4)}$$

From these and similar basic power series expansions we can often obtain power series of other functions.

EXAMPLE 1

Find the Maclaurin series expansion for $f(x) = \cos 3x$.

Substituting $3x$ for x in Equation (3), we obtain

$$\cos 3x = 1 - \frac{(3x)^2}{2!} + \frac{(3x)^4}{4!} - \cdots$$

$$= 1 - \frac{9x^2}{2!} + \frac{81x^4}{4!} - \cdots$$

$$= 1 - \frac{9x^2}{2} + \frac{27x^4}{8} - \cdots$$

Compare this result with Example 2, Section 4.5.

EXAMPLE 2

Find a power series expansion for $f(x) = \dfrac{\ln(1 + x)}{x}$.

Dividing each side of Equation (4) by x, we have

$$\frac{\ln(1 + x)}{x} = \frac{x}{x} - \frac{x^2}{2x} + \frac{x^3}{3x} - \frac{x^4}{4x} + \cdots$$

$$= 1 - \frac{x}{2} + \frac{x^2}{3} - \frac{x^3}{4} + \cdots$$

EXAMPLE 3

Find the Maclaurin series expansion for $f(x) = e^{-3x}$.

Substituting $-3x$ for x in Equation (1), we have

$$e^{-3x} = 1 + (-3x) + \frac{(-3x)^2}{2!} + \frac{(-3x)^3}{3!} + \frac{(-3x)^4}{4!} + \cdots$$

$$= 1 - 3x + \frac{9x^2}{2} - \frac{9x^3}{2} + \frac{27x^4}{8} - \cdots$$

EXAMPLE 4

Compare the graph of $f(x) = \sin x$ (shown with a dotted line) with the graphs of its first-, third-, and fifth-degree Taylor polynomials.

green diamond Y= x ENTER x-x^3/3 **green diamond** ÷ ENTER, *etc.* F2 7

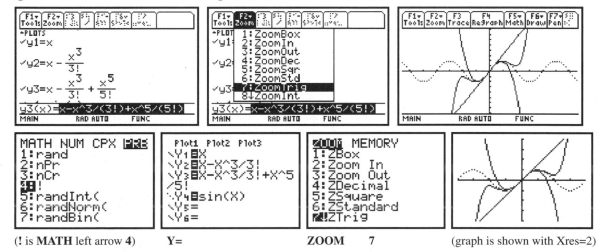

(**!** is **MATH** left arrow **4**)   Y=   ZOOM   7   (graph is shown with Xres=2)

A similar pattern can be found in Example 6 in Appendix C, Section C.12, which shows the graphs of $f(x) = \cos x$ and its 2nd-, 4th-, 6th-, 8th-, and 20th-degree Taylor polynomials.

EXAMPLE 5

Evaluate $\displaystyle\int_0^1 \frac{\sin x}{x}\,dx$.

We use the function $\dfrac{\sin x}{x}$ to find the derivative of $y = \sin x$. We have no trouble differentiating this function, but none of the techniques of integration introduced in the preceding chapters leads to finding the integral $\displaystyle\int_0^1 \frac{\sin x}{x}\,dx$. However, if we divide each side of Equation (2) by x, we have

$$\frac{\sin x}{x} = \frac{x}{x} - \frac{x^3}{3!x} + \frac{x^5}{5!x} - \frac{x^7}{7!x} + \cdots$$

$$= 1 - \frac{x^2}{3!} + \frac{x^4}{5!} - \frac{x^6}{7!} + \cdots$$

Then,

$$\int_0^1 \frac{\sin x}{x}\,dx = \int_0^1 \left(1 - \frac{x^2}{3!} + \frac{x^4}{5!} - \frac{x^6}{7!} + \cdots\right)dx$$

$$= \left(x - \frac{x^3}{3!3} + \frac{x^5}{5!5} - \frac{x^7}{7!7} + \cdots\right)\Bigg|_0^1$$

$$= \left(1 - \frac{1}{18} + \frac{1}{600} - \frac{1}{35{,}280} + \cdots\right) - (0)$$

$$= 0.946083 \qquad \text{(sum of the first four nonzero terms)}$$

EXAMPLE 6

Evaluate $\displaystyle\int_{0.1}^1 \frac{e^{-x} - 1}{x}\,dx$.

Using Equation (1), we have

$$\frac{e^{-x}}{x} = \frac{1}{x} + \frac{-x}{x} + \frac{(-x)^2}{2!x} + \frac{(-x)^3}{3!x} + \frac{(-x)^4}{4!x} + \cdots$$

$$= \frac{1}{x} - 1 + \frac{x}{2!} - \frac{x^2}{3!} + \frac{x^3}{4!} - \cdots$$

So

$$\frac{e^{-x} - 1}{x} = \frac{e^{-x}}{x} - \frac{1}{x} = \left(\frac{1}{x} - 1 + \frac{x}{2!} - \frac{x^2}{3!} + \frac{x^3}{4!} - \cdots\right) - \frac{1}{x}$$

$$= -1 + \frac{x}{2!} - \frac{x^2}{3!} + \frac{x^3}{4!} - \cdots$$

$$\int_{0.1}^1 \frac{(e^{-x} - 1)}{x}\,dx = \int_{0.1}^1 \left(-1 + \frac{x}{2!} - \frac{x^2}{3!} + \frac{x^3}{4!} - \cdots\right)dx$$

$$= \left(-x + \frac{x^2}{4} - \frac{x^3}{18} + \frac{x^4}{96} - \cdots\right)\Bigg|_{0.1}^1$$

$$= \left(-1 + \frac{1}{4} - \frac{1}{18} + \frac{1}{96} - \cdots \right)$$

$$- \left(-0.1 + \frac{0.01}{4} - \frac{0.001}{18} + \frac{0.0001}{96} - \cdots \right)$$

$$= -0.6976 \qquad \text{(using the first four terms)}$$

The exponential form of a complex number is based on the expression

$$e^{j\theta} = \cos \theta + j \sin \theta, \qquad \text{where } j = \sqrt{-1}$$

We will now show that this is a valid identity. Recall from Equations (1) through (3) that

$$e^x = 1 + x + \frac{x^2}{2!} + \frac{x^3}{3!} + \frac{x^4}{4!} + \frac{x^5}{5!} + \cdots \tag{1}$$

$$\cos x = 1 - \frac{x^2}{2!} + \frac{x^4}{4!} - \cdots \tag{3}$$

$$\sin x = x - \frac{x^3}{3!} + \frac{x^5}{5!} - \cdots \tag{2}$$

If we let $x = j\theta$ in Equation (1) and $x = \theta$ in Equations (3) and (2), then we have the following equations, respectively:

$$e^{j\theta} = 1 + j\theta + \frac{(j\theta)^2}{2!} + \frac{(j\theta)^3}{3!} + \frac{(j\theta)^4}{4!} + \frac{(j\theta)^5}{5!} + \cdots$$

$$= 1 + j\theta - \frac{\theta^2}{2!} - j\frac{\theta^3}{3!} + \frac{\theta^4}{4!} + j\frac{\theta^5}{5!} - \cdots \tag{5}$$

$$\cos \theta = 1 - \frac{\theta^2}{2!} + \frac{\theta^4}{4!} - \cdots \tag{6}$$

$$j \sin \theta = j \left(\theta - \frac{\theta^3}{3!} + \frac{\theta^5}{5!} - \cdots \right)$$

$$= j\theta - j\frac{\theta^3}{3!} + j\frac{\theta^5}{5!} - \cdots \tag{7}$$

Adding Equations (6) and (7), we have

$$\cos \theta + j \sin \theta = \left(1 - \frac{\theta^2}{2!} + \frac{\theta^4}{4!} - \cdots \right) + \left(j\theta - j\frac{\theta^3}{3!} + j\frac{\theta^5}{5!} - \cdots \right)$$

$$= 1 + j\theta - \frac{\theta^2}{2!} - j\frac{\theta^3}{3!} + \frac{\theta^4}{4!} + j\frac{\theta^5}{5!} - \cdots \qquad [\text{same as Equation (5)}]$$

$$= e^{j\theta}$$

Exercises 4.6

Find a Maclaurin series expansion for each function.

1. $f(x) = e^{-x}$ **2.** $f(x) = \cos \sqrt{x}$ **3.** $f(x) = e^{x^2}$

4. $f(x) = \sin x^2$ **5.** $f(x) = \ln (1 - x)$ **6.** $f(x) = e^{-4x}$

7. $f(x) = \cos 5x^2$ **8.** $f(x) = \ln (1 + 3x)$ **9.** $f(x) = \sin x^3$

10. $f(x) = e^{-2x^2}$ **11.** $f(x) = xe^x$ **12.** $f(x) = x^2 \sin x$

13. $f(x) = \dfrac{\cos x - 1}{x}$ **14.** $f(x) = \dfrac{e^x}{x - 1}$

15. Evaluate $\displaystyle\int_0^1 e^{-x^2}\,dx$. (Use first four nonzero terms.)

16. Evaluate $\displaystyle\int_0^1 \frac{\cos x - 1}{x}\,dx$. (Use first three nonzero terms.)

17. Evaluate $\displaystyle\int_2^3 \frac{e^{x-1}}{x-1}\,dx$. (Use first three nonzero terms.)

18. Evaluate $\displaystyle\int_0^1 \cos x^2\,dx$. (Use first four nonzero terms.)

19. Evaluate $\displaystyle\int_0^1 \sin \sqrt{x}\,dx$. (Use first three nonzero terms.)

20. Evaluate $\displaystyle\int_0^{\pi/2} \sqrt{x}\cos x\,dx$. (Use first six nonzero terms.)

21. The hyperbolic sine function is defined by $\sinh x = \frac{1}{2}(e^x - e^{-x})$. Find its Maclaurin series.

22. The hyperbolic cosine function is defined by $\cosh x = \frac{1}{2}(e^x + e^{-x})$. Find its Maclaurin series.

23. If $i = \sin t^2$ amperes, find the amount of charge q (in coulombs) transmitted by this current
from $t = 0$ to $t = 0.5$ s. *Note:* $q = \displaystyle\int i\,dt$.

24. The current supplied to a capacitor is given by $i = \dfrac{1 - \cos t}{t}$ amperes. Find the voltage V
across the capacitor after 0.1 s, where the capacitance $C = 1 \times 10^{-6}$ F. *Note:* $V = \dfrac{1}{C}\displaystyle\int i\,dt$.

Using power series for sin x, cos x, and e^x, show that

25. $\sin x = \dfrac{e^{jx} - e^{-jx}}{2j}$ **26.** $\cos x = \dfrac{e^{jx} + e^{-jx}}{2}$

4.7 TAYLOR SERIES

When a function $f(x)$ is repeatedly differentiable at a number a and at x as well as all numbers between a and x, then the function usually has a Taylor series expansion that is a valid representation of the given function at x.

TAYLOR SERIES

A Taylor series expansion of a function $f(x)$ is a power series in the form

$$f(x) = f(a) + f'(a)(x - a) + \frac{f''(a)}{2!}(x - a)^2 + \frac{f'''(a)}{3!}(x - a)^3 + \cdots$$
$$+ \frac{f^{(n)}(a)}{n!}(x - a)^n + \cdots$$

Note that a Maclaurin series is a special case of a Taylor series with $a = 0$.

EXAMPLE 1

Find the Taylor series expansion for $f(x) = \ln x$ with $a = 2$.

$$f(x) = \ln x \qquad f(2) = \ln 2$$

$$f'(x) = \frac{1}{x} \qquad f'(2) = \frac{1}{2}$$

$$f''(x) = -\frac{1}{x^2} \qquad f''(2) = -\frac{1}{4}$$

$$f'''(x) = \frac{2}{x^3} \qquad f'''(2) = \frac{2}{8} = \frac{1}{4}$$

$$f^{(4)}(x) = -\frac{6}{x^4} \qquad f^{(4)}(2) = -\frac{6}{16} = -\frac{3}{8}$$

So,

$$f(x) = \ln x = \ln 2 + \frac{1}{2}(x-2) + \frac{(-\frac{1}{4})}{2!}(x-2)^2 + \frac{\frac{1}{4}}{3!}(x-2)^3 + \frac{(-\frac{3}{8})}{4!}(x-2)^4 + \cdots$$

$$= \ln 2 + \frac{1}{2}(x-2) - \frac{1}{8}(x-2)^2 + \frac{1}{24}(x-2)^3 - \frac{1}{64}(x-2)^4 + \cdots$$

EXAMPLE 2

Find the Taylor series expansion for $f(x) = e^x$ with $a = 1$.

Since $\frac{d}{dx}(e^x) = e^x$, we have

$$f(1) = f'(1) = f''(1) = f'''(1) = \cdots = f^{(n)}(1) = e^1 = e$$

So,

$$f(x) = e^x = e + e(x-1) + \frac{e}{2!}(x-1)^2 + \frac{e}{3!}(x-1)^3 + \cdots + \frac{e}{n!}(x-1)^n + \cdots$$

$$= e\left[1 + (x-1) + \frac{1}{2!}(x-1)^2 + \frac{1}{3!}(x-1)^3 + \cdots + \frac{1}{n!}(x-1)^n + \cdots\right]$$

EXAMPLE 3

Find the Taylor series expansion for $f(x) = \sin x$ at $a = \pi/2$.

$$f(x) = \sin x \qquad f\left(\frac{\pi}{2}\right) = 1$$

$$f'(x) = \cos x \qquad f'\left(\frac{\pi}{2}\right) = 0$$

$$f''(x) = -\sin x \qquad f''\left(\frac{\pi}{2}\right) = -1$$

$$f'''(x) = -\cos x \qquad f'''\left(\frac{\pi}{2}\right) = 0$$

$$f^{(4)}(x) = \sin x \qquad f^{(4)}\left(\frac{\pi}{2}\right) = 1$$

So,

$$f(x) = \sin x = 1 - \frac{1}{2!}\left(x - \frac{\pi}{2}\right)^2 + \frac{1}{4!}\left(x - \frac{\pi}{2}\right)^4 - \cdots$$

Exercises 4.7

Find the Taylor series expansion for each function for the given value of a.

1. $f(x) = \cos x, a = \dfrac{\pi}{2}$ 　　**2.** $f(x) = \sin x, a = \dfrac{\pi}{4}$ 　　**3.** $f(x) = e^x, a = 2$

4. $f(x) = \sqrt{x}, a = 4$ 　　**5.** $f(x) = \sqrt{x}, a = 9$ 　　**6.** $f(x) = \tan x, a = \dfrac{\pi}{4}$

7. $f(x) = \dfrac{1}{x}, a = 2$ 　　**8.** $f(x) = e^{-x}, a = 1$ 　　**9.** $f(x) = \ln x, a = 1$

10. $f(x) = x \ln x, a = 1$ 　　**11.** $f(x) = \dfrac{1}{\sqrt{x}}, a = 1$ 　　**12.** $f(x) = \dfrac{1}{1 + 2x}, a = 1$

13. $f(x) = \dfrac{1}{x^2}, a = 1$ 　　**14.** $f(x) = \cos x, a = \dfrac{\pi}{3}$ 　　**15.** $f(x) = \cos x, a = \pi$

16. $f(x) = e^{-x}, a = -3$

4.8　COMPUTATIONAL APPROXIMATIONS

One important use of power series expansions is to compute the numerical values of transcendental functions. Unlike the geometric series, it is difficult to compute the sum of a power series. Usually we must settle for an approximate value by simply evaluating only the first few terms of the series.

EXAMPLE 1

Calculate ln 1.1.

From Exercise 9 in Section 4.7 we found that

$$\ln x = (x - 1) - \frac{(x - 1)^2}{2} + \frac{(x - 1)^3}{3} - \frac{(x - 1)^4}{4} + \cdots$$

Then,

$$\ln 1.1 = (1.1 - 1) - \frac{(1.1 - 1)^2}{2} + \frac{(1.1 - 1)^3}{3} - \frac{(1.1 - 1)^4}{4} + \cdots$$

$$= 0.1 - \frac{(0.1)^2}{2} + \frac{(0.1)^3}{3} - \frac{(0.1)^4}{4} + \cdots$$

$$= 0.095308 \qquad \text{(sum of the first four terms)}$$

From the alternating series test, we know that the absolute error in this estimate is less than the numerical value of the next term in the series.

$$|S - S_n| < a_{n+1} \qquad \text{(alternating series test)}$$

$$|S - S_4| < a_5 \qquad \text{(for } n = 4\text{)}$$

$$|\text{error}| < \frac{(0.1)^5}{5} = 2 \times 10^{-6}$$

Thus, the last digit shown is off by no more than 2 (and all other digits are accurate). We can conclude that $\ln 1.1 \cong 0.09351$.

EXAMPLE 2

Calculate $e^{-0.2}$.

From

$$e^x = 1 + x + \frac{x^2}{2!} + \frac{x^3}{3!} + \cdots$$

we find

$$e^{-0.2} = 1 - 0.2 + \frac{(-0.2)^2}{2!} + \frac{(-0.2)^3}{3!} + \cdots$$

$$= 0.81867 \qquad \text{(sum of the first four terms)}$$

To analyze the error in this estimate, note that

$$|S - S_4| < a_5 \qquad \text{(alternating series test, } n = 4\text{)}$$

$$|\text{error}| < \frac{(-0.2)^4}{4!} = 0.0000667$$

Thus, the last digit shown is off by less than 7 (and all other digits are accurate). We can immediately conclude that $e^{-0.2}$ is either 0.8186 or 0.8187 when rounded to four decimal places. More subtly, we can tell if an estimate obtained from an alternating series is too large or too small by noting whether the final term in the estimate is positive or negative, respectively. Since the fourth and final term, $\dfrac{(-0.2)^3}{3!}$, is negative, we know that the estimate 0.81867 is too small. So *adding* the error estimate (or anything smaller), we can actually infer that $e^{-0.2} = 0.8187$ to four decimal place accuracy.

EXAMPLE 3

Calculate $\sin 3°$.

From

$$\sin x = x - \frac{x^3}{3!} + \frac{x^5}{5!} - \cdots$$

and the first two terms, we have

$$\sin 3° = \sin \frac{\pi}{60} = \frac{\pi}{60} - \frac{\left(\frac{\pi}{60}\right)^3}{3!} + \cdots \qquad \left(3° = \frac{\pi}{60}\,\text{rad}\right)$$

$$= 0.0523599 - 0.0000239$$

$$= 0.0523360$$

Error analysis:

$$|S - S_2| < a_3 \qquad\qquad \text{(alternating series test, } n = 2)$$

$$|\text{error}| < \frac{\left(\frac{\pi}{60}\right)^5}{5!} = 3.3 \times 10^{-9}$$

Thus, *all* of the decimal digits shown are accurate.

EXAMPLE 4

Calculate cos 32°.

The Taylor series expansion for $f(x) = \cos x$ at $a = \pi/6$ is found as follows:

$$f(x) = \cos x \qquad f\!\left(\frac{\pi}{6}\right) = \frac{\sqrt{3}}{2}$$

$$f'(x) = -\sin x \qquad f'\!\left(\frac{\pi}{6}\right) = -\frac{1}{2}$$

$$f''(x) = -\cos x \qquad f''\!\left(\frac{\pi}{6}\right) = -\frac{\sqrt{3}}{2}$$

$$f'''(x) = \sin x \qquad f'''\!\left(\frac{\pi}{6}\right) = \frac{1}{2}$$

So,

$$\cos x = \frac{\sqrt{3}}{2} - \frac{1}{2}\left(x - \frac{\pi}{6}\right) - \frac{\sqrt{3}}{2}\frac{(x - \pi/6)^2}{2!} + \frac{1}{2}\frac{(x - \pi/6)^3}{3!} - \cdots$$

Note: We need to write $x = 32° = 30° + 2° = \frac{\pi}{6} + \frac{\pi}{90}$.

Then,

$$x - a = x - \frac{\pi}{6} = \left(\frac{\pi}{6} + \frac{\pi}{90}\right) - \frac{\pi}{6} = \frac{\pi}{90}$$

and

$$\cos 32° = \frac{\sqrt{3}}{2} - \frac{1}{2}\left(\frac{\pi}{90}\right) - \frac{\sqrt{3}}{2}\frac{(\pi/90)^2}{2!} + \frac{1}{2}\frac{(\pi/90)^3}{3!} - \cdots$$

$$= 0.848048 \qquad \text{(using the first four nonzero terms)}$$

Since this is not an alternating series, we will not attempt to analyze the error.

More advanced texts explain how many terms need to be used in approximating the value of a function to a desired accuracy. In the exercises that follow, the number of terms to be used will be specified.

If one desires to evaluate $e^{1.1}$, then it is better to use the Taylor expansion with $a = 1$,

$$e^x = e\left[1 + (x - 1) + \frac{1}{2!}(x - 1)^2 + \frac{1}{3!}(x - 1)^3 + \cdots\right]$$

rather than the Maclaurin series,

$$e^x = 1 + x + \frac{x^2}{2!} + \frac{x^3}{3!} + \cdots$$

because the powers of $x - 1$ become smaller faster than do the powers of x when $x = 1.1$. Thus, an accurate approximation can be obtained with the Taylor expansion using fewer terms. This observation illustrates the importance of the Taylor series expansion.

Exercises 4.8

Calculate the value of each expression.

1. $e^{0.1}$ (Use first four nonzero terms.)
2. $e^{-0.3}$ (Use first four nonzero terms.)
3. $\cos 1°$ (Use first two nonzero terms.)
4. $\sin 2°$ (Use first two nonzero terms.)
5. $\ln 0.5$ (Use first four nonzero terms.)
6. $\ln 1.5$ (Use first four nonzero terms.)
7. $\sqrt{1.1}$ (Use first four nonzero terms.)
8. $\sqrt{0.9}$ (Use first four nonzero terms.)
9. $e^{1.3}$ (Use first four nonzero terms.)
10. $\sqrt{3.9}$ (Use first four nonzero terms.)
11. $\sin 29°$ (Use first three nonzero terms.)
12. $e^{0.9}$ (Use first four nonzero terms.)
13. Find the value of a current $i = \sin \omega t$ when $\omega t = 0.03$ rad.
14. Find the value of a current $i = 3e^{t^2}$ when $t = 0.1$ s.

4.9 FOURIER SERIES

One of the difficulties with Taylor series expansions is that, in general, they can be used to represent a given function only for values of x close to a [when expanded in powers of $(x - a)$]. A Fourier series expansion is often used when it is necessary to approximate a function over a larger interval of values of x.

The following expression is called a *Fourier series expansion* representing $f(x)$:

Four of the basic periodic waves that commonly occur in the analysis of electric and mechanical systems are shown in Fig. 4.1.

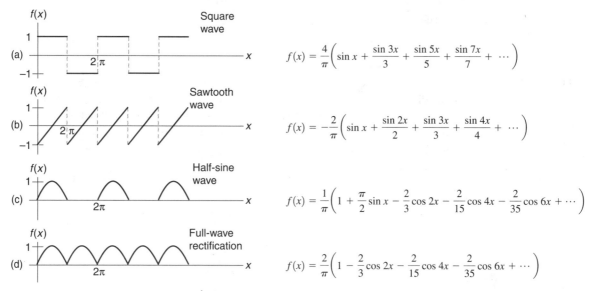

$$f(x) = \frac{4}{\pi}\left(\sin x + \frac{\sin 3x}{3} + \frac{\sin 5x}{5} + \frac{\sin 7x}{7} + \cdots\right)$$

$$f(x) = -\frac{2}{\pi}\left(\sin x + \frac{\sin 2x}{2} + \frac{\sin 3x}{3} + \frac{\sin 4x}{4} + \cdots\right)$$

$$f(x) = \frac{1}{\pi}\left(1 + \frac{\pi}{2}\sin x - \frac{2}{3}\cos 2x - \frac{2}{15}\cos 4x - \frac{2}{35}\cos 6x + \cdots\right)$$

$$f(x) = \frac{2}{\pi}\left(1 - \frac{2}{3}\cos 2x - \frac{2}{15}\cos 4x - \frac{2}{35}\cos 6x + \cdots\right)$$

Figure 4.1   Four basic periodic waves.

EXAMPLE 1

Find the Fourier series that represents the square wave of period 2π and amplitude 3 shown in Fig. 4.2. Its formula is given by

$$f(x) = \begin{cases} 3 & 0 < x < \pi \\ -3 & \pi \leq x < 2\pi \end{cases}$$

To calculate the coefficients, we will need to split up all of the integrals at $x = \pi$.

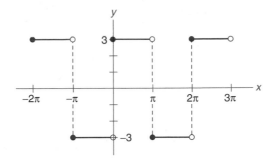

Figure 4.2

Finding a_0: $\displaystyle a_0 = \frac{1}{2\pi} \int_0^{2\pi} f(x)\, dx$

$$= \frac{1}{2\pi} \left(\int_0^{\pi} 3\, dx + \int_{\pi}^{2\pi} -3\, dx \right)$$

$$= \frac{1}{2\pi} \left[3x \Big|_0^{\pi} + (-3x) \Big|_{\pi}^{2\pi} \right]$$

$$- \frac{1}{2\pi} [3\pi - 0 + (-6\pi) - (-3\pi)]$$

$$= 0$$

Finding a_n: $\displaystyle a_n = \frac{1}{\pi} \int_0^{2\pi} f(x) \cos nx\, dx \qquad\qquad (n = 1, 2, 3, \dots)$

$$= \frac{1}{\pi} \left(\int_0^{\pi} 3 \cos nx\, dx + \int_{\pi}^{2\pi} -3 \cos nx\, dx \right)$$

$$= \frac{1}{\pi} \left(\frac{3 \sin nx}{n} \Big|_0^{\pi} + \frac{-3 \sin nx}{n} \Big|_{\pi}^{2\pi} \right)$$

$$= \frac{1}{\pi} \left(\frac{3 \sin n\pi}{n} - \frac{3 \sin 0}{n} + \frac{-3 \sin 2n\pi}{n} - \frac{-3 \sin n\pi}{n} \right)$$

$$= \frac{1}{\pi}(0 - 0 + 0 - 0)$$

$$= 0$$

Therefore, the constant coefficient and all of the coefficients of the cosine terms are zero.

Finding b_n: $\displaystyle b_n = \frac{1}{\pi} \int_0^{2\pi} f(x) \sin nx\, dx \qquad\qquad (n = 1, 2, 3, \dots)$

$$= \frac{1}{\pi} \left(\int_0^{\pi} 3 \sin nx\, dx + \int_{\pi}^{2\pi} -3 \sin nx\, dx \right)$$

$$= \frac{1}{\pi} \left(\frac{-3 \cos nx}{n} \Big|_0^{\pi} + \frac{3 \cos nx}{n} \Big|_{\pi}^{2\pi} \right)$$

$$= \frac{1}{\pi} \left(\frac{-3 \cos n\pi}{n} - \frac{-3 \cos 0}{n} + \frac{3 \cos 2n\pi}{n} - \frac{3 \cos n\pi}{n} \right)$$

$$= \frac{1}{\pi} \left(\frac{6}{n} - \frac{6 \cos n\pi}{n} \right) \qquad (\cos 0 = 1 \text{ and } \cos 2n\pi = 1)$$

$$= \begin{cases} \dfrac{1}{\pi} \left(\dfrac{6}{n} - \dfrac{6}{n} \right) = 0 & \text{if } n \text{ is even} \\[3mm] \dfrac{1}{\pi} \left(\dfrac{6}{n} + \dfrac{6}{n} \right) = \dfrac{12}{n\pi} & \text{if } n \text{ is odd} \end{cases}$$

Therefore, the Fourier series is

$$f(x) = \frac{12}{(1)\pi} \sin 1x + \frac{12}{(3)\pi} \sin 3x + \frac{12}{(5)\pi} \sin 5x + \frac{12}{(7)\pi} \sin 7x + \cdots$$

$$= \frac{12}{\pi} \left(\sin x + \frac{\sin 3x}{3} + \frac{\sin 5x}{5} + \frac{\sin 7x}{7} + \cdots \right)$$

Note that this is just 3 times the formula for the square wave of period 2π and amplitude 1 given in the table in Fig. 4.1.

Using a graphing calculator to visualize an approximation of the square wave by the first three terms of the series, we have

green diamond Y=   **F2   7**

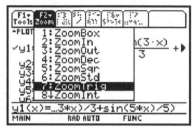
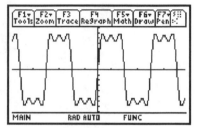

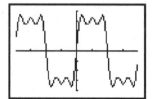

Y=   **ZOOM   7**

EXAMPLE 2

Find the Fourier series which represents the wave function $f(x) = x \ (0 \leq x < 2\pi)$ with period 2π shown in Fig. 4.3.

Finding a_0: $a_0 = \dfrac{1}{2\pi} \displaystyle\int_0^{2\pi} x \, dx = \dfrac{1}{2\pi} \dfrac{x^2}{2} \Big|_0^{2\pi} = \pi$

Finding a_n: $a_n = \dfrac{1}{\pi} \displaystyle\int_0^{2\pi} x \cos nx \, dx$

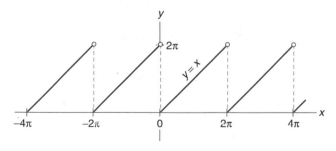

Figure 4.3

From Appendix B, Formula 81, we have

$$\int u \cos u \, du = \cos u + u \sin u + C$$

$$\int x \cos nx \, dx = \int \frac{u}{n} \cos u \, \frac{du}{n}$$
$$\boxed{\begin{array}{l} u = nx \\ du = n \, dx \end{array}}$$

$$= \frac{1}{n^2} \int u \cos u \, du$$

$$= \frac{1}{n^2} (\cos u + u \sin u) + C$$

$$= \frac{1}{n^2} (\cos nx + nx \sin nx) + C$$

Thus,

$$a_n = \frac{1}{\pi n^2} (\cos nx + nx \sin nx) \Big|_0^{2\pi}$$

$$= \frac{1}{\pi n^2} \{(\cos 2n\pi + 2n\pi \sin 2n\pi) - [\cos 0 + n(0) \sin 0]\}$$

$$= \frac{1}{\pi n^2} (1 + 0 - 1 - 0) = 0 \qquad \text{(Recall that } n \text{ is a positive integer.)}$$

Finding b_n: $\quad b_n = \frac{1}{\pi} \int_0^{2\pi} x \sin nx \, dx$

From Appendix B, Formula 80, we have

$$\int u \sin u \, du = \sin u - u \cos u + C$$

So,

$$\int x \sin nx \, dx = \int \frac{u}{n} \sin u \, \frac{du}{n}$$
$$\boxed{\begin{array}{l} u = nx \\ du = n \, dx \end{array}}$$

$$= \frac{1}{n^2} \int u \sin u \, du$$

$$= \frac{1}{n^2} (\sin u - u \cos u) + C$$

$$= \frac{1}{n^2} (\sin nx - nx \cos nx) + C$$

Thus,

$$b_n = \frac{1}{\pi n^2} (\sin nx - nx \cos nx) \Big|_0^{2\pi}$$

$$= \frac{1}{\pi n^2} \{(\sin 2n\pi - 2n\pi \cos 2n\pi) - [\sin 0 - n(0) \cos 0]\}$$

$$= \frac{1}{\pi n^2} (0 - 2n\pi - 0 + 0)$$

$$= -\frac{2}{n}$$

That is, $b_1 = -\frac{2}{1} = -2$, $b_2 = -\frac{2}{2} = -1$, $b_3 = -\frac{2}{3}, \ldots$, and the Fourier series is

$$f(x) = \pi - 2 \sin x - \sin 2x - \frac{2}{3} \sin 3x - \cdots$$

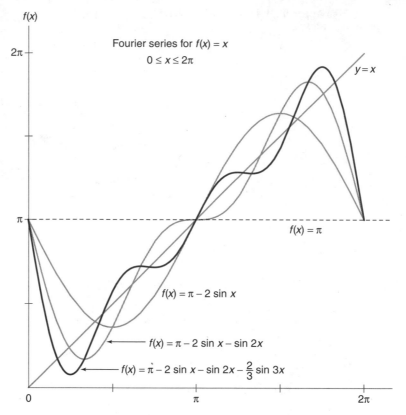

Fourier series for $f(x) = x$

$0 \le x \le 2\pi$

$y = x$

$f(x) = \pi$

$f(x) = \pi - 2 \sin x$

$f(x) = \pi - 2 \sin x - \sin 2x$

$f(x) = \pi - 2 \sin x - \sin 2x - \dfrac{2}{3} \sin 3x$

Figure 4.4

Note: There are no terms involving cosine because $a_1 = a_2 = a_3 = \cdots = a_n = 0$. The graphs of the sums of the first few terms are sketched in Fig. 4.4.

EXAMPLE 3

Find the Fourier series for the wave function given by

$$f(x) = \begin{cases} \pi, & 0 \le x < \pi \\ 2\pi - x, & \pi \le x < 2\pi \end{cases}$$

First, sketch several periods of $f(x)$ as in Fig. 4.5.

Finding a_0:
$$a_0 = \frac{1}{2\pi} \int_0^{\pi} \pi \, dx + \frac{1}{2\pi} \int_{\pi}^{2\pi} (2\pi - x) \, dx$$

$$= \frac{1}{2\pi} (\pi x) \Big|_0^{\pi} + \frac{1}{2\pi} \left(2\pi x - \frac{x^2}{2} \right) \Big|_{\pi}^{2\pi}$$

$$= \frac{\pi}{2} + \frac{\pi}{4} = \frac{3\pi}{4}$$

Note: Two separate integrals must be used to determine the coefficients. This is because the function is defined differently on the two intervals $0 \le x < \pi$ and $\pi \le x < 2\pi$.

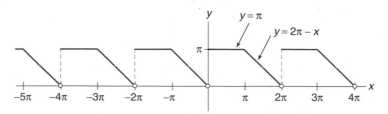

y

$y = \pi$

$y = 2\pi - x$

π

-5π -4π -3π -2π $-\pi$ π 2π 3π 4π x

Figure 4.5

Finding a_n: $a_n = \dfrac{1}{\pi} \displaystyle\int_0^{\pi} \pi \cos nx \, dx + \dfrac{1}{\pi} \int_{\pi}^{2\pi} (2\pi - x) \cos nx \, dx$

$$= \int_0^{\pi} \cos nx \, dx + 2 \int_{\pi}^{2\pi} \cos nx \, dx - \frac{1}{\pi} \int_{\pi}^{2\pi} x \cos nx \, dx$$

$$= \frac{1}{n}(\sin nx) \Big|_0^{\pi} + \frac{2}{n}(\sin nx) \Big|_{\pi}^{2\pi}$$

$$- \frac{1}{\pi n^2}(\cos nx + nx \sin nx) \Big|_{\pi}^{2\pi} \qquad \text{(from Example 2)}$$

$$= \begin{cases} 0 + 0 - \dfrac{2}{\pi n^2} = -\dfrac{2}{\pi n^2} & \text{if } n \text{ is odd} \\ 0 & \text{if } n \text{ is even} \end{cases}$$

Finding b_n: $b_n = \dfrac{1}{\pi} \displaystyle\int_0^{\pi} \pi \sin nx \, dx + \dfrac{1}{\pi} \int_{\pi}^{2\pi} (2\pi - x) \sin nx \, dx$

$$= \int_0^{\pi} \sin nx \, dx + 2 \int_{\pi}^{2\pi} \sin nx \, dx - \frac{1}{\pi} \int_{\pi}^{2\pi} x \sin nx \, dx$$

$$= \left(-\frac{1}{n}\right)(\cos nx) \Big|_0^{\pi} + \left(-\frac{2}{n}\right)(\cos nx) \Big|_{\pi}^{2\pi}$$

$$- \frac{1}{\pi n^2}(\sin nx - nx \cos nx) \Big|_{\pi}^{2\pi} \qquad \text{(from Example 2)}$$

$$= \begin{cases} \dfrac{2}{n} - \dfrac{4}{n} + \dfrac{3}{n} = \dfrac{1}{n} & \text{if } n \text{ is odd} \\ 0 & \text{if } n \text{ is even} \end{cases}$$

We thus obtain the Fourier series

$$f(x) = \frac{3\pi}{4} - \frac{2}{\pi}\left(\cos x + \frac{1}{9}\cos 3x + \frac{1}{25}\cos 5x + \cdots\right)$$

$$+ \left(\sin x + \frac{1}{3}\sin 3x + \frac{1}{5}\sin 5x + \cdots\right)$$

We will now show how the formulas for the coefficients a_0, a_n, and b_n are obtained. Note that if we integrate each side of the equation

$$f(x) = a_0 + a_1 \cos x + a_2 \cos 2x + a_3 \cos 3x + \cdots$$
$$+ b_1 \sin x + b_2 \sin 2x + b_3 \sin 3x + \cdots \qquad \textbf{(1)}$$

from 0 to 2π, then the integrals should be equal. That is,

$$\int_0^{2\pi} f(x) \, dx = \int_0^{2\pi} a_0 \, dx + \int_0^{2\pi} a_1 \cos x \, dx + \int_0^{2\pi} a_2 \cos 2x \, dx + \cdots$$

$$+ \int_0^{2\pi} b_1 \sin x \, dx + \int_0^{2\pi} b_2 \sin 2x \, dx + \cdots$$

All terms on the right-hand side are zero except for $\displaystyle\int_0^{2\pi} a_0 \, dx = 2\pi a_0$, so

$$\int_0^{2\pi} f(x) \, dx = 2\pi a_0$$

$$a_0 = \frac{1}{2\pi} \int_0^{2\pi} f(x) \, dx$$

Multiply each side of Equation (1) by cos nx. Then integrate each term to obtain

$$\int_0^{2\pi} f(x) \cos nx \, dx = \int_0^{2\pi} a_0 \cos nx \, dx + \int_0^{2\pi} a_1(\cos nx) \cos x \, dx$$

$$+ \int_0^{2\pi} a_2(\cos nx) \cos 2x \, dx + \cdots$$

$$+ \int_0^{2\pi} b_1(\cos nx) \sin x \, dx$$

$$+ \int_0^{2\pi} b_2(\cos nx) \sin 2x \, dx + \cdots$$

All terms on the right-hand side are zero except the term

$$\int_0^{2\pi} a_n(\cos nx)(\cos nx) \, dx = \pi a_n$$

So,

$$\int_0^{2\pi} f(x) \cos nx \, dx = \pi a_n$$

$$a_n = \frac{1}{\pi} \int_0^{2\pi} f(x) \cos nx \, dx$$

In a similar manner [multiplying each side of the Fourier series equation (1) by sin nx and integrating each term], we can show that

$$b_n = \frac{1}{\pi} \int_0^{2\pi} f(x) \sin nx \, dx$$

Note: If the function to be analyzed ranges periodically from $-\pi$ to π, then the coefficients become

$$a_0 = \frac{1}{2\pi} \int_{-\pi}^{\pi} f(x) \, dx$$

$$a_n = \frac{1}{\pi} \int_{-\pi}^{\pi} f(x) \cos nx \, dx$$

$$b_n = \frac{1}{\pi} \int_{-\pi}^{\pi} f(x) \sin nx \, dx$$

In general, if you need to find a Fourier series of a function which ranges periodically from $-L$ to L, the coefficients become

$$a_0 = \frac{1}{2L} \int_{-L}^{L} f(x) \, dx$$

$$a_n = \frac{1}{L} \int_{-L}^{L} f(x) \cos \frac{n\pi x}{L} \, dx$$

$$b_n = \frac{1}{L} \int_{-L}^{L} f(x) \sin \frac{n\pi x}{L} \, dx$$

The period of the function is $2L$. The Fourier series is

$$f(x) = a_0 + a_1 \cos \frac{\pi x}{L} + a_2 \cos \frac{2\pi x}{L} + a_3 \cos \frac{3\pi x}{L} + \cdots + a_n \cos \frac{n\pi x}{L} + \cdots$$

$$+ b_1 \sin \frac{\pi x}{L} + b_2 \sin \frac{2\pi x}{L} + b_3 \sin \frac{3\pi x}{L} + \cdots + b_n \sin \frac{n\pi x}{L} + \cdots$$

Exercises 4.9

Sketch several periods of each given function and find its Fourier series expansion.

1. $f(x) = -x, 0 \le x < 2\pi$

2. $f(x) = 2x, 0 \le x < 2\pi$

3. $f(x) = \frac{1}{3}x, 0 \le x < 2\pi$

4. $f(x) = 2x, -\pi \le x < \pi$

$a_n = 0 \rightarrow odd$

5. $f(x) = \begin{cases} 0 & 0 \le x < \pi \\ 1 & \pi \le x < 2\pi \end{cases}$

6. $f(x) = \begin{cases} \pi & 0 \le x < \pi \\ 0 & \pi \le x < 2\pi \end{cases}$ $\rangle odd\ also$

7. $f(x) = \begin{cases} 1 & 0 \le x < \pi \\ -1 & \pi \le x < 2\pi \end{cases}$

8. $f(x) = \begin{cases} x & 0 \le x < \pi \\ \pi & \pi \le x < 2\pi \end{cases}$

9. $f(x) = \begin{cases} 0 & -5 \le x < 0 \\ 6 & 0 \le x < 5 \end{cases}$

10. $f(x) = \begin{cases} 1 & -4 \le x < 0 \\ -1 & 0 \le x < 4 \end{cases}$

11. $f(x) = \begin{cases} x & 0 \le x < \pi \\ 2\pi - x & \pi \le x < 2\pi \end{cases}$

12. $f(x) = \begin{cases} 0 & 0 \le x < \pi \\ x & \pi \le x < 2\pi \end{cases}$

13. $f(x) = e^x, 0 \le x < 2\pi$

14. $f(x) = e^{-2x}, 0 \le x < 2\pi$

15. $f(x) = \begin{cases} \sin x & 0 \le x < \pi \\ 0 & \pi \le x < 2\pi \end{cases}$

16. $f(x) = \begin{cases} \sin x & 0 \le x < \pi \\ -\sin x & \pi \le x < 2\pi \end{cases}$

CHAPTER 4 SUMMARY

1. *Definition of convergence and divergence:*

$$\sum_{n=1}^{\infty} a_n = a_1 + a_2 + a_3 + \cdots$$

Then,

$$S_1 = a_1$$
$$S_2 = a_1 + a_2$$
$$S_3 = a_1 + a_2 + a_3$$
$$.$$
$$.$$
$$.$$
$$S_n = a_1 + a_2 + a_3 + \cdots + a_n$$
$$.$$
$$.$$
$$.$$

where S_1 is the sum of the first term, S_2 is the sum of the first two terms, S_3 is the sum of the first three terms, ..., S_n is the sum of the first n terms (or sometimes called the nth partial sum).

(a) If $\lim\limits_{n\to\infty} S_n = S$ (where S is finite), the series $\sum\limits_{n=1}^{\infty} a_n$ *converges* and S is the *sum of the*

infinite series.

(b) If $\lim\limits_{n\to\infty} S_n$ does not exist, the series $\sum\limits_{n=1}^{\infty} a_n$ *diverges.*

2. *nth-Term Test for divergence of a series:* If $\lim\limits_{n\to\infty} a_n \neq 0$, then the series *diverges.* Stated

another way, if the series $\sum\limits_{n=1}^{\infty} a_n$ converges, then $\lim\limits_{n\to\infty} a_n = 0$.

3. *Convergence and divergence of a p-series:* Any series in the form

$\sum\limits_{n=1}^{\infty} \dfrac{1}{n^p} = \dfrac{1}{1^p} + \dfrac{1}{2^p} + \dfrac{1}{3^p} + \cdots$, where p is a real number, is called a *p-series.* The
p-series
(a) converges for $p > 1$ and
(b) diverges for $p \leq 1$.

4. *Comparison test for convergence and divergence:* Let N be a positive integer, $\sum\limits_{n=1}^{\infty} a_n$
and $\sum\limits_{n=1}^{\infty} b_n$ be series of positive terms, and $0 \leq a_n \leq b_n$ for all $n > N$.
(a) If $\sum\limits_{n=1}^{\infty} b_n$ converges, then $\sum\limits_{n=1}^{\infty} a_n$ also converges.
(b) If $\sum\limits_{n=1}^{\infty} a_n$ diverges, then $\sum\limits_{n=1}^{\infty} b_n$ also diverges.
In other words, the comparison test says
(a) A series of positive terms that is term by term smaller than a known convergent series must also converge.
(b) A series of positive terms that is term by term larger than a known divergent series must also diverge.

5. *Order of magnitude:* Let $\sum\limits_{n=1}^{\infty} a_n$ and $\sum\limits_{n=1}^{\infty} b_n$ be two series of positive terms.

(a) Then $\sum\limits_{n=1}^{\infty} a_n$ and $\sum\limits_{n=1}^{\infty} b_n$ have the *same order of magnitude* if $\lim\limits_{n\to\infty} \dfrac{a_n}{b_n} = L$, where
L is a real number and $L \neq 0$.

(b) The series $\sum\limits_{n=1}^{\infty} a_n$ has a *lesser order of magnitude* than $\sum\limits_{n=1}^{\infty} b_n$ if $\lim\limits_{n\to\infty} \dfrac{a_n}{b_n} = 0$.

(c) The series $\sum\limits_{n=1}^{\infty} a_n$ has a *greater order of magnitude* than $\sum\limits_{n=1}^{\infty} b_n$ if $\lim\limits_{n\to\infty} \dfrac{a_n}{b_n} = \infty$.

6. *Limit comparison test:* Let $\sum\limits_{n=1}^{\infty} a_n$ and $\sum\limits_{n=1}^{\infty} b_n$ be series of positive terms.
(a) If these series have the same order of magnitude, then either both series converge or both series diverge.

(b) If the series $\sum\limits_{n=1}^{\infty} a_n$ has a lesser order of magnitude than $\sum\limits_{n=1}^{\infty} b_n$ and $\sum\limits_{n=1}^{\infty} b_n$ is

known to converge, then $\sum\limits_{n=1}^{\infty} a_n$ also converges.

(c) If $\sum\limits_{n=1}^{\infty} a_n$ has a greater order of magnitude than $\sum\limits_{n=1}^{\infty} b_n$ and $\sum\limits_{n=1}^{\infty} b_n$ is known to

diverge, then $\sum\limits_{n=1}^{\infty} a_n$ also diverges.

7. *Ratio test for convergence and divergence:* Let $\sum\limits_{n=1}^{\infty} a_n$ be a series of positive terms and

$$r = \lim_{n \to \infty} \frac{a_{n+1}}{a_n}$$

(a) If $r < 1$, the series converges.
(b) If $r > 1$ (including $r = \infty$), the series diverges.
(c) If $r = 1$, the test fails. Some other test must be used.

8. *Integral test for convergence and divergence:* Let $\sum\limits_{n=1}^{\infty} a_n$ be a series of positive terms and $f(x)$ be a continuous, decreasing function for $x \geq 1$ such that $f(n) = a_n$ for all positive integers n. Then $\sum\limits_{n=1}^{\infty} a_n$ and $\int_{1}^{\infty} f(x)\,dx$ both converge or both diverge.

9. *Alternating series test:* The alternating series

$$\sum_{n=1}^{\infty} (-1)^{n+1} a_n = a_1 - a_2 + a_3 - a_4 + \cdots \qquad (a_n > 0 \text{ for each } n)$$

converges provided that both of the following conditions are fulfilled:
(a) $0 < a_{n+1} \leq a_n$ for $n \geq 1$
(b) $\lim\limits_{n \to \infty} a_n = 0$
In addition, if S is the sum of the infinite series and S_n is the nth partial sum, then

$$|S - S_n| \leq a_{n+1}$$

10. *Absolute and conditional convergence:* Suppose that $\sum\limits_{n=1}^{\infty} a_n$ converges.

(a) If $\sum\limits_{n=1}^{\infty} |a_n|$ converges, then $\sum\limits_{n=1}^{\infty} a_n$ *converges absolutely.*

(b) If $\sum\limits_{n=1}^{\infty} |a_n|$ diverges, then $\sum\limits_{n=1}^{\infty} a_n$ *converges conditionally.*

11. A *power series* is an infinite series in the form

$$\sum_{n=0}^{\infty} a_n x^n = a_0 + a_1 x + a_2 x^2 + \cdots + a_n x^n + \cdots$$

A series in the form

$$\sum_{n=0}^{\infty} a_n(x - a)^n = a_0 + a_1(x - a) + a_2(x - a)^2 + a_3(x - a)^3$$
$$+ \cdots + a_n(x - a)^n + \cdots$$

is called a *power series centered at a.* Let

$$\lim_{n = \infty} \left| \frac{u_{n+1}}{u_n} \right| = r(x)$$

where u_{n+1} is the $(n + 1)$st term and u_n is the nth term of a power series. Note that the ratio will most often be a function of x, namely $r(x)$. Then the series
(a) converges absolutely for $r(x) < 1$ and
(b) diverges for $r(x) > 1$.
Recall that the ratio test is not valid for $r = 1$ or $r(x) = 1$. These values of x must be checked individually by other methods.

12. A power series converges on an interval, called the *interval of convergence*. The interval of convergence may include both endpoints, only one endpoint, or neither endpoint. The interval of convergence of the power series

$$\sum_{n=0}^{\infty} a_n(x - a)^n$$

is centered at $x = a$. The *radius of convergence* is the distance from the point $x = a$ to either endpoint of the interval. Thus the radius of convergence is one-half the length of the interval of convergence.

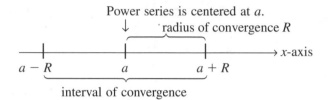

13. The *Maclaurin series expansion* of the function $f(x)$ is

$$f(x) = f(0) + f'(0)x + \frac{f''(0)}{2!}x^2 + \frac{f'''(0)}{3!}x^3 + \cdots + \frac{f^{(n)}(0)}{n!}x^n + \cdots$$

The expansion is valid for all values of x for which the power series converges and for which the function $f(x)$ is repeatedly differentiable.

14. A *Taylor series expansion* of $f(x)$ is a power series in the form

$$f(x) = f(a) + f'(a)(x - a) + \frac{f''(a)}{2!}(x - a)^2 + \frac{f'''(a)}{3!}(x - a)^3 + \cdots$$
$$+ \frac{f^{(n)}(a)}{n!}(x - a)^n + \cdots$$

Note that a Maclaurin series is a special case of a Taylor series with $a = 0$.

15. The *Fourier series expansion* of the function $f(x)$ is

$$f(x) = a_0 + a_1 \cos x + a_2 \cos 2x + \cdots + a_n \cos nx + \cdots$$
$$+ b_1 \sin x + b_2 \sin 2x + \cdots + b_n \sin nx + \cdots$$

The coefficients are determined as follows:

$$a_0 = \frac{1}{2\pi} \int_0^{2\pi} f(x)\, dx$$

$$a_n = \frac{1}{\pi} \int_0^{2\pi} f(x) \cos nx\, dx$$

$$b_n = \frac{1}{\pi} \int_0^{2\pi} f(x) \sin nx\, dx$$

Note that n is a positive integer and that the Fourier series expansion is periodic with period 2π.

CHAPTER 4 REVIEW

Write the expanded form of each series.

1. $\displaystyle\sum_{n=1}^{6} (1 - 3n)$

2. $\displaystyle\sum_{k=1}^{n} \frac{k + 1}{k}$

Write each sum using sigma notation.

3. $\dfrac{1}{3} + \dfrac{1}{9} + \dfrac{1}{27} + \cdots + \dfrac{1}{2187}$

4. $\dfrac{1}{4} + \dfrac{2}{5} + \dfrac{3}{6} + \dfrac{4}{7} + \cdots + \dfrac{10}{13}$

Determine whether each series converges or diverges.

5. $\displaystyle\sum_{n=1}^{\infty} \frac{1}{n^3}$

6. $\displaystyle\sum_{n=1}^{\infty} \frac{1}{\sqrt[4]{n}}$

7. $\displaystyle\sum_{n=1}^{\infty} \frac{1}{6n^2 + 2}$

8. $\displaystyle\sum_{n=2}^{\infty} \frac{\sqrt{n}}{n^2 - 1}$

9. $\displaystyle\sum_{n=2}^{\infty} \frac{n}{\ln n}$

10. $\displaystyle\sum_{n=1}^{\infty} \frac{5n + 2}{(3n + 1)\, 4^n}$

11. $\displaystyle\sum_{n=1}^{\infty} \frac{n^3}{2^n}$

12. $\displaystyle\sum_{n=1}^{\infty} \frac{3n + 1}{4n - 5}$

13. $\displaystyle\sum_{n=1}^{\infty} \frac{n + 1}{n^2 + 4n}$

14. $\displaystyle\sum_{n=1}^{\infty} \frac{\sin n}{n^2 + 1}$

Determine whether each alternating series converges or diverges. If it converges, find whether it converges absolutely or converges conditionally.

15. $\displaystyle\sum_{n=1}^{\infty} \frac{(-1)^{n+1}\, 3^n}{n!}$

16. $\displaystyle\sum_{n=1}^{\infty} \frac{(-1)^{n+1}\, 2^n}{5^n\, (n + 1)}$

17. $\displaystyle\sum_{n=2}^{\infty} (-1)^n \frac{n + 1}{n - 1}$

18. $\displaystyle\sum_{n=1}^{\infty} (-1)^{n+1} \frac{n + 2}{n(n + 3)}$

Find the interval of convergence of each series.

19. $\displaystyle\sum_{n=0}^{\infty} \frac{n}{2}(x - 2)^n$

20. $\displaystyle\sum_{n=0}^{\infty} n^2 (x - 3)^n$

21. $\displaystyle\sum_{n=1}^{\infty} \frac{(x - 1)^n}{n!}$

22. $\displaystyle\sum_{n=1}^{\infty} \frac{3^n (x - 4)^n}{n^2}$

Find a Maclaurin series expansion for each function.

23. $f(x) = \dfrac{1}{1 - x}$

24. $f(x) = \sqrt{x + 1}$

25. $f(x) = \sin x + \cos x$

26. $f(x) = e^x \sin x$

27. $f(x) = \dfrac{1 - e^x}{x}$

28. $f(x) = \cos x^2$

29. $f(x) = \sin 3x$

30. $f(x) = e^{\sin x}$

31. Evaluate $\displaystyle\int_{0}^{0.1} \frac{\ln(x + 1)}{x}\, dx.$ (Use first four nonzero terms.)

32. If $i = \dfrac{\sin t}{t}$ amperes, find the amount of charge q (in coulombs) transmitted by this current from $t = 0$ to $t = 0.1$ s. *Note:* $q = \displaystyle\int i\, dt.$

Find the Taylor series expansions for each function for the given value of a.

33. $f(x) = \cos 2x$, $a = \dfrac{\pi}{6}$

34. $f(x) = \ln x$, $a = 4$

35. $f(x) = e^{x^2}$, $a = 1$

36. $f(x) = \sin x$, $a = \dfrac{3\pi}{2}$

Calculate the value of each expression.

37. $\sin 31°$ (Use first three nonzero terms.)

38. $e^{1.2}$ (Use first four nonzero terms.)

39. $\ln 1.2$ (Use first four nonzero terms.)

40. $\sqrt{4.1}$ (Use first four nonzero terms.)

Find the Fourier series for each function.

41. $f(x) = \begin{cases} 0 & 0 \le x < \pi \\ -1 & \pi \le x < 2\pi \end{cases}$

42. $f(x) = \begin{cases} x^2 & 0 \le x < \pi \\ 0 & \pi \le x < 2\pi \end{cases}$

5

First-Order Differential Equations

INTRODUCTION

Often in physics, engineering, and other technical areas, we need to search for an unknown function. In many cases, this search leads to an equation involving derivatives (or differentials) of the unknown function. Such equations involving derivatives (or differentials) are called differential equations.

Objectives

- Solve differential equations by the method of separation of variables.
- Solve differential equations by using an integrating factor.
- Use differential equations to solve applications problems.

5.1 SOLVING DIFFERENTIAL EQUATIONS

In Chapters 5 and 6 we present methods of solving differential equations; that is, we find ways to use differential equations to determine an unknown function.

EXAMPLE 1

The following are examples of differential equations:

(a) $\dfrac{dy}{dx} = x^2 y$

(b) $\dfrac{dy}{dx} = \sin x$

(c) $\dfrac{d^2 y}{dx^2} + x\dfrac{dy}{dx} + y = 0$

(d) $x^2 \dfrac{d^3 y}{dx^3} + 2y\dfrac{d^2 y}{dx^2} - \left(\dfrac{dy}{dx}\right)^4 + 3 = 0$

(e) $e^x\,dy - x^2 y\,dx = 2$

The *order of a differential equation* is n if n is the highest order derivative that appears in the equation.

151

EXAMPLE 2

Determine the order of the differential equation

$$\frac{d^2y}{dx^2} + 2\left(\frac{dy}{dx}\right)^3 + 5 = 0$$

The order is 2 since the second derivative $\frac{d^2y}{dx^2}$ (order 2 derivative) is the highest-order derivative appearing in the equation.

The *degree of a differential equation* is the highest power of the derivative of highest order.

EXAMPLE 3

Determine the degree and order of each differential equation:

$$\frac{d^2y}{dx^2} - 7\frac{dy}{dx} + \left(\frac{dy}{dx}\right)^3 = 0 \tag{1}$$

$$\left(\frac{dy}{dx}\right)^2 - 3\frac{dy}{dx} + y = 0 \tag{2}$$

Equation (1) is a first-degree differential equation of order 2 since $\frac{d^2y}{dx^2}$ is the highest-order derivative in the equation and is raised to the first power. Note that the third power of $\frac{dy}{dx}$ has no effect on the degree of Equation (1) because $\frac{dy}{dx}$ is of lesser order than $\frac{d^2y}{dx^2}$.

Equation (2) is a second-degree, first-order differential equation. $\frac{dy}{dx}$ is the highest-order derivative (order 1), and 2 is the highest power of $\frac{dy}{dx}$ appearing in the equation.

A *solution* of a differential equation is a function $y = f(x)$ that together with its derivatives satisfies the given differential equation.

EXAMPLE 4

Verify that $y = x^2 + 5x$ is a solution of the second-order, first-degree differential equation

$$x\frac{d^2y}{dx^2} - \frac{dy}{dx} + 5 = 0$$

First, $\frac{dy}{dx} = 2x + 5$ and $\frac{d^2y}{dx^2} = 2$. Then substitute in the differential equation:

$$x\frac{d^2y}{dx^2} - \frac{dy}{dx} + 5 = 0$$
$$x(2) - (2x + 5) + 5 = 0$$
$$2x - 2x - 5 + 5 = 0$$
$$0 = 0$$

EXAMPLE 5

Verify that $y = \dfrac{1}{x^2 + C}$ is a solution of the first-order, first-degree differential equation

$$\frac{dy}{dx} = -2xy^2$$

First, $\dfrac{dy}{dx} = -\dfrac{2x}{(x^2 + C)^2}$. Substitute this result in the given differential equation:

$$\frac{dy}{dx} = -2xy^2$$

$$\frac{-2x}{(x^2 + C)^2} = -2x\left(\frac{1}{x^2 + C}\right)^2$$

$$\frac{-2x}{(x^2 + C)^2} = \frac{-2x}{(x^2 + C)^2}$$

The solution $y = x^2 + 5x$ in Example 4 is an example of a *particular solution* of a differential equation. One can verify that $y = x^2 + 5x - 7$ is also a particular solution of the differential equation in Example 4. A differential equation can have infinitely many particular solutions.

A solution $y = f(x)$ of a differential equation of order n containing n arbitrary constants is called a *general solution*. Thus, the solution $y = \dfrac{1}{x^2 + C}$ in Example 5 or $y = x^2 + 5x + C$ in Example 4 is an example of a general solution.

We will solve only first-degree equations. Differential equations that do not contain partial derivatives are called *ordinary differential equations*. We restrict our considerations to first-degree ordinary differential equations.

Recall the use of other notations for derivatives:

$$y' = \frac{dy}{dx} \qquad y'' = \frac{d^2y}{dx^2} \qquad y''' = \frac{d^3y}{dx^3} \qquad \cdots$$

EXAMPLE 6

Verify that $y = C_1 + C_2x + C_3e^x$ is a general solution of the differential equation $y''' = y''$.

First, find the first three derivatives of the given function:

$$y' = C_2 + C_3e^x$$
$$y'' = C_3e^x$$
$$y''' = C_3e^x$$

Substituting in the differential equation, we have

$$y''' = y''$$
$$C_3e^x = C_3e^x$$

Therefore, $y = C_1 + C_2x + C_3e^x$ is a general solution of the given differential equation because it has three distinct arbitrary constants.

Exercises 5.1

State the order and degree of each differential equation.

1. $\dfrac{dy}{dx} = x^2 - y^2$

2. $\left(\dfrac{dy}{dx}\right)^2 - 3x\,\dfrac{dy}{dx} + 2 = 0$

3. $\dfrac{d^2y}{dx^2} + 5xy\,\dfrac{dy}{dx} = x^2y$

4. $x^2\,\dfrac{dy}{dx} + y\left(\dfrac{dy}{dx}\right)^2 = 0$

5. $y''' - 4y'' + xy = 0$

6. $y' + x\cos x = 0$

7. $(y'')^3 - xy' + y'' = 0$

8. $y'' + e^xy = 2$

Verify that each function y = f(x) is a solution of the differential equation.

9. $\dfrac{dy}{dx} = 3$; $y = 3x - 7$

10. $\dfrac{dy}{dx} + y + 2x + 4 = x^2$; $y = x^2 - 4x$

11. $x\dfrac{dy}{dx} - 2y = 4x$; $y = x^2 - 4x$

12. $\dfrac{d^2y}{dx^2} + y = 0$; $y = 2\sin x + 3\cos x$

13. $\dfrac{dy}{dx} + y = e^{-x}$; $y = (x + 2)e^{-x}$

14. $x\dfrac{dy}{dx} = x^2 + y$; $y = x^2 + Cx$

15. $\dfrac{d^2y}{dx^2} + 16y = 0$; $y = C_1\sin 4x + C_2\cos 4x$

16. $\dfrac{d^2y}{dx^2} = 20x^3$; $y = x^5 + 3x - 2$

17. $\dfrac{dy}{dx} + y - 2\cos x = 0$; $y = \sin x + \cos x - e^{-x}$

18. $\dfrac{d^2y}{dx^2} - y + x^2 = 2$; $y = e^{-x} + x^2$

19. $\left(\dfrac{d^2y}{dx^2}\right)^2 + 4\left(\dfrac{dy}{dx}\right)^2 = 4$; $y = \sin x\cos x$

20. $\dfrac{d^2y}{dx^2} = 9y$; $y = e^{3x}$

21. $\dfrac{d^2y}{dx^2} - 5\left(\dfrac{dy}{dx}\right) + 4y = 0$; $y = e^{4x}$

22. $\dfrac{d^2y}{dx^2} + 2\left(\dfrac{dy}{dx}\right) + y = 0$; $y = e^{-x}$

23. $\dfrac{d^2y}{dx^2} + 2\left(\dfrac{dy}{dx}\right) + y = 0$; $y = xe^{-x}$

24. $\dfrac{d^2y}{dx^2} - 2\left(\dfrac{dy}{dx}\right) + y = -\dfrac{e^{-x}}{x^2}$; $y = e^x\ln x$

5.2 SEPARATION OF VARIABLES

There are numerous methods for solving ordinary differential equations. We present a few of these methods. Certain first-order differential equations can be solved most easily by using the method of separation of variables.

A first-order differential equation is an equation involving a function and its first derivative. That is, it can be written in the form

$$N(x, y)\dfrac{dy}{dx} + M(x, y) = 0 \tag{1}$$

or (by multiplying each side by the differential dx, where $dx \neq 0$)

$$M(x, y)\,dx + N(x, y)\,dy = 0 \tag{2}$$

where $M(x, y)$ and $N(x, y)$ are functions involving the variables x and y.

EXAMPLE 1

Rewrite the first-degree differential equation $x^2y' - e^{xy} = 0$ in the form of Equation (2).

$$x^2y' - e^{xy} = 0$$
$$x^2\dfrac{dy}{dx} - e^{xy} = 0$$
$$x^2\,dy - e^{xy}\,dx = 0 \quad\text{(Multiply each side by } dx.)$$
$$-e^{xy}\,dx + x^2\,dy = 0$$

In this example, $M(x, y) = -e^{xy}$ and $N(x, y) = x^2$.

Some first-degree equations in the form $M(x, y)\,dx + N(x, y)\,dy = 0$ can be rewritten in the form

$$f(x)\,dx + g(y)\,dy = 0 \tag{3}$$

where $f(x)$ is a function of x alone and $g(y)$ is a function of y alone.

EXAMPLE 2

Rewrite the first-degree differential equation $x^2yy' - 2xy^3 = 0$ in the form of Equation (3).

$$x^2yy' - 2xy^3 = 0$$

$$x^2y\frac{dy}{dx} - 2xy^3 = 0$$

$$x^2y\,dy - 2xy^3\,dx = 0 \qquad\text{(Multiply each side by } dx.)$$

$$\left(\frac{1}{x^2y^3}\right)(x^2y\,dy - 2xy^3\,dx) = (0)\left(\frac{1}{x^2y^3}\right) \qquad\text{(Divide each side by } x^2y^3.)$$

$$\frac{1}{y^2}\,dy - \frac{2}{x}\,dx = 0$$

or

$$-\frac{2}{x}\,dx + \frac{1}{y^2}\,dy = 0$$

The process demonstrated in Example 2 is called *separating the variables*. By appropriate multiplications and divisions, we separate the equation into terms such that each term involves only one variable and its corresponding differential. Because of the expression e^{xy} in Example 1, it is impossible to separate the variables.

When a first-order differential equation can be separated so that we can collect all y terms with dy and all x terms with dx, then the general solution can be obtained by integrating each term. If we separate the variables to opposite sides of the equation, the general solution of a differential equation in the form

$$f(x)\,dx = g(y)\,dy$$

is

$$\int f(x)\,dx = \int g(y)\,dy$$

$$F(x) = G(y) + C$$

where $F(x)$ is the antiderivative of $f(x)$, $G(y)$ is the antiderivative of $g(y)$, and C is the constant of integration.

EXAMPLE 3

Find the general solution of the differential equation $x^2yy' - 2xy^3 = 0$.

In Example 2 we wrote $x^2yy' - 2xy^3 = 0$ as

$$-\frac{2}{x}\,dx + \frac{1}{y^2}\,dy = 0$$

$$\frac{1}{y^2}\,dy = \frac{2}{x}\,dx$$

$$\int \frac{1}{y^2}\,dy = \int \frac{2}{x}\,dx \qquad\text{(Integrate each side of the equation.)}$$

$$-\frac{1}{y} = 2\ln x + C$$

$$y = -\frac{1}{2\ln x + C}$$

Note: When the solution of a differential equation involves integrating a term in the form $\frac{du}{u}$, we will now write $\int \frac{du}{u} = \ln u + C$ rather than $\int \frac{du}{u} = \ln |u| + C$. We now assume that the solution is valid only when u is positive. Remember also to include the constant of integration C.

EXAMPLE 4

Solve the differential equation $y' = \dfrac{y}{x^2 + 1}$.

Rewriting, we have

$$\frac{dy}{dx} = \frac{y}{x^2 + 1}$$

$$dy = \frac{y}{x^2 + 1}\, dx \qquad \text{(Multiply each side by } dx.)$$

$$\frac{dy}{y} = \frac{dx}{x^2 + 1} \qquad \left(\text{Multiply each side by } \frac{1}{y}.\right)$$

$$\int \frac{dy}{y} = \int \frac{dx}{x^2 + 1} \qquad \text{(Integrate each side.)}$$

$$\ln y = \arctan x + C$$

Using a calculator, we have

2nd 7 1/y,y)= **2nd 7** 1/(x^2+1),x,c) **ENTER**   **F3**   **alpha C**   y **2nd =** =y/(x^2+1),x,y) **ENTER**

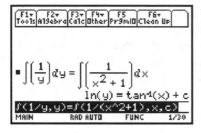 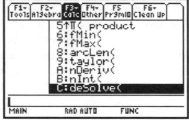

Note that if we use both sides of the implicit solution $\ln y = \arctan x + C$ as exponents for e, we get the solution shown in the last frame, that is,

$$e^{\ln y} = e^{\arctan x + C}$$

$$y = e^C \cdot e^{\arctan x}$$

$$y = C_1 e^{\arctan x}, \qquad \text{where } C_1 = e^C$$

EXAMPLE 5

Solve the differential equation $x(1 + y^2) - y(1 + x^2)y' = 0$.

Rewriting, we have

$$x(1 + y^2) - y(1 + x^2)\frac{dy}{dx} = 0$$

$$x(1 + y^2)\, dx - y(1 + x^2)\, dy = 0$$

$$\frac{x}{1 + x^2}\, dx - \frac{y}{1 + y^2}\, dy = 0 \qquad [\text{Divide each side by } (1 + y^2)(1 + x^2).]$$

$$\frac{x}{1 + x^2}\, dx = \frac{y}{1 + y^2}\, dy$$

$$\int \frac{x}{1 + x^2}\, dx = \int \frac{y}{1 + y^2}\, dy \qquad \frac{1}{2}\int \frac{1}{u}\, du = \frac{1}{2}\int \frac{1}{v}\, dv$$

$$\frac{1}{2}\ln (1 + x^2) = \frac{1}{2}\ln (1 + y^2) + C$$

$$\frac{1}{2}\ln(1+x^2) - \frac{1}{2}\ln(1+y^2) = C$$

$$\frac{1}{2}\ln\left(\frac{1+x^2}{1+y^2}\right) = C$$

$$\ln|AB| = \ln|A| + \ln|b|$$

$$\ln\left|\frac{A}{B}\right| = \ln|A| - \ln|b|$$

Since C is an arbitrary constant, we could rewrite this constant as $C = \frac{1}{2}\ln k$, where $k > 0$. Then we have

$$\frac{1}{2}\ln\left(\frac{1+x^2}{1+y^2}\right) = \frac{1}{2}\ln k$$

$$\frac{1+x^2}{1+y^2} = k$$

$$1 + x^2 = k + ky^2$$

$$x^2 - ky^2 + 1 - k = 0$$

This last equation is easier to work with since it no longer involves natural logarithms. The equations $\frac{1}{2}\ln\left(\frac{1+x^2}{1+y^2}\right) = C$ and $x^2 - ky^2 + 1 - k = 0$ are equivalent. They differ only in the form of the constant of integration. By working the exercises, you will gain experience in choosing the most appropriate form for this arbitrary constant.

EXAMPLE 6

Solve the differential equation $y' - 2x = 0$.

Rewriting, we have

$$\frac{dy}{dx} = 2x$$

$$dy = 2x\,dx$$

$$\int dy = \int 2x\,dx$$

$$y = x^2 + C$$

This general solution represents a family of functions where each function $y = f(x)$ is a particular solution of the differential equation $y' - 2x = 0$. In this case, the solution is a family of parabolas some of which are sketched in Fig. 5.1.

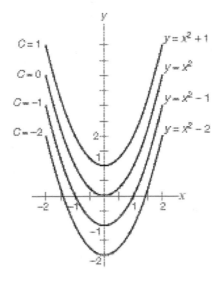

Figure 5.1 Family of parabolas $y = x^2 + C$.

A unique particular solution can be obtained if certain initial conditions are given. An *initial condition* of a differential equation is a condition that specifies a particular value of y, y_0, corresponding to a particular value of x, x_0. That is, if $y = f(x)$ is a solution of the differential equation, then the function must satisfy the condition $y_0 = f(x_0)$. A differential equation with initial conditions is called an *initial value problem*.

EXAMPLE 7

Solve the differential equation $y' - 2x = 0$ subject to the initial condition that $y = 1$ when $x = 2$.

From Example 6 the general solution is

$$y = x^2 + C$$

Substituting $y = 1$ and $x = 2$, we have

$$1 = (2)^2 + C$$
$$-3 = C$$

So, the particular solution is

$$y = x^2 - 3$$

EXAMPLE 8

Solve the differential equation $y + xy' = 0$ subject to the initial condition that $y = 2$ when $x = 3$, which may also be written $y(3) = 2$.

Rewriting, we have

$$y + x\,\frac{dy}{dx} = 0$$

$$y\,dx + x\,dy = 0$$

$$\frac{dx}{x} + \frac{dy}{y} = 0$$

$$\frac{dx}{x} = -\frac{dy}{y}$$

$$\int \frac{dx}{x} = -\int \frac{dy}{y}$$

$$\ln x = -\ln y + C$$

$$\ln x + \ln y = C$$

$$\ln xy = C$$

or

$$\ln xy = \ln k, \qquad \text{where } C = \ln k$$

$$xy = k$$

Substituting $y = 2$ when $x = 3$, we have

$$(3)(2) = k$$
$$6 = k$$

So, the required particular solution is

$$xy = 6$$

or

$$y = \frac{6}{x}$$

Exercises 5.2

Solve each differential equation.

1. $x \, dy - y^2 \, dx = 0$ **2.** $3x^3y^2 \, dx - xy \, dy = 0$ **3.** $x \, dy + y \, dx = 0$

4. $\sec x \, dy + \csc y \, dx = 0$ **5.** $\dfrac{dy}{dx} = y^{3/2}$ **6.** $(y^2 - 4)\dfrac{dy}{dx} = 1$

7. $\dfrac{dy}{dx} = x^2 + x^2y^2$ **8.** $y\dfrac{dy}{dx} = \sin x$ **9.** $x\dfrac{dy}{dx} + y = 3$

10. $\dfrac{dy}{dx} = 1 - y$ **11.** $\dfrac{dy}{dx} = \dfrac{x^2}{y}$ **12.** $\dfrac{dy}{dx} = \dfrac{xy}{x^2 + 3}$ $\longrightarrow \dfrac{dy}{y} = \dfrac{x}{x^2+3}\,dx$

13. $\dfrac{dy}{dx} + y^3 \cos x = 0$ **14.** $\dfrac{dy}{dx} - \dfrac{e^x}{y^2} = 0$ **15.** $e^{3x}\dfrac{dy}{dx} - e^x = 0$

16. $x\sqrt{1 - y^2}\, dx - 3\, dy = 0$ **17.** $(1 + x^2)\, dy - dx = 0$ **18.** $(1 + x^2)\, dy + x\, dx = 0$

19. $\dfrac{dy}{dx} = 1 + x^2 + y^2 + x^2y^2$ **20.** $\dfrac{dy}{dx} = e^{x+y}$ **21.** $y' = e^{x-y}$

22. $y' = xe^{x^2 + 2y}$ **23.** $(x + 1)y' = y^2 + 4$ **24.** $\sqrt{1 - 16y^2} = (4x^2 + 9)y'$

25. $(4xy + 12x)\, dx = (5x^2 + 5)\, dy$ **26.** $8x^3(1 - y^2) = 3y(1 + x^4)y'$

Find the particular solution of each differential equation subject to the given conditions.

27. $\dfrac{dy}{dx} = x^2y^4$; $y = 1$ when $x = 1$ **28.** $ye^{-x}\dfrac{dy}{dx} + 2 = 0$; $y = 2$ when $x = 0$

29. $\dfrac{dy}{dx} = \dfrac{2x}{y + x^2y}$; $y = 4$ when $x = 0$ **30.** $x^2 \, dy = y \, dx$; $y = 1$ when $x = 1$

31. $y\dfrac{dy}{dx} = e^x$; $y(0) = 6$ **32.** $y^2x\dfrac{dy}{dx} - 2x + 4 = 0$; $y(1) = 3$

33. $\sqrt{x} + \sqrt{y}\dfrac{dy}{dx} = 0$; $y(1) = 4$ **34.** $e^{-2y}\dfrac{dy}{dx} = x - 2$; $y(1) = 0$

35. $xy\dfrac{dy}{dx} = \ln x$; $y(1) = 0$ **36.** $\dfrac{dy}{dx} = e^{x-y}$; $y(0) = 1$

5.3 USE OF EXACT DIFFERENTIALS

Not all differential equations can be solved by separating the variables. There are some differential equations, however, that can be solved by recognizing a combination of differentials that can be integrated. For example, we recognize the left-hand side of the differential equation

$$\frac{x \, dy - y \, dx}{x^2} = 3 \, dx$$

as

$$d\left(\frac{y}{x}\right) = \frac{x \, dy - y \, dx}{x^2}$$

so we can integrate as follows:

$$\int \frac{x \, dy - y \, dx}{x^2} = \int 3 \, dx$$

$$\int d\left(\frac{y}{x}\right) = \int 3 \, dx$$

$$\frac{y}{x} = 3x + C$$

$$y = 3x^2 + Cx$$

is the general solution.

Some easily recognizable differentials are expressed below:

1. $d\left(\dfrac{x}{y}\right) = \dfrac{y \, dx - x \, dy}{y^2}$

2. $d\left(\dfrac{y}{x}\right) = \dfrac{x \, dy - y \, dx}{x^2} = -\left(\dfrac{y \, dx - x \, dy}{x^2}\right)$

3. $d\left(\arctan \dfrac{y}{x}\right) = \dfrac{x \, dy - y \, dx}{x^2 + y^2}$

4. $d\left(\arctan \dfrac{x}{y}\right) = \dfrac{y \, dx - x \, dy}{x^2 + y^2}$

5. $d(xy) = x \, dy + y \, dx$

6. $d\left(\ln \sqrt{x^2 + y^2}\right) = \dfrac{x \, dx + y \, dy}{x^2 + y^2}$

7. $d(x^2 + y^2) = 2(x \, dx + y \, dy)$

Thus, be on the lookout for the terms $x \, dy - y \, dx$, $x \, dy + y \, dx$, and $x \, dx + y \, dy$ appearing in a differential equation. It may be possible to integrate the differential equation after multiplying or dividing the equation by an appropriate expression, called the *integrating factor.*

EXAMPLE 1

Solve the differential equation

$$x \, dy - y \, dx = (x^2 + y^2) \, dy$$

Divide each side of the equation by $(x^2 + y^2)$.

$$\frac{x \, dy - y \, dx}{x^2 + y^2} = dy$$

$$d\left(\arctan \frac{y}{x}\right) = dy$$

$$\int d\left(\arctan \frac{y}{x}\right) = \int dy$$

Then

$$\arctan \frac{y}{x} = y + C$$

is the general solution.

EXAMPLE 2

Solve the differential equation

$$x \, dy + y \, dx = 3xy \, dx$$

Divide each side of the equation by xy.

$$\frac{x \, dy + y \, dx}{xy} = 3 \, dx$$

$$\frac{d(xy)}{xy} = 3 \, dx \qquad [d(xy) = x \, dy + y \, dx]$$

$$\int \frac{d(xy)}{xy} = \int 3 \, dx$$

Then

$$\ln xy = 3x + C$$

is the general solution.

EXAMPLE 3

Find the particular solution of the differential equation

$$y \, dx - x \, dy + dx = 4x^4 \, dx$$

subject to the initial condition that $y = \frac{1}{3}$ when $x = 1$.

Rewriting, we have

$$y \, dx - x \, dy = 4x^4 \, dx - dx$$

$$\frac{y \, dx - x \, dy}{x^2} = 4x^2 \, dx - \frac{dx}{x^2} \qquad \text{(Divide each side by } x^2 \text{.)}$$

$$-d\left(\frac{y}{x}\right) = 4x^2 \, dx - \frac{dx}{x^2}$$

$$-\int d\left(\frac{y}{x}\right) = \int 4x^2 \, dx - \int \frac{dx}{x^2}$$

$$-\frac{y}{x} = \frac{4x^3}{3} + \frac{1}{x} + C$$

and $y = -\frac{4}{3}x^4 - 1 - Cx$ is the general solution. Substituting $y = \frac{1}{3}$ when $x = 1$, we have

$$\left(\frac{1}{3}\right) = -\frac{4}{3}(1)^4 - 1 - C(1)$$

$$\frac{1}{3} = -\frac{4}{3} - 1 - C$$

$$-\frac{8}{3} = C$$

So,

$$y = -\frac{4}{3}x^4 + \frac{8}{3}x - 1$$

is the desired particular solution.

Exercises 5.3

Solve each differential equation.

1. $x\,dy + y\,dx = y^2\,dy$
2. $x\,dx + y\,dy = (x^2 + y^2)\,dx$
3. $x\,dy - y\,dx = 5x^2\,dy$
4. $x\,dx + y\,dy = x^3\,dx$
5. $y\,dx - x\,dy + y^2\,dx = 3\,dy$
6. $x\,dy - y\,dx = x^4\,dx + x^2y^2\,dx$
7. $x\sqrt{x^2 + y^2}\,dx - 2x\,dx = 2y\,dy$
8. $x\,dy - y\,dx + x^4y^2\,dx = 0$
9. $x\,dx + y\,dy = (x^3 + xy^2)\,dy + (x^2y + y^3)\,dx$
10. $(y + x)\,dx + (y - x)\,dy = (x^2 + y^2)\,dx$

Find the particular solution of each differential equation for the given initial conditions.

11. $x\,dy + y\,dx = 2x\,dx + 2y\,dy$ for $y = 1$ when $x = 0$
12. $y\,dx - x\,dy = y^2\,dx$ for $y = 3$ when $x = 1$
13. $x\,dy - 4\,dx = (x^3 + xy^2)\,dy + (x^2y + y^3)\,dx$ for $y = 2$ when $x = 2$
14. $x\,dy - y\,dx = x^5\,dx$ for $y = 4$ when $x = 1$

5.4 LINEAR EQUATIONS OF FIRST ORDER

A differential equation where both the unknown function $y = f(x)$ and its derivatives are of first degree is called a *linear differential equation*. A linear differential equation of first order can be written in the form

$$\frac{dy}{dx} + y\,P(x) = Q(x) \tag{1}$$

or

$$dy + y\,P(x)\,dx = Q(x)\,dx \tag{2}$$

where $P(x)$ and $Q(x)$ are functions of x.

A method has been devised for solving linear equations of first order. *An integrating factor* is an expression that, when multiplied on both sides of a differential equation, gives a differential equation that can be integrated to find its solution. We will show that $e^{\int P(x)\,dx}$ is an integrating factor for these equations. Multiplying each side of Equation (2) by $e^{\int P(x)\,dx}$, we have

$$e^{\int P(x)\,dx}\,dy + e^{\int P(x)\,dx}\,y\,P(x)\,dx = e^{\int P(x)\,dx}\,Q(x)\,dx$$

First, observe that

$$d\big(ye^{\int P(x)\,dx}\big) = y\,d\big(e^{\int P(x)\,dx}\big) + e^{\int P(x)\,dx}\,dy$$
$$= ye^{\int P(x)\,dx}\,d\left[\int P(x)\,dx\right] + e^{\int P(x)\,dx}\,dy$$
$$= ye^{\int P(x)\,dx}\,P(x)\,dx + e^{\int P(x)\,dx}\,dy$$
$$= e^{\int P(x)\,dx}\big[yP(x)\,dx + dy\big]$$
$$= e^{\int P(x)\,dx}\,Q(x)\,dx \qquad \big[\text{from Equation (2)}\big]$$

Thus,

$$d\big(ye^{\int P(x)\,dx}\big) = \big[Q(x)e^{\int P(x)\,dx}\big]\,dx$$
$$\int d\big(ye^{\int P(x)\,dx}\big) = \int \big[Q(x)e^{\int P(x)\,dx}\big]\,dx \qquad \text{(Integrate each side.)}$$

$$y e^{\int P(x)\,dx} = \int Q(x) e^{\int P(x)\,dx}\,dx$$

So $e^{\int P(x)\,dx}$ is an integrating factor. The general solution of the first-order linear differential equation

$$\frac{dy}{dx} + y\,P(x) = Q(x)$$

is

$$y e^{\int P(x)\,dx} = \int Q(x) e^{\int P(x)\,dx}\,dx$$

EXAMPLE 1

Solve $\dfrac{dy}{dx} + 2xy = 5x$.

Here, $P(x) = 2x$, $Q(x) = 5x$, and $\int P(x)\,dx = \int 2x\,dx = x^2$. We do not write a constant of integration for $\int P(x)\,dx$ because we are merely obtaining an integrating factor. The solution is

$$y e^{\int P(x)\,dx} = \int Q(x) e^{\int P(x)\,dx}\,dx$$

$$y e^{x^2} = \int 5x e^{x^2}\,dx$$

$$y e^{x^2} = \int \frac{5}{2} e^{u}\,du$$

$$y e^{x^2} = \frac{5}{2} e^{u} + C$$

$$y e^{x^2} = \frac{5}{2} e^{x^2} + C$$

$$y = \frac{5}{2} + C e^{-x^2}$$

$$\boxed{\begin{aligned}\text{let } u &= x^2 \\ du &= 2x\,dx\end{aligned}}$$

EXAMPLE 2

Solve $y' + y = e^{-x}\cos x$.

Here $P(x) = 1$, $Q(x) = e^{-x}\cos x$, and $\int P(x)\,dx = \int dx = x$. The solution is

$$y e^{\int P(x)\,dx} = \int Q(x) e^{\int P(x)\,dx}\,dx$$

$$y e^{x} = \int (e^{-x}\cos x)(e^{x})\,dx$$

$$y e^{x} = \int \cos x\,dx$$

$$y e^{x} = \sin x + C$$

$$y = e^{-x}\sin x + C e^{-x}$$

EXAMPLE 3

Solve $(2y - 6x^2)\,dx + x\,dy = 0$.

Rewriting this equation, we obtain

$$dy + \frac{2y}{x}\,dx = 6x\,dx$$

where $P(x) = \dfrac{2}{x}$, $Q(x) = 6x$, and

$$\int P(x)\, dx = \int \frac{2}{x}\, dx = 2 \ln x = \ln x^2$$

The solution is then

$$ye^{\int P(x)\, dx} = \int Q(x)e^{\int P(x)\, dx}\, dx$$

$$ye^{\ln x^2} = \int 6xe^{\ln x^2}\, dx$$

$$yx^2 = \int 6x^3\, dx \qquad (\text{since } e^{\ln x^2} = x^2)$$

$$yx^2 = \frac{3}{2}x^4 + C$$

$$y = \frac{3}{2}x^2 + \frac{C}{x^2}$$

Exercises 5.4

Solve each differential equation.

1. $\dfrac{dy}{dx} - 5y = e^{3x}$

2. $\dfrac{dy}{dx} + 3y = e^{-2x}$

3. $\dfrac{dy}{dx} + \dfrac{3y}{x} = x^3 - 2$

4. $\dfrac{dy}{dx} - \dfrac{2y}{x} = x^2 + 5$

5. $y' + 2xy = e^{3x}(3 + 2x)$

6. $y' - 3x^2 y = e^x(3x^2 - 1)$

7. $dy - 4y\, dx = x^2 e^{4x}\, dx$

8. $dy - 3x^2 y\, dx = x^2\, dx$

9. $x\, dy - 5y\, dx = (x^6 + 4x)\, dx$

10. $x\dfrac{dy}{dx} + 2y = (x^2 + 4)^3$

11. $(1 + x^2)\, dy + 2xy\, dx = 3x^2\, dx$

12. $\dfrac{dy}{dx} - y \tan x = \sin x$

13. $x^2 y' + 2xy = x^4 - 7$

14. $x^2 y' - 2xy = x^3 + 5$

15. $\dfrac{dy}{dx} + 2y = e^{-x}$

16. $(x + 1)\dfrac{dy}{dx} + 5y = 10$

17. $x\dfrac{dy}{dx} - y = 3x^2$

18. $\dfrac{dy}{dx} + \dfrac{y}{3x - 1} = 8$

19. $y' + y \cos x = \cos x$

20. $\dfrac{dy}{dx} + y \sec^2 x = \sec^2 x$

Find a particular solution of each differential equation subject to the given initial conditions.

21. $\dfrac{dy}{dx} - 3y = e^{2x}$; $y = 2$ when $x = 0$

22. $\dfrac{dy}{dx} - \dfrac{y}{x} = x^2 + 3$; $y = 3$ when $x = 1$

23. $\dfrac{dy}{dx} = \csc x - y \cot x$; $y\left(\dfrac{\pi}{2}\right) = \dfrac{3\pi}{2}$

24. $dy = (x - 3y)\, dx$; $y(0) = 1$

25. $y' = e^x - y$; $y(0) = \dfrac{3}{2}$

26. $y' + 8x^2 y = 4x^2$; $y(0) = 2$

27. $x\dfrac{dy}{dx} + y = 3$; $y(1) = -2$

28. $\dfrac{dy}{dx} - \dfrac{3y}{x - 4} = (x - 4)^2$; $y(5) = 3$

29. $xy' + y = 4x^3$; $y(2) = 3$

30. $y' + y \sin x = \sin x$; $y(\pi/2) = 3$

5.5 APPLICATIONS OF FIRST-ORDER DIFFERENTIAL EQUATIONS

Many technical problems involve first-order, first-degree differential equations. In the applications that follow, observe that certain phenomena involve a rate of change (a derivative). The presence of a derivative often leads to a differential equation that describes the physical situation in mathematical terms. We solve the differential equation, and the mathematical solution is given a physical interpretation that provides a solution to the original technical problem.

As with all mathematical applications, we create a mathematical model of a certain physical phenomenon. The mathematical model is usually an approximation. The model is only as accurate as the interpretation given the physical phenomena.

EXAMPLE 1   RADIOACTIVE DECAY

Radioactive material decays at a rate proportional to the amount present. For example, consider a certain radioactive substance for which approximately 10% of the original quantity decomposes in 25 years. Find the half-life of this radioactive material. That is, find the time that elapses for the quantity of material to decay to one-half of its original quantity.

Step 1: Set up the mathematical model.

Let Q_0 represent the original quantity present and Q the amount present at any time t in years. The mathematical model describing the observed rate of decay process is

$$\frac{dQ}{dt} = kQ$$

where k is the constant of proportionality of decay.

Step 2: Solve the differential equation.

Separate the variables:

$$dQ = kQ \, dt$$
$$\frac{dQ}{Q} = k \, dt$$

Then,

$$\int \frac{dQ}{Q} = \int k \, dt$$
$$\ln Q = kt + \ln C$$

We have the initial condition that $Q = Q_0$ when $t = 0$. So,

$$\ln Q_0 = k(0) + \ln C$$
$$\ln Q_0 = \ln C$$
$$C = Q_0$$

We then have

$$\ln Q = kt + \ln Q_0$$
$$\ln Q - \ln Q_0 = kt$$
$$\ln \frac{Q}{Q_0} = kt$$
$$\frac{Q}{Q_0} = e^{kt} \qquad \text{(Rewrite each side as a power of } e\text{.)}$$
$$Q = Q_0 e^{kt}$$

which is an expression for the amount of radioactive material present after t years, where k is the constant of proportionality of decay.

Step 3: Solve the particular problem in question.

To find t, the material's half-life, first find k. We are given that after 25 years, 10% of the material has decayed. That is, at $t = 25$ years, $Q = (1 - 0.1)Q_0 = 0.9Q_0$. Thus,

$$0.9Q_0 = Q_0e^{25k}$$

$$0.9 = e^{25k}$$

$$\ln 0.9 = 25k \qquad \text{(Take the ln of each side.)}$$

$$\frac{\ln 0.9}{25} = k$$

$$-0.00421 = k$$

Now determine the half-life. Since the **half-life** represents the time for the material to decay to half its original quantity (that is, $Q = Q_0/2$), the half-life can be determined by substituting $Q = Q_0/2$ in the equation $Q = Q_0e^{kt}$.

$$\frac{Q_0}{2} = Q_0e^{kt}$$

$$\frac{1}{2} = e^{kt}$$

$$\ln\frac{1}{2} = kt \qquad \text{(Take the ln of each side.)}$$

$$-\ln 2 = kt \qquad (\ln\tfrac{1}{2} = \ln 1 - \ln 2 = 0 - \ln 2)$$

$$\frac{-\ln 2}{k} = t \qquad \textbf{(half-life formula)}$$

$$\frac{-\ln 2}{-0.00421} = t$$

$$t = 165 \text{ years}$$

EXAMPLE 2   ELECTRIC CIRCUIT

The current i in a series circuit with constant inductance L, constant resistance R, and a constant applied voltage V is described by the differential equation

$$L\frac{di}{dt} + Ri = V$$

Find an equation for the current i as a function of time t.

Rewrite the equation as

$$\frac{di}{dt} + \frac{R}{L}i = \frac{V}{L}$$

and apply the method described in Section 5.4:

$$P(t) = \frac{R}{L} \qquad Q(t) = \frac{V}{L}$$

and

$$\int P(t)\, dt = \int \frac{R}{L}\, dt = \frac{R}{L}t$$

and

$$ie^{(R/L)t} = \int \frac{V}{L}e^{(R/L)t}\, dt$$

$$= \frac{V}{L}\int e^{(R/L)t}\, dt$$

$$= \frac{V}{L} \cdot \frac{L}{R} e^{(R/L)t} + C$$

$$= \frac{V}{R} e^{(R/L)t} + C$$

If there is no initial current, then $i = 0$ when $t = 0$. So we have

$$0 \cdot e^{(R/L)(0)} = \frac{V}{R} e^{(R/L)(0)} + C$$

$$0 = \frac{V}{R} + C$$

$$C = -\frac{V}{R}$$

Finally, we solve for i:

$$ie^{(R/L)t} = \frac{V}{R} e^{(R/L)t} - \frac{V}{R}$$

$$i = \frac{\frac{V}{R}(e^{(R/L)t} - 1)}{e^{(R/L)t}}$$

$$i = \frac{V}{R}(1 - e^{-(R/L)t})$$

This shows that V/R is a limiting value for the current i. As $t \to \infty$,

$$e^{-(R/L)t} = \frac{1}{e^{(R/L)t}} \to 0$$

and

$$i = \frac{V}{R}\left(1 - \frac{1}{e^{(R/L)t}}\right) \to \frac{V}{R}(1 - 0) = \frac{V}{R} \qquad \text{(See Fig. 5.2.)}$$

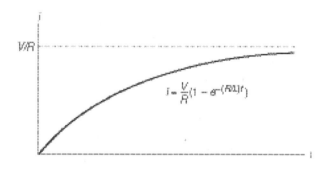

Figure 5.2 As $t \to \infty$, $i \to \dfrac{V}{R}$.

The equation for i involves two terms, V/R and $(V/L)e^{-(R/L)t}$. The limit V/R is called the *steady state solution* and represents the solution when no inductance is present ($Ri = V$); the other term, $(V/R)e^{-(R/L)t}$, represents the effect of inductance. The addition of this term gives what is called the *transient solution*. Thus, the study of this type of differential equation enables us to understand the effect of inductance in an electric circuit.

EXAMPLE 3 MIXTURES

Salt is being dissolved in a tank filled with 100 gallons (gal) of water. Originally 25 lb of salt was dissolved in the tank. Saltwater containing 1 lb of salt per gallon is poured in at the rate of

3 gal/min; the solution is kept well stirred, and the mixture is poured out at the same rate of 3 gal/min. Find an expression for the amount of salt Q in the tank at time t. How much salt remains after 1 h?

The rate of change of the amount of salt $\dfrac{dQ}{dt}$ is equal to the rate at which salt enters the tank minus the rate at which it leaves. That is,

$$\frac{dQ}{dt} = \text{rate of gain} - \text{rate of loss}$$

$$\text{rate of gain} = (1 \text{ lb/gal})(3 \text{ gal/min}) = 3 \text{ lb/min}$$

$$\text{rate of loss} = \left(\frac{Q \text{ lb}}{100 \text{ gal}}\right)(3 \text{ gal/min}) = \frac{3Q}{100} \text{ lb/min}$$

so

$$\frac{dQ}{dt} = 3 - \frac{3Q}{100}$$

$$\frac{dQ}{dt} = 3\left(1 - \frac{Q}{100}\right)$$

$$\frac{dQ}{dt} = 3\left(\frac{100 - Q}{100}\right)$$

Separating the variables, we have

$$\frac{dQ}{100 - Q} = \frac{3}{100} dt$$

or, after rewriting, we obtain

$$\int \frac{dQ}{Q - 100} = \int -\frac{3}{100} dt$$

$$\ln(Q - 100) = -\frac{3}{100}t + \ln C$$

$$\ln(Q - 100) - \ln C = -\frac{3}{100}t$$

$$\ln\left(\frac{Q - 100}{C}\right) = -\frac{3}{100}t$$

$$\frac{Q - 100}{C} = e^{-(3/100)t}$$

$$Q = Ce^{-(3/100)t} + 100$$

At $t = 0$, $Q = 25$, so

$$25 = Ce^{-(3/100)(0)} + 100$$

$$25 = C + 100$$

$$C = -75$$

So,

$$Q = -75e^{-(3/100)t} + 100$$

After 1 h = 60 min, we have

$$Q = -75e^{-(3/100)(60)} + 100$$

$$= -75e^{-1.8} + 100$$

$$= -12.4 + 100$$

$$= 87.6 \text{ lb}$$

EXAMPLE 4   TEMPERATURE CHANGE

The temperature of an object changes at a rate proportional to the difference between the temperature surrounding the object and the temperature of the object itself (Newton's law of cooling). A thermometer registering 75°F is taken outside where the temperature is 40°F. After 5 min, the thermometer registers 60°F. Find the temperature reading on the thermometer 7 min after having been outside.

Let T represent the temperature reading of the thermometer at any time t. Then,

$$\frac{dT}{dt} = k(T - T_{\text{outside}})$$

$$\frac{dT}{dt} = k(T - 40)$$

The equation is subject to the conditions $T = 75$ when $t = 0$ and $T = 60$ when $t = 5$.

Separating the variables, we obtain

$$\frac{dT}{T - 40} = k\,dt$$

$$\int \frac{dT}{T - 40} = \int k\,dt$$

$$\ln(T - 40) = kt + \ln C$$

or

$$T = Ce^{kt} + 40$$

Since $T = 75$ when $t = 0$, we can find C:

$$75 = Ce^{k(0)} + 40$$

$$75 - 40 = C$$

$$35 = C$$

So,

$$T = 35e^{kt} + 40$$

Now, determine k. Since $T = 60$ when $t = 5$, we have

$$60 = 35e^{k(5)} + 40$$

$$\frac{20}{35} = e^{5k}$$

$$\ln\frac{20}{35} = 5k$$

$$k = -0.11$$

So,

$$T = 35e^{-0.11t} + 40$$

After 7 min, we have

$$T = 35e^{(-0.11)(7)} + 40$$
$$= 35e^{-0.77} + 40$$
$$= 56°F$$

Exercises 5.5

1. Find the rate of change of velocity with respect to time of a body moving along a straight line with acceleration $a = \dfrac{dv}{dt}$. A body is moving along a straight line with constant acceleration $a = 5$ m/s^2. If the body had an initial velocity of $v = 10$ m/s (when $t = 0$), find the equation for velocity. Find the velocity at $t = 3$ s.

2. Find the equation for the velocity of an object moving along a straight line with acceleration $a = t^2$ m/s^2 if the object started moving from rest. Find the velocity at $t = 2$ s. (See Exercise 1.)

3. Find the equation of the curve passing through the point $(1, 1)$ with slope $\dfrac{x^2 - y}{x}$.

4. Find the equation of the curve passing through the point $(-1, 0)$ with slope $\dfrac{x^2}{y^3}$.

5. Find the equation for the current i in a series circuit with inductance $L = 0.1$ H, resistance $R = 80$ Ω, and voltage $V = 120$ V if the initial current $i_0 = 2$ A when $t = 0$. (See Example 2.)

6. Find the equation relating charge q in terms of time t in a series circuit containing only a resistance and a capacitance if the initial charge $q_0 = 3$ C when $t = 0$. This circuit is described by the differential equation $Ri + \dfrac{q}{C} = 0$, where $i = \dfrac{dq}{dt}$.

7. Find the equation for the current i in a series circuit with inductance $L = 1$ H, resistance $R = 4$ Ω, and voltage $V = 10 \sin 2t$ V. The initial current $i_0 = 0$ when $t = 0$.

8. Find the equation for the current i in a series circuit with inductance $L = 0.1$ H, resistance $R = 300$ Ω, and voltage $V = 120$ V. The initial current $i_0 = 0$ when $t = 0$.

9. The isotope ^{238}U of uranium has a half-life of 4.5×10^9 years. Determine the amount of ^{238}U left after t years if the initial quantity is 1 g. ^{238}U decays at a rate proportional to the amount present. (See Example 1.)

10. The isotope ^{234}U of uranium has a half-life of 2.7×10^5 years. Determine the amount of ^{234}U left after t years if the initial quantity is 2 g. ^{234}U decays at a rate proportional to the amount present.

11. A radioactive material with mass 5 g decays 10% after 36 h. The material decays at a rate proportional to the amount present. Find an equation expressing the amount of material present at any given time t. Find its half-life.

12. A radioactive material with an original mass of 10 g has a mass of 8 g after 50 years. The material decays at a rate proportional to the amount present. Find an expression for the amount of material present at any time t. Find its half-life.

13. Fifty gallons of brine originally containing 10 lb of salt is in a tank. Saltwater containing 2 lb of salt per gallon is poured in at the rate of 2 gal/min, the solution is kept well stirred, and the mixture is poured out at the same rate of 2 gal/min. Find the amount of salt remaining after 30 min. (See Example 3.)

14. One hundred gallons of brine originally containing 20 lb of salt are in a tank. Pure water is poured in at the rate of 1 gal/min, the solution is kept well stirred, and the mixture is poured out at the same rate of 1 gal/min. Find the amount of salt remaining after 1 h.

15. An object at 90°C is cooled in air, which is at 10°C. If the temperature of the object is 70°C after 5 min, find the temperature of the object after 30 min. (See Example 4.)

16. A thermometer registering 80°F is taken outside, where the temperature is 35°F. After 3 min, the thermometer registers 50°F. Find the temperature reading on the thermometer 5 min after having been outside.

17. Populations tend to have a growth rate that is proportional to the present population. That is, $y' = ky$, where y is the present population. Suppose that the population of a country has doubled in the past 20 years. Find the expected population in 80 years if the current population is 2,000,000. (*Hint:* First solve the differential equation $y' = ky$ before determining k.)

18. An amount of money earning compound interest continuously also satisfies the growth equation $y' = ky$ (see Exercise 17), where k is the rate of compound interest. Find the value of a deposit of $500 after 10 years if it is earning 5% interest compounded continuously.

19. A gas undergoing an adiabatic change (a thermodynamic process occurring without heat gain or loss) has a rate of change of pressure with respect to volume that is directly proportional to the pressure and inversely proportional to the volume. Solve the resulting differential equation and express the pressure in terms of the volume.

20. A lake contains 5×10^7 litres (L) of water. Industrial waste in the form of a chemical compound begins to be dumped into the lake at the rate of 5 L/h. A freshwater stream feeds the lake at a rate of 345 L/h. Determine how long it will take for the lake in Fig. 5.3 to become polluted if the lake is considered polluted when the water contains 0.2% of the chemical compound. (*Hint:* $Q' = 5 - 7 \times 10^{-6}Q$, where Q is the amount of the chemical compound present in the water at any time t.)

Figure 5.3

CHAPTER 5 SUMMARY

1. The *order of a differential equation* is n if n is the highest-order derivative that appears in the equation.

2. The *degree of a differential equation* is the highest power of the derivative of highest order.

3. A *solution of a differential equation* is a function $y = f(x)$ that together with its derivatives satisfies the given differential equation.

4. *Separation of variables method:* By appropriate multiplications and divisions, separate the differential equation into terms where each term involves only one variable and its differential.

5. Some easily recognizable differentials:

(a) $d\left(\dfrac{x}{y}\right) = \dfrac{y\,dx - x\,dy}{y^2}$

(b) $d\left(\dfrac{y}{x}\right) = \dfrac{x\,dy - y\,dx}{x^2} = -\left(\dfrac{y\,dx - x\,dy}{x^2}\right)$

(c) $d\left(\arctan\dfrac{y}{x}\right) = \dfrac{x\,dy - y\,dx}{x^2 + y^2}$

(d) $d\left(\arctan\dfrac{x}{y}\right) = \dfrac{y\,dx - x\,dy}{x^2 + y^2}$

(e) $d(xy) = x\,dy + y\,dx$

(f) $d\left(\ln\sqrt{x^2 + y^2}\right) = \dfrac{x\,dx + y\,dy}{x^2 + y^2}$

(g) $d(x^2 + y^2) = 2(x\,dx + y\,dy)$

6. *Linear differential equation of the first order:* a differential equation where both the unknown function $y = f(x)$ and its derivative are of first power. A method for solving such equations involves using the integrating factor $e^{\int P(x)\,dx}$. The general solution of $\dfrac{dy}{dx} + y\,P(x) = Q(x)$ is

$$ye^{\int P(x)\,dx} = \int Q(x)e^{\int P(x)\,dx}\,dx$$

CHAPTER 5 REVIEW

State the order and degree of each differential equation.

1. $\dfrac{d^2y}{dx^2} - 3x\dfrac{dy}{dx} + x^2y^3 = 0$

2. $\left(\dfrac{dy}{dx}\right)^2 - xy\dfrac{dy}{dx} = 3$

3. $(y'')^3 - 3y' + x^2y^5 = 2$

4. $\left(\dfrac{dy}{dx}\right)^2 + 3y^3 = 7$

Verify that each function $y = f(x)$ is a solution of the given differential equation.

5. $\dfrac{d^2y}{dx^2} + 3y = 3x^3;\ y = x^3 - 2x$

6. $y'' - 2y' + y = 4e^{-x};\ y = 2e^x - 3xe^x + e^{-x}$

7. $y'' + y = x^2 + 2;\ y = \sin x + x^2$

8. $\dfrac{dy}{dx} - 2y = 5x^4e^{2x};\ y = e^{2x}(x^5 - 1)$

Solve each differential equation.

9. $x^3\dfrac{dy}{dx} - y = 0$

10. $e^{2x}\dfrac{dy}{dx} - 3y = 0$

11. $(9 + x^2)y^2\,dy + x\,dx = 0$

12. $\dfrac{dy}{dx} = e^y\sec^2 x$

13. $x\,dy - y\,dx = 3x^4\,dx$

14. $\dfrac{dy}{dx} + 6x^2y = 12x^2$

15. $\dfrac{dy}{dx} - \dfrac{y}{x^2} = \dfrac{5}{x^2}$

16. $x\,dx + y\,dy - (x^2y + y^3)\,dy$

17. $x\,dy - y\,dx - (x^4 + x^2y^2)\,dx$

18. $x\,dy + y\,dx = 14x^5\,dx$

19. $dy + 3y\,dx = e^{-2x}\,dx$

20. $\dfrac{dy}{dx} - \dfrac{5y}{x} = x^3 + 7$

21. $x\,dy - 3y\,dx = (4x^3 - x^2)\,dx$

22. $\dfrac{dy}{dx} + y\cot x = \cos x$

Find a particular solution of each differential equation subject to the given initial conditions.

23. $3x^2y^3\,dx - xy\,dy = 0;\ y = -1$ when $x = -2$

24. $ye^{2x}\,dy + 3\,dx = 0;\ y = -2$ when $x = 0$

25. $x\,dy - y\,dx = x^5\,dx;\ y(1) = 1$

26. $x\,dy + y\,dx = x\ln x\,dx;\ y(1) = \frac{3}{4}$

27. $\dfrac{dy}{dx} - y = e^{5x};\ y(0) = -3$

28. $\dfrac{dy}{dx} - \dfrac{2y}{x} = x^3 - 5x;\ y(1) = 3$

29. Find the equation for the current i in a series circuit with inductance $L = 0.2$ H, resistance $R = 60\ \Omega$, and voltage $V = 120$ V if the initial current $i = 1$ A when $t = 0$.

30. The isotope ^{235}U of uranium has a half-life of 8.8×10^8 years. Determine the amount of ^{235}U left after t years if the initial quantity is 1 g. ^{235}U decays at a rate proportional to the amount present.

31. Two hundred litres of brine originally containing 5 kg of salt are in a tank. Pure water is poured in at the rate of 1 L/min, the solution is kept well stirred, and the mixture is poured out at the same rate of 1 L/min. Find the amount of salt remaining after 20 min.

32. The temperature of a block of material registers 30°C. The block is cooled in air, which is at 12°C. If the block is at 25°C after 20 min, find the temperature of the material after 45 min.

33. Find the equation of the curve passing through the point $(0, 2)$ and having slope x^2y.

34. Find the equation for the velocity of an object moving along a straight line with acceleration $a = 4t^3$ m/s^2 if the object started moving from rest. Find the velocity after $t = 3$ s.

CHAPTER **5**

SPECIAL NASA APPLICATION
Under the Sea: Carbon Dioxide Buildup*

The Scott Carpenter Space Analog Station, created in 1997, is an example of an underwater habitat that is closely related to living conditions in space. In both environments inhabitants are isolated and it is necessary to import a breathable atmosphere, food, water, and power. Underwater and space environments also require special systems for regulating and monitoring the environment, protecting occupants from heat and cold, communication, and waste removal. Finally, an underwater environment can be used to simulate weightlessness.

The Station can go to a depth of up to 27 ft due to decompression constraints. It is an ambient pressure habitat, not designed to have a cabin that is maintained at atmospheric pressure. The aquanauts breathe air that is pumped into the top of the cabin in a steady stream. This in turn pushes air out an open hatch at the bottom of the cabin and keeps the surrounding water from entering the cabin. Therefore, the pressure inside the cabin must be equal to the pressure outside the hatch.

PART A

The cabin of the Station has an approximate volume of 7000 L, into which air flows through a line from the surface at a rate of 15 ft^3/min, or 424.65 L/min. Air bubbles out through the open hatch at the bottom of the cabin at the same rate. The air flowing in has a carbon dioxide (CO_2) concentration of 0.04%. An aquanaut in the Station exhales air with a carbon dioxide concentration of 4%. This excess CO_2 must be removed before it reaches a level that is dangerous to the aquanauts, which is 20,000 parts per million or 2%. This means that 2% of 7000 L or 140 L would be dangerous to the aquanauts.

We will determine the amount of CO_2 normally present in the cabin, and then see what happens if the supply of fresh air is cut off. We will assume that all air mixes instantaneously in the cabin. This inquiry is developed through a series of questions and exercises. Try to formulate your own response before looking at the answers.

1. How many litres of CO_2 are in the air in the cabin when no aquanauts are present, assuming the air flow from the surface is constant? $[0.04\%(7000 \text{ L}) = 2.8 \text{ L}]$

*From NASA–AMATYC–NSF project Mathematics Explorations II, grant principals John S. Pazdar, Patricia L. Hirschy, and Peter A. Wursthorn; copyright Capital Community College, 2000.

2. How many litres of CO_2 are flowing into the cabin each minute?
   [0.04%(424.65) L/min = 0.17 L/min]

3. If an aquanaut breathes 16 times per minute and each breath has a volume of 0.5 L, how many litres of CO_2 are exhaled by one aquanaut each minute?
   [16(0.5)(4%) = 0.32 L/min]

4. What is the total amount of CO_2 coming into the cabin each minute, both from the air flowing in from the surface and from the breathing of the aquanaut?
   [0.17 + 0.32 = 0.49 L/min]

5. Let A = the amount of CO_2 in the cabin t minutes after an aquanaut has entered the Station. The notation $A(t)$ could also be used to emphasize that the amount is a function of time. Write an expression in terms of A for the amount of CO_2 bubbling out of the hatch at the bottom of the cabin.
   $$\left[\frac{A}{7000}(424.65)\ \text{L/min} = 0.06\,A\ \text{L/min}\right]$$

6. Use this information to write an expression for dA/dt, the rate of change in the amount of CO_2 in the cabin at time t. $[dA/dt = 0.49 - 0.06A$ where $A = 2.8$ at $t = 0]$

   Next, we solve the differential equation

   $$\frac{dA}{dt} + 0.06\,A = 0.49$$

Let

$$P(t) = 0.06 \quad \text{and} \quad Q(t) = 0.49$$

The solution is

$$Ae^{\int P(t)\,dt} = \int Q(t)e^{\int P(t)\,dt}\,dt$$

$$Ae^{0.06t} = \int 0.49e^{0.06t}\,dt$$

$$Ae^{0.06t} = \frac{0.49}{0.06}e^{0.06t} + K$$

$$A = 8.17 + Ke^{-0.06t}$$

At $t = 0, A = 2.8$, so $K = -5.37$. Thus,

$$A = 8.17 - 5.37e^{-0.06t}$$

The CO_2 reaches a limit of approximately 8.17 L, which is below the danger level of 140 L.

If three aquanauts occupy the cabin, then 3(16)(0.5)(4%) or 0.96 L of CO_2 is exhaled in 1 min. The amount of CO_2 entering the cabin per minute is then 0.96 + 0.17 or 1.13 L. The corresponding differential equation is

$$\frac{dA}{dt} = 1.13 - 0.06\,A$$

Its solution is $A = 18.8 - 16.0e^{-0.06t}$. The CO_2 level reaches a limit of approximately 18.8 L; we see that if more aquanauts are in the cabin, the CO_2 level increases.

Now consider a situation where three aquanauts occupy the cabin. Assume they leave the cabin when the level of CO_2 reaches 18 L. Air continues to be pumped through the cabin at the same rate. Let t = the time in minutes after the aquanauts depart.

7. Write and solve a differential equation involving $A(t)$, the amount of CO_2 in the cabin at time t. $[dA/dt = 0.17 - 0.06 A$. Its solution is $A = 2.8 - 15e^{-0.06t}$, which reaches a limit of approximately 2.8 L.$]$

PART B

Now look at what would happen if the supply of fresh air from the surface were stopped. Let $A(t) =$ the amount of CO_2 in the cabin and $t =$ the time in minutes after the air supply is cut off.

1. Suppose that one aquanaut has been working in the Station for several hours. What is the amount of CO_2 present? $[8.17$ L, the approximate limit to the solution of Exercise 6$]$

2. If the supply of fresh air from the surface is cut off, the air in the cabin will stop bubbling out the bottom of the cabin and the CO_2 level will rise. With the fresh air cut off, what is the amount of CO_2 entering the cabin each minute? Where does it come from? $[4\% (16)(0.5) = 0.32$ L/min from the aquanaut's breathing$]$

3. How much CO_2 is removed from the cabin? Why? [None. No air is being pushed out the bottom.]

4. Write an expression for dA/dt and solve it. What does the solution tell you? $[dA/dt = 0.32$, where $A = 8.17$ at $t = 0$. The solution is $A = 0.32t + 8.17$. Danger occurs when $A = 140$, thus there are approximately 412 min before the aquanaut is in danger.$]$

6

Second-Order Differential Equations

INTRODUCTION

In Chapter 5, we studied first-order differential equations. However, problems in mechanical vibrations, buoyancy, and electric circuits require the use of second-order differential equations, discussed in this chapter.

Objectives

- Solve homogeneous linear differential equations.
- Solve nonhomogeneous second-order linear differential equations.
- Use linear differential equations to solve application problems.
- Find Laplace transforms of functions using a table.
- Use Laplace transforms to solve linear differential equations subject to initial conditions.

6.1   HIGHER-ORDER HOMOGENEOUS DIFFERENTIAL EQUATIONS

We now consider higher-order linear differential equations, that is, equations that have derivatives of an unknown function with order higher than first order. These equations are called *linear* because they contain no powers of the unknown function and its derivatives higher than the first power. Thus, a linear differential equation of order n is represented by the form

$$a_0 \frac{d^n y}{dx^n} + a_1 \frac{d^{n-1} y}{dx^{n-1}} + \cdots + a_{n-1} \frac{dy}{dx} + a_n y = b$$

where $a_0, a_1, a_2, \ldots, a_{n-1}, a_n$, and b can be either functions of x or constants. If $b = 0$, the linear differential equation is called *homogeneous*. If $b \neq 0$, the equation is called *nonhomogeneous*.

We have already seen linear differential equations in which the coefficients of y and $\frac{dy}{dx}$ were not constants. However, in this chapter we consider only equations in which the coefficients a_i are constants.

EXAMPLE 1

The following are examples of linear differential equations with constant coefficients and with *b* constant:

$$3\frac{d^4y}{dx^4} - 2\frac{d^2y}{dx^2} + 5\frac{dy}{dx} + 3y = 7 \tag{1}$$

$$y''' + 2y'' - 5y = 2 \tag{2}$$

$$4\frac{d^5y}{dx^5} - \frac{dy}{dx} + y = 0 \tag{3}$$

$$y'' - 3y' + 2y = 0 \tag{4}$$

Equations (1) and (2) are nonhomogeneous, whereas Equations (3) and (4) are homogeneous.

We now present a method of solving homogeneous linear differential equations with constant coefficients. These equations arise in many practical situations. Although this method is applicable to equations with order higher than the second, we cover only second-order equations in the remaining sections.

We introduce a *differential operator D*, which operates on a function $y = f(x)$ as follows:

$$Dy = \frac{dy}{dx} \qquad D^2y = \frac{d^2y}{dx^2} \qquad D^3y = \frac{d^3y}{dx^3} \qquad \cdots$$

For example, if $y = 2x^3 + 5 \ln x$, then

$$Dy = D(2x^3 + 5 \ln x) = 6x^2 + \frac{5}{x}$$

and

$$D^2y = D(Dy) = D\left(6x^2 + \frac{5}{x}\right) = 12x - \frac{5}{x^2}$$

Operator *D* is an example of a linear operator. An algebraic expression in the form $ax + by$ where *a* and *b* are constants is called a *linear combination*. A *linear operator* is any process that after operating on a linear combination results in another linear combination. We thus observe that for the operator *D*, we have

$$D[a\,f(x) + b\,g(x)] = a\,D[f(x)] + b\,D[g(x)]$$

We can apply algebraic operations to linear operators. In particular, we can factor expressions involving the differential operator *D*. For example, $(D^2 - 2D - 3)y = (D - 3)(D + 1)y$, which can be used to solve differential equations. The method is explained in Example 2.

EXAMPLE 2

Solve the differential equation

$$y'' - 2y' - 3y = 0$$

Step 1: First, rewrite this equation using the differential operator *D*.

$$y'' - 2y' - 3y = D^2y - 2Dy - 3y = 0$$
$$(D^2 - 2D - 3)y = 0$$

Factor:

$$(D - 3)(D + 1)y = 0$$

Step 2: Next, let $z = (D + 1)y = Dy + y$. Note that z is a function of x and is a linear combination of the functions $\dfrac{dy}{dx}$ and y, that is,

$$z = \frac{dy}{dx} + y$$

Step 3: Then, $(D - 3)(D + 1)y = (D - 3)z = 0$. The equation $(D - 3)z = 0$ is a linear differential equation of first order which can be solved by the method of separation of variables:

$$(D - 3)z = 0$$
$$Dz - 3z = 0$$
$$\frac{dz}{dx} - 3z = 0$$
$$dz = 3z\,dx$$
$$\frac{dz}{z} = 3\,dx$$
$$\int \frac{dz}{z} = \int 3\,dx$$

$$\ln z = 3x + \ln C_1 \qquad \text{(We use } \ln C_1 \text{ instead of } C_1 \text{ as our}$$
$$\ln z - \ln C_1 = 3x \qquad\qquad \text{constant of integration to obtain a}$$
$$\qquad\qquad\qquad\qquad \text{simpler expression for } z.)$$
$$\ln \frac{z}{C_1} = 3x$$
$$\frac{z}{C_1} = e^{3x}$$
$$z = C_1 e^{3x}$$

Step 4: Now replace z by $(D + 1)y$ and obtain

$$(D + 1)y = C_1 e^{3x}$$
$$\frac{dy}{dx} + y = C_1 e^{3x}$$

which is another differential equation of first order.

Step 5: Next, solve this differential equation by the method shown in Section 5.4.

$$P(x) = 1 \qquad Q(x) = C_1 e^{3x} \qquad \int P(x)\,dx = \int dx = x$$

Then,

$$ye^x = \int (C_1 e^{3x})e^x\,dx$$
$$ye^x = \int C_1 e^{4x}\,dx$$
$$ye^x = \frac{C_1}{4}e^{4x} + C_2$$
$$y = \frac{C_1}{4}e^{3x} + C_2 e^{-x}$$

or

$$y = k_1 e^{3x} + k_2 e^{-x}$$

where

$$k_1 = C_1/4 \quad \text{and} \quad k_2 = C_2.$$

Let's consider a second, simpler method. The general solution $y = k_1e^{3x} + k_2e^{-x}$ of the differential equation $D^2y - 2Dy - 3y = 0$ in Example 2 suggests that $y = ke^{mx}$ is a particular solution of a second-order linear differential equation

$$a_0 D^2y + a_1 Dy + a_2y = 0$$

Since $Dy = D(ke^{mx}) = mke^{mx}$ and $D^2y = D[D(ke^{mx})] = D(mke^{mx}) = m^2ke^{mx}$, we can write

$$a_0 D^2y + a_1 Dy + a_2y = 0$$
$$a_0(m^2ke^{mx}) + a_1(mke^{mx}) + a_2ke^{mx} = 0$$
$$(a_0m^2 + a_1m + a_2)ke^{mx} = 0$$

Note: $ke^{mx} \neq 0$ (e^{mx} is never zero and k cannot be zero if $y \neq 0$).

Thus, $a_0m^2 + a_1m + a_2 = 0$ if $y = ke^{mx}$ is a solution.

The equation $a_0m^2 + a_1m + a_2 = 0$ is called the *auxiliary equation* (*characteristic equation*) for the differential equation

$$a_0 D^2y + a_1 Dy + a_2y = 0$$

Observe that $y = ke^{mx}$ is a solution if m satisfies the auxiliary equation $a_0m^2 + a_1m + a_2 = 0$. To find a solution of the differential equation, find the two roots m_1 and m_2 of the auxiliary equation.

EXAMPLE 3

Solve the differential equation $y'' - 2y' - 3y = 0$ by solving its auxiliary equation.

The auxiliary equation is $m^2 - 2m - 3 = 0$. Since this factors as $(m - 3)(m + 1) = 0$, the roots are $m_1 = 3$ and $m_2 = -1$. Thus,

$$y = k_1e^{m_1x} = k_1e^{3x}$$

and

$$y = k_2e^{m_2x} = k_2e^{-x}$$

are both solutions of the differential equation. Since the sum of the solutions of a homogeneous linear differential equation can also be shown to be a solution, $y = k_1e^{3x} + k_2e^{-x}$ is the general solution. Note that this is the same solution as in Example 2, as should be the case.

GENERAL SOLUTION OF A HOMOGENEOUS LINEAR DIFFERENTIAL EQUATION

1. Write the auxiliary equation for a given differential equation

$$a_0 D^2y + a_1 Dy + a_2y = 0$$

   as

$$a_0m^2 + a_1m + a_2 = 0$$

   Note that the power of m corresponds to the order of the derivative.

2. Find the two roots m_1 and m_2 of the auxiliary equation.

3. Write the general solution as

$$y = k_1e^{m_1x} + k_2e^{m_2x}$$

EXAMPLE 4

Solve the differential equation $y'' + 3y' = 0$.

Step 1: Since $D^2y + 3 Dy = 0$, the auxiliary equation is $m^2 + 3m = 0$.

Step 2: Solve for m:

$$m^2 + 3m = 0$$
$$m(m + 3) = 0$$
$$m_1 = 0 \quad \text{and} \quad m_2 = -3$$

Step 3: The general solution is

$$y = k_1 e^{m_1 x} + k_2 e^{m_2 x}$$
$$y = k_1 e^0 + k_2 e^{-3x}$$
$$y = k_1 + k_2 e^{-3x} \qquad (\text{since } e^0 = 1)$$

EXAMPLE 5

Solve the differential equation $\dfrac{d^2 y}{dx^2} - 5 \dfrac{dy}{dx} + 4y = 0$ subject to the initial conditions that

$y = -2$ and $\dfrac{dy}{dx} = 1$ when $x = 0$.

Step 1: $\quad D^2 y - 5 \, Dy + 4y = 0$
$$m^2 - 5m + 4 = 0$$

Step 2: $\quad (m - 4)(m - 1) = 0$
$$m_1 = 4 \quad \text{and} \quad m_2 = 1$$

Step 3: The general solution is

$$y = k_1 e^{m_1 x} + k_2 e^{m_2 x}$$
$$y = k_1 e^{4x} + k_2 e^x \tag{1}$$

Now find the particular solution subject to the conditions that $y = -2$ and $\dfrac{dy}{dx} = 1$ when $x = 0$. First, find $\dfrac{dy}{dx}$ from Equation (1).

$$\frac{dy}{dx} = 4k_1 e^{4x} + k_2 e^x$$

Next, substitute $y = -2$, $\dfrac{dy}{dx} = 1$, and $x = 0$ into the equations for y and $\dfrac{dy}{dx}$:

$$y = k_1 e^{4x} + k_2 e^x$$
$$-2 = k_1 e^{4(0)} + k_2 e^0$$
$$-2 = k_1 + k_2 \qquad (\text{since } e^0 = 1)$$

and

$$\frac{dy}{dx} = 4k_1 e^{4x} + k_2 e^x$$
$$1 = 4k_1 e^{4(0)} + k_2 e^0$$
$$1 = 4k_1 + k_2$$

Now, solve the resulting system of equations for k_1 and k_2:

$$-2 = k_1 + k_2$$
$$1 = 4k_1 + k_2$$

The solution of this system is $k_1 = 1$ and $k_2 = -3$. The particular solution is then

$$y = e^{4x} - 3e^x$$

Exercises 6.1

State whether each differential equation is homogeneous or nonhomogeneous. Also state the order of each equation.

1. $3y^{(4)} - 7y''' + 2y = 0$

2. $y'' - 7y' + 3y = 2$

3. $y''' - 5y' + 2y + 6 = 0$

4. $y^{(5)} - 6y''' - y = 0$

5. $4y'' - y' + 3y = 0$

6. $y''' - y' + 2 = 0$

7. $y''' - y'' - 5y = 3$

8. $y'' - 2y' = 3y$

Solve each differential equation.

9. $\dfrac{d^2y}{dx^2} - 5\dfrac{dy}{dx} - 14y = 0$

10. $\dfrac{d^2y}{dx^2} + 4\dfrac{dy}{dx} - 5y = 0$

11. $y'' - 2y' - 8y = 0$

12. $y'' - y' - 6y = 0$

13. $y'' - y = 0$

14. $y'' - 9y = 0$

15. $\dfrac{d^2y}{dx^2} - 3\dfrac{dy}{dx} = 0$

16. $\dfrac{d^2y}{dx^2} + 2\dfrac{dy}{dx} = 0$

17. $2D^2y - 13Dy + 15y = 0$

18. $3D^2y + 2Dy - 5y = 0$

19. $3\dfrac{d^2y}{dx^2} - 7\dfrac{dy}{dx} + 2y = 0$

20. $2y'' + y' - 15y = 0$

Find the particular solution of each differential equation subject to the given conditions.

21. $y'' - 4y' = 0$; $y = 3$ and $y' = 4$ when $x = 0$

22. $y'' + 3y' = 0$; $y = -1$ and $y' = 6$ when $x = 0$

23. $y'' - y' - 2y = 0$; $y = 2$ and $y' = 1$ when $x = 0$

24. $y'' + 3y' - 10y = 0$; $y = 7$ and $y' = 0$ when $x = 0$

25. $y'' - 8y' + 15y = 0$; $y = 4$ and $y' = 2$ when $x = 0$

26. $y'' + y' = 0$; $y = 2$ and $y' = 1$ when $x = 1$

6.2 REPEATED ROOTS AND COMPLEX ROOTS

When the auxiliary equation of a differential equation results in a repeated root ($m_1 = m_2 = m$), then the general solution has the following form:

> **REPEATED ROOTS**
>
> $$y = k_1 e^{mx} + k_2 x e^{mx}$$

Note that the second term includes the factor x.

EXAMPLE 1

Solve the differential equation

$$y'' - 2y' + y = 0$$

Since $D^2y - 2\,Dy + y = 0$, the auxiliary equation is

$$m^2 - 2m + 1 = 0$$
$$(m - 1)^2 = 0$$
$$m_1 = m_2 = 1$$

The general solution is

$$y = k_1e^{mx} + k_2xe^{mx}$$
$$y = k_1e^x + k_2xe^x$$
$$y = e^x(k_1 + k_2x)$$

EXAMPLE 2

Solve the differential equation $y'' + 4y' + 4y = 0$ subject to the conditions that $y = 2$ and $y' = 1$ when $x = 0$.

$$D^2y + 4\,Dy + 4y = 0$$
$$m^2 + 4m + 4 = 0$$
$$(m + 2)^2 = 0$$
$$m = -2$$

The general solution is

$$y = k_1e^{-2x} + k_2xe^{-2x}$$

Next,

$$y' = -2k_1e^{-2x} - 2k_2xe^{-2x} + k_2e^{-2x}$$

Substitute $y = 2$, $y' = 1$, and $x = 0$ in the equations for y and y':

$$y = k_1e^{-2x} + k_2xe^{-2x}$$
$$2 = k_1e^{-2(0)} + k_2(0)e^{-2(0)}$$
$$2 = k_1$$
$$y' = -2k_1e^{-2x} - 2k_2xe^{-2x} + k_2e^{-2x}$$
$$1 = -2k_1e^{-2(0)} - 2k_2(0)e^{-2(0)} + k_2e^{-2(0)}$$
$$1 = -2k_1 + k_2$$

But since $k_1 = 2$, we have

$$1 = -4 + k_2, \qquad \text{so} \quad k_2 = 5$$

The desired particular solution is then

$$y = 2e^{-2x} + 5xe^{-2x}, \qquad \text{so} \quad y = e^{-2x}(2 + 5x)$$

When the roots of the auxiliary equation of a differential equation are complex numbers, the method used in Section 6.1 still applies.

EXAMPLE 3

Solve the differential equation $y'' - y' + 2y = 0$.

Solve the auxiliary equation $m^2 - m + 2 = 0$ using the quadratic formula,

$$m = \frac{-(-1) \pm \sqrt{(-1)^2 - 4(1)(2)}}{2(1)}$$

$$= \frac{1 \pm \sqrt{1 - 8}}{2} = \frac{1 \pm \sqrt{-7}}{2} = \frac{1}{2} \pm \frac{j\sqrt{7}}{2}$$

So the general solution is

$$y = k_1 e^{[(1/2) + (j\sqrt{7}/2)]x} + k_2 e^{[(1/2) - (j\sqrt{7}/2)]x}$$

Simplify this expression as follows:

$$y = k_1 e^{x/2} e^{j(\sqrt{7}/2)x} + k_2 e^{x/2} e^{-j(\sqrt{7}/2)x}$$

$$y = e^{x/2}(k_1 e^{j(\sqrt{7}/2)x} + k_2 e^{-j(\sqrt{7}/2)x})$$

Recall that $z = re^{j\theta}$ represents the trigonometric form of a complex number. That is,

$$z = re^{j\theta} = r(\cos\theta + j\sin\theta) \qquad \text{(See Section 10.6.)}$$

or

$$e^{j\theta} = \cos\theta + j\sin\theta$$

For $\theta = \dfrac{\sqrt{7}}{2}x$,

$$e^{j(\sqrt{7}/2)x} = \cos\frac{\sqrt{7}}{2}x + j\sin\frac{\sqrt{7}}{2}x$$

and for $\theta = -\dfrac{\sqrt{7}}{2}x$,

$$e^{-j(\sqrt{7}/2)x} = \cos\left(-\frac{\sqrt{7}}{2}x\right) + j\sin\left(-\frac{\sqrt{7}}{2}x\right)$$

$$= \cos\frac{\sqrt{7}}{2}x - j\sin\frac{\sqrt{7}}{2}x$$

But then

$$k_1 e^{j(\sqrt{7}/2)x} = k_1\cos\frac{\sqrt{7}}{2}x + jk_1\sin\frac{\sqrt{7}}{2}x \qquad\qquad \textbf{(1)}$$

$$k_2 e^{-j(\sqrt{7}/2)x} = k_2\cos\frac{\sqrt{7}}{2}x - jk_2\sin\frac{\sqrt{7}}{2}x \qquad\qquad \textbf{(2)}$$

Adding Equations (1) and (2), we have

$$k_1 e^{j(\sqrt{7}/2)x} + k_2 e^{-j(\sqrt{7}/2)x} = (k_1 + k_2)\cos\frac{\sqrt{7}}{2}x + j(k_1 - k_2)\sin\frac{\sqrt{7}}{2}x$$

$$= C_1\cos\frac{\sqrt{7}}{2}x + C_2\sin\frac{\sqrt{7}}{2}x$$

where $C_1 = k_1 + k_2$ and $C_2 = j(k_1 - k_2)$.
The general solution can now be written as

$$y = e^{x/2}\left[C_1\cos\left(\frac{\sqrt{7}}{2}x\right) + C_2\sin\left(\frac{\sqrt{7}}{2}x\right)\right]$$

In general, if the auxiliary equation of a differential equation has complex roots $m = a \pm bj$, the solution of the differential equation is as follows:

COMPLEX ROOTS

$$y = e^{ax}(k_1\sin bx + k_2\cos bx)$$

where k_1 and k_2 are arbitrary constants.

EXAMPLE 4

Solve the differential equation $y'' - 2y' + 3y = 0$.
   The auxiliary equation is $m^2 - 2m + 3 - 0$. So

$$m = \frac{2 \pm \sqrt{-8}}{2} = 1 \pm j\sqrt{2}$$

Then, $a = 1$ and $b = \sqrt{2}$, and the general solution is

$$y = e^x(k_1 \sin \sqrt{2}x + k_2 \cos \sqrt{2}x)$$

EXAMPLE 5

Solve the differential equation $y'' + 9y = 0$.
   The auxiliary equation is $m^2 + 9 = 0$. So $m = \pm 3j$. Since $a = 0$ and $b = 3$, the general solution is

$$y = e^{0x}(k_1 \sin 3x + k_2 \cos 3x)$$
$$y = k_1 \sin 3x + k_2 \cos 3x$$

Exercises 6.2

Solve each differential equation.

1. $\dfrac{d^2y}{dx^2} - 4\dfrac{dy}{dx} + 4y = 0$
2. $\dfrac{d^2y}{dx^2} + 6\dfrac{dy}{dx} + 9y = 0$
3. $y'' - 4y' + 5y = 0$

4. $y'' - 2y' + 4y = 0$
5. $4y'' - 4y' + y = 0$
6. $y'' - 8y' + 16y = 0$

7. $\dfrac{d^2y}{dx^2} - 4\dfrac{dy}{dx} + 13y = 0$
8. $\dfrac{d^2y}{dx^2} + 2\dfrac{dy}{dx} + y = 0$
9. $D^2y - 10\,Dy + 25y = 0$

10. $D^2y + 12\,Dy + 36y = 0$
11. $D^2y + 9y = 0$
12. $D^2y + 16y = 0$

13. $\dfrac{d^2y}{dx^2} = 0$
14. $9\dfrac{d^2y}{dx^2} + 16y = 0$

Find the particular solution of each differential equation satisfying the given conditions.

15. $y'' - 6y' + 9y = 0$; $y = 2$ and $y' = 4$ when $x = 0$
16. $D^2y + 10\,Dy + 25y = 0$; $y = 0$ and $y' = 3$ when $x = 0$
17. $y'' + 25y = 0$; $y = 2$ and $y' = 0$ when $x = 0$
18. $y'' + 16y = 0$; $y = 1$ and $y' = -4$ when $x = 0$
19. $D^2y - 12\,Dy + 36y = 0$; $y = 1$ and $y' = 0$ when $x = 0$
20. $y'' - 6y' + 25y = 0$; $y = 0$ and $y' = 8$ when $x = 0$

6.3 NONHOMOGENEOUS EQUATIONS

Now consider the solutions of nonhomogeneous second-order linear differential equations with constant coefficients. We represent such an equation in the form

$$a_0 D^2 y + a_1 Dy + a_2 y = b$$

where $b = g(x)$ is a function of x (b may be a constant).

Obtaining a solution of a nonhomogeneous differential equation involves two basic steps. First, obtain a solution called the *complementary solution* (denoted y_c). This is the solution of the homogeneous equation obtained by substituting 0 for b, that is,

$$a_0 D^2 y + a_1 Dy + a_2 y = 0$$

Next, obtain a *particular solution* (denoted y_p) for the given nonhomogeneous equation. The general solution of the nonhomogeneous equation will then be

$$y = y_c + y_p$$

Since we have shown methods of obtaining the complementary solution y_c in Sections 6.1 and 6.2, our only problem is to determine a particular solution of a given nonhomogeneous equation. We find y_p using the *method of undetermined coefficients*.

The method relies on inspecting the expression $b = g(x)$ and determining a family of functions that contains $g(x)$ and all of its derivatives. In most applications, $g(x)$ involves polynomials, exponentials, sines, and cosines. For these functions, see Table 6.1 for finding y_p.

To show how to use Table 6.1, six examples of a differential equation and its corresponding trial solution for y_p are shown in Example 1.

TABLE 6.1 Finding y_p [a,b]

If $g(x) =$	Try $y_p =$
$b_n x^n + b_{n-1} x^{n-1} + \cdots + b_2 x^2 +$ $b_1 x + b_0$ (polynomial of degree n)	$A_n x^n + A_{n-1} x^{n-1} + \cdots + A_2 x^2 + A_1 x + A_0$
be^{nx}	Ae^{nx}
$b \sin nx$ $b \cos nx$ $b \sin nx + c \cos nx$	$A \sin nx + B \cos nx$

[a] If $g(x)$ is the sum of two or more types in the left column, try the corresponding sum in the right column.

[b] If a term of $g(x)$ is a solution of the homogeneous equation, try multiplying y_p by x or some higher power of x.

EXAMPLE 1

Find the trial solution y_p using Table 6.1 for each differential equation.

Differential equation	$g(x) =$	Try $y_p =$
(a) $y'' - 4y' - 5y - 6x^2 - 1$	$6x^2 - 1$	$Ax^2 + Bx + C$
(b) $y'' - y = 3e^{-4x}$	$3e^{-4x}$	Ae^{-4x}
(c) $y'' + 16y = 3 \sin 5x$	$3 \sin 5x$	$A \sin 5x + B \cos 5x$

Differential equation	$g(x) =$	Try $y_p =$
(d) $y'' - 9y = 2e^{3x}$	$2e^{3x}$	Axe^{3x}

Note: $2e^{3x}$ is a solution of the homogeneous equation.

(e) $y'' + y' = 6x + 4$	$6x + 4$	$x(Ax + B) = Ax^2 + Bx$

Note: 4 is a solution of the homogeneous equation.

(f) $y'' + 9y = \cos 3x$	$\cos 3x$	$Ax \sin 3x + Bx \cos 3x$

Note: $\cos 3x$ is a solution of the homogeneous equation.

The method of undetermined coefficients is illustrated in the following examples.

EXAMPLE 2

Find a particular solution of the differential equation

$$y'' - 2y' - 3y = e^x$$

Try $y_p = Ae^x$. We need to find the value of A. First, find $y'_p = Ae^x$ and $y''_p = Ae^x$. If y_p is a solution, it must satisfy the given differential equation.

$$y''_p - 2y'_p - 3y_p = e^x$$
$$Ae^x - 2Ae^x - 3Ae^x = e^x$$
$$-4Ae^x = e^x$$
$$-4A = 1$$
$$A = -\frac{1}{4}$$

Then,

$$y_p = -\frac{1}{4}e^x$$

EXAMPLE 3

Find a particular solution of the differential equation

$$y'' - 2y' - 3y = x^2 + e^{-2x}$$

Try $y_p = Ax^2 + Bx + C + De^{-2x}$, which is the sum of a second-degree polynomial and an exponential that appears in $g(x)$. To find the values of A, B, C, and D, we first find

$$y'_p = 2Ax + B - 2De^{-2x}$$

and

$$y''_p = 2A + 4De^{-2x}$$

Then, substitute into the given differential equation,

$$y''_p - 2y'_p - 3y_p = x^2 + e^{-2x}$$

Then,

$$(2A + 4De^{-2x}) - 2(2Ax + B - 2De^{-2x}) - 3(Ax^2 + Bx + C + De^{-2x}) = x^2 + e^{-2x}$$
$$(2A - 2B - 3C) + (-4A - 3B)x + (-3A)x^2 + (4D + 4D - 3D)e^{-2x} = x^2 + e^{-2x}$$

We equate the coefficients on the two sides of the last equation.

$$2A - 2B - 3C = 0 \qquad \text{(constants)} \tag{1}$$
$$-4A - 3B = 0 \qquad \text{(coefficients of } x) \tag{2}$$
$$-3A = 1 \qquad \text{(coefficients of } x^2) \tag{3}$$
$$5D = 1 \qquad \text{(coefficients of } e^{-2x}) \tag{4}$$

Solving this system of four equations, we find that

$$D = \frac{1}{5} \qquad A = -\frac{1}{3} \qquad B = \frac{4}{9} \qquad C = -\frac{14}{27}$$

The particular solution is then

$$y_p = -\frac{1}{3}x^2 + \frac{4}{9}x - \frac{14}{27} + \frac{1}{5}e^{-2x}$$

GENERAL SOLUTION OF A NONHOMOGENEOUS DIFFERENTIAL EQUATION

To find the general solution of the nonhomogeneous equation

$$a_0 D^2 y + a_1 Dy + a_2 y = b$$

1. Find the complementary solution y_c by solving the homogeneous equation $a_0 D^2 y + a_1 Dy + a_2 y = 0$ using the methods developed in Sections 6.1 and 6.2.

2. Find a particular solution y_p by using the method of undetermined coefficients described in Examples 2 and 3.

3. Find the general solution y by adding the complementary solution y_c from Step 1 and the particular solution y_p from Step 2:

$$y = y_c + y_p$$

EXAMPLE 4

Find the general solution of

$$y'' - 2y' - 3y = e^x$$

Step 1: Find the complementary solution y_c which is the solution of the homogeneous equation $y'' - 2y' - 3y = 0$. We solved this equation in Example 2, Section 6.1:

$$y_c = k_1 e^{3x} + k_2 e^{-x}$$

Step 2: Find a particular solution y_p, which we obtained in Example 2 of this section:

$$y_p = -\frac{1}{4}e^x$$

Step 3: The desired general solution is

$$y = y_c + y_p$$
$$y = k_1 e^{3x} + k_2 e^{-x} - \frac{1}{4}e^x$$

EXAMPLE 5

Find the general solution of $y'' - 2y' - 3y = x^2 + e^{-2x}$.

Step 1: From Example 4, the complementary solution is

$$y_c = k_1 e^{3x} + k_2 e^{-x}$$

Step 2: From Example 3, a particular solution is

$$y_p = -\frac{1}{3}x^2 + \frac{4}{9}x - \frac{14}{27} + \frac{1}{5}e^{-2x}$$

Step 3: The general solution is

$$y = y_c + y_p$$

$$y = k_1 e^{3x} + k_2 e^{-x} - \frac{1}{3}x^2 + \frac{4}{9}x - \frac{14}{27} + \frac{1}{5}e^{-2x}$$

EXAMPLE 6

Solve the differential equation

$$y'' + 6y' + 9y = x + \sin x$$

Step 1: Find y_c:

$$y'' + 6y' + 9y = 0$$
$$m^2 + 6m + 9 = 0$$
$$(m + 3)^2 = 0$$
$$m = -3 \qquad \text{(a repeated root)}$$
$$y_c = e^{mx}(k_1 + k_2 x)$$
$$= e^{-3x}(k_1 + k_2 x)$$

Step 2: Find y_p. Try $y_p = Ax + B + C \sin x + D \cos x$. Differentiating y_p, we have

$$y_p' = A + C \cos x - D \sin x$$
$$y_p'' = -C \sin x - D \cos x$$

Substitute y_p, y_p', and y_p'' in the given differential equation

$$y'' + 6y' + 9y = x + \sin x$$

$$(-C \sin x - D \cos x) + 6(A + C \cos x - D \sin x)$$
$$+ 9(Ax + B + C \sin x + D \cos x) = x + \sin x$$

$$(6A + 9B) + 9Ax + (-C - 6D + 9C)\sin x + (-D + 6C + 9D)\cos x = x + \sin x$$

Equating coefficients, we have

$$6A + 9B = 0$$
$$9A \qquad = 1$$
$$8C - 6D = 1$$
$$6C + 8D = 0$$

Solving for A, B, C, and D, we have

$$A = \frac{1}{9} \qquad B = -\frac{2}{27} \qquad C = \frac{2}{25} \qquad D = -\frac{3}{50}$$

The particular solution is then

$$y_p = \frac{1}{9}x - \frac{2}{27} + \frac{2}{25}\sin x - \frac{3}{50}\cos x$$

Step 3: The general solution is then

$$y = y_c + y_p$$

$$y = e^{-3x}(k_1 + k_2x) + \frac{1}{9}x - \frac{2}{27} + \frac{2}{25}\sin x - \frac{3}{50}\cos x$$

EXAMPLE 7

Solve the differential equation

$$y'' - 3y' - 4y = e^{4x}$$

Step 1: Find y_c:

$$m^2 - 3m - 4 = 0$$

$$(m - 4)(m + 1) = 0$$

$$m_1 = 4 \quad \text{and} \quad m_2 = -1$$

$$y_c = k_1e^{4x} + k_2e^{-x}$$

Step 2: Find y_p: First, note that $g(x) = e^{4x}$ is a solution of the homogeneous equation

$$y'' - 3y' - 4y = 0$$

$$16e^{4x} - 3(4e^{4x}) - 4(e^{4x}) = 0$$

Then, following note b to Table 6.1 for finding y_p, we try

$$y_p = Axe^{4x}$$

$$y_p' = 4Axe^{4x} + Ae^{4x}$$

$$y_p'' = 16Axe^{4x} + 4Ae^{4x} + 4Ae^{4x} = 16Axe^{4x} + 8Ae^{4x}$$

Substituting into the differential equation, we have

$$y'' - 3y' - 4y = e^{4x}$$

$$(16Axe^{4x} + 8Ae^{4x}) - 3(4Axe^{4x} + Ae^{4x}) - 4(Axe^{4x}) = e^{4x}$$

$$16Axe^{4x} + 8Ae^{4x} - 12Axe^{4x} - 3Ae^{4x} - 4Axe^{4x} = e^{4x}$$

$$5Ae^{4x} = e^{4x}$$

$$5A = 1$$

$$A = \frac{1}{5}$$

Step 3: The general solution is

$$y = y_c + y_p$$

$$y = k_1e^{4x} + k_2e^{-x} + \frac{1}{5}xe^{4x}$$

Exercises 6.3

Solve each differential equation.

1. $y'' + y' = \sin x$

2. $y'' + 4y = 3e^{-x}$

3. $y'' - y' - 2y = 4x$

4. $y'' - 4y' + 4y = e^x$

5. $y'' - 10y' + 25y = x$

6. $y'' - 2y' - 3y = 3x^2$

7. $y'' - y = x^2$

8. $y'' + y = e^x$

9. $y'' + 4y = e^x - 2$

10. $y'' + 4y = e^x - 2x$

11. $y'' - 3y' - 4y = 6e^x$

12. $y'' - 4y' + 3y - 20\cos x$

13. $y'' + y = 5 + \sin 3x$

14. $y'' - y' - 6y = x + \cos x$

15. $y'' - y = e^x$

16. $y'' + 6y' = 18x^2 - 6x + 3$

17. $y'' + 4y = \cos 2x$

18. $y'' - 4y = e^{-2x}$

Find the particular solution of each differential equation satisfying the given conditions.

19. $y'' + y = 10e^{2x}$; $y = 0$ and $y' = 0$ when $x = 0$

20. $y'' + y' = \sin x$; $y = 0$ and $y' = 0$ when $x = 0$

21. $y'' + y = e^x$; $y = 0$ and $y' = 3$ when $x = 0$

22. $y'' - 4y = 2 - 8x$; $y = 0$ and $y' = 5$ when $x = 0$

6.4 APPLICATIONS OF SECOND-ORDER DIFFERENTIAL EQUATIONS

Mathematical models of numerous technical applications result in second-order linear differential equations. We focus on three basic applications: mechanical vibrations, buoyancy, and electric circuits.

The force required to stretch or compress a spring obeys Hooke's law, that is, the required force $F = f(x)$ is directly proportional to the distance x that the spring is stretched or compressed:

$$f(x) = kx$$

where k is called the *spring constant*.

Another basic mechanical principle, Newton's law, states that the force F acting on a mass m at any time t is equal to the product of the mass m and the acceleration a of the mass:

$$F = ma$$

We now relate these two mechanical principles and investigate the motion of a vibrating spring. Consider a spring hanging downward with a natural length l. If a weight W is attached to the spring, the force of gravity acting on the weight will stretch the spring downward a distance s until it comes to rest (see Fig. 6.1).

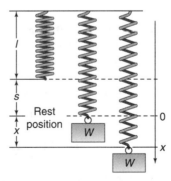

Figure 6.1

By Hooke's law the force used to stretch the spring a distance s to this rest position is

$$F = ks$$

and by Newton's law this same force is

$$F = mg$$

where m is the mass of the weight and g is the acceleration of the weight as a result of gravity (approximately 32 ft/s^2). Then,

$$mg = ks$$

If the spring is now stretched beyond the rest length $l + s$ and then released, a vibrating motion will result. When in motion, at any time t, the force F acting on the weight is

$$F = mg - k(s + x)$$

where x is the distance measured from the rest position at time t. The term mg represents the force of gravity acting downward on the weight. The term $-k(s + x)$ represents the spring tension, which is a force acting to restore the system to the rest position.

Again, by Newton's law this same force acting on the weight is given by

$$F = ma$$

$$F = m\frac{d^2x}{dt^2}$$

since $\dfrac{d^2x}{dt^2}$ is the acceleration of the weight at any time t. Then

$$m\frac{d^2x}{dt^2} = mg - k(s + x)$$

$$= mg - ks - kx$$

$$= mg - mg - kx \qquad \text{(since } mg = ks\text{)}$$

$$= -kx$$

Then,

$$m\frac{d^2x}{dt^2} + kx = 0$$

$$\frac{d^2x}{dt^2} + \frac{k}{m}x = 0$$

This is a second-order linear differential equation whose solution $x = f(t)$ describes the vibrating motion of the weight and spring. The motion described by this differential equation is called *simple harmonic motion.* Another visual example of simple harmonic motion is the motion of a simple pendulum like the pendulum of a clock.

The solution of this differential equation is obtained by using the methods of Section 6.2. The solution is

$$x = C_1 \sin \sqrt{\frac{k}{m}}\, t + C_2 \cos \sqrt{\frac{k}{m}}\, t$$

The period (time for one complete oscillation) of this simple harmonic motion is given by

$$P = \frac{2\pi}{\sqrt{\dfrac{k}{m}}}$$

since the period for $y = A \sin Bt$ and $y = A \cos Bt$ is $\dfrac{2\pi}{|B|}$.

EXAMPLE 1

Find the equation expressing the simple harmonic motion of a weight attached to a spring. A 32 lb weight stretches the spring 6 in. to a rest position. The motion is started by stretching the spring an additional 3 in. and then releasing the spring.

We have

$$m = \frac{W}{g} = \frac{32 \text{ lb}}{32 \text{ ft/s}^2} = 1 \text{ lb-s}^2/\text{ft}$$

$$k = \frac{F}{s} = \frac{32 \text{ lb}}{6 \text{ in.}} = \frac{32 \text{ lb}}{\frac{1}{2} \text{ ft}} = 64 \text{ lb/ft}$$

Then

$$x = C_1 \sin \sqrt{\frac{k}{m}} t + C_2 \cos \sqrt{\frac{k}{m}} t$$

$$x = C_1 \sin \sqrt{64} t + C_2 \cos \sqrt{64} t$$

$$x = C_1 \sin 8t + C_2 \cos 8t$$

To find constants C_1 and C_2, differentiate the preceding equation.

$$\frac{dx}{dt} = 8C_1 \cos 8t - 8C_2 \sin 8t$$

Substitute $x = 3$ in. $= 0.25$ ft and $\frac{dx}{dt} = 0$ when $t = 0$.

$$0.25 = C_1 \sin 0 + C_2 \cos 0$$

$$0 = 8C_1 \cos 0 - 8C_2 \sin 0$$

We find $C_1 = 0$ and $C_2 = 0.25$. The solution is

$$x = 0.25 \cos 8t \qquad \text{(See Fig. 12.2.)}$$

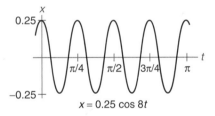

$$x = 0.25 \cos 8t$$

Figure 6.2

However, in reality, the vibrations do not continue forever. Resistant forces to the motion of vibration exist. The effect of these forces is called the *damping effect*. These resistant forces, such as friction, will cause the vibration to decrease. In many situations this force of resistance is directly proportional to the velocity of the vibrating system. That is, the damping force equals $p \frac{dx}{dt}$, where p is a constant.

The differential equation expressing the total forces acting on the system becomes

$$m \frac{d^2x}{dt^2} = -kx - p \frac{dx}{dt}$$

$$\frac{d^2x}{dt^2} + \frac{p}{m} \frac{dx}{dt} + \frac{k}{m} x = 0$$

The auxiliary equation is

$$\overline{m}^2 + \frac{p}{m}\overline{m} + \frac{k}{m}x = 0$$

(We use $\overline{m}$ in place of m in the auxiliary equation so it will not be confused with the mass m.) Solving for $\overline{m}$, we have

$$\overline{m} = \frac{-\dfrac{p}{m} \pm \sqrt{\left(\dfrac{p}{m}\right)^2 - \dfrac{4k}{m}}}{2} = -\frac{p}{2m} \pm \sqrt{\left(\frac{p}{2m}\right)^2 - \frac{k}{m}}$$

Now, let

$$d = \left(\frac{p}{2m}\right)^2 - \frac{k}{m}$$

Case 1, d > 0: There are two real roots of the auxiliary equation:

$$\overline{m}_1 = -\frac{p}{2m} + \sqrt{d}$$

$$\overline{m}_2 = -\frac{p}{2m} - \sqrt{d}$$

The solution of the differential equation is

$$x = C_1 e^{\overline{m}_1 t} + C_2 e^{\overline{m}_2 t}$$

This case is called *overdamped* (see Fig. 6.3).

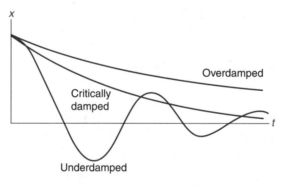

Figure 6.3   Damping effect.

Case 2, d = 0: There is a repeated real root of the auxiliary equation. The solution is

$$x = (C_1 + C_2 t)e^{\overline{m}t}, \qquad \text{where } \overline{m} = -\frac{p}{2m}$$

This case is called *critically damped*.

Case 3, d < 0: There are two complex roots of the auxiliary equation. The solution is

$$x = e^{-[p/(2m)]t}(C_1 \sin \omega t + C_2 \cos \omega t), \qquad \text{where } \omega = \sqrt{|d|}$$

This case is called *underdamped* (see Fig. 6.3).

EXAMPLE 2

Find the general equation for the motion of the vibrating spring of Example 1 if there is a resistant force that exerts a force of 0.04 lb with a velocity of 2 in./s.

Since

$$F_{\text{resistant}} = p \frac{dx}{dt}$$

we have

$$p = \frac{F_{\text{resistant}}}{\dfrac{dx}{dt}} = \frac{0.04 \text{ lb}}{2 \text{ in./s}} = \frac{0.04 \text{ lb-s}}{\frac{1}{6} \text{ ft}} = 0.24 \text{ lb-s/ft}$$

$$d = \left(\frac{p}{2m}\right)^2 - \frac{k}{m}$$

$$d = \left(\frac{0.24}{2(1)}\right)^2 - 64$$

$$d = -63.99 \quad \text{and} \quad \omega = \sqrt{|d|} = \sqrt{63.99} = 8$$

Case 3 applies and the general solution is

$$x = e^{-[p/(2m)]t}(C_1 \sin \omega t + C_2 \cos \omega t)$$
$$x = e^{-0.12t}(C_1 \sin 8t + C_2 \cos 8t) \qquad \text{(since } m = 1\text{)}$$

EXAMPLE 3

A cylindrical buoy with radius 1 ft is floating in water with the axis of the buoy vertical as in Fig. 6.4. If the buoy is pushed a small distance into the water and released, the period of vibration is found to be 4 s. Find the weight of the buoy given that the density of water is 62.4 lb/ft^3.

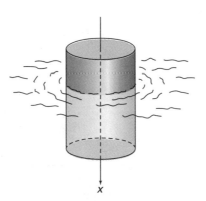

Figure 6.4

Let the origin be at the intersection of the axis of the buoy and the water when the buoy is in equilibrium. Let's choose the downward direction to be positive.

A body partly or wholly submerged in a fluid is buoyed up by a force equal to the weight of the fluid it displaces (Archimedes' principle). If the downward displacement is x, the change in submerged volume is $\pi(1)^2 x$ and the change in the buoyant force is $62.4 \, \pi(1)^2 x$. If we let W (in pounds) be the weight of the buoy, then its mass is W/g, where $g = 32.2$ ft/s^2. The equation $F = ma$ thus becomes

$$-62.4\pi x = \frac{W}{g}\frac{d^2x}{dt^2}$$

$$\frac{d^2x}{dt^2} + \frac{2009\pi}{W}x = 0$$

By the methods of Section 6.2, the solution of this differential equation is

$$x = C_1 \sin\sqrt{\frac{2009\pi}{W}}\,t + C_2 \cos\sqrt{\frac{2009\pi}{W}}\,t$$

Recall that the period is 4 s, so

$$P = \frac{2\pi}{\sqrt{\dfrac{2009\pi}{W}}} = 4$$

or

$$\frac{\pi}{2} = \sqrt{\frac{2009\pi}{W}}$$

$$\frac{\pi^2}{4} = \frac{2009\pi}{W} \qquad \text{(Square each side.)}$$

$$W = 2560 \text{ lb}$$

Electric circuits provide another example of the use of second-order linear differential equations. Kirchhoff's law states that the sum of the voltage drops across the elements of an electric circuit equals the voltage source V. If a circuit (as in Fig. 6.5) contains a capacitor C (in farads), an inductance L (in henrys), and a resistance R (in ohms), then Kirchhoff's law results in the differential equation:

$$L\frac{di}{dt} + Ri + \frac{1}{C}\int_0^t i\,dt = V$$

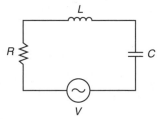

Figure 6.5 Circuit with capacitance, inductance, and resistance.

If the voltage source V is constant, then by differentiating we obtain

$$L\frac{d^2i}{dt^2} + R\frac{di}{dt} + \frac{1}{C}i = \frac{dV}{dt} = 0$$

$$\frac{d^2i}{dt^2} + \frac{R}{L}\frac{di}{dt} + \frac{1}{CL}i = 0$$

The auxiliary equation is $m^2 + \dfrac{R}{L}m + \dfrac{1}{CL} = 0$, whose roots are

$$m = \frac{-\dfrac{R}{L} \pm \sqrt{\left(\dfrac{R}{L}\right)^2 - \dfrac{4}{CL}}}{2} = -\frac{R}{2L} \pm \sqrt{\frac{R^2}{4L^2} - \frac{1}{CL}}$$

The form of the solution depends on the value of $d = \dfrac{R^2}{4L^2} - \dfrac{1}{CL}$

Case 1, $d > 0$ (overdamped):

$$i = k_1 e^{m_1 t} + k_2 e^{m_2 t}$$

where

$$m_1 = -\frac{R}{2L} + \sqrt{d} \quad \text{and} \quad m_2 = -\frac{R}{2L} - \sqrt{d}$$

Case 2, $d = 0$ (critically damped):

$$i = (k_1 + k_2 t)e^{-[R/(2L)]t}$$

Case 3, $d < 0$ (underdamped):

$$i = e^{-[R/(2L)]t}(k_1 \sin \omega t + k_2 \cos \omega t), \qquad \text{where } \omega = \sqrt{|d|}$$

EXAMPLE 4

Find an expression for the current in an electric circuit containing an inductor of 0.2 H, a capacitor of 10^{-5} F, and a resistor of 300 Ω. The voltage source is 12 V. Assume that $i = 0$ and $q = 0$ at $t = 0$.

$$d = \frac{R^2}{4L^2} - \frac{1}{CL}$$

$$d = \frac{(300)^2}{4(0.2)^2} - \frac{1}{0.2 \times 10^{-5}} = 62{,}500 > 0$$

Then, by Case 1, we have

$$-\frac{R}{2L} = -\frac{300}{2(0.2)} = -750$$

$$m_1 = -750 + \sqrt{62{,}500} = -500$$

$$m_2 = -750 - \sqrt{62{,}500} = -1000$$

The solution is then

$$i = k_1 e^{-500t} + k_2 e^{-1000t}$$

Differentiating, we have

$$\frac{di}{dt} = -500 k_1 e^{-500t} - 1000 k_2 e^{-1000t}$$

Using

$$L\frac{di}{dt} + Ri + \frac{1}{C}q = V$$

and the conditions $i = 0$ and $q = 0$ at $t = 0$, we have

$$(0.2)\frac{di}{dt} + 300(0) + \left(\frac{1}{10^{-5}}\right)(0) = 12$$

$$\frac{di}{dt} = 60$$

Then, substituting $t = 0$ in the preceding equations for i and $\dfrac{di}{dt}$, we have

$$0 = k_1 + k_2$$
$$60 = -500k_1 - 1000k_2$$

Then,

$$k_1 = 0.12$$
$$k_2 = -0.12$$

The particular solution is

$$i = 0.12e^{-500t} - 0.12e^{-1000t}$$

If the voltage source V in the electric circuit is not constant, then $\dfrac{dV}{dt}$ is not zero, and we obtain a nonhomogeneous differential equation:

$$\frac{d^2i}{dt^2} + \frac{R}{L}\frac{di}{dt} + \frac{1}{CL}i = \frac{1}{L}\frac{dV}{dt}$$

Similarly, if a force $f(t)$ external to a vibrating system of simple harmonic motion is applied (such as a periodic push or pull on the weight), then we also obtain a nonhomogeneous equation:

$$\frac{d^2x}{dt^2} + \frac{p}{m}\frac{dx}{dt} + \frac{k}{m}x = \frac{1}{m}f(t)$$

Exercises 6.4

1. A spring is stretched $\frac{1}{4}$ ft by a weight of 4 lb. If the weight is displaced a distance of 2 in. from the rest position and then released, find the equation of motion.

2. A spring is stretched 6 in. by a weight of 10 lb. If the weight is displaced a distance of 6 in. from the rest position and then released, find the equation of motion.

3. A spring is stretched 6 in. by a weight of 20 lb. A damping force exerts a force of 5 lb for a velocity of 4 in./s. If the weight is displaced from the rest position and then released, find the general equation of motion.

4. A spring is stretched 2 in. by a weight of 8 lb. A damping force exerts a force of 4 lb for a velocity of 6 in./s. If the weight is displaced from the rest position and then released, find the general equation of motion.

5. A cylindrical buoy with a radius of 1.5 ft is floating in water with the axis of the buoy vertical. When the buoy is pushed a small distance into the water and released, the period of vibration is 6 s. Find the weight of the buoy.

6. A cylindrical buoy with a radius of 2 ft is floating in water with the axis of the buoy vertical. When the buoy is pushed a small distance into the water and released, the period of vibration is 1.6 s. Find the weight of the buoy.

7. A cylindrical buoy weighing 1000 lb is floating in water with the axis of the buoy vertical. When the buoy is pushed a small distance into the water and released, the period of vibration is 2 s. Find the radius of the buoy.

8. A cylindrical buoy weighing 1600 lb is floating in water with the axis of the buoy vertical. When the buoy is pushed a small distance into the water and released, the period of vibration is 1.5 s. Find the radius of the buoy.

9. An electric circuit has an inductance $L = 0.1$ H, a resistance $R = 50\ \Omega$, a capacitance $C = 2 \times 10^{-4}$ F, and a voltage source of 12 V. Find the equation for the current i.

10. An electric circuit has an inductance $L = 0.2$ H, a resistance $R = 400\ \Omega$, a capacitance $C = 5 \times 10^{-4}$ F, and a voltage source of 12 V. Find the equation for the current i.

11. An electric circuit has an inductance $L = 0.4$ H, a resistance $R = 200\ \Omega$, and a capacitance $C = 5 \times 10^{-5}$ F. Find the equation for the current i if the voltage source is 12 V, given that $i = 0$ and $q = 0$ at $t = 0$.

12. An electric circuit has an inductance $L = 0.5$ H, a resistance $R = 1000\ \Omega$, and a capacitance $C = 5.6 \times 10^{-6}$ F. Find the equation for the current i if the voltage source is 12 V, given that $i = 0$ and $q = 0$ at $t = 0$.

6.5 THE LAPLACE TRANSFORM

The linear operator $\mathcal{L}$, called the *Laplace transform*, is very useful in solving differential equations with given initial conditions. The Laplace transform $\mathcal{L}$, like the differential operator D, operates on functions. The Laplace transform operates on a function $f(t)$ and transforms it into another function $F(s)$. That is, $\mathcal{L}[f(t)] = F(s)$. The transform is defined by means of integration:

LAPLACE TRANSFORM

$$F(s) = \mathcal{L}[f(t)] = \int_0^\infty e^{-st} f(t)\, dt$$

Note that this equation involves an integral with an infinite upper limit (∞). Such an integral is called an *improper integral*, whose value is found by a special limit process. In general, an integral of the form

$$\int_0^\infty g(t)\, dt$$

is evaluated by considering the limit of the integral $\displaystyle\int_0^b g(t)\, dt$ as $b \to \infty$ (as b takes on positive values without bound), that is,

$$\int_0^\infty g(t)\, dt = \lim_{b \to \infty} \int_0^b g(t)\, dt$$

If $G(t)$ is an antiderivative of $g(t)$, then

$$\int_0^\infty g(t)\, dt = \lim_{b \to \infty} \int_0^b g(t)\, dt$$
$$= \lim_{b \to \infty} \left[G(t) \right] \Big|_0^b$$
$$= \lim_{b \to \infty} \left[G(b) - G(0) \right]$$

We illustrate this method of integration by using examples of Laplace transforms.

EXAMPLE 1

Find the Laplace transform of the function $f(t) = e^{at}$,

$$\mathcal{L}(e^{at}) = \int_0^\infty e^{-st}(e^{at})\, dt \qquad \text{(Assume that } s > a.)$$

$$= \int_0^\infty e^{-st+at}\, dt$$

$$= \int_0^\infty e^{-(s-a)t}\, dt$$

$$= \lim_{b\to\infty} \int_0^b e^{-(s-a)t}\, dt$$

$$= \lim_{b\to\infty} \left(\frac{-e^{-(s-a)t}}{s-a} \bigg|_0^b \right)$$

$$= \lim_{b\to\infty} \left(\frac{-e^{-(s-a)b}}{s-a} - \frac{-e^0}{s-a} \right)$$

$$= \lim_{b\to\infty} \left[\frac{1}{s-a} \left(\frac{-1}{e^{(s-a)b}} + 1 \right) \right]$$

$$= \frac{1}{s-a}(0+1) \qquad \left(\frac{-1}{e^{(s-a)b}} \to 0 \text{ as } b \to \infty \right)$$

$$\mathscr{L}(e^{at}) = \frac{1}{s-a} \qquad (s > a)$$

EXAMPLE 2

Find the Laplace transform of the function $f(t) = 1$.

This is a special case of Example 1. If $a = 0, f(t) = e^{(0)t} = e^0 = 1$. Then

$$\mathscr{L}(1) = \mathscr{L}(e^{0t})$$

$$\mathscr{L}(1) = \frac{1}{s-0}$$

$$\mathscr{L}(1) = \frac{1}{s} \qquad (s > 0)$$

EXAMPLE 3

Find $\mathscr{L}(\sin kt)$.

$$\mathscr{L}(\sin kt) = \int_0^\infty e^{-st} \sin kt\, dt$$

$$= \lim_{b\to\infty} \int_0^b e^{-st} \sin kt\, dt$$

$$= \lim_{b\to\infty} \left[\frac{e^{-st}(-s \sin kt - k \cos kt)}{s^2 + k^2} \bigg|_0^b \right] \qquad \text{(Use Formula 78, Appendix B.)}$$

$$= 0 - \frac{1(0-k)}{s^2+k^2} \qquad (\text{For } s > 0, e^{-sb} \to 0 \text{ as } b \to \infty.)$$

$$\mathscr{L}(\sin kt) = \frac{k}{s^2+k^2}$$

We now develop the expression for the Laplace transform of the derivative $f'(t)$ of a function $f(t)$:

$$\mathcal{L}[f'(t)] = \int_0^\infty e^{-st} f'(t)\, dt$$

Integrating by parts, we let $u = e^{-st}$ and $dv = f'(t)\, dt$. Then,

$$\int u\, dv \qquad\qquad \int v\, du$$

$$\boxed{\begin{aligned} u &= e^{-st} \\ dv &= f'(t)\, dt \end{aligned}} \longrightarrow \boxed{\begin{aligned} du &= -se^{-st}\, dt \\ v &= f(t) \end{aligned}}$$

$$\int u\, dv = uv - \int v\, du$$

$$\mathcal{L}[f'(t)] = \int_0^\infty e^{-st} f'(t)\, dt = f(t)e^{-st}\Big|_0^\infty - \int_0^\infty - se^{-st} f(t)\, dt$$

$$= \lim_{b \to \infty}\left[\frac{f(t)}{e^{st}}\Big|_0^b\right] + s \int_0^\infty e^{-st} f(t)\, dt$$

$$= \lim_{b \to \infty}\left[\frac{f(b)}{e^{sb}} - \frac{f(0)}{e^0}\right] + s\,\mathcal{L}[f(t)]$$

$$= s\,\mathcal{L}[f(t)] - f(0) \qquad \left[\lim_{b \to \infty}\frac{f(b)}{e^{sb}} = 0\right]$$

One can show that the Laplace transform of the second derivative is given as follows:

$$\mathcal{L}[f''(t)] = s^2\,\mathcal{L}[f(t)] - s\,f(0) - f'(0)$$

One can also show that the Laplace transform is a linear operator, that is,

$$\mathcal{L}[a\,f(t) + b\,g(t)] = a\,\mathcal{L}[f(t)] + b\,\mathcal{L}[g(t)]$$

where $a\,f(t)$ represents a constant multiple of the function $f(t)$ and $b\,g(t)$ represents a constant multiple of the function $g(t)$.

Using this linearity property and the Laplace transforms for derivatives, we can obtain a Laplace transform for any linear combination of a function $y = f(t)$ and its first and second derivatives. Table 6.2 lists some commonly used Laplace transforms. A more complete table can be found in standard books of mathematical tables.

EXAMPLE 4

Express the Laplace transform for $y'' - 3y' + 2y$ in terms of $\mathcal{L}(y)$ and s, where $y = 2$ and $y' = 1$ when $t = 0$, that is, $y(0) = 2$ and $y'(0) = 1$.

$$\begin{aligned} \mathcal{L}(y'' - 3y' + 2y) &= \mathcal{L}(y'') - 3\,\mathcal{L}(y') + 2\,\mathcal{L}(y) \\ &= [s^2\,\mathcal{L}(y) - s\,y(0) - y'(0)] - 3[s\,\mathcal{L}(y) - y(0)] + 2\,\mathcal{L}(y) \\ &= [s^2\,\mathcal{L}(y) - s(2) - 1] - 3[s\,\mathcal{L}(y) - 2] + 2\,\mathcal{L}(y) \\ &= (s^2 - 3s + 2)\,\mathcal{L}(y) - 2s + 5 \end{aligned}$$

EXAMPLE 5

Find the Laplace transform of $f(t) = te^{-3t}$

Using Formula 15 in Table 6.2, we have $a = -3$ and

$$\mathcal{L}(te^{-3t}) = \frac{1}{(s + 3)^2}$$

TABLE 6.2 Laplace Transforms

$f(t) = \mathcal{L}^{-1}[F(s)]$	$\mathcal{L}[f(t)] = F(s)$
1. $a\,f(t) + b\,g(t)$	$a\,\mathcal{L}[f(t)] + b\,\mathcal{L}[g(t)]$
2. $f'(t)$	$s\,\mathcal{L}[f(t)] - f(0)$
3. $f''(t)$	$s^2\,\mathcal{L}[f(t)] - s\,f(0) - f'(0)$
4. 1	$\dfrac{1}{s}$
5. t	$\dfrac{1}{s^2}$
6. $\dfrac{t^{n-1}}{(n-1)!}$	$\dfrac{1}{s^n} \quad n = 1, 2, 3, \ldots$
7. e^{at}	$\dfrac{1}{s-a}$
8. $\sin kt$	$\dfrac{k}{s^2 + k^2}$
9. $e^{at}\sin kt$	$\dfrac{k}{(s-a)^2 + k^2}$
10. $\cos kt$	$\dfrac{s}{s^2 + k^2}$
11. $e^{at}\cos kt$	$\dfrac{s-a}{(s-a)^2 + k^2}$
12. $e^{at} - e^{bt}$	$\dfrac{a-b}{(s-a)(s-b)}$
13. $1 - e^{at}$	$\dfrac{-a}{s(s-a)}$
14. $ae^{at} - be^{bt}$	$\dfrac{s(a-b)}{(s-a)(s-b)}$
15. te^{at}	$\dfrac{1}{(s-a)^2}$
16. $\dfrac{t^{n-1}e^{at}}{(n-1)!}$	$\dfrac{1}{(s-a)^n} \quad n = 1, 2, 3, \ldots$
17. $e^{at}(1 + at)$	$\dfrac{s}{(s-a)^2}$
18. $t \sin kt$	$\dfrac{2ks}{(s^2 + k^2)^2}$
19. $t \cos kt$	$\dfrac{s^2 - k^2}{(s^2 + k^2)^2}$
20. $\sin kt - kt\cos kt$	$\dfrac{2k^3}{(s^2 + k^2)^2}$
21. $\sin kt + kt\cos kt$	$\dfrac{2ks^2}{(s^2 + k^2)^2}$
22. $1 - \cos kt$	$\dfrac{k^2}{s(s^2 + k^2)}$
23. $kt - \sin kt$	$\dfrac{k^3}{s^2(s^2 + k^2)}$

When using the method of Laplace transforms to solve differential equations, we usually need to invert a transform at the end of the process, that is, we need to find the *inverse transform*

$$\mathcal{L}^{-1}[F(s)] = f(t)$$

where the symbol $\mathcal{L}^{-1}$ denotes an inverse transform.

If $F(s)$ is a function of s and $f(t)$ is a function of t such that

$$\mathcal{L}[f(t)] = F(s)$$

then

$$\mathcal{L}^{-1}[F(s)] = f(t) \text{ is the inverse transform}$$

EXAMPLE 6

Find the inverse transform of $F(s) = \dfrac{5}{s(s + 5)}$.

Using Formula 13 in Table 6.2, we have $a = -5$ and

$$-\left\{\mathcal{L}^{-1}\left[\frac{-5}{s(s + 5)}\right]\right\} = -(1 - e^{-5t}) = -1 + e^{-5t}$$

EXAMPLE 7

Find the inverse transform of $\mathcal{L}[f(t)]$, where

$$s(s^2 + 9)\,\mathcal{L}[f(t)] - 9 = 0$$

Solving for $\mathcal{L}[f(t)]$, we have

$$\mathcal{L}[f(t)] = \frac{9}{s(s^2 + 9)} = F(s)$$

Applying Formula 22 in Table 6.2 with $k = 3$, we obtain

$$\mathcal{L}^{-1}[F(s)] = \mathcal{L}^{-1}\left[\frac{9}{s(s^2 + 9)}\right]$$

$$= 1 - \cos 3t$$

An inverse transform cannot always be found directly by using Table 6.2. Sometimes the method of completing the square or partial fractions can be used to rewrite a function $F(s)$ in a form applicable to the table.

EXAMPLE 8

Find the inverse transform of $F(s) = \dfrac{s + 1}{s^2 - 4s + 5}$.

Completing the square, we have

$$s^2 - 4s + 5 = (s^2 - 4s + 4) + 1 = (s - 2)^2 + 1$$

Then, we can write

$$F(s) = \frac{s + 1}{s^2 - 4s + 5} = \frac{(s - 2) + 3}{(s - 2)^2 + 1}$$

$$= \frac{s - 2}{(s - 2)^2 + 1} + \frac{3}{(s - 2)^2 + 1}$$

and

$$\mathcal{L}^{-1}[F(s)] = \mathcal{L}^{-1}\left[\frac{s-2}{(s-2)^2+1} + \frac{3}{(s-2)^2+1}\right]$$

$$= \mathcal{L}^{-1}\left[\frac{s-2}{(s-2)^2+1}\right] + \mathcal{L}^{-1}\left[\frac{3}{(s-2)^2+1}\right]$$

$$= e^{2t}\cos t + 3(e^{2t}\sin t)$$

where the first term is found from Formula 11 using $a = 2$ and $k = 1$ and the second term is found from Formula 9 using $a = 2$ and $k = 1$.

Exercises 6.5

1. Derive the Laplace transform for $f(t) = t$.

2. Derive the Laplace transform for $f(t) = \cos kt$.

Using Table 6.2, find the Laplace transform of each function f(t).

3. $f(t) = \sin 3t$ **4.** $f(t) = e^{5t}$ **5.** $f(t) = 1 - e^{4t}$

6. $f(t) = 1 - \cos 7t$ **7.** $f(t) = t^2$ **8.** $f(t) = te^{3t}$

9. $f(t) = \sin 2t - 2t \cos t$ **10.** $f(t) = e^{3t}\sin 5t$ **11.** $f(t) = t - e^{2t}$

12. $f(t) = t + \sin 3t$ **13.** $f(t) = t \sin 4t$ **14.** $f(t) = 6t - \sin 6t$

15. $f(t) = e^{-3t}\cos 5t$ **16.** $f(t) = t^5$ **17.** $f(t) = 8t + 4t^3$

18. $f(t) = t \sin 4t + t \cos 4t$

Express the Laplace transform of each expression with the given conditions in terms of $\mathcal{L}(y)$ and s.

19. $y'' - 3y'$; $y(0) = 0$ and $y'(0) = 0$ **20.** $y'' - y' + 2y$; $y(0) = 0$ and $y'(0) = 0$

21. $y'' + y' + y$; $y(0) = 0$ and $y'(0) = 1$ **22.** $y'' - 2y$; $y(0) = -1$ and $y'(0) = 2$

23. $y'' - 3y' + y$; $y(0) = 1$ and $y'(0) = 0$ **24.** $y'' + 4y$; $y(0) = 2$ and $y'(0) = -3$

25. $y'' + 8y' + 2y$; $y(0) = 4$ and $y'(0) = 6$ **26.** $y'' - 3y' + 6y$; $y(0) = 7$ and $y'(0) = -3$

27. $y'' - 6y'$; $y(0) = 3$ and $y'(0) = 7$ **28.** $y'' + 2y' + 3y$; $y(0) = -4$ and $y'(0) = 5$

29. $y'' + 8y' - 3y$; $y(0) = -6$ and $y'(0) = 2$ **30.** $y'' + 3y' - 2y$; $y(0) = -5$ and $y'(0) = -3$

Using Table 6.2, find the inverse transform of each function F(s).

31. $F(s) = \dfrac{1}{s}$ **32.** $F(s) = \dfrac{4}{s^2+16}$ **33.** $F(s) = \dfrac{1}{(s-5)^2}$

34. $F(s) = \dfrac{2}{s(s+2)}$ **35.** $F(s) = \dfrac{s}{s^2+64}$ **36.** $F(s) = \dfrac{1}{s^4}$

37. $F(s) = \dfrac{4}{(s-6)(s-2)}$ **38.** $F(s) = \dfrac{1}{s^2} - \dfrac{3}{(s-2)^2+9}$ **39.** $F(s) = \dfrac{2}{s^2-6s+13}$

40. $F(s) = \dfrac{1}{s^2+4s+13}$ **41.** $F(s) = \dfrac{2}{(s^2+1)^2}$ **42.** $F(s) = \dfrac{9s^2+3s+62}{(s^2+9)(s+5)}$

43. $F(s) = \dfrac{2}{(s-1)(s^2+1)}$ **44.** $F(s) = \dfrac{11s-3}{s^2-s-6}$ **45.** $F(s) = \dfrac{6s^2+42s+54}{s^3+9s^2+18s}$

46. $F(s) = \dfrac{4s^2-22s+38}{(s+1)(s-3)^2}$ **47.** $F(s) = \dfrac{s+11}{s^2+10s+29}$ **48.** $F(s) = \dfrac{3s-4}{(s+2)(s^2+s+3)}$

49. Show: $\mathcal{L}[f''(t)] = s^2\mathcal{L}[f(t)] - sf(0) - f'(0)$

6.6 SOLUTIONS BY THE METHOD OF LAPLACE TRANSFORMS

We find particular solutions y_p of linear differential equations using Laplace transforms as follows:

SOLVING LINEAR DIFFERENTIAL EQUATIONS USING LAPLACE TRANSFORMS

To solve $a_0 D^2 y + a_1 Dy + a_2 y = b$ subject to initial conditions $y(0) = c$ and $y'(0) = d$:

1. Take the Laplace transform of each side of the linear differential equation $a_0 D^2 y + a_1 Dy + a_2 y = b$. Substitute the initial values c for $y(0)$ and d for $y'(0)$ in this new equation.

2. Solve the resulting equation in Step 1 for $\mathcal{L}(y)$ to obtain an equation in the form $\mathcal{L}(y) = F(s)$.

3. Find the inverse transform of $\mathcal{L}(y) = F(s)$ from Step 2 to obtain the particular solution $y = \mathcal{L}^{-1}[F(s)]$.

EXAMPLE 1

Solve the homogeneous differential equation $y'' + 4y' + 4y = 0$ subject to the initial conditions that $y = 2$ and $y' = 1$ when $x = 0$ [write this as $y(0) = 2$ and $y'(0) = 1$].

Step 1: Take the Laplace transform of each side of the equation.

$$\mathcal{L}(y'' + 4y' + 4y) = \mathcal{L}(0)$$
$$[s^2 \mathcal{L}(y) - s\, y(0) - y'(0)] + 4[s\, \mathcal{L}(y) - y(0)] + 4\, \mathcal{L}(y) = 0$$
$$(s^2 + 4s + 4)\, \mathcal{L}(y) + (-s - 4)y(0) - y'(0) = 0$$
$$(s^2 + 4s + 4)\, \mathcal{L}(y) - (s + 4)(2) - 1 = 0$$
$$(s^2 + 4s + 4)\, \mathcal{L}(y) - 2s - 9 = 0$$

Step 2: Solve for $\mathcal{L}(y)$:

$$\mathcal{L}(y) = \frac{2s + 9}{s^2 + 4s + 4}$$

Step 3: Find the inverse transform of $\mathcal{L}(y) = F(s)$.

Although $F(s) = \dfrac{2s + 9}{s^2 + 4s + 4}$ does not appear in Table 6.2, we can rewrite $F(s)$ as follows:

$$F(s) = \frac{2s + 9}{s^2 + 4s + 4} = \frac{2s}{(s + 2)^2} + \frac{9}{(s + 2)^2}$$

Then,

$$y = \mathcal{L}^{-1}[F(s)]$$
$$= \mathcal{L}^{-1}\left[\frac{2s}{(s + 2)^2} + \frac{9}{(s + 2)^2}\right]$$
$$= 2\, \mathcal{L}^{-1}\left[\frac{s}{(s + 2)^2}\right] + 9\, \mathcal{L}^{-1}\left[\frac{1}{(s + 2)^2}\right]$$
$$= 2\left[e^{-2t}(1 - 2t)\right] + 9(te^{-2t})$$
$$= 2e^{-2t} - 4te^{-2t} + 9te^{-2t}$$

or

$$y = (2 + 5t)e^{-2t}$$

We used Formulas 15 and 17 with $a = -2$. Compare this result with the solution obtained in Example 2, Section 6.2.

EXAMPLE 2

Solve the nonhomogeneous differential equation

$$y'' + y = \sin t \quad \text{if} \quad y(0) = 1 \quad \text{and} \quad y'(0) = -1$$

Step 1: Take the Laplace transform of each side of the equation.

$$\mathcal{L}(y'' + y) = \mathcal{L}(\sin t)$$

$$\mathcal{L}(y'') + \mathcal{L}(y) = \mathcal{L}(\sin t)$$

$$s^2 \mathcal{L}(y) - s\, y(0) - y'(0) + \mathcal{L}(y) = \frac{1}{s^2 + 1}$$

$$s^2 \mathcal{L}(y) - s(1) - (-1) + \mathcal{L}(y) = \frac{1}{s^2 + 1}$$

$$(s^2 + 1)\, \mathcal{L}(y) - s + 1 = \frac{1}{s^2 + 1}$$

Step 2: Solve for $\mathcal{L}(y)$.

$$(s^2 + 1)\, \mathcal{L}(y) = \frac{1}{s^2 + 1} + s - 1$$

$$\mathcal{L}(y) = \frac{1}{(s^2 + 1)^2} + \frac{s - 1}{s^2 + 1}$$

Step 3: Find the inverse Laplace transform of $\mathcal{L}(y) = F(s)$.

$$y = \mathcal{L}^{-1}[F(s)]$$

$$= \mathcal{L}^{-1}\left[\frac{1}{(s^2 + 1)^2} + \left(\frac{s - 1}{s^2 + 1}\right)\right]$$

$$= \mathcal{L}^{-1}\left[\frac{1}{(s^2 + 1)^2}\right] + \mathcal{L}^{-1}\left(\frac{s - 1}{s^2 + 1}\right)$$

$$= \mathcal{L}^{-1}\left[\frac{1}{(s^2 + 1)^2}\right] + \mathcal{L}^{-1}\left(\frac{s}{s^2 + 1} - \frac{1}{s^2 + 1}\right)$$

$$= \mathcal{L}^{-1}\left[\frac{1}{(s^2 + 1)^2}\right] + \mathcal{L}^{-1}\left(\frac{s}{s^2 + 1}\right) - \mathcal{L}^{-1}\left(\frac{1}{s^2 + 1}\right)$$

Since

$$\mathcal{L}^{-1}\left[\frac{1}{(s^2 + 1)^2}\right] = \frac{1}{2}(\sin t - t \cos t) \qquad \text{(Formula 20 with } k = 1\text{)}$$

$$\mathcal{L}^{-1}\left(\frac{s}{s^2 + 1}\right) = \cos t \qquad \text{(Formula 10 with } k = 1\text{)}$$

$$\mathcal{L}^{-1}\left(\frac{s}{s^2 + 1}\right) = \sin t \qquad \text{(Formula 8 with } k = 1\text{)}$$

we have

$$y = \frac{1}{2}(\sin t - t \cos t) + \cos t - \sin t$$

$$y = -\frac{1}{2}\sin t + \left(1 - \frac{t}{2}\right)\cos t$$

EXAMPLE 3

Solve the differential equation $y'' + 4y' - 5y = 0$ with $y(0) = 1$ and $y'(0) = -4$.

Step 1: Take the Laplace transform of each side of the equation.

$$\mathcal{L}(y'' + 4y' - 5y) = \mathcal{L}(0)$$

$$[s^2\,\mathcal{L}(y) - s\,y(0) - y'(0)] + 4[s\,\mathcal{L}(y) - y(0)] - 5\,\mathcal{L}(y) = 0$$

$$(s^2 + 4s - 5)\,\mathcal{L}(y) + (-s - 4)y(0) - y'(0) = 0$$

$$(s^2 + 4s - 5)\,\mathcal{L}(y) - (s + 4)(1) - (-4) = 0$$

$$(s^2 + 4s - 5)\,\mathcal{L}(y) - s = 0$$

Step 2: Solve for $\mathcal{L}(y)$.

$$(s^2 + 4s - 5)\,\mathcal{L}(y) = s$$

$$\mathcal{L}(y) = \frac{s}{s^2 + 4s - 5}$$

Step 3: Find the inverse Laplace transform of $\mathcal{L}(y) = F(s)$. $F(s) = \dfrac{s}{s^2 + 4s - 5}$ does not appear in Table 6.2. However, using partial fractions, we express $F(s)$ as a sum of two fractions:

$$\frac{s}{s^2 + 4s - 5} = \frac{s}{(s + 5)(s - 1)}$$

$$= \frac{A}{s + 5} + \frac{B}{s - 1}$$

$$= \frac{A(s - 1)}{(s + 5)(s - 1)} + \frac{B(s + 5)}{(s + 5)(s - 1)}$$

$$= \frac{As - A + Bs + 5B}{(s + 5)(s - 1)}$$

$$= \frac{(A + B)s + (-A + 5B)}{(s + 5)(s - 1)}$$

Setting

$$A + B = 1$$

$$-A + 5B = 0$$

we solve for A and B and find $A = \frac{5}{6}$ and $B = \frac{1}{6}$.
Then,

$$y = \mathcal{L}^{-1}[F(s)]$$

$$= \mathcal{L}^{-1}\left(\frac{s}{s^2 + 4s - 5}\right)$$

$$= \mathcal{L}^{-1}\left[\left(\frac{\frac{5}{6}}{s + 5}\right) + \left(\frac{\frac{1}{6}}{s - 1}\right)\right]$$

$$= \frac{5}{6}\,\mathcal{L}^{-1}\left(\frac{1}{s + 5}\right) + \frac{1}{6}\,\mathcal{L}^{-1}\left(\frac{1}{s - 1}\right)$$

or

$$y = \frac{5}{6}e^{-5t} + \frac{1}{6}e^t \qquad \text{(Formula 7 with } a = -5 \text{ and } a = 1\text{)}$$

EXAMPLE 4

Use Laplace transforms to find an expression for the current in an *RL* circuit containing an inductor of 0.1 H and a resistor of 8 Ω if the voltage source is 12 V and $i = 2$ A at $t = 0$.

By Kirchhoff's law,

$$L\frac{di}{dt} + Ri = V$$

$$0.1\frac{di}{dt} + 8i = 12$$

$$\frac{di}{dt} + 80i = 120$$

$$\mathscr{L}\left(\frac{di}{dt} + 80i\right) = \mathscr{L}(120) \qquad \text{(Transform both sides.)}$$

$$s\mathscr{L}(i) - 2 + 80\mathscr{L}(i) = \frac{120}{s} \qquad (i = 2 \text{ when } t = 0)$$

$$(s + 80)\mathscr{L}(i) = \frac{120}{s} + 2$$

$$\mathscr{L}(i) = \frac{120 + 2s}{s(s + 80)}$$

$$\mathscr{L}(i) = \frac{1.5}{s} + \frac{0.5}{s + 80} \qquad \text{(partial fractions)}$$

$$i = 1.5 + 0.5e^{-80t} \qquad \text{(Formula 4; Formula 7 with } k = -80\text{)}$$

EXAMPLE 5

Use Laplace transforms to find an expression for the current in an electric circuit containing an inductor of 0.2 H, a capacitor of 10^{-5} F, and a resistor of 300 Ω. The voltage source is a 12-V battery. Assume that $i = 0$ and $q = 0$ at $t = 0$.

By Kirchhoff's law,

$$L\frac{di}{dt} + Ri + \frac{1}{C}q = V$$

$$0.2\frac{di}{dt} + 300i + \frac{1}{10^{-5}}q = 12 \qquad \text{(1)}$$

$$0.2\frac{di}{dt} + 300(0) + \frac{1}{10^{-5}}(0) = 12 \qquad (i = 0 \text{ and } q = 0 \text{ when } t = 0)$$

$$\frac{di}{dt} = 60 \qquad \text{(when } t = 0\text{)}$$

$$0.2\frac{d^2i}{dt^2} + 300\frac{di}{dt} + \frac{1}{10^{-5}}i = 0 \qquad \text{[Differentiate both sides of Equation (1) with respect to } t.]$$

$$\frac{d^2i}{dt^2} + 1500\frac{di}{dt} + 500,000\,i = 0 \qquad \text{(Multiply both sides by 5.)}$$

$$\mathscr{L}\left(\frac{d^2i}{dt^2} + 1500\frac{di}{dt} + 500,000\,i\right) = \mathscr{L}(0) \qquad \text{(Transform both sides.)}$$

$$s^2\mathscr{L}(i) - 0s - 60 + 1500\,s\mathscr{L}(i) - 0 + 500,000\,\mathscr{L}(i) = 0 \qquad \left(i = 0 \text{ and } \frac{di}{dt} = 60 \text{ when } t = 0.\right)$$

$$(s^2 + 1500s + 500,000)\mathscr{L}(i) = 60$$

$$\mathscr{L}(i) = \frac{60}{(s + 1000)(s + 500)}$$

$$\mathscr{L}(i) = \frac{-0.12}{s + 1000} + \frac{0.12}{s + 500} \qquad \text{(partial fractions)}$$

$$i = -0.12e^{-1000t} + 0.12e^{-500t} \qquad \text{(Formula 7 with } a = -1000 \text{ and}$$
$$a = -500)$$

For comparison, see Example 4 of Section 6.4, where this same problem is solved by classical methods.

Exercises 6.6

Solve each differential equation subject to the given conditions by using Laplace transforms.

1. $y' - y = 0; y(0) = 2$ 2. $y' + 3y = 0; y(0) = -1$

3. $4y' + 3y = 0; y(0) = 1$ 4. $y' - 2y = 0; y(0) = 5$

5. $y' - 7y = e^t; y(0) = 5$ 6. $y' + 2y = 3; y(0) = 0$

7. $y'' + y = 0; y(0) = 1$ and $y'(0) = 0$ 8. $y'' + 3y = 0; y(0) = 2$ and $y'(0) = 5$

9. $y'' - 2y' = 0; y(0) = 1$ and $y'(0) = -1$ 10. $y'' + 3y' = 0; y(0) = 0$ and $y'(0) = 2$

11. $y'' + 2y' + y = 0; y(0) = 1$ and $y'(0) = 0$ 12. $y'' - 6y' + 9y = 0; y(0) = 1$ and $y'(0) = 2$

13. $y'' - 4y' + 4y = te^{2t}; y(0) = 0$ and $y'(0) = 0$

14. $y'' + 10y' + 25y = e^{-5t}; y(0) = 0$ and $y'(0) = 0$

15. $y'' + 2y' + y = 3te^{-t}; y(0) = 4$ and $y'(0) = 2$

16. $y'' - 6y' + 9y = e^{3t}; y(0) = 1$ and $y'(0) = 2$

17. $y'' + 3y' - 4y = 0; y(0) = 1$ and $y'(0) = -2$

18. $y'' - y' - 2y = 0; y(0) = 2$ and $y'(0) = 3$

19. Find the equation for the current i in an RL circuit with inductance $L = 0.2$ H, resistance $R = 20 \ \Omega$, and voltage $V = 12$ V if $i = 3$ at $t = 0$.

20. Find the equation for the current i in an RL circuit with inductance $L = 0.1$ H, resistance $R = 300 \ \Omega$, and voltage $V = 120$ V if $i = 0$ at $t = 0$.

21. Find the equation for the current i in an RLC circuit with inductance $L = 0.1$ H, resistance $R = 45 \ \Omega$, capacitance $C = 2 \times 10^{-4}$ F, and voltage $V = 12$ V if $i = 0$ and $q = 0$ at $t = 0$.

CHAPTER 6 SUMMARY

1. A linear differential equation of order n is represented by the form

$$a_0 \frac{d^n y}{dx^n} + a_1 \frac{d^{n-1}y}{dx^{n-1}} + \cdots + a_{n-1} \frac{dy}{dx} + a_n y = b$$

where $a_0, a_1, a_2, \ldots, a_{n-1}, a_n$, and b can be either functions of x or constants. If $b = 0$, the linear differential equation is called *homogeneous*. If $b \neq 0$, the equation is called *nonhomogeneous*.

2. *Differential operator D operates on a function* $y = f(x)$ *as follows:*

$$Dy = \frac{dy}{dx} \qquad D^2 y = \frac{d^2 y}{dx^2} \qquad D^3 y = \frac{d^3 y}{dx^3} \qquad \cdots$$

Operator D is an example of a linear operator. An algebraic expression in the form $ax + by$ where a and b are constants is called a *linear combination*. A *linear operator* is any process which after operating on a linear combination results in another linear combination. For the linear operator D, we have

$$D[a f(x) + b g(x)] = a D[f(x)] + b D[g(x)]$$

We are able to apply algebraic operations to linear operators.

3. The equation $a_0 m^2 + a_1 m + a_2 = 0$ is called the *auxiliary equation (characteristic equation)* for the differential equation

$$a_0 D^2 y + a_1 Dy + a_2 y = 0$$

Observe that $y = ke^{mx}$ will be a solution if m satisfies the auxiliary equation $a_0 m^2 + a_1 m + a_2 = 0$. The problem of determining a solution of the differential equation is now a problem of finding the two roots m_1 and m_2 of the auxiliary equation.

The method may be summarized as follows:

(a) Write the auxiliary equation for a given differential equation:

$$a_0 D^2 y + a_1 Dy + a_2 y = 0$$
$$a_0 m^2 + a_1 m + a_2 = 0$$

(b) Determine the two roots m_1 and m_2 of the auxiliary equation.
(c) Write the general solution as

$$y = k_1 e^{m_1 x} + k_2 e^{m_2 x}$$

4. When the auxiliary equation of a differential equation results in a *repeated root* $(m_1 = m_2 = m)$, then the general solution is in the form

$$y = k_1 e^{mx} + k_2 x e^{mx}$$

Note carefully that the second term includes the factor x.

5. If the auxiliary equation of a differential equation has *complex roots* in the form $m = a \pm bj$, then the solution of the differential equation is

$$y = e^{ax}(k_1 \sin bx + k_2 \cos bx)$$

where k_1 and k_2 are arbitrary constants.

6. To find the *general solution of the nonhomogeneous equation*

$$a_0 D^2 y + a_1 Dy + a_2 y = b$$

(a) Find the complementary solution y_c by solving the homogeneous equation $a_0 D^2 y + a_1 Dy + a_2 y = 0$ using the methods summarized in items 3 through 5 above.
(b) Find a particular solution y_p by using the method of undetermined coefficients.
(c) Find the general solution y by adding the complementary solution y_c from Step (a) and the particular solution y_p from Step (b):

$$y = y_c + y_p$$

7. The *Laplace transform* $\mathcal{L}$, like the differential operator D, operates on functions. The Laplace transform operates on a function $f(t)$ and transforms it into another function $F(s)$, that is, $\mathcal{L}[f(t)] = F(s)$. The transform is defined by means of integration:

$$F(s) = \mathcal{L}[f(t)] = \int_0^\infty e^{-st} f(t)\, dt$$

8. The *particular solution* y_p of a linear differential equation $a_0D^2y + a_1Dy + a_2y = b$ subject to given initial conditions $y(0) = c$ and $y'(0) - d$ can be found by using Laplace transforms as follows:

(a) Take the Laplace transform of each side of the linear differential equation $a_0D^2y + a_1Dy + a_2y = b$. Substitute the initial values c for $y(0)$ and d for $y'(0)$ in this new equation.

(b) Solve the resulting equation in Step (a) for $\mathcal{L}(y)$ to obtain an equation in the form $\mathcal{L}(y) = F(s)$.

(c) Find the inverse transform of $\mathcal{L}(y) = F(s)$ from Step (b) to obtain the particular solution $y = \mathcal{L}^{-1}[F(s)]$.

CHAPTER 6 REVIEW

State whether each differential equation is homogeneous or nonhomogeneous. Also state the order of each equation.

1. $2y'' + y' - 7y = 0$
2. $\dfrac{d^2y}{dx^2} - 7y = 8$

3. $\dfrac{dy}{dx} - 3y - 5 = 0$
4. $y''' - y'' + y = 0$

Solve each differential equation.

5. $\dfrac{d^2y}{dx^2} + 4\dfrac{dy}{dx} - 5y = 0$ 6. $\dfrac{d^2y}{dx^2} - 5\dfrac{dy}{dx} + 6y = 0$ 7. $y'' - 6y' = 0$

8. $2y'' - y' - 3y = 0$ 9. $y'' - 6y' + 9y = 0$ 10. $D^2y + 10\,Dy + 25y = 0$

11. $D^2y - 2\,Dy + y = 0$ 12. $9\,D^2y - 6\,Dy + y = 0$ 13. $y'' + 16y = 0$

14. $4\,D^2y + 25y = 0$ 15. $D^2y - 2\,Dy + 3y = 0$ 16. $y'' - 3y' + 8y = 0$

17. $D^2y + Dy - 2y = x$ 18. $y'' - 6y' + 9y = e^x$ 19. $y'' + 4y = \cos x$

20. $y'' - 2y' + 3y = 6e^{2x}$

Find the particular solution of each differential equation satisfying the given conditions.

21. $\dfrac{d^2y}{dx^2} + 2\dfrac{dy}{dx} - 8y = 0$; $y = 6$ and $y' = 0$ when $x = 0$

22. $D^2y - 3\,Dy = 0$; $y = 3$ and $y' = 6$ when $x = 0$

23. $D^2y - 4\,Dy + 4y = 0$; $y = 0$ and $y' = 3$ when $x = 0$

24. $y'' + 6y' + 9y = 0$; $y = 8$ and $y' = 0$ when $x = 0$

25. $y'' + 4y = 0$; $y = 1$ and $y' = -4$ when $x = 0$

26. $D^2y - 8\,Dy + 25y = 0$; $y = 2$ and $y' = 11$ when $x = 0$

27. $y'' - y' = e^{2x}$; $y = 1$ and $y' = 0$ when $x = 0$

28. $D^2y + 4y = \sin x$; $y = 2$ and $y' = \frac{7}{3}$ when $x = 0$

29. A spring is stretched 4 in. by a weight of 16 lb. If the weight is displaced a distance of 6 in. from the rest position and then released, determine the equation of motion.

30. A spring is stretched 2 in. by a weight of 12 lb. A damping force exerts a force of 8 lb for a velocity of 4 in./s. If the weight is displaced from the rest position and then released, determine the equation of motion.

31. An electric circuit has an inductance $L = 2$ H, a resistance $R = 400\ \Omega$, a capacitance $C = 10^{-5}$ F, and a voltage source of 12 V. Find the equation for the current i.

32. An electric circuit has an inductance $L = 1$ H, a resistance $R = 2000\ \Omega$, a capacitance $C = 4 \times 10^{-6}$ F, and a voltage source of 12 V. Find the equation for the current i.

Using Table 6.2, find the Laplace transform for each function f(t).

33. $f(t) = e^{6t}$ **34.** $f(t) = e^{-2t} \cos 3t$ **35.** $f(t) = t^3 + \cos t$ **36.** $f(t) = 3t - e^{5t}$

Using Table 6.2, find the inverse transform for each function F(s).

37. $F(s) = \dfrac{1}{s^2}$ **38.** $F(s) = \dfrac{3}{s(s-2)}$ **39.** $F(s) = \dfrac{2}{(s-3)(s-4)}$ **40.** $F(s) = \dfrac{3}{s^2+9}$

Solve each differential equation subject to the given conditions by using Laplace transforms.

41. $4y' - 5y = 0;\ y(0) = 2$

42. $y'' + 9y = 0;\ y(0) = 3$ and $y'(0) = 0$

43. $y'' + 5y' = 0;\ y(0) = 0$ and $y'(0) = 2$

44. $y'' + 4y' + 4y = e^{-2t};\ y(0) = 0$ and $y'(0) = 0$

APPLICATION
Differential Equations and the Gateway Arch

The Gateway Arch to the West in St. Louis, Missouri, rises 630 ft and spans 630 ft at ground level. Its design is based on the fact that when a uniform flexible cable hangs freely, there are no transverse forces pushing the cable out of shape and all internal forces are in equilibrium. The plane curve in which a uniform cable hangs when suspended from two points is called a **catenary.** When a catenary is turned upside down the forces are reversed, but are still in equilibrium. The stability of this shape is the reason architect Eero Saarinen chose it for his design of the Gateway Arch to the West.

To study the tension of a uniform cable hanging from two points, we consider the lowest point Q to be on the y-axis with the x-axis parallel to the tangent line at Q as shown below.

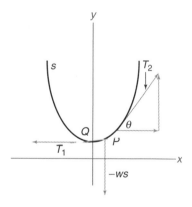

Catenary

Let $P(x, y)$ be any other point on the cable. The three forces acting on the cable are its weight and the resulting tensions on Q and P. If T_1 is the magnitude of the horizontal force at Q, then its x-component is $-T_1$ and its y-component is zero.

If T_2 is the magnitude of the force at P and θ is the angle of inclination at P, then the x-component of the force at P is $T_2 \cos \theta$ and the y-component is $T_2 \sin \theta$. The magnitude of the gravitational pull is the unit weight of the cable w times the length of the curve s. The downward force has an x-component of zero and a y-component of $-ws$.

Since the cable is at rest, the sum of the x-components of the forces must be zero and the sum of the y-components of the forces must be zero. That is,

$$-T_1 + T_2 \cos \theta + 0 = 0$$

and

$$0 + T_2 \sin \theta - ws = 0$$

Thus,

$$T_2 \cos \theta = T_1 \quad \text{and} \quad T_2 \sin \theta = ws$$

$$\frac{T_2 \sin \theta}{T_2 \cos \theta} = \frac{ws}{T_1}$$

$$\tan \theta = \frac{ws}{T_1}$$

Since we assume that the cable lies along a differentiable curve, the slope $\frac{dy}{dx}$ of the curve has the value $\tan \theta$ at P. Now, x and y are included in our equations since

$$\frac{dy}{dx} = \tan \theta = \frac{ws}{T_1}$$

It can be shown that s, the length of a curve, is related to x and y by the equation

$$\frac{ds}{dx} = \sqrt{1 + \left(\frac{dy}{dx}\right)^2}$$

Differentiating $\frac{dy}{dx} = \frac{w}{T_1} s$ with respect to x yields

$$\frac{d^2y}{dx^2} = \frac{w}{T_1} \frac{ds}{dx}$$

$$\frac{d^2y}{dx^2} = \frac{w}{T_1} \sqrt{1 + \left(\frac{dy}{dx}\right)^2}$$

The solution to this second-order differential equation (including the determination of initial values) is

$$y = \frac{T_1}{2w} \left(e^{\frac{w}{T_1}x} + e^{-\frac{w}{T_1}x} \right)$$

which is the equation of a catenary.

Weights and Measures

TABLE 1   U.S. Weights and Measures

Units of length	Units of weight
Standard unit–inch (in. or ″)	Standard unit–pound (lb)
12 inches = 1 foot (ft or ′)	16 ounces (oz) = 1 pound
3 feet = 1 yard (yd)	2000 pounds = 1 ton (T)
$5\frac{1}{2}$ yards or $16\frac{1}{2}$ feet = 1 rod (rd)	
5280 feet = 1 mile (mi)	

Volume measure

Liquid

16 ounces (fl oz) = 1 pint (pt)
2 pints = 1 quart (qt)
4 quarts = 1 gallon (gal)

Dry

2 pints (pt) = 1 quart (qt)
8 quarts = 1 peck (pk)
4 pecks = 1 bushel (bu)

TABLE 2   Conversion Tables

Length

	cm	m	km	in.	ft	mi
1 centimetre	1	10^{-2}	10^{-5}	0.394	3.28×10^{-2}	6.21×10^{-6}
1 metre	100	1	10^{-3}	39.4	3.28	6.21×10^{-4}
1 kilometre	10^5	1000	1	3.94×10^4	3280	0.621
1 inch	2.54	2.54×10^{-2}	2.54×10^{-5}	1	8.33×10^{-2}	1.58×10^{-5}
1 foot	30.5	0.305	3.05×10^{-4}	12	1	1.89×10^{-4}
1 mile	1.61×10^5	1610	1.61	6.34×10^4	5280	1

Area

Metric	*U.S.*
$1\ m^2 = 10{,}000\ cm^2$	$1\ ft^2 = 144\ in^2$
$\quad = 1{,}000{,}000\ mm^2$	$1\ yd^2 = 9\ ft^2$
$1\ cm^2 = 100\ mm^2$	$1\ rd^2 = 30.25\ yd^2$
$\quad = 0.0001\ m^2$	$1\ acre = 160\ rd^2$
$1\ km^2 = 1{,}000{,}000\ m^2$	$\quad = 4840\ yd^2$
$1\ ha = 10{,}000\ m^2$	$\quad = 43{,}560\ ft^2$
	$1\ mi^2 = 640\ acres$

	m^2	cm^2	ft^2	in^2
$1\ m^2$	1	10^4	10.8	1550
$1\ cm^2$	10^{-4}	1	1.08×10^{-3}	0.155
$1\ ft^2$	9.29×10^{-2}	929	1	144
$1\ in^2$	6.45×10^{-4}	6.45	6.94×10^{-3}	1

$1\ mi^2 = 2.79 \times 10^7\ ft^2 = 640\ acres$

$1\ circular\ mil = 5.07 \times 10^{-6}\ cm^2 = 7.85 \times 10^{-7}\ in^2$

$1\ hectare = 2.47\ acres$

Volume

	m^3	cm^3	L	ft^3	in^3
	Metric			*U.S.*	
	1 m³ = 10⁶ cm³			1 ft³ = 1728 in³	
	1 cm³ = 10⁻⁶ m³			1 yd³ = 27 ft³	
	= 10³ mm³				

	m^3	cm^3	L	ft^3	in^3
1 m³	1	10⁶	1000	35.3	6.10×10^4
1 cm³	10⁻⁶	1	1.00×10^{-3}	3.53×10^{-5}	6.10×10^{-2}
1 L	1.00×10^{-3}	1000	1	3.53×10^{-2}	61.0
1 ft³	2.83×10^{-2}	2.83×10^4	28.3	1	1728
1 in³	1.64×10^{-5}	16.4	1.64×10^{-2}	5.79×10^{-4}	1

1 U.S. fluid gallon = 4 U.S. fluid quarts = 8 U.S. pints = 128 U.S. fluid ounces = 231 in³ = 0.134 ft³ = 3.79 litres

1 L = 1000 cm³ = 1.06 qt

Other useful conversion factors

1 newton (N) = 0.225 lb
1 pound (lb) = 4.45 N
1 slug = 14.6 kg
1 joule (J) = 0.738 ft-lb
        = 2.39×10^{-4} kcal
1 calorie (cal) = 4.185 J
1 kilocalorie (kcal) = 4185 J
1 foot-pound (ft-lb) = 1.36 J
1 watt (W) = 1 J/s = 0.738 ft-lb/s
1 kilowatt (kW) = 1000 W
        = 1.34 hp
1 hp = 550 ft-lb/s = 746 W

1 atm = 101.32 kpa
    = 14.7 lb/in²
1 Btu = 0.252 kcal
1 kcal = 3.97 Btu
$F = \frac{9}{5}C + 32°$
$C = \frac{5}{9}(F - 32°)$
1 kg = 2.20 lb (on the earth's surface)
1 lb = 454 g
   = 16 oz
1 metric ton = 1000 kg
        = 2200 lb

Table of Integrals

1. $\displaystyle\int u^n\,du = \frac{u^{n+1}}{n+1} + C \qquad (n \neq -1)$

2. $\displaystyle\int \frac{du}{a+bu} = \frac{1}{b}\ln|a+bu| + C$

3. $\displaystyle\int \frac{u}{a+bu}\,du = \frac{1}{b^2}\big[(a+bu) - a\ln|a+bu|\big] + C$

4. $\displaystyle\int \frac{u^2\,du}{a+bu} = \frac{1}{b^3}\left[\frac{1}{2}(a+bu)^2 - 2a(a+bu) + a^2\ln|a+bu|\right] + C$

5. $\displaystyle\int \frac{du}{u(a+bu)} = \frac{1}{a}\ln\left|\frac{u}{a+bu}\right| + C$

6. $\displaystyle\int \frac{du}{u^2(a+bu)} = -\frac{1}{au} + \frac{b}{a^2}\ln\left|\frac{a+bu}{u}\right| + C$

7. $\displaystyle\int \frac{u\,du}{(a+bu)^2} = \frac{1}{b^2}\left(\ln|a+bu| + \frac{a}{a+bu}\right) + C$

8. $\displaystyle\int \frac{u^2\,du}{(a+bu)^2} = \frac{1}{b^3}\left(a+bu - \frac{a^2}{a+bu} - 2a\ln|a+bu|\right) + C$

9. $\displaystyle\int \frac{du}{u(a+bu)^2} = \frac{1}{a(a+bu)} + \frac{1}{a^2}\ln\left|\frac{u}{a+bu}\right| + C$

10. $\displaystyle\int \frac{du}{u^2(a+bu)^2} = -\frac{a+2bu}{a^2u(a+bu)} + \frac{2b}{a^3}\ln\left|\frac{a+bu}{u}\right| + C$

Forms containing $\sqrt{a+bu}$

---

11. $\displaystyle\int u\sqrt{a+bu}\,du = -\frac{2(2a-3bu)(a+bu)^{3/2}}{15b^2} + C$

12. $\displaystyle\int u^2\sqrt{a+bu}\,du = \frac{2(8a^2 - 12abu + 15b^2u^2)(a+bu)^{3/2}}{105b^3} + C$

13. $\displaystyle\int \frac{u\,du}{\sqrt{a+bu}} = -\frac{2(2a-bu)\sqrt{a+bu}}{3b^2} + C$

14. $\displaystyle\int \frac{u^2\,du}{\sqrt{a+bu}} = \frac{2(3b^2u^2 - 4abu + 8a^2)\sqrt{a+bu}}{15b^3} + C$

15. $\displaystyle\int \frac{du}{u\sqrt{a+bu}} = \frac{1}{\sqrt{a}}\ln\left|\frac{\sqrt{a+bu}-\sqrt{a}}{\sqrt{a+bu}+\sqrt{a}}\right| + C \qquad (a>0)$

16. $\displaystyle\int \frac{du}{u\sqrt{a + bu}} = \frac{2}{\sqrt{-a}} \arctan \sqrt{\frac{a + bu}{-a}} + C \qquad (a < 0)$

17. $\displaystyle\int \frac{\sqrt{a + bu}\, du}{u} = 2\sqrt{a + bu} + a \int \frac{du}{u\sqrt{a + bu}} + C$

Rational forms containing $a^2 \pm u^2$ and $u^2 \pm a^2$

---

18. $\displaystyle\int \frac{du}{a^2 + u^2} = \frac{1}{a} \arctan \frac{u}{a} + C$

19. $\displaystyle\int \frac{du}{a^2 - u^2} = \frac{1}{2a} \ln \left| \frac{a + u}{a - u} \right| + C \qquad (a^2 > u^2)$

20. $\displaystyle\int \frac{du}{u^2 - a^2} = \frac{1}{2a} \ln \left| \frac{u - a}{u + a} \right| + C \qquad (a^2 < u^2)$

Irrational forms containing $\sqrt{a^2 - u^2}$

---

21. $\displaystyle\int (a^2 - u^2)^{1/2}\, du = \frac{u}{2} \sqrt{a^2 - u^2} + \frac{a^2}{2} \arcsin \frac{u}{a} + C$

22. $\displaystyle\int \frac{du}{(a^2 - u^2)^{1/2}} = \arcsin \frac{u}{a} + C \qquad (a > 0)$

23. $\displaystyle\int \frac{du}{(a^2 - u^2)^{3/2}} = \frac{u}{a^2\sqrt{a^2 - u^2}} + C$

24. $\displaystyle\int \frac{u^2\, du}{(a^2 - u^2)^{1/2}} = -\frac{u}{2} \sqrt{a^2 - u^2} + \frac{a^2}{2} \arcsin \frac{u}{a} + C$

25. $\displaystyle\int \frac{u^2\, du}{(a^2 - u^2)^{3/2}} = \frac{u}{\sqrt{a^2 - u^2}} - \arcsin \frac{u}{a} + C$

26. $\displaystyle\int \frac{du}{u(a^2 - u^2)^{1/2}} = -\frac{1}{a} \ln \left| \frac{a + \sqrt{a^2 - u^2}}{u} \right| + C$

27. $\displaystyle\int \frac{du}{u^2(a^2 - u^2)^{1/2}} = -\frac{\sqrt{a^2 - u^2}}{a^2 u} + C$

28. $\displaystyle\int \frac{(a^2 - u^2)^{1/2}\, du}{u} = \sqrt{a^2 - u^2} - a \ln \left| \frac{a + \sqrt{a^2 - u^2}}{u} \right| + C$

29. $\displaystyle\int \frac{(a^2 - u^2)^{1/2}\, du}{u^2} = -\frac{\sqrt{a^2 - u^2}}{u} - \arcsin \frac{u}{a} + C$

Irrational forms containing $\sqrt{u^2 \pm a^2}$

---

30. $\displaystyle\int \sqrt{u^2 \pm a^2}\, du = \tfrac{1}{2}\left(u\sqrt{u^2 \pm a^2} \pm a^2 \ln \left| u + \sqrt{u^2 \pm a^2} \right| \right) + C$

31. $\displaystyle\int u^2\sqrt{u^2 \pm a^2}\, du = \tfrac{1}{8}u(2u^2 \pm a^2)\sqrt{u^2 \pm a^2} - \tfrac{1}{8}a^4 \ln \left| u + \sqrt{u^2 \pm a^2} \right| + C$

32. $\displaystyle\int \frac{\sqrt{u^2 + a^2}}{u}\, du = \sqrt{u^2 + a^2} - a \ln \left| \frac{a + \sqrt{u^2 + a^2}}{u} \right| + C$

33. $\displaystyle\int \frac{\sqrt{u^2 - a^2}}{u}\, du = \sqrt{u^2 - a^2} - a \arccos \frac{a}{u} + C$

34. $\displaystyle\int \frac{\sqrt{u^2 \pm a^2}}{u^2}\, du = -\frac{\sqrt{u^2 \pm a^2}}{u} + \ln \left| u + \sqrt{u^2 \pm a^2} \right| + C$

35. $\displaystyle\int \frac{du}{\sqrt{u^2 \pm a^2}} = \ln\left|u + \sqrt{u^2 \pm a^2}\right| + C$

36. $\displaystyle\int \frac{du}{u\sqrt{u^2 - a^2}} - \frac{1}{a}\arccos\frac{a}{u} + C$

37. $\displaystyle\int \frac{du}{u\sqrt{u^2 + a^2}} = \frac{1}{a}\ln\left|\frac{u}{a + \sqrt{u^2 + a^2}}\right| + C$

38. $\displaystyle\int \frac{u^2\,du}{\sqrt{u^2 \pm a^2}} = \frac{1}{2}\left(u\sqrt{u^2 \pm a^2} \pm a^2\ln\left|u + \sqrt{u^2 \pm a^2}\right|\right) + C$

39. $\displaystyle\int \frac{du}{u^2\sqrt{u^2 \pm a^2}} = -\frac{\pm\sqrt{u^2 \pm a^2}}{a^2 u} + C$

40. $\displaystyle\int \frac{du}{(u^2 \pm a^2)^{3/2}} = \frac{\pm u}{a^2\sqrt{u^2 \pm a^2}} + C$

41. $\displaystyle\int \frac{u^2\,du}{(u^2 \pm a^2)^{3/2}} = \frac{-u}{\sqrt{u^2 \pm a^2}} + \ln\left|u + \sqrt{u^2 \pm a^2}\right| + C$

Forms containing $a + bu \pm cu^2$ $\quad(c > 0)$

---

42. $\displaystyle\int \frac{du}{a + bu + cu^2} = \frac{2}{\sqrt{4ac - b^2}}\arctan\frac{2cu + b}{\sqrt{4ac - b^2}} + C \quad (b^2 < 4ac)$

43. $\displaystyle\int \frac{du}{a + bu + cu^2} = \frac{1}{\sqrt{b^2 - 4ac}}\ln\left|\frac{2cu + b - \sqrt{b^2 - 4ac}}{2cu + b + \sqrt{b^2 - 4ac}}\right| + C \quad (b^2 > 4ac)$

44. $\displaystyle\int \frac{du}{a + bu - cu^2} = \frac{1}{\sqrt{b^2 + 4ac}}\ln\left|\frac{\sqrt{b^2 + 4ac} + 2cu - b}{\sqrt{b^2 + 4ac} - 2cu + b}\right| + C$

45. $\displaystyle\int \sqrt{a + bu + cu^2}\,du = \frac{2cu + b}{4c}\sqrt{a + bu + cu^2} - \frac{b^2 - 4ac}{8c^{3/2}}\ln\left|2cu + b + 2\sqrt{c}\sqrt{a + bu + cu^2}\right| + C$

46. $\displaystyle\int \sqrt{a + bu - cu^2}\,du = \frac{2cu - b}{4c}\sqrt{a + bu - cu^2} + \frac{b^2 + 4ac}{8c^{3/2}}\arcsin\left(\frac{2cu - b}{\sqrt{b^2 + 4ac}}\right) + C$

47. $\displaystyle\int \frac{du}{\sqrt{a + bu + cu^2}} = \frac{1}{\sqrt{c}}\ln\left|2cu + b + 2\sqrt{c}\sqrt{a + bu + cu^2}\right| + C$

48. $\displaystyle\int \frac{du}{\sqrt{a + bu - cu^2}} = \frac{1}{\sqrt{c}}\arcsin\left(\frac{2cu - b}{\sqrt{b^2 + 4ac}}\right) + C$

49. $\displaystyle\int \frac{u\,du}{\sqrt{a + bu + cu^2}} = \frac{\sqrt{a + bu + cu^2}}{c} - \frac{b}{2c^{3/2}}\ln\left|2cu + b + 2\sqrt{c}\sqrt{a + bu + cu^2}\right| + C$

50. $\displaystyle\int \frac{u\,du}{\sqrt{a + bu - cu^2}} = -\frac{\sqrt{a + bu - cu^2}}{c} + \frac{b}{2c^{3/2}}\arcsin\left(\frac{2cu - b}{\sqrt{b^2 + 4ac}}\right) + C$

Exponential and logarithmic forms

---

51. $\displaystyle\int e^u\,du = e^u + C$

52. $\displaystyle\int a^u\,du = \frac{a^u}{\ln a} + C \quad (a > 0, a \neq 1)$

53. $\displaystyle\int ue^{au}\,du = \frac{e^{au}}{a^2}(au - 1) + C$

54. $\displaystyle\int u^n e^{au}\,du = \frac{u^n e^{au}}{a} - \frac{n}{a}\int u^{n-1}e^{au}\,du$

55. $\displaystyle\int \frac{e^{au}}{u^n}\, du = -\frac{e^{au}}{(n-1)u^{n-1}} + \frac{a}{n-1}\int \frac{e^{au}}{u^{n-1}}\, du$

56. $\displaystyle\int \ln u\, du = u \ln u - u + C$

57. $\displaystyle\int u^n \ln u\, du = \frac{u^{n+1} \ln u}{n+1} - \frac{u^{n+1}}{(n+1)^2} + C$

58. $\displaystyle\int \frac{du}{u \ln u} = \ln|\ln u| + C$

59. $\displaystyle\int e^{au} \sin nu\, du = \frac{e^{au}(a \sin nu - n \cos nu)}{a^2 + n^2} + C$

60. $\displaystyle\int e^{au} \cos nu\, du = \frac{e^{au}(n \sin nu + a \cos nu)}{a^2 + n^2} + C$

Trigonometric forms

---

61. $\displaystyle\int \sin u\, du = -\cos u + C$

62. $\displaystyle\int \cos u\, du = \sin u + C$

63. $\displaystyle\int \tan u\, du = -\ln|\cos u| + C = \ln|\sec u| + C$

64. $\displaystyle\int \cot u\, du = \ln|\sin u| + C$

65. $\displaystyle\int \sec u\, du = \ln|\sec u + \tan u| + C$

66. $\displaystyle\int \csc u\, du = \ln|\csc u - \cot u| + C$

67. $\displaystyle\int \sec^2 u\, du = \tan u + C$

68. $\displaystyle\int \csc^2 u\, du = -\cot u + C$

69. $\displaystyle\int \sec u \tan u\, du = \sec u + C$

70. $\displaystyle\int \csc u \cot u\, du = -\csc u + C$

71. $\displaystyle\int \sin^2 u\, du = \tfrac{1}{2}u - \tfrac{1}{4}\sin 2u + C$

72. $\displaystyle\int \cos^2 u\, du = \tfrac{1}{2}u + \tfrac{1}{4}\sin 2u + C$

73. $\displaystyle\int \cos^n u \sin u\, du = -\frac{\cos^{n+1} u}{n+1} + C$

74. $\displaystyle\int \sin^n u \cos u\, du = \frac{\sin^{n+1} u}{n+1} + C$

75. $\displaystyle\int \sin mu \sin nu\, du = -\frac{\sin(m+n)u}{2(m+n)} + \frac{\sin(m-n)u}{2(m-n)} + C$

76. $\displaystyle\int \cos mu \cos nu\, du = \frac{\sin(m+n)u}{2(m+n)} + \frac{\sin(m-n)u}{2(m-n)} + C$

77. $\displaystyle\int \sin mu \; \cos nu \; du = -\frac{\cos(m+n)u}{2(m+n)} - \frac{\cos(m-n)u}{2(m-n)} + C$

78. $\displaystyle\int e^{au} \sin nu \; du = \frac{e^{au}(a \sin nu - n \cos nu)}{a^2 + n^2} + C$

79. $\displaystyle\int e^{au} \cos nu \; du = \frac{e^{au}(n \sin nu + a \cos nu)}{a^2 + n^2} + C$

80. $\displaystyle\int u \sin u \; du = \sin u - u \cos u + C$

81. $\displaystyle\int u \cos u \; du = \cos u + u \sin u + C$

82. $\displaystyle\int \sin^m u \cos^n u \; du = \frac{\sin^{m+1} u \cos^{n-1} u}{m+n} + \frac{n-1}{m+n} \int \sin^m u \cos^{n-2} u \; du$

83. $\displaystyle\int \sin^n u \; du = -\frac{1}{n} \sin^{n-1} u \cos u + \frac{n-1}{n} \int \sin^{n-2} u \; du$

84. $\displaystyle\int \cos^n u \; du = \frac{1}{n} \cos^{n-1} u \sin u + \frac{n-1}{n} \int \cos^{n-2} u \; du$

85. $\displaystyle\int \tan^n u \; du = \frac{\tan^{n-1} u}{n-1} - \int \tan^{n-2} u \; du$

86. $\displaystyle\int \cot^n u \; du = -\frac{\cot^{n-1} u}{n-1} - \int \cot^{n-2} u \; du$

87. $\displaystyle\int \sec^n u \; du = \frac{\sec^{n-2} u \tan u}{n-1} + \frac{n-2}{n+1} \int \sec^{n-2} u \; du$

88. $\displaystyle\int \csc^n u \; du = -\frac{\csc^{n-2} u \cot u}{n-1} + \frac{n-2}{n-1} \int \csc^{n-2} u \; du$

APPENDIX C

Using a Graphing Calculator

This appendix is included to provide faculty with the flexibility of integrating graphing calculators in their classes. Each section explains and illustrates important features of the Texas Instruments TI 83 and TI-84 Plus. Though this appendix was specifically designed to supplement the graphing calculator examples found throughout the text, the material is organized so that an interested student could also study it as a separate chapter.

C.1 INTRODUCTION TO THE TI-83 KEYBOARD

This section provides a guided tour of the keyboard of the TI-83 Plus and TI-84 Plus graphing calculators (including their Silver Editions). In this and the following sections, please have your calculator in front of you and be sure to try out the features as they are discussed.

First, notice that the keys forming the bottom six rows of the keyboard perform the standard functions of a scientific calculator. The thin blue keys that form the very top row allow functions to be defined and their graphs to be drawn (see Section C.3 for details). The second, third, and fourth rows of keys provide access to menus full of advanced features and perform special tasks such as **INS**ert, **DEL**ete, **CLEAR**, and **QUIT** (to leave a menu, an editor, or a graph, and return to the home screen). Also found in these rows are the **2nd** and **ALPHA** shift keys, which give additional, color-coded meanings to almost every key on the calculator.

The **ON** key is in the lower left-hand corner. Note that pressing the (golden yellow) **2nd** key followed by the **ON** key will turn the calculator **OFF**. If the calculator is left unattended (or no buttons are pressed for a couple of minutes), the calculator will shut itself off. No work is lost when the unit is turned off. Just turn the calculator back **ON** and the display will be exactly as you left it. Due to different lighting conditions and battery strengths, the screen contrast needs adjustment from time to time. Press the **2nd** key, then *press and hold* the up (or down) arrow key to darken (or lighten) the screen contrast.

The **ENTER** key in the lower right-hand corner is like the = key on many scientific calculators; it signals the calculator to perform the calculation that you've been typing. Its (shifted) **2nd** meaning, **ENTRY**, gives you access to previously entered formulas, starting with the most recent one. If you continue to press **2nd ENTRY** you can access previous entries up to an overall memory limit of 128 characters. Depending on the length of your formulas, this means that about 10 to 15 of your most recent entries can be retrieved from the calculator's memory to be reused or modified.

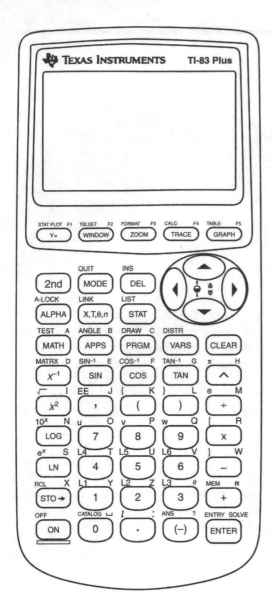
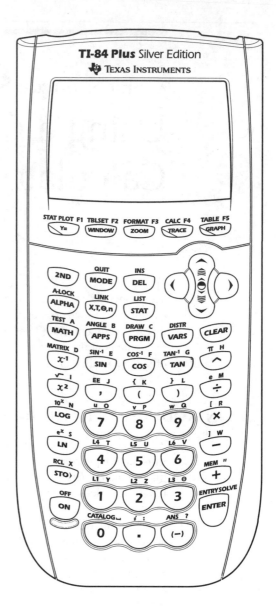

Courtesy of Texas Instruments

Just above **ENTER** is a column of four other blue keys that perform the standard operations of arithmetic. Note, though, that the multiplication key, indicated by an ×, prints an asterisk on the screen and the division key prints a slash on the screen. Just above these four is the ^ key, which indicates that you're raising something to the power that follows; for example, 2^5 would mean 2^5. Moving to the left across that row, you will see the keys for the trigonometric functions: **SIN**, **COS**, and **TAN** (note that their standard setting is radians, but you can specify degrees by using the degree symbol, which is option 1 in the **ANGLE** menu, or the calculator can be set to always think in degrees by specifying that option in the **MODE** menu). Always press the trig key before typing the angle, as in $\cos(\pi)$ or $\sin(30°)$. Notice that the left-hand parenthesis is automatically included when you press any of the trig keys. To the left of these three is a key labeled x^{-1}, which acts as a reciprocal key for ordinary arithmetic. It will also invert a matrix, as in $[A]^{-1}$, which explains why the key isn't labeled **1/x**, as it would be on many scientific calculators. Beneath that key is x^2

(the squaring key), whose shifted **2nd** meaning is square root. Below in that column are keys for logs, whose shifted **2nd** versions give exponential functions. Like the trig keys, the square root, **LOG, LN,** and exponential keys also precede their arguments. For example, log(2) will find the common logarithm of 2.

Between **LN** and **ON** is the **STO>** key, which is used to store a number (possibly the result of a calculation) into any of the 27 memory locations whose names are A, B, C, . . . , Z, and θ. First indicate the number or calculation, then press **STO>** (which just prints an arrow on the screen) followed by the (green) **ALPHA** key, then the (green) letter name you want the stored result to have, and finally press **ENTER.** The computation will be performed and the result will be stored in the desired memory location as well as being displayed on the screen. If you have just performed a calculation and now wish that you had stored it, don't worry. Just press **STO>** on the next line followed by **ALPHA** and the letter name you want to give this quantity, then press **ENTER.**

Here are some examples:

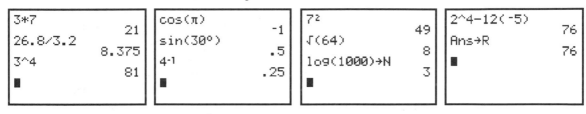

If you watched the last **STO>** example closely, you may have noticed that the calculator prints **Ans** (which stands for "the previous answer") on the screen whenever you don't indicate the first operand on a given line. For example, if you begin a formula with a plus sign, the calculator assumes that you want to add something to the previous result, so it displays "Ans+" instead of just "+." At times, you'll want to refer to the previous result somewhere other than at the beginning of your formula. In that case, press **2nd ANS** (the shifted version of the key to the left of **ENTER**) wherever you want the previous answer to appear in the computation.

The shifted **2nd** meaning of the **STO>** key is **RCL** (recall), as in **RCL Z**, which would display the *contents* of memory location Z at the current cursor position in your formula. It is usually easier to write the letter Z itself (press **ALPHA** followed by **Z**) in formulas instead of the current value that's stored there, so this recall feature isn't the best choice in most computations. However, the **RCL** feature is very useful in creating instant copies of functions (Rcl Y1) and programs (Rcl prgmSIMPSON) so that newly modified versions don't have to destroy the old ones.

The key that changes the sign of a number is labeled **(-)** and is located just to the left of the **ENTER** key. Don't confuse this white (or gray) key with the dark blue subtraction key! Note also that the calculator consistently views the lack of an indicated operation between two quantities as an intended multiplication.

The parentheses keys are just above the 8 and 9 keys. These are used for all levels of parentheses. Do not be confused by symbols such as { } and [ ], which are the shifted **2nd** versions of these and other nearby keys. Braces { } are used *only* to indicate lists, and brackets [ ] are used *only* for matrices. Once again, these special symbols *cannot* be used to indicate higher levels of parentheses; just nest ordinary parentheses to show several levels of quantification. Also note that the comma key is used only with matrices, lists, multiple-argument functions, and certain commands in the calculator's programming language. Never use commas to separate digits within a number. The number three thousand should always be typed 3000 (not 3,000). The shifted **2nd** meaning of the comma key is **EE** (enter exponent), which is used to enter data in scientific notation; for example, **1.3** followed by **2nd EE (-)8** would be the keystrokes needed to enter 1.3×10^{-8} in a formula. It would be displayed on the screen as 1.3E-8.

The shifted **2nd** versions of the numbers 1 through 9 provide keyboard access to lists and sequences. The shifted **ALPHA** version of the zero key prints a blank space on the display. The shifted **2nd** version of the zero key is **CATALOG,** which provides alphabetical access to every feature of the calculator. Just press the first letter of the desired feature (without pressing **ALPHA**), then scroll from there using the down arrow key. Press **ENTER** when the desired feature is marked by the small arrow. The shifted **2nd** version of the decimal point is *i*, the imaginary unit (which is often called *j* in electronics applications). This symbol can be used in computations involving imaginary and complex numbers even when **MODE Real** has been selected.

The shifted **2nd** version of the plus sign is **MEM** (the memory management menu), which gives you a chance to erase programs, lists, and anything else stored in memory. Use this menu sparingly (remember, your calculator has a fairly large memory, so you don't usually need to be in a hurry to dispose of things which might prove useful later). If you get into **MEM** by accident, just press **2nd QUIT** to get back to the home screen. **2nd QUIT** always takes you back to the home screen from any menu, editor, or graph, but it will not terminate a running program on a TI-83 or TI-84 Plus. To interrupt a running program, just press the **ON** button, then choose "Quit" in the menu you'll see.

If you're looking for keys that will compute cube roots, absolute values, complex conjugates, permutations, combinations, or factorials, press the **MATH** key, and you'll see four submenus (selectable by using the right or left arrow key) which give you these options and many more. Especially interesting is >**Frac** (convert to fraction), which will convert a decimal to its simplified fractional form, provided that the denominator would be less than 10,000 (otherwise, it just writes the decimal form of the number). Other examples are also included below to give you a better idea of just how many options are available in the **MATH** menu.

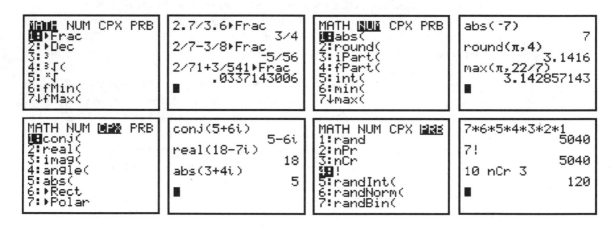

C.2 COMPUTATIONAL EXAMPLES

EXAMPLE 1

Compute the following:
(a) 7×6

(b) $3 \times 7 + 6(3 - 5)$

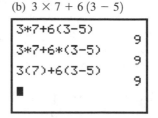

EXAMPLE 2

Compute $8\{3 + 5[2 - 7(8 - 9)]\}$.

```
8(3+5(2-7(8-9)))
                384
■
```

Note: The calculator uses only ordinary parentheses.

EXAMPLE 3

Express the following as a decimal and as a simplified fraction:

(a) $\dfrac{105}{100}$ 　　　　　　　　　　(b) $\dfrac{3}{8} + \dfrac{21}{10} - \dfrac{17}{25}$

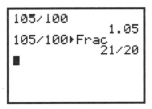

```
105/100
            1.05
105/100▶Frac
            21/20
■
```

```
3/8+21/10-17/25
            1.795
3/8+21/10-17/25▶
Frac
            359/200
■
```

Note that a fraction is an indicated division operation and that the division key always prints a diagonal fraction bar line on the screen. The convert to fraction feature is the first item in the **MATH** menu and is accessed by pressing **MATH** then **1** (or **MATH** then **ENTER**) at the end of a formula. Note also that simplified improper fractions are the intended result. *Mixed numbers are not supported.* A decimal result would mean that the answer cannot be written as a simplified fraction with a denominator less than 10,000.

EXAMPLE 4

Compute the following, expressing the answer as a simplified fraction:

(a) $\dfrac{2^5}{6^2}$ 　　　　　　　　　　(b) $\dfrac{5 - (-7)}{-2 - 12}$

```
2^5/6²▶Frac
            8/9
2^5/6^2▶Frac
            8/9
■
```

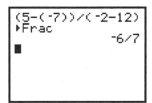

```
(5-(-7))/(-2-12)
▶Frac       -6/7
■
```

Squares can be computed by pressing the x^2 key; similarly, a third power can be indicated by pressing **MATH** then **3**. Most other exponents require the use of the $\wedge$ key (found between **CLEAR** and the division key). In Part (b), notice the calculator's need for additional parentheses which enclose the numerator and denominator of the fraction. Also notice the difference between the calculator's negative sign (the key below **3**) and its subtraction symbol (the key to the right of **6**).

EXAMPLE 5

Compute the following complex numbers:

(a) $(3 + 4i)(-2 - 5i)$ 　　　　　　　　　(b) $\dfrac{7 + 29i}{30 + 10i}$

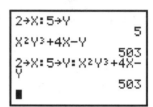

```
(3+4i)(-2-5i)
              14-23i
(3+4i)*(-2-5i)
              14-23i
■
```

```
(7+29i)/(30+10i)
              .5+.8i
(7+29i)/(30+10i)
▶Frac
          1/2+4/5i
■
```

Note that the calculator key for the imaginary unit i is the shifted **2nd** version of the decimal point. This imaginary number is often called j in electronics applications.

EXAMPLE 6

Evaluate these expressions:
(a) $x^2 + 5x - 8$ when $x = 4$ 　　　　(b) $x^2 y^3 + 4x - y$ when $x = 2$ and $y = 5$

```
4→X
              4
X²+5X-8
              28
4→X:X²+5X-8
              28
■
```

```
2→X:5→Y
              5
X²Y³+4X-Y
              503
2→X:5→Y:X²Y³+4X-
Y
              503
■
```

The **STO>** key (just above **ON**) is used to print the arrow symbol on the screen. The letter x can be typed on the screen by pressing the key next to **ALPHA**, labeled **X,T,θ,n,** or by pressing **ALPHA**, then **X**. Note that several steps can be performed on one line if the steps are separated by a colon (the shifted **ALPHA** version of the decimal point key). In such cases, all steps are performed in sequence, but only the result of the very last step is displayed on the screen.

EXAMPLE 7

Given that $f(x) = x^4 - 7x + 11$, find $f(3), f(5),$ and $f(-1)$.

Y=	**2nd QUIT**	**VARS**	right arrow 　 **1**	**1**

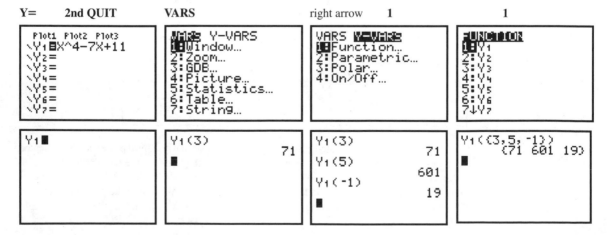

Note that using a stored function requires entering the function in the **Y=** menu, pressing **2nd QUIT** to return to the home screen, then finding the name of that function in the **FUNCTION** submenu under **Y-VARS**. Function evaluation requires the use of parentheses; without parentheses around the argument, multiplication would be assumed. To type the second and third uses of Y_1, press **2nd ENTRY**, then left arrow twice, modifying only the argument from the previous formula. The last screen shows how a list of arguments can be used to calculate a list of function values. Your list entries must be enclosed by braces { } and separated by commas (list entries output by the calculator are separated by spaces instead of commas).

C.3   GRAPHING FEATURES

The thin blue buttons along the top row of the calculator do most of its graphical work. The **Y=** key provides access to the calculator's list of 10 functions (assuming that the calculator is set in **MODE Func**). Pressing the **Y=** key will reveal functions Y_1 through Y_7; the other three functions, Y_8, Y_9, and Y_0, can be seen by pressing the (blue) down arrow key nine times (or just press and hold the down arrow key). These functions are part of the calculator's memory, but the information stored on this screen can be easily edited, overwritten, or **CLEAR**ed. Functions are selected for graphing (turned "on") by highlighting their equal sign. This is done automatically when you type in a new function or modify an old one. In other cases, to change the status of a function (from "off" to "on" or vice versa), you will need to use the arrow keys to position the cursor over the equal sign (making it blink); then press **ENTER**. Functions marked with an ordinary equal sign are stored in memory but will *not* be graphed. To the left of each function name is a symbol indicating how it will be graphed. The normal setting looks like a backslash, \, and simply indicates that the graph will be drawn with a thin line. Other settings include a thicker line, shading above the graph, shading below the graph, two animated settings (one marks the path of motion on the screen; the other just shows the motion without marking its path), and finally an option that graphs with a dotted line. To switch from one option to another, just press the left-arrow key until the cursor is over the option marking (at the far left of that function's name), then press **ENTER** repeatedly until the desired option appears. One warning about the **Y=** menu is that the names Plot1, Plot2, and Plot3 at the top of the function list refer only to the calculator's **STAT**istical **PLOT**s. They have nothing to do with ordinary graphing and should *not* be highlighted if you are just trying to graph some functions.

The **WINDOW** key allows you to *manually* specify the extents of the *x*- and *y*-values that will be visible on the calculator's graphing screen (see **ZOOM** for *automatic* ways of doing this). The Xscl and Yscl options specify the meaning of a mark on the *x*- or *y*-axis. For example Xscl=5 means that each mark shown on the *x*-axis will mean an increment of 5 units (Xscl=1 is a common setting for algebraic functions; Xscl=$\pi/2$ is commonly used when graphing trigonometric functions). The last option, Xres, allows you to control how many points will actually be calculated when a graph is drawn. Xres=1 means that an accurate point will be calculated for each pixel on the *x*-axis (somewhat slow, but very accurate). Xres=2 will calculate only at every other pixel, and so on; Xres=8 only calculates a point for every eighth pixel (this is the fastest setting, but also the least accurate). In the examples that follow, all graphs are shown with Xres=1.

Pressing **2nd FORMAT** (the shifted version of the **ZOOM** key), reveals additional graphing options that allow you to change the way coordinates are displayed (polar instead of rectangular), turn coordinates off completely (inhibiting some **TRACE** features), provide a coordinate grid, hide the axes, label the axes, or inhibit printing expressions which describe the graphs. If you find your graphs looking cluttered or notice that axes, coordinates, or algebraic expressions are missing, the "standard" settings are all in the left-hand column. Like other menus where the options aren't numbered (**MODE** is similar), use your arrow keys to make a new option blink, then select it by pressing **ENTER**.

ZOOM accesses a menu full of *automatic* ways to set the graphical viewing window. **ZStandard** (option 6) is usually a good place to start, but you should consider option 7, **ZTrig**, if you're graphing trigonometric functions. **ZStandard** shows the origin in the exact center of the screen with x- and y-values both ranging from -10 to 10. From here you can **Zoom In** or **Zoom Out** (options 2 and 3), or draw a box around a portion of the graph that you would like magnified to fit the entire screen (option 1, **ZBox**). There is also an option to "square up" your graph so that units along the x-axis are equal in length to units along the y-axis (option 5, **ZSquare**); the *smaller* unit length from the axes of the previous graph will now be used on both axes. This option makes the graph look more like it would on regular graph paper; for example, circles really look like circles. **ZDecimal** and **ZInteger** (options 4 and 8) prepare the screen for **TRACE**s, which will utilize x-coordinates at exact tenths or integer values, respectively. Option 9, **ZoomStat**, makes sure that all of the data in a statistical plot will fit in the viewing window. Option 0, **ZoomFit**, calculates a viewing window using the present x-axis, but adjusts the y-axis so that the function fits neatly within the viewing window. All of these options work by making automatic changes to the **WINDOW** settings. Want to go back to the view you had before? The **MEMORY** submenu (press the right arrow key after pressing **ZOOM**) contains options to go back to your immediately previous view (option 1, **ZPrevious**) or to a window setting you saved a while ago (option 3, **ZoomRcl**). **ZoomSto** (option 2) is the way to save the current window setting for later (note that it can only retain one window setting, so the new information replaces whatever setting you had saved before). Option 4, **SetFactors...**, gives you the chance to control how dramatically your calculator will **Zoom In** or **Zoom Out**. These zoom factors are set by Texas Instruments for a magnification ratio of 4 on each axis. Many people prefer smaller factors, such as 2 on each axis. It is possible to set either factor to any number greater than or equal to 1; they don't need to be whole numbers, and they don't necessarily have to be equal.

The **TRACE** key takes you from any screen or menu to the current graph, displaying the x- and y-coordinates of specific points as you trace along a curve using the left and right arrow keys. Note that in **TRACE**, the up and down arrow keys are used to jump from one curve to another when several curves have been drawn on the same screen. The expression (formula) for the function you are presently tracing is shown in the upper left-hand corner of the screen (or its subscript number is shown in the upper right-hand corner if you have selected the **ExprOff** option from the **FORMAT** menu). If you press **ENTER** while in **TRACE**, the graph will be redrawn with the currently selected point in the exact center of the screen, even if that point is presently outside the current viewing window. This feature is a convenient way to pan up or down to see higher or lower portions of the graph. It is also the easiest way to locate a "lost" graph that doesn't appear anywhere in the current viewing window (just press **TRACE**, then **ENTER**). To pan left or right, just press and hold the left or right arrow key until new portions of the graph come into view. These useful features change the way the graph is centered on the screen without changing its magnification. Note also that these recentering features work *only* in **TRACE**. To exit **TRACE** without disturbing your view of the graph, just press **GRAPH** (or **CLEAR**). To return to the home screen, abandoning both **TRACE** and the graph, just press **2nd QUIT** (or press **CLEAR** twice). Note that using any **ZOOM** feature also causes an exit from **TRACE** (to resume tracing on the new zoomed version, you must press **TRACE** again).

The **GRAPH** key takes the calculator from any screen or menu to the current graph. Note that the calculator is smart enough that it will redraw the curves only if changes have been made to the function list (**Y=**). As previously mentioned, the **GRAPH** key can be used to turn off **TRACE**. You can also hide an unwanted free cursor by pressing **GRAPH**. When you're finished with viewing a graph, press **CLEAR** or **2nd QUIT** to return to the home screen.

C.4 EXAMPLES OF GRAPHING

This appendix is designed to explain graphing calculator features rather than mathematics itself. Accordingly, the example format in this and subsequent sections is different from that found in the body of the text.

EXAMPLE 1

To graph $y = x^2 - 5x$, first press **Y=**, then press **CLEAR** to erase the current formula in Y_1 (or use the down arrow key to find a blank function), then press the **X,T,θ,n** key (**ALPHA** then **X** will also work), followed by the **x²** button; now press the (blue) minus sign key, then **5**, followed immediately by the **X,T,θ,n** key (a multiplication sign is not needed). Your screen should look very much like the first one shown below. There is no need to press **ENTER** when you have finished typing a function's formula. To set up a good graphing window, press **ZOOM** and then **6** to choose **ZStandard**. This causes the graph to be immediately drawn on axes that range from -10 to 10. Notice that you did not have to press the **GRAPH** key; the **ZOOM** menu items and the **TRACE** key also activate the graphing screen. *Note:* If you have one or more unwanted graphs drawn on top of this one, go back to your function list (**Y=**) and turn "off" the unwanted functions by placing the cursor over their highlighted equal signs and pressing **ENTER**. After you have turned off the unwanted functions, just press **GRAPH** and you will finally see the last screen below.

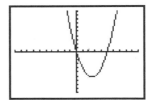

EXAMPLE 2

To modify this function to be $y = -x^2 + 4$, press **Y=**, then insert the negative sign by pressing **2nd INS** followed by the white (or gray) sign change key (**-**); now press the right arrow key twice to skip over the parts of the formula that are to be preserved. Note that the arrow keys also take you out of insert mode. Now type the plus sign and the 4 (replacing the -5), and finally press **DEL** to delete the extra X at the end of the formula. Press **TRACE** to plot this function. **TRACE** gives the added bonus of a highlighted point, with its coordinates shown at the bottom of the screen. Press the right or left arrow keys to highlight other points on the curve.

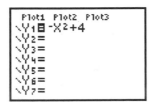
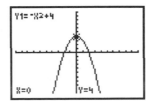
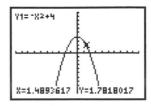

Perhaps $x = 1.4893617$, $y = 1.7818017$ was not a coordinate pair you had expected to investigate. Two special **ZOOM** features (options 4 and 8) can be used to make the **TRACE** option more predictable. Press **ZOOM**, then **4** to select **ZDecimal**; now press **TRACE**.

ZOOM   4   **TRACE**   right arrows

 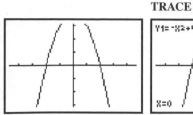 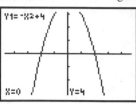 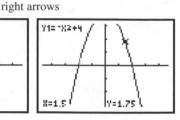

Try pressing the right or left arrow key about 15 times while watching the values at the bottom of the screen. You'll quickly notice that the *x*-values are now all *exact tenths* (**ZOOM** option 8, **ZInteger**, produces **TRACE**able *x*-values which are all integers). Another nice thing about **ZDecimal** is that the graph is "square" in the sense that units on the *x*- and *y*-axes have the same length. The main disadvantage to **ZDecimal** is that the graphing window is "small," displaying only points with *x*-values between -4.7 and 4.7 and *y*-values between -3.1 and 3.1. This disadvantage is apparent on the current graph, which runs off the top of the screen. To demonstrate how this problem can be overcome, **TRACE** the graph to the point $x = 1.5$, $y = 1.75$, and then press **ENTER**. This special feature of **TRACE** causes the graph to be redrawn with the highlighted point in the exact center of the screen (with no change in the magnification of the graph). This is the way to pan up or down from the current viewing window (to pan left or right, see Example 6).

ENTER

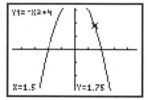 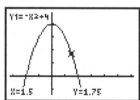

EXAMPLE 3

Another way to deal with the preceding problem is to **Zoom Out**, but first you'll want to set your ZOOM FACTORS to 2 (the factory setting is 4). Press **ZOOM**, then the right arrow key (**MEMORY**), then press **4** (**SetFactors**). To change the factors to 2, just type **2**, press **ENTER**, and then type another **2**.

ZOOM   right arrow   4   2 **ENTER**   2

Now to reproduce our problem, press **ZOOM**, then **4** (**ZDecimal**). However, this time correct it by pressing **ZOOM** followed by **3** (**Zoom Out**). At first glance, it looks like nothing has happened, except that X=0 Y=0 is displayed at the bottom of the screen. The calculator is waiting for you to use your arrow keys to locate the point in the current window where you would like the exact center of the new graph to be (then press **ENTER**). Of course, if you like the way the graph is already centered, you will still have to press **ENTER** (you'll just skip pressing the arrow keys).

ZOOM   4

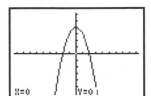
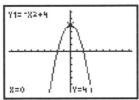

ZOOM   3

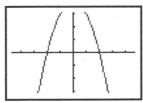
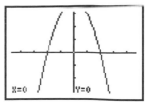

ENTER

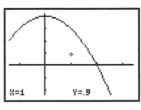

TRACE   right arrows

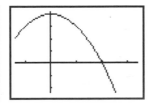
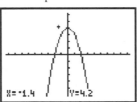
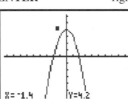
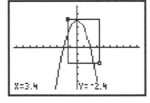

This extra keystroke has proven to be a bit confusing to beginners who think that **Zoom In**, **Zoom Out**, and **ZInteger** should work like the six zoom options (4, 5, 6, 7, 9, and 0) that do their job without pressing **ENTER**. Perhaps more interesting is the fact that you can continue to **Zoom Out** just by pressing **ENTER** again and again (of course, you can also press some arrow keys to recenter between zooms if you wish). Before you experiment with that feature, press **TRACE** and notice, by pressing the left or right arrow key a few times, that the *x*-values are now changing by .2 (instead of .1) and the graph is still "square." Other popular square window settings can be obtained by repeating this example with both zoom factors set to 2.5 or 5. These give "larger" windows where the *x*-values change by .25 or .5, respectively, during a **TRACE**.

EXAMPLE 4

The only other zoom option that needs extra keystrokes is **ZBox** (option 1). This is a very powerful option that lets you draw a box around a part of the graph which you would like enlarged to fit the entire screen. After selecting this option, use the arrow keys to locate the position of one corner of the box and press **ENTER**. Now use the arrow keys to locate the *opposite* corner, and press **ENTER** again.

ZOOM   1   left and up arrows   **ENTER**   right and down arrows

ENTER   **GRAPH**

Note that the resulting graph has a free cursor identifying the point in the exact center of the screen. What may not be apparent is that your calculator is ready for you to draw another box if you wish to zoom in closer. To get rid of this free cursor, just press **GRAPH** (or **CLEAR**).

EXAMPLE 5

Sometimes, you will know the precise interval on the *x*-axis (the domain) that you want for a graph, but a corresponding interval for the *y*-values (the range) may not be obvious. **ZoomFit** (the 10th **ZOOM** option) is designed for this circumstance. For example, to graph $f(x) = 2x^3 - 8x + 9$ on the interval $[-3, 2]$, manually set the **WINDOW** so that Xmin=-3 and Xmax=2 (the other values shown in the second frame are just leftovers from **ZStandard**). Now press **ZOOM**, then **0** to select **ZoomFit**. There is a noticeable pause while appropriate values of Ymin and Ymax are calculated, then the graph is drawn. To view the values calculated for the range, just press **WINDOW**. The minimum value of this function on the interval $[-3, 2]$ is -21 and its maximum value is approximately 15.16.

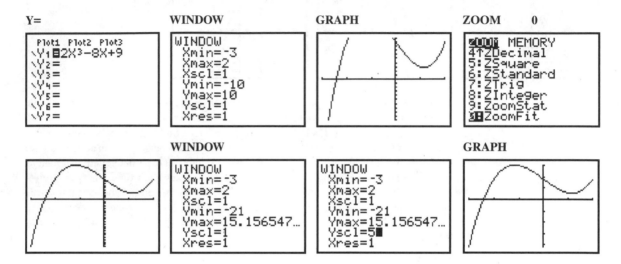

Note that **ZoomFit** changes only Ymin and Ymax. You may also wish to change Yscl.

EXAMPLE 6

Panning to the right is done by tracing a curve off the right-hand edge of the screen:

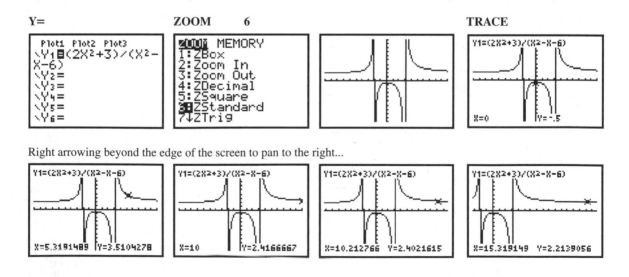

Right arrowing beyond the edge of the screen to pan to the right...

Panning to the left is done similarly. To pan *up or down*, see the last part of Example 2.

EXAMPLE 7

Creating, storing, and retrieving viewing windows:

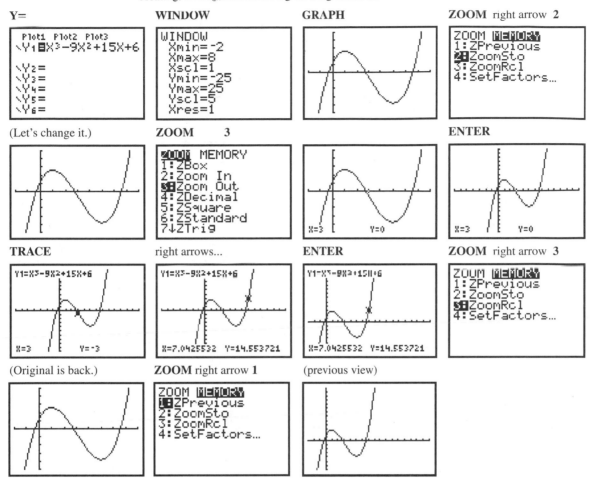

Y=   **WINDOW**   **GRAPH**   **ZOOM** right arrow **2**

(Let's change it.)   **ZOOM**   **3**   **ENTER**

TRACE   right arrows...   **ENTER**   **ZOOM** right arrow **3**

(Original is back.)   **ZOOM** right arrow **1**   (previous view)

EXAMPLE 8

Graphing and tracing more than one function:

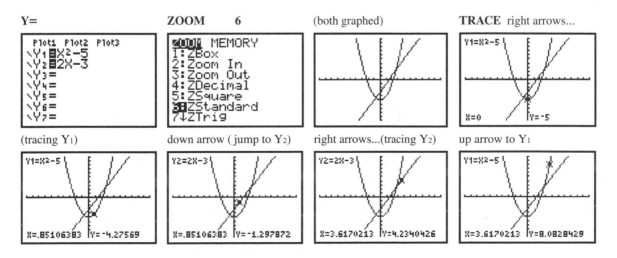

Y=   **ZOOM**   **6**   (both graphed)   **TRACE** right arrows...

(tracing Y₁)   down arrow (jump to Y₂)   right arrows...(tracing Y₂)   up arrow to Y₁

Note that the down arrow increases the subscript of the function being traced and the up arrow decreases the subscript. The result has nothing to do with which graph is above or below the other.

EXAMPLE 9

Finding a point of intersection:

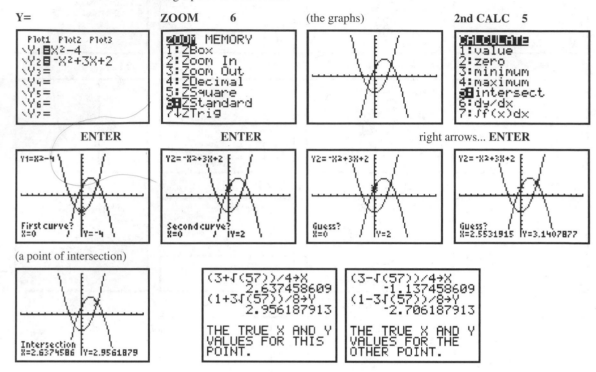

(a point of intersection)

Note that the *Guess* was very important in determining which point of intersection would be calculated. Now find the other intersection point using **intersect**.

EXAMPLE 10

Calculating *y*-values and locating the resulting points on your graphs:
If you have just completed Example 9, please skip to the fourth frame.

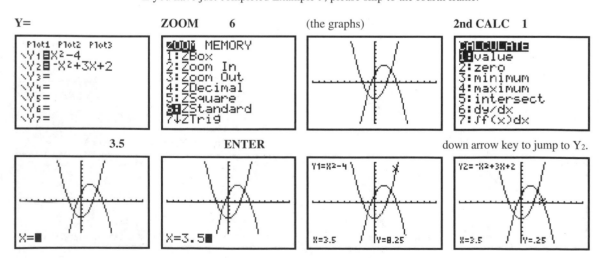

The *x*-value entered must be in the current viewing **WINDOW** (but the resulting *y*-value need not be). This *x*-value can be investigated for any of the functions that are presently graphed by pressing the up or down arrow keys. Note again that the subscript of a function increases as you jump from one curve to another by pressing the down arrow key. The up arrow key decreases this number, and either key can be used to wrap around and start over.

EXAMPLE 11

Another way to calculate a specific value of a function is to press **TRACE**, then type the *x*-value and press **ENTER**. The main difference between the **CALCULATE value** feature (see Example 10) and this special **TRACE** feature is that **TRACE** does *not* preserve the entered *x*-value if you jump from one curve to another (you would usually need to retype that *x*-value). The following frames assume **ZStandard (ZOOM 6) WINDOW** settings.

Y=   **TRACE**   **3.5**   **ENTER**

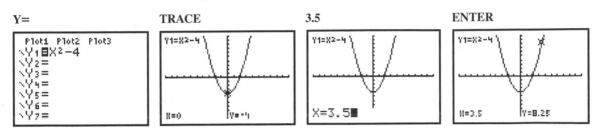

EXAMPLE 12

Using **TRACE** to quickly locate a "lost" graph that doesn't appear anywhere in the current viewing window:

Y=   **ZOOM   6**   (no visible graph)   **TRACE   ENTER**

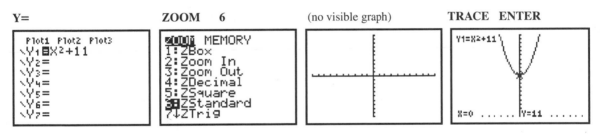

C.5   TRIGONOMETRIC FUNCTIONS AND POLAR COORDINATES

For calculating and graphing trigonometric functions on the TI-83 and TI-84 Plus, the standard default setting is **Radian** mode. To set the calculator to **Degree** mode, press the **MODE** key, arrow down and over to **Degree**, then press **ENTER**.

MODE down arrow *twice*, right arrow **ENTER**   **CLEAR** (or **2nd QUIT**) to exit

 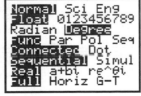

EXAMPLE 1

Evaluating trigonometric functions using degrees, minutes, and seconds:

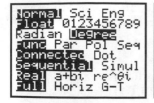
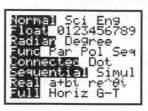

The symbols for degrees and minutes are the first two options in the menu found by pressing **2nd ANGLE** (just to the right of the **MATH** key). The symbol for seconds is the shifted **ALPHA** version of the addition key. Note that in **Radian MODE**, degrees can still be used, but an *additional* degree symbol must follow the angle's measure.

EXAMPLE 2

To graph $y = \sin x$, first press **Y=**, then press **CLEAR** to erase the current formula in Y₁ (or use the arrow keys to find a blank function), then press the **SIN** key followed by the **X,T,θ,n** key (**ALPHA X** will also work), and finally press the right parenthesis key. Your screen should look very much like the first one in the following figure. To set up a good graphing window, press **ZOOM** and then press **7** to choose **ZTrig**. This causes the graph to be immediately drawn on axes that range from roughly -2π to 2π (actually from $-352.5°$ to $352.5°$) in the x-direction and from -4 to 4 in the y-direction. Each mark along the x-axis represents a multiple of $\pi/2$ radians (90°). Notice also that you did not need to press the **GRAPH** key; the **ZOOM** menu items and the **TRACE** key also activate the graphing screen. *Note*: If you have one or more unwanted graphs drawn on top of this one, go back to your function list (**Y=**) and turn "off" the unwanted functions by placing the cursor over their highlighted equal signs and pressing **ENTER**. After you have turned off the unwanted functions, press **GRAPH** and you will finally see the last frame below.

Y=   **ZOOM 7**

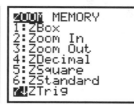
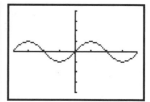

EXAMPLE 3

To modify this function to be $y = -3 \sin 2x$, press **Y=**, then insert the -3 by pressing **2nd INS** followed by the white (or gray) sign change key **(-)** then the number **3**. Now press the right arrow key to skip over the part of the formula that's OK. Note that the arrow keys take you out of insert mode. Now type **2nd INS** then the **2**. Press **ZOOM 7**, then **TRACE** to plot this function. **TRACE** gives the added bonus of a highlighted point with its coordinates shown at the bottom of the screen. Press the right or left arrow keys to highlight other points on the curve. The highlighted coordinate pair in the 4th frame that follows is $x = 5\pi/12$, $y = -1.5$. **ZTrig** allows **TRACE** to display all points whose x-values are multiples of $\pi/24$ (of course, this includes such special values as 0, $\pi/6$, $\pi/4$, $\pi/3$, $\pi/2$, etc.), written in their decimal forms. In degrees, follow the same directions. The only difference is that the traced x-values are now multiples of 7.5° (which is the equivalent of $\pi/24$ radians). As this example illustrates, **ZTrig** has been carefully designed to produce the same graph for both radians and degrees. Other automatic ways of establishing a viewing window, such as **ZStandard** and **ZDecimal**, ignore the **MODE** setting and are not recommended for graphing trigonometric functions in degrees.

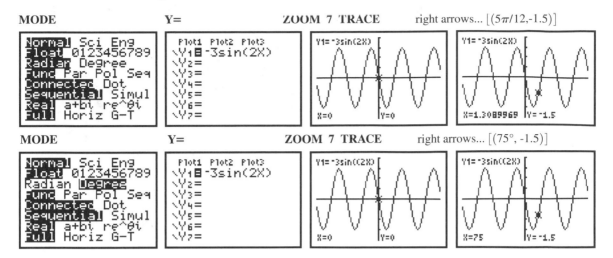

| MODE | Y= | ZOOM 7 TRACE | right arrows... $[(5\pi/12,-1.5)]$ |
| MODE | Y= | ZOOM 7 TRACE | right arrows... $[(75°, -1.5)]$ |

EXAMPLE 4

Several related trig functions can be drawn on the same screen, either by typing them separately in the function list **Y=** or by using a list of coefficients as shown in the following figures. A list consists of numbers separated by commas which are enclosed by braces { }. The braces are the shifted **2nd** versions of the parentheses keys. The first two frames indicate how to efficiently graph $y = \sin(x)$, $y = 2\sin(x)$, and $y = 4\sin(x)$ on the same screen. The last two frames graph $y = 2\sin(x)$ and $y = 2\sin(3x)$.

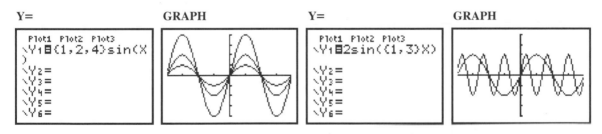

| Y= | GRAPH | Y= | GRAPH |

EXAMPLE 5

Multiple lists are allowed, but are not highly recommended. For example, to graph the two functions $y = 2\sin 3x$ and $y = 4\sin x$, you could do what's shown in the first frame or type them separately as shown in the third frame.

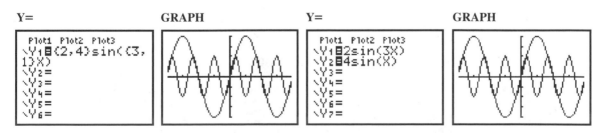

| Y= | GRAPH | Y= | GRAPH |

EXAMPLE 6

When graphing trig functions that have vertical asymptotes, remember that your calculator just evaluates individual points and arbitrarily assumes that it should connect those points if it is set in **Connected MODE**. The effect is shown in the following graph of $y = \sec x$. Some people like these "vertical asymptotes" being shown on the graph (they are really just nearly vertical lines which are trying to connect two points on the curve). The last frame shows the same graph in **Dot MODE**.

Y=

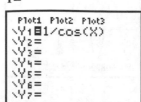

ZOOM   7

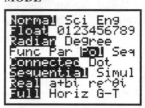

MODE

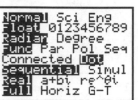

GRAPH

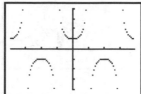

EXAMPLE 7

To graph in polar coordinates, the calculator's **MODE** must be changed from **Func** to **Pol**. You may also wish to change your **2nd FORMAT** options from **RectGC** to **PolarGC**, which will show values of r and θ (instead of x and y) when you **TRACE** your polar graphs. Note that the calculator treats these as two completely separate issues (it is possible to graph in one coordinate system and trace in the other). Pressing **Y=** will reveal the calculator's six polar functions $r_1, r_2, \ldots, r_6$. The **X,T,θ,n** key now prints θ on the screen.

MODE

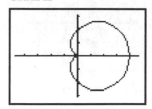

2nd FORMAT

Y= ZOOM   4

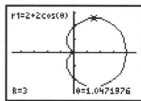

WINDOW

GRAPH

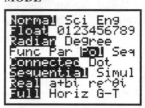

TRACE

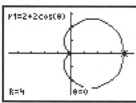

right arrows

Note in the preceding frames that the standard radian values of θmin, θmax, and θstep are 0, 2π, and $\pi/24$, respectively. A more accurate, smoother graph can be obtained by using θstep$=\pi/48$ or $\pi/96$. Also note that the *right* arrow key is used to **TRACE** in the standard, counterclockwise direction.

EXAMPLE 8

Graphing polar equations in **Degree MODE**:

Y= ZOOM   4

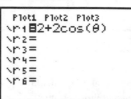

MODE

WINDOW

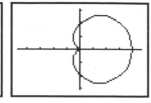

GRAPH

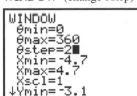
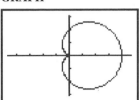

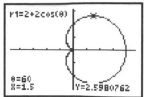

The standard degree values of θmin, θmax, and θstep are 0, 360, and 7.5, respectively. Smoother (but slower) graphs can be obtained by using smaller values of θstep. The last two frames show a polar graph traced in **RectGC FORMAT**.

C.6 EQUATION-SOLVING AND TABLE FEATURES

EXAMPLE 1

Solving an equation on the home screen:
(a) Rewrite the equation on paper in the form $f(x) = 0$; for example, rewrite

$$x^3 + 15x = 9x^2 - 6$$

as

$$x^3 - 9x^2 + 15x + 6 = 0$$

(b) From the home screen, press **2nd CATALOG**, then press the letter **T** (the **4** key), next press the up arrow repeatedly until **solve(** comes into view; then press **ENTER**. You should now see **solve(** on the home screen.

(c) Finish the statement so that it looks like one of the following: **solve($X^3 - 9X^2 + 15X + 6$, X, 3)** or **solve (Y_1, X, 3)**, presuming you've entered the function in Y_1 (to type the symbol Y_1 in a formula, press **VARS** then the right arrow key, then **1**, then **1** again).

Y=	**WINDOW**	**GRAPH**	**2nd CATALOG T** up arrows

```
Plot1 Plot2 Plot3
\Y1■X^3-9X^2+15X+6
\Y2=
\Y3=
\Y4=
\Y5=
\Y6=
```

```
WINDOW
 Xmin=-2
 Xmax=8
 Xscl=1
 Ymin=-25
 Ymax=25
 Yscl=5
 Xres=1
```

```
CATALOG
▶solve(
 SortA(
 SortD(
 stdDev(
 Stop
 StoreGDB
 StorePic
```

ENTER (home screen)	**VARS** right arrow **1** **1**		etc.

```
solve(■
```

```
VARS Y-VARS
1■Function...
2:Parametric...
3:Polar...
4:On/Off...
```

```
FUNCTION
1■Y1
2:Y2
3:Y3
4:Y4
5:Y5
6:Y6
7↓Y7
```

```
solve(Y1,X,3)
        2.748677137
solve(Y1,X,7)
         6.58291867
■
```

(d) Press **ENTER** and the calculator will try to find a zero of this function near 3 (answer: 2.748677137).
(e) Press **2nd ENTRY** to bring back your formula, then arrow left and change the 3 to a 7.
(f) Press **ENTER** and it will now find the zero near 7 (answer: 6.58291867).
(g) See if you can use the **solve** feature to find the other zero (answer: −.3315958073).

   Notice that the **solve** feature finds solutions of an equation *one at a time*, with each new solution requiring its own estimate. Graphing the function and noticing where it crosses the x-axis is usually the easiest way to discover good estimates. If you prefer the **TABLE** feature (see Example 3), look for sign changes in the list of y-values; the corresponding x-values should be good estimates. Random guesses, although not recommended, can be effective when the equation has very few solutions.

EXAMPLE 2

Solving an equation on the graphics screen:

(a) As in Example 1(a), be sure to rewrite the equation as a function set equal to zero.

(b) Enter this function in your (**Y=**) list of functions and make sure that it is the only one selected for graphing.

(c) Press **2nd CALC** (the shifted **TRACE** key), and choose option 2, **zero**.

(d) The prompt "Left Bound?" is asking you to trace the curve using the arrow keys until you are just to the *left* of the desired zero (then press **ENTER**). Again, "Left Bound" just refers to an *x*-value that's too small to be the solution; do not consider whether the curve is above the axis or below the axis at that point. Similarly, the prompt "Right Bound?" is asking you to trace the curve until you are just to the *right* of the desired zero (then press **ENTER**). You'll notice in each case that a bracketing arrow is displayed near the top of the screen to graphically document the interval which will be searched for a solution.

(e) The prompt "Guess?" is asking you to trace the curve to a point as close as possible to where it crosses the axis (then press **ENTER**). This Guess is just an approximate solution like the **solve** feature uses (see Example 1).

(f) The solution (the "Zero") is displayed at the bottom of the screen (using 7 or 8 significant digits rather than the 10 digits you get on the home screen). An added bonus is that the *y*-value is also included (it should be exactly zero or extremely close to zero like "1E-12," which means 10^{-12}). Two of the solutions are found below. Try the third one on your own. The **WINDOW** from the previous example is assumed.

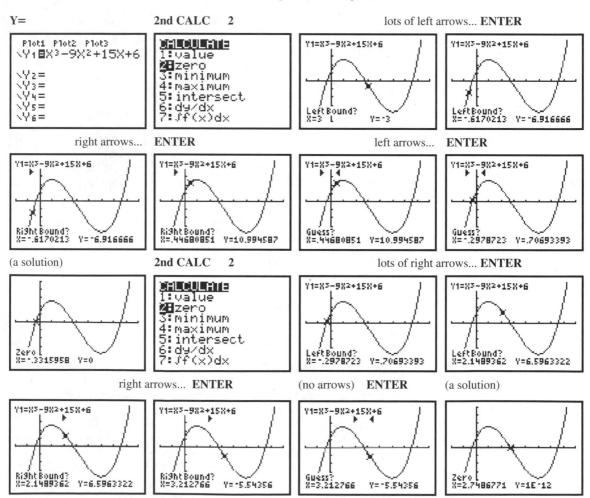

Note that a Right Bound can also be used as the Guess (see the last three frames).

EXAMPLE 3

Basic **TABLE** features:

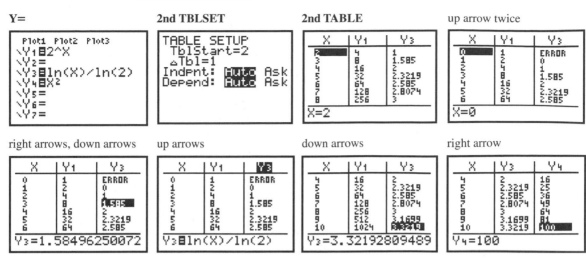

Note that functions to be investigated using a **TABLE** need to be entered and turned on in the same sense as those you want to graph. To get to the TABLE SETUP screen, press **2nd TBLSET** (the shifted version of the **WINDOW** key). TblStart is just a beginning x-value for the table; you can scroll up or down using the arrow keys. ΔTbl is the incremental change in x. You can use ΔTbl=1 (as in the preceding example) to calculate the function at consecutive integers; in calculus, you could use 0.001 to investigate what is happening to a function as it approaches a limit; or you could use a larger number like 10 or 100 to study the function's numerical behavior as x goes to ∞.

EXAMPLE 4

Split-screen graphing with a table (**MODE G-T**):

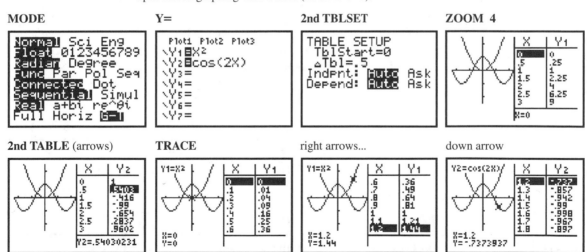

In **MODE G-T**, the graph and a corresponding table share the screen, but only one of them is "active" at any given moment. The **ZOOM** commands and the **GRAPH** key give control to the graphical side of the screen. This just means that the arrow keys refer to the graph rather than the table. Pressing **2nd TABLE** enables the arrow keys to be used to scroll through its values. The **TRACE** key links the table to the graph, with the graph in control (all previous TABLE SETUP specifications are replaced with values related to the **TRACE**).

Note in the last frame that jumping to a different function will display a different column of the table (the same value of x is highlighted).

C.7 THE NUMERIC SOLVER

The TI-83 and TI-84 Plus are equipped with a numeric **Solver** feature (press **MATH**, then **0**), composed of two specialized screens. One is an equation editor that shows **eqn:0=** on the screen, expecting you to fill in the right-hand side. To use the formula for the total surface area of a cylinder, $A = 2\pi R(R + H)$, you must first set one side equal to zero, entering the formula as $0 = 2\pi R(R + H) - A$ or $0 = A - 2\pi R(R + H)$. Pressing **ENTER** takes you to the second screen, where you can enter values and solve for a variable. Enter a value for each letter name except the variable you want to solve for. If there is more than one possible solution for that variable, you can control which one will be found by typing an estimate of it. Use the up and down arrow keys to place the cursor on the line which contains the variable you want to solve for, and press **ALPHA SOLVE (ALPHA**, then the **ENTER** key). The solution is marked by a small square to its left. Also marked (at the bottom of the screen) is a "check" of this solution, indicating the difference between the left- and right-hand sides of the equation using all of the values shown (this should be zero or something very close to zero, such as $1\text{E}-12$). Fourteen significant digits are calculated and displayed for the solution variable. Press **2nd**, then the right arrow key to view the last several digits or to perform arithmetic on the solution; for example, you could divide a solution by π to see *what multiple* of π it is.

The **bound=** option near the bottom of the screen allows you to specify an interval to be searched for the solution. The default interval $\{-1\text{E}99,1\text{E}99\}$ essentially considers any number that the calculator is capable of representing. When solving trigonometric equations, a limited **bound** like the interval $\{0,2\pi\}$ might be better, but in most cases, the default interval works well. If you accidentally erase this line and can't remember the syntax, just exit the **Solver** by pressing **2nd QUIT** and reenter it by pressing **MATH 0**. The default **bound** is restored whenever you enter the **Solver** (any **bound** interval you specify is valid only for that **Solver** session). The equation, however, stays in memory until you **CLEAR** it or replace it with another. Press the up arrow until the top line is reached. The calculator will switch immediately to the equation editor page, where you can modify or **CLEAR** the old equation. The following example assumes that you are starting with a blank equation (as if **Solver** has never been used before); you may **CLEAR** the present equation to achieve the same effect (if an equation is stored, you will always start on the solving screen).

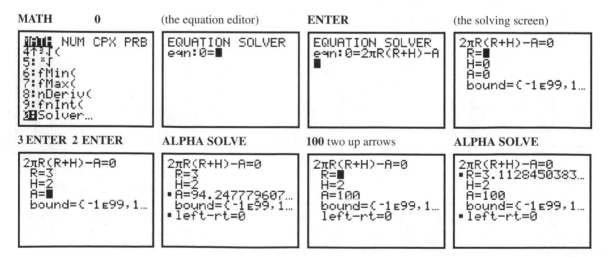

| **MATH** 0 | (the equation editor) | **ENTER** | (the solving screen) |

| **3 ENTER 2 ENTER** | **ALPHA SOLVE** | **100** two up arrows | **ALPHA SOLVE** |

The first two frames in the bottom row of the previous example found the total surface area of a cylinder whose radius is 3 and whose height is 2. The last two frames found the radius of a cylinder whose height is 2 and whose total surface area is 100 square units. Use the **Solver** to find the height of a cylinder whose radius is 5 and whose total surface area is 440 square units (the answer is about 9).

The **Solver** can also be used on equations which contain only one variable, but think about the previous example (which had several variables) to understand why the **Solver** works as it does. In particular, it would seem natural to press **ENTER** after typing an estimate for the solution variable; instead, you must press **ALPHA SOLVE** (press **ALPHA**, *then* the **ENTER** key). If you accidentally press **ENTER** first, you will have to press the up arrow key to get back to the solution variable's line (if the cursor is on **bound=** rather than a variable's line, pressing **ALPHA SOLVE** does *nothing*). For direct comparison, the next example solves the same equation that was solved on both the home screen and the graphics screen in Section C.6. All three methods need one side to be zero and require each solution to be estimated. To solve

$$x^3 + 15x = 9x^2 - 6$$

rewrite it as

$$x^3 - 9x^2 + 15x + 6 = 0$$

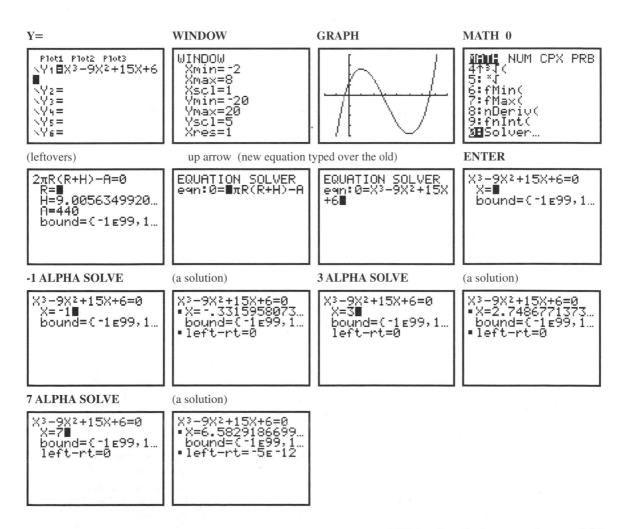

C.8 MATRIX FEATURES

Start by pressing the **MATRX** key on the TI-83 or **2nd MATRX** on the TI-83 Plus. This is the main keyboard difference between these two models. In the remainder of this section, directions will just refer to **MATRX**, which should be interpreted as **2nd MATRX** if you are using a TI-83 Plus (**2nd MATRIX** on Silver Edition). **MATRX** gives you access to three submenus: NAMES, MATH, and EDIT (which can be selected by pressing the right or left arrow keys). The MATH submenu has 16 options, but only 7 of them will fit on the screen at any one time (the arrows next to the 7 in the second frame and the 8 and D in the third frame indicate that there are additional options in those directions).

MATRX   right arrow   down arrows...

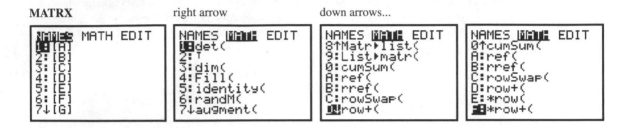

NAMES gives you the ability to insert the name of any one of the 10 user-address-able matrices into a formula on the home screen (or into a program statement in the **PRGM Edit**or). Choosing an item from this submenu is the *only* way to type the name of a matrix on a TI-83 or TI-83 Plus. In particular, typing a left bracket, followed by the letter A, followed by a right bracket, *looks* like the name of the matrix [A], but it will *not* be interpreted as a matrix by the calculator. Either dimension of a matrix can be as large as 99 (note, however, that there is not enough memory to handle a full 99 by 99 matrix). The EDIT submenu allows you to specify the dimensions and entries of the selected matrix. This example shows how to define matrix [C]:

MATRX left arrow **3**   **2 ENTER 3 ENTER**   **1 ENTER -4 ENTER**, etc.

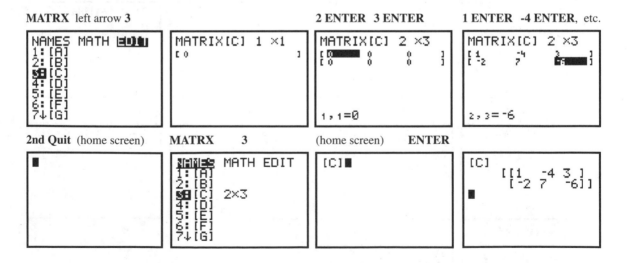

Note that the calculator left-justifies each column, which can make some matrices look a little bit ragged (as in the last frame). Note also that once a matrix has been defined, its dimensions appear in the NAMES and EDIT submenus (see the sixth frame).

The EDIT submenu can also be used to make changes to an existing matrix.

MATRX left arrow **3**   arrow to the incorrect entry, type the new value...**ENTER**

  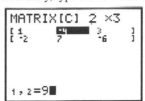

Press **2nd QUIT** to return to the home screen after you finish editing a matrix.

You can also create a new matrix or overwrite an existing one on the home screen (for most purposes, the matrix editor is much more convenient; see the previous example). Type each *row* within brackets, with the entries separated by commas, and enclose the entire matrix within an outer set of brackets. Typically, you'll want to store it in one of the 10 matrix variables [A], . . . , [J], but as the third and fourth frames show, there is also **Ans**, which stores the most recent computational result, even if it's a matrix result:

type entries...**STO**>   **MATRX 2 ENTER**   type entries   **ENTER**   **2nd ANS ENTER**

 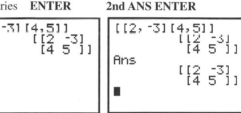

To multiply matrices, just type their names in the proper order (with or without a multiplication sign in between). You can square a matrix using the x^2 button. Multiplication by a scalar is shown in the final frame below:

MATRX 3 MATRX 2 ENTER   **MATRX 2 x^2 ENTER**   **1000 MATRX 2 ENTER**

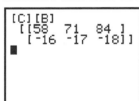 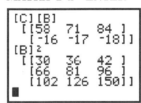 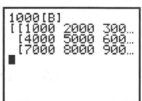

Notice that the three dots at the right of each row of the last frame indicate that there is more of the matrix in that direction; just use the right arrow key to reveal the hidden columns. To find the inverse of a (square) matrix, use the x^{-1} key following the name of the matrix. Fractional forms can be obtained by pressing **MATH 1**, then **ENTER**.

(edit [A]) **2nd Quit**   **MATRX 1 ENTER**   **MATRX 1 x^{-1} ENTER**   **MATH 1 ENTER**

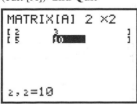 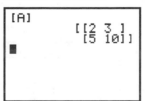 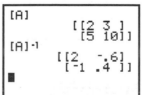 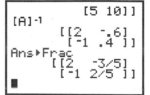

The determinant of a (square) matrix is available as a feature in the MATH submenu.

MATRX right arrow **1**   (home screen)   **MATRX 1**   **) ENTER**

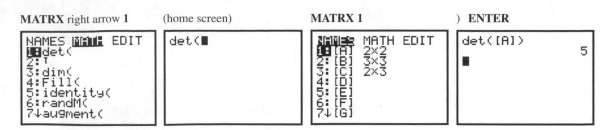

To row-reduce a matrix which might represent a system of equations, the option **rref(** is available in the MATH submenu.

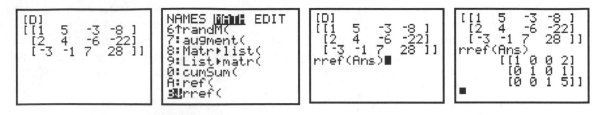

If a matrix has more rows than will fit on the viewing screen, an arrow appears to indicate that there are hidden rows in that direction. Just use the down (or up) arrow key to scroll to these hidden rows.

MATRX 5   (home screen) **ENTER**   down arrow

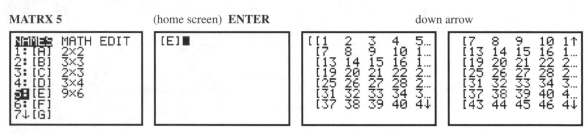

C.9   LIST FEATURES AND DESCRIPTIVE STATISTICS

The TI-83 has six built-in lists, named $L_1, L_2, \ldots, L_6$, which can be accessed from the keyboard by pressing **2nd** followed by the subscript number of the list. You can create and name other lists (starting with a letter and using no more than five characters) and access them by pressing **2nd LIST** (**2nd**, then the **STAT** key). The TI-83 Plus and its Silver Edition will show $L_1, L_2, \ldots, L_6$ in the **LIST** NAMES submenu, but an ordinary TI-83 will not. New list names can be created most easily in the **STAT Edit**or (press **STAT** then **1**). In this editor, go to the very top of any column and press **2nd INS** to create a new list. The example below creates a list named "RBI" and computes its descriptive statistics.

2nd LIST   **STAT 1**   up arrow

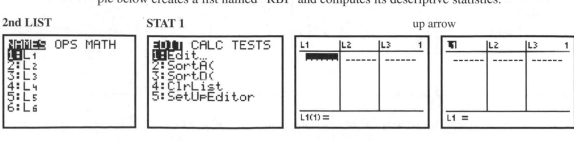

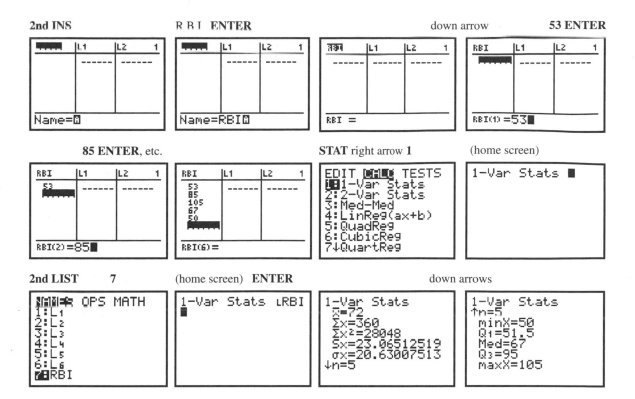

Note that when a list name is shown on the home screen, it is preceded by a small L. This character is available in the **LIST OPS** menu (press **2nd LIST**, right arrow, up arrow, **ENTER**), and is also in the **CATALOG** (press **2nd CATALOG L ENTER**). You can create a list from the home screen by enclosing your data in braces { }, separating the items with commas, and **STO**ring them in a new list name (preceded by the small L). However, a list created in this manner will *not* appear in the **STAT Edit**or until you include its name in a **SetUpEditor** command or **INS**ert its name along the top row of the **STAT Edit**or. To restore the standard setup, which shows just $L_1, L_2, \ldots, L_6$, execute **SetUpEditor** without specifying any list names. Deleting a list from the editor in this way (or by arrowing up to a list name at the top of the editor and pressing **DEL**) does not erase any data or delete the list from the **LIST NAMES** submenu. The list simply doesn't appear in the *editor* for the time being. To erase all data from a list (leaving it empty), arrow up to its name in the top row of the editor and press **CLEAR**, then **ENTER** (or **CLEAR**, then down arrow). To completely dispose of a list (name and all) on a TI-83 Plus, press **2nd MEM 2 4** and down arrow until the marker points at the name of the list you wish to get rid of, then press **DEL** (*not* **ENTER**). On an ordinary TI-83, press **ENTER** instead of **DEL**.

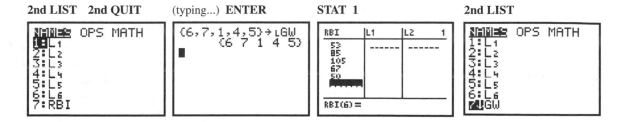

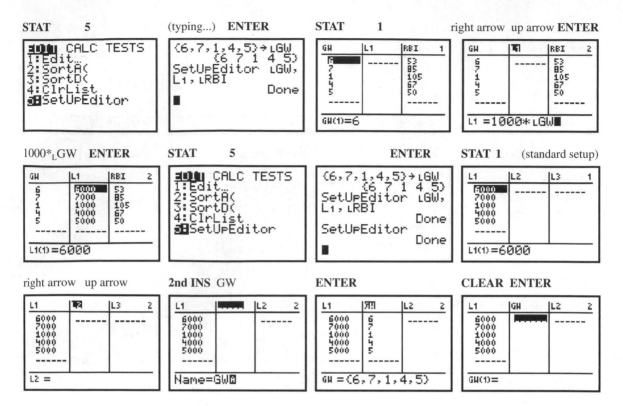

STAT 5   (typing...) **ENTER**   **STAT 1**   right arrow up arrow **ENTER**

1000*$_L$GW **ENTER**   **STAT 5**   **ENTER**   **STAT 1**   (standard setup)

right arrow up arrow   **2nd INS** GW   **ENTER**   **CLEAR ENTER**

The first three frames in the bottom row show how to insert a preexisting list into the **STAT Edit**or. The last frame illustrates how to **CLEAR** a list, leaving it empty, but still named. If you highlight a list's name (in the very top row of the editor), you will be able to wrap around using the right or left arrow keys. If you wrap around using the *right* arrow, you will also notice a new blank list in the editor, ready to be named and filled with data. Just press **ENTER** or down arrow when it is highlighted, and you will be given a chance to name it. The **STAT Edit**or can hold up to 20 lists at once. Each list stored in a TI-83 or TI-83 Plus can have as many as 999 elements.

C.10 THE LINE OF BEST FIT (LINEAR REGRESSION)

EXAMPLE

Find and graph the equation of the line of best fit for the following data:

x	5	7	9	12	14
y	40	58	62	74	80

STAT 1   **5 ENTER 7 ENTER**, etc.   right arrow   **40 ENTER**, etc.

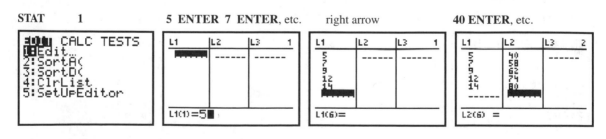

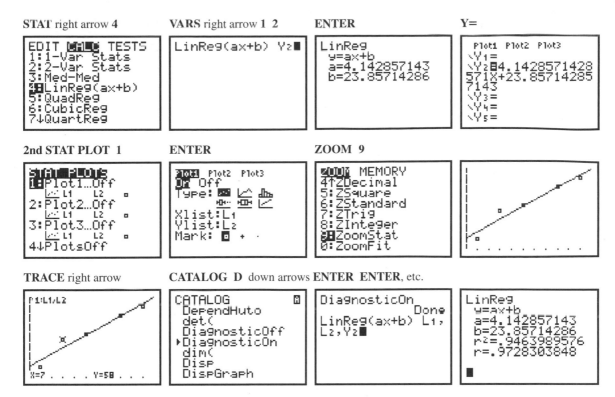

STAT right arrow **4**

```
EDIT CALC TESTS
1:1-Var Stats
2:2-Var Stats
3:Med-Med
4▉LinReg(ax+b)
5:QuadReg
6:CubicReg
7↓QuartReg
```

VARS right arrow **1 2**

```
LinReg(ax+b) Y2▉
```

ENTER

```
LinReg
  y=ax+b
  a=4.142857143
  b=23.85714286
```

Y=

```
Plot1 Plot2 Plot3
\Y1=
\Y2▉4.1428571428
571X+23.85714285
7143
\Y3=
\Y4=
\Y5=
```

2nd STAT PLOT 1

```
STAT PLOTS
1▉Plot1…Off
    ⊾ L1  L2   ▫
2:Plot2…Off
    ⊾ L1  L2   ▫
3:Plot3…Off
    ⊾ L1  L2   ▫
4↓PlotsOff
```

ENTER

```
Plot1 Plot2 Plot3
On Off
Type: ▨ ⊾ ▥
      ▥ ▥ ▥
Xlist:L1
Ylist:L2
Mark: ▫ + ·
```

ZOOM 9

```
ZOOM MEMORY
4↑ZDecimal
5:ZSquare
6:ZStandard
7:ZTrig
8:ZInteger
9▉ZoomStat
0:ZoomFit
```

TRACE right arrow

```
P1:L1/L2




X=7 . . . . Y=58 . . .
```

CATALOG D down arrows **ENTER ENTER**, etc.

```
CATALOG        ▣
  DependAuto
  det(
  DiagnosticOff
▸ DiagnosticOn
  dim(
  Disp
  DispGraph
```

```
DiagnosticOn
            Done
LinReg(ax+b) L1,
L2,Y2▉
```

```
LinReg
  y=ax+b
  a=4.142857143
  b=23.85714286
  r²=.9463989576
  r=.9728303848
▉
```

Turn **STAT PLOT 1 Off** *now* (before trying to graph anything else).

In the last three frames, this linear regression is shown in more detail. **DiagnosticOn** enables the calculator to compute and print correlation coefficients. **DiagnosticOff** is the default setting. These options appear only in the **CATALOG**. The last linear regression command shows the full syntax of the **LinReg(ax+b)** statement. All three parameters are optional. The name of the first list provides the x-values, the second list provides the y-values, and the third parameter is the name of the function where the regression equation will be stored. If you omit the two list names, the calculator will use list L_1 for the x-values and list L_2 for the y-values (see the sixth frame of the example). If you don't plan to use or graph the regression equation, you may omit the function name. To turn **PLOT 1 Off**, press **Y=**, up arrow, then **ENTER**.

C.11 CALCULUS FEATURES

EXAMPLE 1

Finding local minimum and maximum values on the graphics screen:

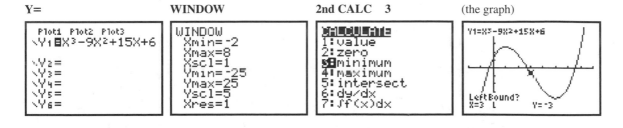

Y=

```
Plot1 Plot2 Plot3
\Y1▉X³-9X²+15X+6

\Y2=
\Y3=
\Y4=
\Y5=
\Y6=
```

WINDOW

```
WINDOW
 Xmin=-2
 Xmax=8
 Xscl=1
 Ymin=-25
 Ymax=25
 Yscl=5
 Xres=1
```

2nd CALC 3

```
CALCULATE
1:value
2:zero
3▉minimum
4:maximum
5:intersect
6:dy/dx
7:∫f(x)dx
```

(the graph)

```
Y1=X³-9X²+15X+6



LeftBound?
X=3  L      Y=-3
```

right arrows... **ENTER**

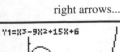

right arrows... **ENTER**

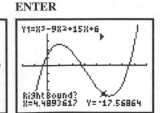

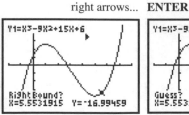

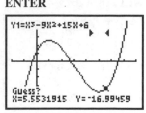

left arrows... **ENTER**

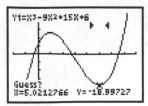

The minimum point is actually $(5, -19)$; tiny errors happen.

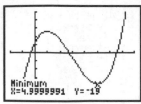

Now use **maximum** to find the local maximum point [answer: $(1, 13)$].

EXAMPLE 2

Finding local minimum and maximum values on the home screen (review Example 1 in Section C.6 if you don't remember how to type the symbol for Y_1 into a formula):

Y= **2nd QUIT**

MATH **6**

VARS right arrow **1** **1** etc.

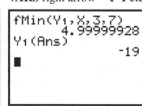

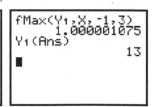

The only intended use of these maximum and minimum routines is to find *local* extreme values using a fairly short bracketing interval. These routines can give unpredictable results if you try to use them to compare local extrema with endpoint extrema on a given interval. Example 5 in Section C.4 shows how **ZoomFit** can be used to estimate the maximum and minimum of a function on a closed interval.

EXAMPLE 3

Finding values of the derivative using the graphics screen:

Y=

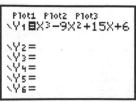

2nd CALC **6**

7

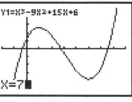

ENTER

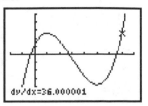

EXAMPLE 4

Finding values of the derivative using the home screen:

Y=   2nd QUIT   MATH   8

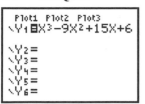   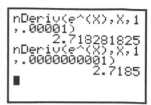

Note that **nDeriv** (numerical derivative) requires three arguments and has an optional fourth. The required arguments are the name of the function you wish to differentiate, the name of the variable to differentiate with respect to, and the value of that variable at the point where the derivative is to be calculated. This routine actually calculates the slope of the line connecting the two points $(x - h, f(x - h))$ and $(x + h, f(x + h))$, which are just a small increment on either side of the point $(x, f(x))$. The optional last argument gives you a chance to say just how small this increment h should be. The default value is .001. An h-value of .00001 often gives better accuracy for commonly studied functions. But don't go overboard on this or any other optional accuracy parameters. You risk severe loss-of-significance errors if you use tiny h-values such as .00000000000001. Note the last frame above. With $h = .00001$, there are nine significant digits in our answer (all but the last digit is correct); but with $h = .0000000001$, we get only four significant digits. In fact, **nDeriv(e^(X), X, 1, 1E-14)** calculates 0, a total loss of significant digits! This phenomenon is typical of computations that involve *subtracting* numbers that are *very* close together on a machine which can only store a limited number of digits.

EXAMPLE 5

Evaluating a function and its first and second derivatives (at $x = 4$):

Y=   2nd QUIT

 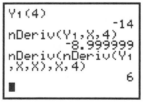

EXAMPLE 6

Graphing a function and its first and second derivatives:

Y=   ZOOM   7

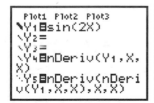 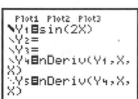  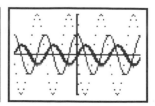

 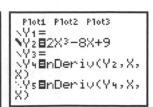 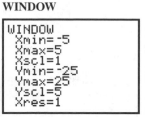 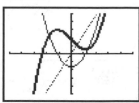

Note that the second derivative Y_5 is shown coded in two different, but equivalent, ways (choose whichever one you like). The first coding style is similar to the home-screen version of the second derivative (see Example 5). The other style exploits the formula for the first derivative, stored in Y_4. It requires less typing, both in the initial example and also when all references to Y_1 are changed to Y_2. Many calculus students keep these derivative-graphing formulas permanently stored in Y_4 and Y_5, just turning them on or off at appropriate times. Third and higher derivatives are *not* supported in either manner of coding.

EXAMPLE 7

Numerical integration on the home screen:

MATH   9

 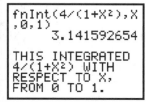 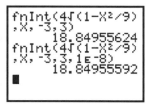

Note that **fnInt** (function integral) needs the name of the function, the name of the variable you're integrating with respect to, the lower limit of integration, and the upper limit of integration (in that order). The optional fifth argument gives you a chance to specify how little error you are willing to tolerate in the numerical result. The standard (default) value is .00001, which usually yields considerably less error than that. In the second frame in the preceding figure, the exact answer is π, which was computed to 14 significant digits (storing your answer in a **LIST** allows you to view all 14 digits that are stored in the calculator). In the last frame, the top calculation took 23 seconds and produced 8 significant digits; the second version produced 11 significant digits, but took 44 seconds to calculate. This is an example of a difficult numerical integration (finding the area enclosed by the ellipse $x^2/9 + y^2/4 = 1$); the exact answer is 6π. Most problems are like the middle frame, where you will get impressive accuracy, very quickly, without needing to specify the optional fifth argument. The **fnInt** feature is based on a powerful Gaussian method that will consistently outperform Simpson's rule and other elementary numerical procedures.

EXAMPLE 8

Numerical integration on the graphics screen:

Y=   **WINDOW**   **2nd CALC   7**   **0**

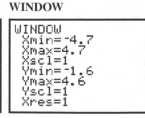 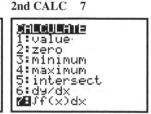 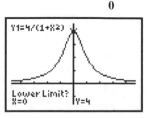

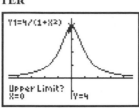
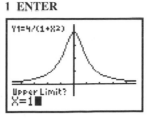
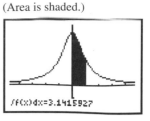

You can enter the lower and upper limits from the keyboard, as shown above or by arrowing over to the proper values using the left or right arrow keys (then pressing **ENTER**). The latter method has the disadvantage that the limits of integration you intended to use often aren't traceable *x*-values in the present viewing window (you can get close, but cannot get the exact limits desired). The result of the numerical integration is shown at the bottom of the screen and can be interpreted as the area of the shaded region. The accuracy of the calculation is the same as the default accuracy for **fnInt** (five decimal places are guaranteed).

C.12   SEQUENCES AND SERIES

On the TI-83 or TI-83 Plus, a sequence (**seq**) can be created and stored as a list. Series can be treated as the **sum** of such a list. Both features are found in the submenus under **2nd LIST** (the shifted version of the **STAT** key).

EXAMPLE 1

Enumerate the sequence of the first six squares ($a_n = n^2$ for $n = 1$ to 6), then evaluate its sum:

2nd LIST   right arrow **5**   etc.

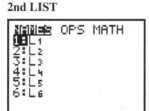
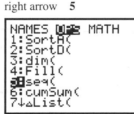
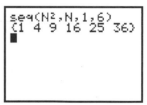

2nd LIST   left arrow **5**   **2nd ANS) ENTER**

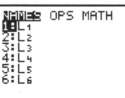

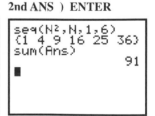

EXAMPLE 2

Evaluate the sum: $7 + 9 + 11 + 13 + 15 + \cdots + 121$.

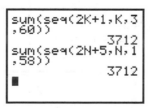

Note that there are many different coding possibilities.

EXAMPLE 3

Estimate the infinite geometric series $\sum_{n=0}^{\infty} (2/3)^n$.

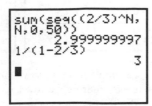

      The top calculation shows the sum of the first 51 terms. The bottom calculation shows that the formula $a_0/(1 - r)$ gives an exact answer of 3.

EXAMPLE 4

Estimate the value of the infinite series $\sum_{n=0}^{\infty} 1/n!$.

      Remember that the factorial symbol can be found by pressing **MATH**, left arrow, **4**, as shown in the first frame below.

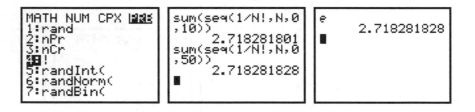

      The exact answer is the number e, the shifted **2nd** version of the division key.

EXAMPLE 5

Use the 7th-degree and 21st-degree Taylor polynomials of $\sin(x)$ to estimate $\sin(\pi/6)$.

7th-degree estimate   21st-degree estimate

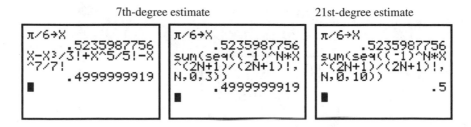

      Note that the degree of the estimate was increased simply by changing the last **seq** index from 3 to 10.

EXAMPLE 6

Graph the 2nd-, 4th-, 6th-, and 8th-degree Taylor polynomials of $\cos(x)$ along with the graph of $y = \cos x$. On a separate screen, graph the 20th-degree Taylor polynomial of $\cos(x)$. Be sure that your calculator is in **Radian MODE**.

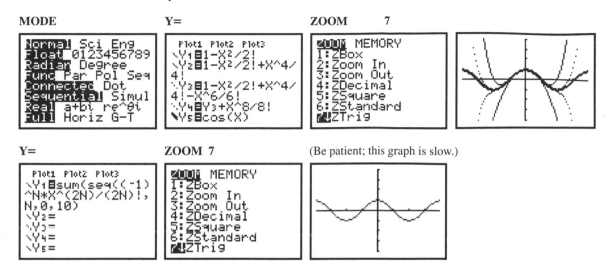

(Be patient; this graph is slow.)

Try a similar exercise for $\sin(x)$, graphing its 1st-, 3rd-, 5th-, 7th-, and 9th-degree Taylor polynomials. See Example 5 for sample formulas.

Answers to Odd-Numbered Exercises and Chapter Reviews

CHAPTER 1

Exercises 1.1, Page 4

1. $\frac{2}{9}(3x+2)^{3/2}+C$ **3.** $2\sqrt{4+x}+C$ **5.** $\frac{2}{7}(x^2+4x)^{7/4}+C$ **7.** $-\frac{1}{4}\cos^4 x+C$ **9.** $\frac{1}{16}\tan^4 4x+C$

11. $-\frac{1}{8}(\cos 4x+1)^2+C$ **13.** $\frac{2}{3}(9+\sec x)^{3/2}+C$ **15.** $\frac{1}{3}(1+e^{2x})^{3/2}+C$ **17.** $\sqrt{1+e^{x^2}}+C$

19. $\frac{1}{6}\ln^2|3x-5|+C$ **21.** $-\dfrac{1}{\ln|x|}+C$ **23.** $\frac{1}{6}\arcsin^2 3x+C$ **25.** $\frac{1}{4}\sin^4 x+C$ **27.** $\frac{1}{3}\arctan^3 x+C$

29. $\frac{64}{3}$ **31.** $\frac{2}{3}(\sqrt{1+e^3}-\sqrt{2})$ **33.** $\frac{1}{4}\ln^2 3$ **35.** $\frac{1}{3}$

Exercises 1.2, Page 8

1. $\frac{1}{3}\ln|3x+2|+C$ **3.** $-\frac{1}{4}\ln|1-4x|+C$ **5.** $-2\ln|1-x^2|+C$ **7.** $\frac{1}{4}\ln|x^4-1|+C$

9. $-\ln|\cot x|+C$ or $\ln|\tan x|+C$ **11.** $\frac{1}{3}\ln|1+\tan 3x|+C$ **13.** $-\ln|1+\csc x|+C$ **15.** $\ln|1+\sin x|+C$

17. $\ln|\ln|x||+C$ **19.** $\frac{1}{2}e^{2x}+C$ **21.** $\dfrac{-1}{4e^{4x}}+C$ **23.** $\frac{1}{2}e^{x^2}+C$ **25.** $-\frac{1}{2}e^{-x^2-9}+C$ **27.** $-e^{\cos x}+C$

29. $\dfrac{e^2}{2}(e^4-1)$ **31.** $\dfrac{4^x}{\ln 4}+C$ **33.** $2\ln|e^x+4|+C$ **35.** $\frac{1}{2}\ln 2$ or 0.347   **37.** $2\ln 9$ or $\ln 81$ or 4.39

39. $2(e-1)$ or 3.44   **41.** $\frac{1}{3}(e-1)$ or 0.573   **43.** $\ln 2$ or 0.693   **45.** $\frac{1}{2}\ln 3$ or 0.549   **47.** $\frac{1}{2}(e^8-1)$ or 1490

Exercises 1.3, Pages 13–14

1. $-\frac{1}{5}\cos 5x+C$ **3.** $\frac{1}{3}\sin(3x-1)+C$ **5.** $-\frac{1}{2}\cos(x^2+5)+C$ **7.** $\sin(x^3-x^2)+C$ **9.** $-\frac{1}{5}\cot 5x+C$

11. $\frac{1}{3}\sec 3x+C$ **13.** $\frac{1}{4}\tan(4x+3)+C$ **15.** $-\frac{1}{2}\csc(2x-3)+C$ **17.** $\frac{1}{2}\tan(x^2+3)+C$

19. $-\frac{1}{3}\csc(x^3-1)+C$ **21.** $-\frac{1}{4}\ln|\cos 4x|+C$ **23.** $\frac{1}{5}\ln|\sec 5x+\tan 5x|+C$ **25.** $\ln|\sin e^x|+C$

27. $x+2\ln|\sec x+\tan x|+\tan x+C$ **29.** $5\ln|\sec x+\tan x|-\ln|\cos x|+C$ **31.** $\frac{1}{2}$ **33.** 3   **35.** 1

37. $\dfrac{\sqrt{2}-1}{2}$ **39.** 2   **41.** 1   **43.** $\frac{1}{2}\ln 2$ **45.** π

Exercises 1.4, Page 17

1. $\frac{1}{3}\cos^3 x-\cos x+C$ **3.** $\sin x-\frac{2}{3}\sin^3 x+\frac{1}{5}\sin^5 x+C$ **5.** $\frac{1}{3}\sin^3 x+C$ **7.** $\dfrac{-1}{2\cos^2 x}+C$

9. $-\frac{1}{3}\cos^3 x+\frac{1}{5}\cos^5 x+C$ **11.** $\dfrac{x}{2}-\frac{1}{4}\sin 2x+C$ **13.** $\dfrac{3x}{8}+\frac{1}{12}\sin 6x+\frac{1}{96}\sin 12x+C$

15. $\dfrac{x}{8}-\frac{1}{32}\sin 4x+C$ **17.** $\dfrac{x}{16}-\frac{1}{64}\sin 4x+\frac{1}{48}\sin^3 2x+C$ **19.** $\frac{1}{2}\tan^2 x+\ln|\cos x|+C$

21. $x-\frac{1}{6}\cot^3 2x+\frac{1}{2}\cot 2x+C$ **23.** $\tan x+\frac{2}{3}\tan^3 x+\frac{1}{5}\tan^5 x+C$

25. $\frac{1}{6}\tan^3 2x-\frac{1}{2}\tan 2x+x+C$ **27.** $\dfrac{\pi}{2}$

Exercises 1.5, Page 20

1. $\frac{1}{3}\arcsin 3x + C$ **3.** $\arcsin\frac{x}{3} + C$ **5.** $\frac{1}{5}\arctan\frac{x}{5} + C$ **7.** $\frac{1}{6}\arctan\frac{3x}{2} + C$ **9.** $\frac{1}{5}\arcsin\frac{5x}{6} + C$

11. $\frac{1}{2\sqrt{3}}\arcsin 2x + C$ **13.** $\frac{1}{2}\arctan\left(\frac{x-1}{2}\right) + C$ **15.** $\frac{1}{4}\arctan\left(\frac{x+3}{4}\right) + C$ **17.** $\arcsin e^x + C$

19. $-\arctan(\cos x) + C$ **21.** $\frac{\pi}{4}$ **23.** 0.215   **25.** 10.9 N

Exercises 1.6, Page 27

1. $\frac{5}{x+2} + \frac{3}{x-7}$ **3.** $\frac{3}{2x+3} - \frac{2}{x-4}$ **5.** $\frac{7}{x} + \frac{2}{3x-4} + \frac{5}{2x+1}$ **7.** $\frac{1}{x+1} + \frac{1}{(x+3)^2}$

9. $\frac{3}{4x-1} + \frac{1}{(4x-1)^2} - \frac{7}{(4x-1)^3}$ **11.** $\frac{3}{x} + \frac{8}{x-1} - \frac{4}{(x-1)^2}$ **13.** $\frac{x-1}{x^2+1} - \frac{x}{x^2-3}$

15. $\frac{4x+1}{x^2+x+1} - \frac{1}{x^2-5}$ **17.** $\frac{5x-2}{x^2+5x+3} + \frac{1}{x+3} - \frac{2}{x-3}$ **19.** $\frac{5}{x} + \frac{3x-1}{x^2+1} - \frac{5}{(x^2+1)^2}$

21. $\frac{1}{x} - \frac{2}{x^2} - \frac{4x}{(x^2+2)^2}$ **23.** $\frac{2}{x+3} + \frac{4}{x-3} - \frac{6x}{x^2+9}$ **25.** $x + \frac{\frac{1}{2}}{x+1} + \frac{\frac{1}{2}}{x-1}$ **27.** $x - 1 + \frac{3}{x-2} + \frac{1}{x+2}$

29. $3x - 2 + \frac{5}{x} - \frac{8x}{x^2+1}$

Exercises 1.7, Pages 29–30

1. $\frac{1}{2}\ln\left|\frac{x+1}{x-1}\right| + C$ **3.** $\frac{1}{6}\ln\left|\frac{x-2}{x+4}\right| + C$ **5.** $2\ln|x-2| - \ln|x-1| + C$ or $\ln\left|\frac{(x-2)^2}{x-1}\right| + C$

7. $\frac{2}{3}\ln|x+5| + \frac{1}{3}\ln|x-1| + C$ or $\frac{1}{3}\ln|(x+5)^2(x-1)| + C$ **9.** $\ln\left|\frac{x}{x+1}\right| + \frac{1}{x+1} + C$

11. $2\ln|x+3| - \frac{1}{x} + C$ **13.** $\frac{x^2}{2} - 3x + \ln\left|\frac{(x+2)^8}{x+1}\right| + C$ **15.** $\frac{3}{2}\ln|x^2+1| - 2\ln|x| + C$

17. $\frac{1}{2}\ln|x^2+9| + \arctan\frac{x}{3} + \frac{1}{x} + C$ **19.** $\frac{1}{2(x^2+1)} + \frac{1}{2}\ln|x^2+1| + C$ **21.** $\frac{3}{2}\ln\frac{2}{3}$ **23.** $\frac{11}{6}\ln 3 - \frac{5}{6}\ln 7$

25. $\ln 3 + 3\ln\frac{7}{5}$

Exercises 1.8, Page 34

1. $x\ln|x| - x + C$ **3.** $xe^x - e^x + C$ **5.** $\frac{2}{3}x^{3/2}\ln|x| - \frac{4}{9}x^{3/2} + C$ **7.** $x\ln x^2 - 2x + C$

9. $x\arccos x - \sqrt{1-x^2} + C$ **11.** $\frac{1}{2}e^x(\sin x + \cos x) + C$ **13.** $x^2\sin x + 2x\cos x - 2\sin x + C$

15. $x\tan x + \ln|\cos x| + C$ **17.** $x(\ln|x|)^2 - 2x\ln|x| + 2x + C$ **19.** $x\sec x - \ln|\sec x + \tan x| + C$

21. $\frac{1}{9}(2e^3 + 1)$ **23.** $\frac{16}{15}$ **25.** $3\ln 3 - 2\ln 2 - 1$ or $\ln\frac{27}{4} - 1$ **27.** $\ln 2 - \frac{1}{2}$ **29.** 2π

Exercises 1.9, Page 39

1. $\frac{1}{2}\ln|2x + \sqrt{9+4x^2}| + C$ **3.** $-\frac{x}{18}\sqrt{4-9x^2} + \frac{2}{27}\arcsin\frac{3x}{2} + C$ **5.** $\arcsin\frac{1}{3}$ **7.** $\frac{1}{4\sqrt{3}}$

9. $\frac{1}{2}\ln\left|\frac{\sqrt{x^2+4}-2}{x}\right| + C$ **11.** $\ln|x + \sqrt{x^2-9}| - \frac{\sqrt{x^2-9}}{x} + C$ **13.** $\frac{-\sqrt{16-x^2}}{16x} + C$

15. $\sqrt{9+x^2} - 3\ln\left|\frac{3+\sqrt{9+x^2}}{x}\right| + C$ **17.** $\frac{x}{25\sqrt{25-x^2}} + C$ **19.** $\ln|x + \sqrt{x^2+9}| + C$

21. $\frac{9x^2-8}{243}\sqrt{9x^2+4} + C$ **23.** $\ln|x - 3 + \sqrt{x^2-6x+8}| + C$ **25.** $-\frac{x+4}{\sqrt{x^2+8x+15}} + C$ **27.** $\ln(1 + \sqrt{2})$

Exercises 1.10, Page 41

1. $\frac{1}{\sqrt{5}}\ln\left|\frac{\sqrt{x+5}-\sqrt{5}}{\sqrt{x+5}+\sqrt{5}}\right| + C;\ 15$ **3.** $\ln|x + \sqrt{x^2-4}| + C;\ 35$ **5.** $-\frac{(3-x)\sqrt{2x+3}}{3};\ 13$

7. $\frac{1}{4}\left(\frac{\sin 4x}{2} - \frac{\sin 10x}{5}\right) + C;\ 75$ **9.** $-\frac{x}{2}\sqrt{9-x^2} + \frac{9}{2}\arcsin\frac{x}{3} + C;\ 24$ **11.** $\frac{1}{1+9x} + \ln\left|\frac{x}{1+9x}\right| + C;\ 9$

13. $\frac{1}{10}\ln\left|\frac{x-5}{x+5}\right| + C;\ 20$ **15.** $\frac{x}{2}\sqrt{x^2+4} + 2\ln|x + \sqrt{x^2+4}| + C;\ 30$ **17.** $\frac{1}{16}\left(\frac{3}{3+4x} + \ln|3+4x|\right) + C;\ 7$

19. $\frac{1}{4}\arccos\frac{4}{3x} + C$; 36   **21.** $\frac{e^{3x}}{25}(3\sin 4x - 4\cos 4x) + C$; 59   **23.** $\frac{1}{2}\sin(2x-3) - \frac{(2x-3)}{2}\cos(2x-3) + C$; 80

25. $-\frac{1}{4}\sin^3 x\cos x + \frac{3x}{8} - \frac{3}{8}\sin x\cos x + C$; 83   **27.** $\sqrt{9x^2 - 16} - 4\arccos\frac{4}{3x} + C$; 33

Exercises 1.11, Pages 46–49

1. 1.117   **3.** 0.783   **5.** 1.913   **7.** 7.395   **9.** 0.925   **11.** 219 ft-lb   **13.** 270   **15.** 1.443   **17.** 0.105
19. 1.464   **21.** 0.186   **23.** 1.910   **25. (a)** 6.889 **(b)** 6.998   **27. (a)** 1.023 **(b)** 1.000
29. (a) 1.006 **(b)** 1.006   **31. (a)** 373,650 ft^2 **(b)** 378,200 ft^2

Exercises 1.12, Pages 55–56

1. $\frac{4\pi}{3}$ **3.** $\frac{9\pi}{4}$ **5.** 9   **7.** $\frac{3\pi}{2}$ **9.** 8π **11.** 8π **13.** $\frac{41\pi}{2}$ **15.** $\frac{1}{4}(e^{2\pi} - 1)$ **17.** $\pi - \frac{3\sqrt{3}}{2}$

19. 2π **21.** $\frac{\pi}{4} - \frac{3\sqrt{3}}{16}$ **23.** $\frac{2\pi}{3} + \sqrt{3}$ **25.** $\frac{11\pi}{12} + \sqrt{3}$ **27.** $9\sqrt{2} + \frac{27\pi}{8} + \frac{9}{4}$

Exercises 1.13, Pages 60–61

1. 1   **3.** $\frac{1}{3}$ **5.** ∞ (diverges)   **7.** $\frac{1}{5}$ **9.** 3   **11.** ∞ (diverges)   **13.** $\frac{1}{2}$ **15.** 2   **17.** $\frac{1}{4}$ **19.** π

Chapter 1 Review, Pages 63–65

1. $\frac{2}{3}\sqrt{2 + \sin 3x} + C$ **2.** $\frac{(5 + \tan 2x)^4}{8} + C$ **3.** $\frac{1}{3}\sin 3x + C$ **4.** $\frac{1}{2}\ln|x^2 - 5| + C$ **5.** $\frac{1}{6}e^{3x^2} + C$

6. $\frac{1}{3}\arctan\frac{2x}{3} + C$ **7.** $\arcsin\frac{x}{4} + C$ **8.** $\frac{1}{7}\tan(7x + 2) + C$ **9.** $\frac{1}{5}\ln|3 + 5\tan x| + C$

10. $-\frac{1}{3}\cos(x^3 + 4) + C$ **11.** $\frac{1}{12}\arctan\frac{3}{4}$ **12.** $\frac{1}{\pi}$ **13.** $-\ln\frac{\sqrt{2}}{2}$ or $\ln\sqrt{2}$ **14.** $\frac{1}{2}\arcsin\frac{2}{3}$

15. $\frac{1}{3}\arccos\frac{3}{4x} + C$ **16.** $-\frac{1}{12}\cos^4 3x + C$ **17.** $\frac{1}{6}\arctan^2 3x + C$ **18.** $\frac{1}{5}\ln|\sec 5x + \tan 5x| + C$

19. $-\frac{1}{2}\ln|\cos x^2| + C$ **20.** $-\frac{\cos^3 2x}{6} + \frac{1}{5}\cos^5 2x - \frac{\cos^7 2x}{14} + C$ **21.** $\frac{x}{16} - \frac{1}{192}\sin 12x + \frac{1}{144}\sin^3 6x + C$

22. $\frac{1}{4}\ln\left|\frac{x-1}{x+3}\right| + C$ **23.** $\frac{e^{3x}}{25}(3\cos 4x + 4\sin 4x)$ **24.** $\cos x(1 - \ln|\cos x|) + C$ **25.** $\frac{\tan^3 x}{3} - \tan x + x + C$

26. $\frac{x}{2} + \frac{\sin 10x}{20} + C$ **27.** $\frac{2}{3}\ln|3x + 1| - \frac{1}{2}\ln|2x - 1| + C$ **28.** $\frac{2}{3}x^{3/2}(\ln|x| - \frac{2}{3}) + C$ **29.** $\frac{\cos^3(e^{-x})}{3} + C$

30. $\ln\left|\frac{x-2}{x+2}\right| + C$ **31.** $-x^2\cos x + 2x\sin x + 2\cos x + C$ **32.** $\frac{1}{10}(\arcsin 5x)^2 + C$ **33.** $\operatorname{arcsec} 3 - \operatorname{arcsec} 2$

34. $\frac{3e^4 + 1}{16}$ **35.** $\ln 2$ **36.** $2\ln 3$ or $\ln 9$ **37.** $\frac{-1}{(x-2)} + 3\ln|x| + C$ **38.** $\frac{1}{4}\ln\left|\frac{4 - \sqrt{16 - 9x^2}}{3x}\right| + C$

39. $\ln 3$ **40.** $e^5 - e^3$ or $e^3(e^2 - 1)$ **41.** $\frac{1}{2}(e^2 - 1)$ **42.** $\frac{\pi}{4}$ **43.** $\frac{\pi}{6}$ **44.** $\frac{1}{2} + \ln 2$ **45.** 1   **46.** $\frac{\pi}{8}$

47. $\frac{1}{2}\ln 2$ **48.** $\pi(2\ln^2 2 - 4\ln 2 + 2)$ **49.** $\frac{\pi}{2}(e^2 - 1)$ **50.** $-\frac{4t}{3}\cos 3t + \frac{4}{9}\sin 3t + C$

51. $3\ln|t + 2| + 2\ln|t - 1| + C$ **52.** $\frac{e}{2}(e^3 - 1)$ **53.** $\frac{1}{5}\ln\left|\frac{x}{5 + 3x}\right| + C$; 5

54. $-\frac{\sqrt{16 - x^2}}{x} - \arcsin\frac{x}{4} + C$; 29   **55.** $\ln|2x + 6 + 2\sqrt{3 + 6x + x^2}| + C$; 47   **56.** $\frac{1}{5}e^x(\sin 2x - 2\cos 2x) + C$; 78

57. $\sqrt{4x^2 - 9} - 3\operatorname{arcsec}\frac{2x}{3} + C$; 33   **58.** $-\frac{1}{15}\cos^5 3x + C$; 73   **59.** $2\sqrt{9 + 4x} + 3\ln\left|\frac{\sqrt{9 + 4x} - 3}{\sqrt{9 + 4x} + 3}\right| + C$; 17, 15

60. $\frac{1}{5}\tan^5 x - \frac{1}{3}\tan^3 x + \tan x - x + C$; 85   **61.** 1.011   **62.** 0.155   **63.** 12.359   **64.** 6.489   **65.** 22.2

66. 0.96   **67.** 18.365   **68.** 5.608   **69.** 0.605   **70.** 71.632   **71.** 4   **72.** $\frac{3\pi}{2}$ **73.** 11π **74.** $\frac{\pi}{16}$

75. $\frac{\pi^3}{8}$ **76.** $\frac{\sqrt{3}}{2} + \frac{\pi}{3}$ **77.** $4\pi - 6\sqrt{3}$ **78.** $2 - \pi/4$ **79.** $4\sqrt{3} - \frac{4\pi}{3}$ **80.** $1 - \sqrt{2}/2$

81. 3   **82.** ∞ (diverges)   **83.** 2   **84.** -1 **85.** 2   **86.** ∞ (diverges)

CHAPTER 2

Exercises 2.1, Page 75

1.

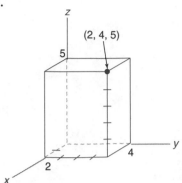

3.

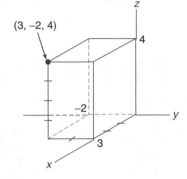

5.

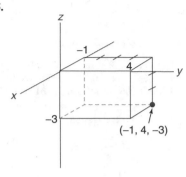

7. Plane

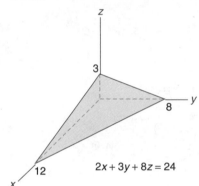

$2x + 3y + 8z = 24$

9. Plane

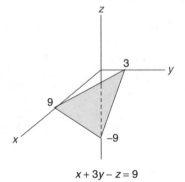

$x + 3y - z = 9$

11. Plane

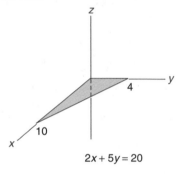

$2x + 5y = 20$

13. Plane

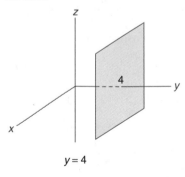

$y = 4$

15. Sphere

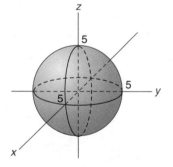

$x^2 + y^2 + z^2 = 25$

17. Sphere

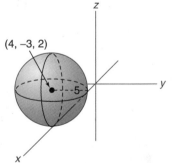

$x^2 + y^2 + z^2 - 8x + 6y - 4z + 4 = 0$

19. Cylindrical surface

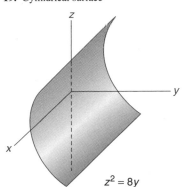

$z^2 = 8y$

21. Cylindrical surface

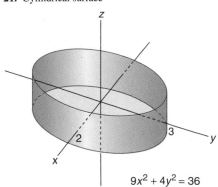

$9x^2 + 4y^2 = 36$

23. Ellipsoid

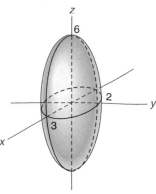

$4x^2 + 9y^2 + z^2 = 36$

25. Elliptic paraboloid

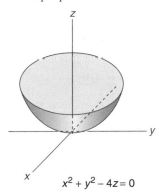

$x^2 + y^2 - 4z = 0$

27. Hyperboloid of two sheets

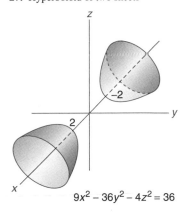

$9x^2 - 36y^2 - 4z^2 = 36$

29. Cylindrical surface

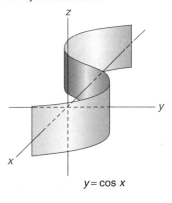

$y = \cos x$

31. Hyperbolic paraboloid

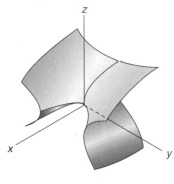

$y^2 - z^2 = 8x$

33. Elliptic cone

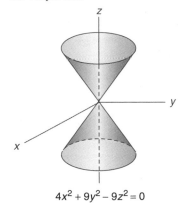

$4x^2 + 9y^2 - 9z^2 = 0$

35. Hyperboloid of one sheet

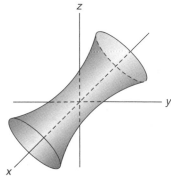

$81y^2 + 36z^2 - 4x^2 = 324$

37. $(x - 3)^2 + (y + 2)^2 + (z - 4)^2 = 36$ **39.** $(x - 3)^2 + (y + 2)^2 + (z - 4)^2 = 16$ **43.** 6

Exercises 2.2, Pages 78–79

1. **(a)** $12x^2y^2$ **(b)** $8x^3y$ **3.** **(a)** $12xy^4 + 2y^2$ **(b)** $24x^2y^3 + 4xy$ **5.** **(a)** $\dfrac{x}{\sqrt{x^2 + y^2}}$ **(b)** $\dfrac{y}{\sqrt{x^2 + y^2}}$

7. (a) $\dfrac{x^2 + y^2}{2x^2 y}$ (b) $\dfrac{-x^2 - y^2}{2xy^2}$ **9.** (a) ay (b) ax **11.** (a) $1/x$ (b) $-1/y$ **13.** (a) $\sec^2(x - y)$ (b) $-\sec^2(x - y)$

15. (a) $e^{3x}(y \cos xy + 3 \sin xy)$ (b) $xe^{3x} \cos xy$ **17.** (a) $\dfrac{e^{xy}(xy - 1)}{x^2 \sin y}$ (b) $\dfrac{e^{xy}(x \sin y - \cos y)}{x \sin^2 y}$

19. (a) $-2 \sin x \sin y$ (b) $2 \cos x \cos y$ **21.** (a) $xy^2 \sec^2 xy + y \tan xy$ (b) $x^2 y \sec^2 xy + x \tan xy$

23. $2IR$ **25.** $\dfrac{-E}{(R + r)^2}$ **27.** $\dfrac{R}{\sqrt{R^2 + X_L^2}}$ **29.** $2\pi E f \cos 2\pi f t$ **31.** $R_2 + R_3$ **33.** $\dfrac{-E}{R^2 C} e^{-t/(RC)}$

35. $Ee^{-t/(RC)}\left(\dfrac{t}{RC} + 1\right)$ **37.** $\dfrac{-X_L}{R^2 + X_L^2}$ **39.** (a) 18   (b) -16 **41.** (a) $\frac{5}{3}$ (b) $-\frac{12}{5}$ **45.** 96π cm^3

Exercises 2.3, Pages 86-87

1. $(6x + 4y)\, dx + (4x + 3y^2)\, dy$ **3.** $2x \cos y\, dx - x^2 \sin y\, dy$ **5.** $\dfrac{1}{x^2}\, dx - \dfrac{1}{y^2}\, dy$

7. $\dfrac{y}{2(1 + xy)}\, dx + \dfrac{x}{2(1 + xy)}\, dy$ **9.** 195 cm^3 **11.** 17 Ω **13.** -64.1 cm^3 **15.** Maximum, $(1, -2, 20)$

17. Minimum, $(1, 1, 3)$ **19.** Saddle point, $(1, -2, -1)$ **21.** Saddle point, $(3, 2, -5)$

23. Minimum, $(3, 1, -109)$; saddle point, $(-1, 1, 19)$ **25.** 10 cm $\times$ 10 cm $\times$ 5 cm   **27.** 10, 10, 10

Exercises 2.4, Page 92

1. 20   **3.** $\frac{17}{8}$ **5.** $\frac{14}{5}$ **7.** $\frac{2}{3}$ **9.** $\frac{1}{2}e^2 - e + \frac{1}{2}$ **11.** $\frac{244}{3}$ **13.** $1 - \pi/4$ **15.** 16   **17.** 2   **19.** 16

Chapter 2 Review, Page 94

1. Plane

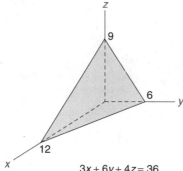

$3x + 6y + 4z = 36$

2. Elliptic paraboloid

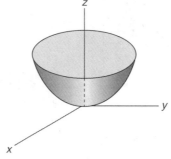

$9x^2 + 9y^2 = 3z$

3. Hyperboloid of one sheet

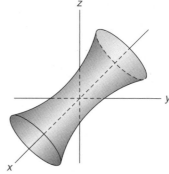

$36y^2 + 9z^2 - 16x^2 = 144$

4. Ellipsoid

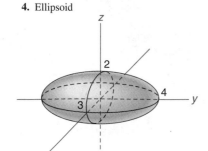

$16x^2 + 9y^2 + 36z^2 = 144$

5. Cylindrical surface

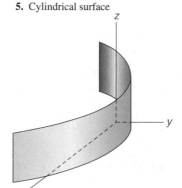

$x^2 = -12y$

6. Hyperbolic paraboloid

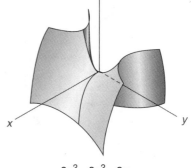

$9x^2 - 9y^2 = 3z$

7. Hyperboloid of two sheets

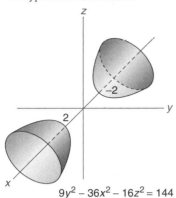

$$9y^2 - 36x^2 - 16z^2 = 144$$

8. Elliptic cone

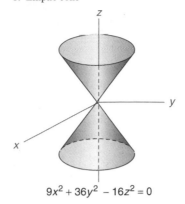

$$9x^2 + 36y^2 - 16z^2 = 0$$

9. $(x + 3)^2 + (y - 2)^2 + (z - 1)^2 = 9$ **10.** $5\sqrt{2}$ **11. (a)** $3x^2 + 6xy$ **(b)** $3x^2 + 4y$
12. (a) $6xe^{2y}$ **(b)** $6x^2e^{2y}$ **13. (a)** $2/x$ **(b)** $1/y$ **14. (a)** $3\cos 3x \sin 3y$ **(b)** $3\sin 3x \cos 3y$
15. (a) $\dfrac{ye^{x^2}(2x^2 - 1)}{x^2 \ln y}$ **(b)** $\dfrac{e^{x^2}(\ln y - 1)}{x \ln^2 y}$ **16. (a)** $\dfrac{e^x \sin y(\sin x - \cos x)}{y \sin^2 x}$ **(b)** $\dfrac{e^x(y \cos y - \sin y)}{y^2 \sin x}$
17. $\dfrac{-p^{1/2}}{2w^{3/2}}$ **18.** LI **19.** $\dfrac{X_C}{\sqrt{R^2 + X_C^2}}$ **20.** $\dfrac{rE}{(R + r)^2}$ **21. (a)** 8 **(b)** 2   **22.** $\dfrac{2x + y}{2(x^2 + xy)}dx + \dfrac{x}{2(x^2 + xy)}dy$
23. $\dfrac{2y}{(x + y)^2}dx - \dfrac{2x}{(x + y)^2}dy$ **24.** 452 L   **25.** 0.000666 A or 0.666 mA   **26.** Saddle point, $(5, 2, -33)$
27. Saddle point, $(1, 2, -7)$ **28.** Maximum, $(0, -4, 25)$ **29.** $2\text{ m} \times 2\text{ m} \times 2\text{ m}$ **30.** $\frac{1}{20}$ **31.** 516
32. $\frac{14}{3}$ **33.** $\ln \sqrt{2}$ or $\frac{1}{2}\ln 2$ **34.** $abc/6$ **35.** $\frac{2}{3}$ **36.** $\frac{4}{15}$

CHAPTER 3

Exercises 3.1, Pages 97–98

1. 17   **3.** 24   **5.** -95 **7.** 57   **9.** 202.5   **11.** -546 **13.** $2, -1, -4, -7, -10$ **15.** $5, 5\frac{2}{3}, 6\frac{1}{3}, 7, 7\frac{2}{3}$
17. 4   **19.** 1,000,000   **21.** $48,600

Exercises 3.2, Pages 101–102

1. $\frac{20}{2187}$ **3.** 8   **5.** $-\frac{1}{64}$ **7.** $\dfrac{65,600}{2187}$ **9.** $7\sqrt{2} + 14$ **11.** $\frac{341}{64}$ **13.** $3, \frac{3}{2}, \frac{3}{4}, \frac{3}{8}, \frac{3}{16}$ **15.** $5, -\frac{5}{4}, \frac{5}{16}, -\frac{5}{64}, \frac{5}{256}$
17. $-4, -12, -36, -108, -324$ **19.** $\frac{1}{2}$ **21.** $13,776   **23.** $\frac{3}{8}$ ft   **25.** 15.1°C   **27.** $\frac{14}{3}$ **29.** $\frac{8}{3}$
31. No sum   **33.** 6.25   **35.** $\frac{1}{3}$ **37.** $\frac{2}{165}$ **39.** $\frac{13}{15}$

Exercises 3.3, Page 105–106

1. $27x^3 + 27x^2y + 9xy^2 + y^3$ **3.** $a^5 - 10a^4 + 40a^3 - 80a^2 + 80a - 32$ **5.** $16x^4 - 32x^3 + 24x^2 - 8x + 1$
7. $64a^6 + 576a^5b + 2160a^4b^2 + 4320a^3b^3 + 4860a^2b^4 + 2916ab^5 + 729b^6$
9. $\frac{32}{243}x^5 - \frac{160}{81}x^4 + \frac{320}{27}x^3 - \frac{320}{9}x^2 + \frac{160}{3}x - 32$ **11.** $a^2 + 12a^{3/2}b^2 + 54ab^4 + 108a^{1/2}b^6 + 81b^8$
13. $\dfrac{x^4}{y^4} - \dfrac{8x^3}{y^3z} + \dfrac{24x^2}{y^2z^2} - \dfrac{32x}{yz^3} + \dfrac{16}{z^4}$ **15.** $-126x^4y^5$ **17.** $41,184a^5b^8$ **19.** $280x^3y^8$ **21.** $4320x^3y^3$
23. $-8064x^5$

Chapter 3 Review, Page 107

1. 47   **2.** $\frac{1}{16}$ **3.** -81 **4.** -62 **5.** $\frac{2}{81}$ **6.** 95   **7.** 300   **8.** $\frac{127}{16}$ **9.** $\dfrac{-80\sqrt{3}}{1 + \sqrt{3}}$ **10.** -348
11. $\frac{728}{81}$ **12.** 500   **13.** 1,001,000   **14.** $2988 (approx.)   **15.** No sum   **16.** $\frac{35}{6}$ **17.** $\frac{3}{2}$ **18.** No sum
19. $\frac{5}{11}$ **20.** $\frac{152}{165}$ **21.** $a^6 - 6a^5b + 15a^4b^2 - 20a^3b^3 + 15a^2b^4 - 6ab^5 + b^6$
22. $32x^{10} - 80x^8 + 80x^6 - 40x^4 + 10x^2 - 1$ **23.** $16x^4 + 96x^3y + 216x^2y^2 + 216xy^3 + 81y^4$
24. $1 + 8x + 28x^2 + 56x^3 + 70x^4 + 56x^5 + 28x^6 + 8x^7 + x^8$ **25.** $90x^2$ **26.** $1280a^3b^3$ **27.** $8064x^5b^{10}$
28. $3,247,695x^{16}$

Exercises 4.1, Pages 114–115

1. $5 + 9 + 13 + 17 + 21 + 25$ **3.** $10 + 17 + 26 + 37 + 50 + 65$

5. $\dfrac{1}{2} + \dfrac{4}{3} + \dfrac{9}{4} + \dfrac{16}{5} + \cdots + \dfrac{n^2}{n+1}$ **7.** $-1 + \dfrac{1}{4} - \dfrac{1}{9} + \dfrac{1}{16} - \dfrac{1}{25} + \cdots$ **9.** $\displaystyle\sum_{n=1}^{12} n$ **11.** $\displaystyle\sum_{n=1}^{50} (2n)$

13. $\displaystyle\sum_{k=1}^{n} (2k-1)$ **15.** $\displaystyle\sum_{k=3}^{n} (k^2+1)$ **17.** Diverges   **19.** Diverges   **21.** Diverges   **23.** Converges

25. Converges   **27.** Converges   **29.** Diverges   **31.** Converges   **33.** Diverges   **35.** Converges

37. Converges   **39.** Diverges   **41.** Converges   **43.** Diverges

Exercises 4.2, Pages 118–119

1. Converges   **3.** Converges   **5.** Converges   **7.** Diverges   **9.** Converges   **11.** Diverges   **13.** Diverges

15. Diverges   **17.** Diverges   **19.** Converges

Exercises 4.3, Page 121

1. Converges conditionally   **3.** Converges absolutely   **5.** Diverges   **7.** Converges conditionally

9. Converges absolutely   **11.** Diverges   **13.** Diverges   **15.** Converges conditionally   **17.** Diverges

19. Converges absolutely

Exercises 4.4, Page 125

1. $-2 < x < 2$ **3.** $x = 0$ **5.** $-\infty < x < \infty$ **7.** $-1 \le x \le 1$ **9.** $-1 \le x < 1$ **11.** $-\dfrac{3}{2} < x < \dfrac{3}{2}$

13. $-2 < x \le 2$ **15.** $1 < x \le 3$ **17.** $-1 \le x \le 1$ **19.** $-\infty < x < \infty$ **21.** $-\dfrac{3}{2} \le x < \dfrac{3}{2}$

23. $2 \le x \le 3$

Exercises 4.5, Page 128

1. $x - \dfrac{x^3}{3!} + \dfrac{x^5}{5!} - \cdots$ **3.** $1 - x + \dfrac{x^2}{2!} - \dfrac{x^3}{3!} + \cdots$ **5.** $x - \dfrac{x^2}{2} + \dfrac{x^3}{3} - \dfrac{x^4}{4} + \cdots$ **7.** $1 - \dfrac{4x^2}{2!} + \dfrac{16x^4}{4!} - \cdots$

9. $x + x^2 + \dfrac{x^3}{2!} + \dfrac{x^4}{3!} + \cdots$ **11.** $2 - \dfrac{x}{4} - \dfrac{x^2}{(32)(2!)} - \dfrac{3x^3}{256(3!)} - \cdots$ **13.** $-1 + \dfrac{x^2}{2!} - \dfrac{x^4}{4!} + \cdots$

15. $1 + 2x + 3x^2 + 4x^3 + \cdots$ **17.** $1 + 5x + 10x^2 + 10x^3 + 5x^4 + x^5$ (Sum is finite.)

19. $x - x^2 + \dfrac{1}{3}x^3 - \dfrac{1}{30}x^5 + \cdots$

Exercises 4.6, Pages 131–132

1. $1 - x + \dfrac{x^2}{2!} - \dfrac{x^3}{3!} + \dfrac{x^4}{4!} - \cdots$ **3.** $1 + x^2 + \dfrac{x^4}{2!} + \dfrac{x^6}{3!} + \cdots$ **5.** $-x - \dfrac{x^2}{2} - \dfrac{x^3}{3} - \dfrac{x^4}{4} - \cdots$

7. $1 - \dfrac{25x^4}{2!} + \dfrac{625x^8}{3!} - \cdots$ **9.** $x^3 - \dfrac{x^9}{3!} + \dfrac{x^{15}}{5!} - \cdots$ **11.** $x + x^2 + \dfrac{x^3}{2!} + \dfrac{x^4}{3!} + \dfrac{x^5}{4!} + \cdots$

13. $-\dfrac{x}{2!} + \dfrac{x^3}{4!} - \dfrac{x^5}{6!} + \cdots$ **15.** 0.743 **17.** $\ln 2 + \dfrac{7}{4}$ **19.** 0.602 **21.** $x + \dfrac{x^3}{3!} + \dfrac{x^5}{5!} + \cdots$

23. 0.041481 C

Exercises 4.7, Page 134

1. $-\left(x - \dfrac{\pi}{2}\right) + \dfrac{\left(x - \dfrac{\pi}{2}\right)^3}{3!} - \dfrac{\left(x - \dfrac{\pi}{2}\right)^5}{5!} + \cdots$ **3.** $e^2\left[1 + (x-2) + \dfrac{(x-2)^2}{2!} + \dfrac{(x-2)^3}{3!} + \cdots\right]$

5. $3 + \dfrac{(x-9)}{6} - \dfrac{(x-9)^2}{108(2!)} + \dfrac{(x-9)^3}{648(3!)} + \cdots$ **7.** $\dfrac{1}{2} - \dfrac{(x-2)}{4} + \dfrac{(x-2)^2}{4(2!)} - \dfrac{3(x-2)^3}{8(3!)} + \cdots$

9. $(x-1) - \dfrac{(x-1)^2}{2!} + \dfrac{2(x-1)^3}{3!} - \dfrac{6(x-1)^4}{4!} + \cdots$ **11.** $1 - \dfrac{1}{2}(x-1) + \dfrac{3}{8}(x-1)^2 - \dfrac{5}{16}(x-1)^3 + \cdots$

13. $1 - 2(x-1) + 3(x-1)^2 - 4(x-1)^3 + \cdots$ **15.** $-1 + \dfrac{(x-\pi)^2}{2!} - \dfrac{(x-\pi)^4}{4!} + \cdots$

Exercises 4.8, Page 137

1. 1.10517 **3.** 0.99985 **5.** -0.68229 **7.** 1.0488 **9.** 3.66832 **11.** 0.48481 **13.** 0.029996

1. $-\pi + 2 \sin x + \sin 2x + \frac{2}{3} \sin 3x + \cdots$

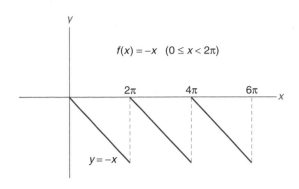

$f(x) = -x \quad (0 \le x < 2\pi)$

$y = -x$

3. $\frac{\pi}{3} \quad \frac{2}{3} \sin x - \frac{1}{3} \sin 2x - \frac{2}{9} \sin 3x - \cdots$

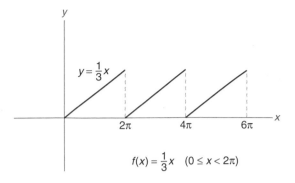

$y = \frac{1}{3} x$

$f(x) = \frac{1}{3} x \quad (0 \le x < 2\pi)$

5. $\frac{1}{2} - \frac{2}{\pi} \sin x - \frac{2}{3\pi} \sin 3x - \frac{2}{5\pi} \sin 5x - \cdots$

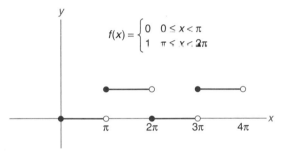

$f(x) = \begin{cases} 0 & 0 \le x < \pi \\ 1 & \pi \le x < 2\pi \end{cases}$

7. $\frac{4}{\pi} \sin x + \frac{4}{3\pi} \sin 3x + \frac{4}{5\pi} \sin 5x + \cdots$

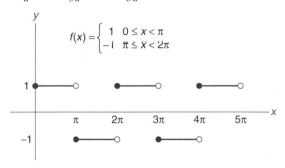

$f(x) = \begin{cases} 1 & 0 \le x < \pi \\ -1 & \pi \le x < 2\pi \end{cases}$

9. $3 + \frac{12}{\pi} \sin \frac{\pi x}{5} + \frac{4}{\pi} \sin \frac{3\pi x}{5} + \frac{12}{5\pi} \sin \pi x + \cdots$

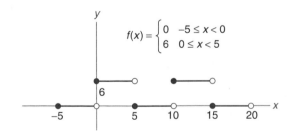

$f(x) = \begin{cases} 0 & -5 \le x < 0 \\ 6 & 0 \le x < 5 \end{cases}$

11. $\frac{\pi}{2} - \frac{4}{\pi} \cos x - \frac{4}{9\pi} \cos 3x - \frac{4}{25\pi} \cos 5x - \cdots$

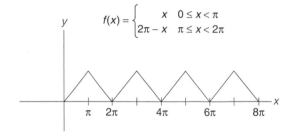

$f(x) = \begin{cases} x & 0 \le x < \pi \\ 2\pi - x & \pi \le x < 2\pi \end{cases}$

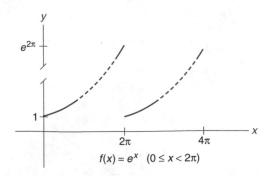

$$f(x) = e^x \quad (0 \leq x < 2\pi)$$

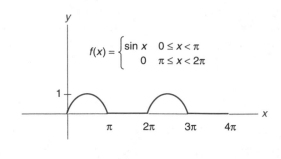

$$f(x) = \begin{cases} \sin x & 0 \leq x < \pi \\ 0 & \pi \leq x < 2\pi \end{cases}$$

13. $\dfrac{e^{2\pi} - 1}{2\pi} + \dfrac{1}{\pi} \cdot \dfrac{e^{2\pi} - 1}{2} \cos x + \dfrac{1}{\pi} \cdot \dfrac{e^{2\pi} - 1}{5} \cos 2x$

$\quad + \dfrac{1}{\pi} \cdot \dfrac{e^{2\pi} - 1}{10} \cos 3x + \cdots + \dfrac{1}{\pi} \cdot \dfrac{1 - e^{2\pi}}{2} \sin x$

$\quad + \dfrac{1}{\pi} \cdot \dfrac{2 - e^{2\pi}}{5} \sin 2x + \cdots$

15. $\dfrac{1}{\pi} + \dfrac{1}{2} \sin x - \dfrac{2}{3\pi} \cos 2x - \dfrac{2}{15\pi} \cos 4x - \cdots$

Chapter 4 Review, Pages 149–150

1. $-2 - 5 - 8 - 11 - 14 - 17$ **2.** $2 + \dfrac{3}{2} + \dfrac{4}{3} + \dfrac{5}{4} + \cdots + \dfrac{n + 1}{n}$ **3.** $\displaystyle\sum_{n=1}^{7} \dfrac{1}{3^n}$ **4.** $\displaystyle\sum_{n=1}^{10} \dfrac{n}{n + 3}$ **5.** Converges

6. Diverges **7.** Converges **8.** Converges **9.** Diverges **10.** Converges **11.** Converges **12.** Diverges

13. Diverges **14.** Converges **15.** Converges absolutely **16.** Converges absolutely **17.** Diverges

18. Converges conditionally **19.** $1 < x < 3$ **20.** $2 < x < 4$ **21.** $-\infty < x < \infty$ **22.** $\dfrac{11}{3} \leq x \leq \dfrac{13}{3}$

23. $1 + x + x^2 + x^3 + \cdots$ **24.** $1 + \dfrac{x}{2} - \dfrac{x^2}{8} + \dfrac{x^3}{16} - \cdots$ **25.** $1 + x - \dfrac{x^2}{2!} - \dfrac{x^3}{3!} + \dfrac{x^4}{4!} + \cdots$ **26.** $x + x^2 + \dfrac{1}{3}x^3 + \cdots$

27. $-1 - \dfrac{x}{2!} - \dfrac{x^2}{3!} - \cdots$ **28.** $1 - \dfrac{x^4}{2!} + \dfrac{x^8}{4!} - \dfrac{x^{12}}{6!} + \cdots$ **29.** $3x - \dfrac{9x^3}{2} + \dfrac{81x^5}{40} - \cdots$

30. $1 + \sin x + \dfrac{\sin^2 x}{2!} + \dfrac{\sin^3 x}{3!} + \cdots$ **31.** 0.09772 **32.** 0.09994

33. $\dfrac{1}{2} - \sqrt{3}\left(x - \dfrac{\pi}{6}\right) - 2\left(x - \dfrac{\pi}{6}\right)^2 + 4\sqrt{3}\left(x - \dfrac{\pi}{6}\right)^3 + 8\left(x - \dfrac{\pi}{6}\right)^4 + \cdots$

34. $\ln 4 + \dfrac{x - 4}{4} - \dfrac{(x - 4)^2}{32} + \dfrac{(x - 4)^3}{192} - \cdots$ **35.** $e\left[1 + 2(x - 1) + \dfrac{6(x - 1)^2}{2!} + \dfrac{20(x - 1)^3}{3!} + \cdots\right]$

36. $-1 + \dfrac{\left(x - \dfrac{3\pi}{2}\right)^2}{2!} - \dfrac{\left(x - \dfrac{3\pi}{2}\right)^4}{4!} + \cdots$ **37.** 0.5150 **38.** 3.3199 **39.** 0.18227 **40.** 2.024846

41. $-\dfrac{1}{2} + \dfrac{2}{\pi} \sin x + \dfrac{2}{3\pi} \sin 3x + \dfrac{2}{5\pi} \sin 5x + \cdots$ **42.** $\dfrac{\pi^2}{6} - 2 \cos x + \dfrac{1}{2} \cos 2x - \dfrac{2}{9} \cos 3x + \cdots$

$\quad + \dfrac{\pi^2 - 4}{\pi} \sin x - \dfrac{\pi}{2} \sin 2x + \dfrac{9\pi^2 - 4}{27\pi} \sin 3x - \cdots$

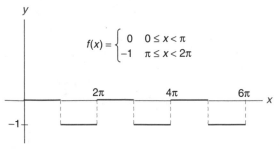

$$f(x) = \begin{cases} 0 & 0 \leq x < \pi \\ -1 & \pi \leq x < 2\pi \end{cases}$$

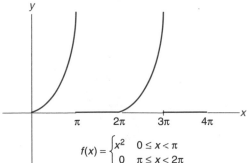

$$f(x) = \begin{cases} x^2 & 0 \leq x < \pi \\ 0 & \pi \leq x < 2\pi \end{cases}$$

CHAPTER 5

Exercises 5.1, Pages 153–154

1. Order 1; degree 1   **3.** Order 2; degree 1   **5.** Order 3; degree 1   **7.** Order 2; degree 3

Exercises 5.2, Page 159

1. $-\dfrac{1}{y} = \ln x - C$ or $y \ln x + 1 = Cy$ **3.** $y = \dfrac{C}{x}$ or $xy = C$ **5.** $-2y^{-1/2} = x + C$ **7.** $\arctan y = \dfrac{x^3}{3} + C$

9. $-\ln(3 - y) = \ln x + C$ or $x(3 - y) = C$ **11.** $3y^2 = 2x^3 + C$ **13.** $1 = 2y^2(\sin x + C)$ **15.** $2y + e^{-2x} = C$

17. $y = \arctan x + C$ **19.** $\arctan y = x + \dfrac{x^3}{3} + C$ **21.** $e^y = e^x + C$ **23.** $\arctan \dfrac{y}{2} = 2 \ln(x + 1) + C$

25. $(x^2 + 1)^2 = C(y + 3)^5$ **27.** $1 = (2 - x^3)y^3$ **29.** $y^2 = 2 \ln(x^2 + 1) + 16$ **31.** $y^2 = 2e^x + 34$
33. $x^{3/2} + y^{3/2} = 9$ **35.** $y^2 = \ln^2 x$

Exercises 5.3, Page 162

1. $3xy = y^3 + C$ **3.** $y = 5xy + Cx$ **5.** $x + xy + Cy + 3 = 0$ **7.** $x^2 = 4\sqrt{x^2 + y^2} + C$

9. $\ln \sqrt{x^2 + y^2} = xy + C$ **11.** $xy = x^2 + y^2 - 1$ **13.** $\arctan \dfrac{y}{x} = xy + \dfrac{\pi - 16}{4}$

Exercises 5.4, Page 164

1. $2y + e^{3x} = Ce^{5x}$ **3.** $14x^3y = 2x^7 - 7x^4 + C$ **5.** $y = e^{3x} + Ce^{-x^2}$ **7.** $3y = x^3e^{4x} + Ce^{4x}$
9. $y = x^6 - x + Cx^5$ **11.** $(1 + x^2)y = x^3 + C$ **13.** $5x^2y = x^5 - 35x + C$ **15.** $y = e^{-x} + Ce^{-2x}$

17. $y = 3x^2 + Cx$ **19.** $(y - 1)e^{\sin x} = C$ **21.** $y = e^{2x}(3e^x - 1)$ **23.** $y \sin x = x + \pi$ **25.** $y = \dfrac{e^x}{2} + e^{-x}$

27. $y = 3 - \dfrac{5}{x}$ **29.** $xy = x^4 - 10$

Exercises 5.5, Pages 170–171

1. $v = 5t + 10$; $v = 25$ m/s   **3.** $3xy = x^3 + 2$ **5.** $i = \frac{1}{2}(3 + e^{-800t})$ **7.** $i = 2 \sin 2t - \cos 2t + e^{-4t}$
9. $Q = e^{-1.54 \times 10^{-10}t}$ **11.** $Q = 5e^{-0.00293t}$; 237 yr   **13.** 72.9 lb   **15.** 24.3°C   **17.** 3.2×10^7 **19.** $P = CV^k$

Chapter 5 Review, Pages 172–173

1. Order 2; degree 1   **2.** Order 1; degree 2   **3.** Order 2; degree 3   **4.** Order 1; degree 2
9. $2x^2 \ln y = -1 + Cx^2$ **10.** $2 \ln y + 3e^{-2x} = C$ **11.** $2y^3 + 3 \ln(9 + x^2) = C$ **12.** $\tan x + e^{-y} = C$
13. $y = x^4 + Cx$ **14.** $(y - 2)e^{2x^3} = C$ **15.** $(y + 5)e^{1/x} = C$ **16.** $\ln(x^2 + y^2) = y^2 + C$

17. $3 \arctan \dfrac{y}{x} = x^3 + C$ **18.** $3xy = 7x^6 + C$ **19.** $ye^{3x} = e^x + C$ **20.** $4y = -4x^4 - 7x + Cx^5$

21. $y = 4x^3 \ln x - x^2 + Cx^3$ **22.** $2y \sin x = \sin^2 x + C$ **23.** $3x^2y - 10y + 2 = 0$ **24.** $y^2 = 3e^{-2x} + 1$

25. $4y - x^5 + 3x$ **26.** $xy = \dfrac{x^2}{4}(2 \ln x - 1) + 1$ **27.** $4y = e^{5x} - 13e^x$ **28.** $2y = x^4 - 10x^2 \ln x + 5x^2$

29. $i = 2 - e^{-300t}$ **30.** $Q = e^{-7.88 \times 10^{-10}t}$ **31.** 4.524 kg   **32.** 20.6°C   **33.** $y^3 = 8e^{x^3}$ **34.** $v = t^4$; 81 m/s²

CHAPTER 6

Exercises 6.1, Page 182

1. Homogeneous, 4   **3.** Nonhomogeneous, 3   **5.** Homogeneous, 2   **7.** Nonhomogeneous, 3
9. $y = k_1e^{7x} + k_2e^{-2x}$ **11.** $y = k_1e^{4x} + k_2e^{-2x}$ **13.** $y = k_1e^x + k_2e^{-x}$ **15.** $y = k_1 + k_2e^{3x}$
17. $y = k_1e^{3x/2} + k_2e^{5x}$ **19.** $y = k_1e^{2x} + k_2e^{x/3}$ **21.** $y = 2 + e^{4x}$ **23.** $y = e^{2x} + e^{-x}$ **25.** $y = 9e^{3x} - 5e^{5x}$

Exercises 6.2, Page 185

1. $y = e^{2x}(k_1 + k_2x)$ **3.** $y = e^{2x}(k_1 \sin x + k_2 \cos x)$ **5.** $y = e^{x/2}(k_1 + k_2x)$ **7.** $y = e^{2x}(k_1 \sin 3x + k_2 \cos 3x)$
9. $y = e^{5x}(k_1 + k_2x)$ **11.** $y = k_1 \sin 3x + k_2 \cos 3x$ **13.** $y = k_1 + k_2x$ **15.** $y = 2e^{3x}(1 - x)$
17. $y = 2 \cos 5x$ **19.** $y = e^{6x}(1 - 6x)$

Exercises 6.3, Pages 190–191

1. $y = k_1 + k_2 e^{-x} - \frac{1}{2}\sin x - \frac{1}{2}\cos x$ **3.** $y = k_1 e^{2x} + k_2 e^{-x} - 2x + 1$ **5.** $y = e^{5x}(k_1 + k_2 x) + \dfrac{x}{25} + \dfrac{2}{125}$

7. $y = k_1 e^x + k_2 e^{-x} - 2 - x^2$ **9.** $y = k_1 \sin 2x + k_2 \cos 2x + \dfrac{e^x}{5} - \dfrac{1}{2}$ **11.** $y = k_1 e^{4x} + k_2 e^{-x} - e^x$

13. $y = k_1 \sin x + k_2 \cos x + 5 - \frac{1}{8}\sin 3x$ **15.** $y = k_1 e^x + k_2 e^{-x} + \frac{1}{2} xe^x$ **17.** $y = k_1 \sin 2x + k_2 \cos 2x + \frac{1}{4} x \sin 2x$

19. $y = 2(e^{2x} - \cos x - 2\sin x)$ **21.** $y = \frac{1}{2}(5\sin x - \cos x + e^x)$

Exercises 6.4, Pages 198–199

1. $x = 0.167 \cos 8\sqrt{2}\,t$ **3.** $x = c_1 e^{-3.06t} + c_2 e^{-20.9t}$ **5.** 13,000 lb   **7.** 1.25 ft   **9.** $i = k_1 e^{-138t} + k_2 e^{-362t}$
11. $i = 0.136 e^{-140t} - 0.136 e^{-360t}$

Exercises 6.5, Page 204

3. $\dfrac{3}{s^2 + 9}$ **5.** $\dfrac{-4}{s(s-4)}$ **7.** $\dfrac{2}{s^3}$ **9.** $\dfrac{16}{(s^2 + 4)^2}$ **11.** $\dfrac{-s^2 + s - 2}{(s-2)s^2}$ **13.** $\dfrac{8s}{(s^2 + 16)^2}$ **15.** $\dfrac{s+3}{s^2 + 6s + 34}$

17. $\dfrac{8s^2 + 24}{s^4}$ **19.** $(s^2 - 3s)\mathscr{L}(y)$ **21.** $(s^2 + s + 1)\mathscr{L}(y) - 1$ **23.** $(s^2 - 3s + 1)\mathscr{L}(y) - s + 3$

25. $(s^2 + 8s + 2)\mathscr{L}(y) - 4s - 38$ **27.** $(s^2 - 6s)\mathscr{L}(y) - 3s + 11$ **29.** $(s^2 + 8s - 3)\mathscr{L}(y) + 6s + 46$

31. 1   **33.** te^{5t} **35.** $\cos 8t$ **37.** $e^{6t} - e^{2t}$ **39.** $e^{3t} \sin 2t$ **41.** $\sin t - t\cos t$ **43.** $e^t - \sin t - \cos t$

45. $2e^{-3t} + e^{-6t} + 3$ **47.** $e^{-5t}(3\sin 2t + \cos 2t)$

Exercises 6.6, Page 209

1. $y = 2e^t$ **3.** $y = e^{-3t/4}$ **5.** $6y = 31e^{7t} - e^t$ **7.** $y = \cos t$ **9.** $2y = 3 - e^{2t}$

11. $y = e^{-t}(1 + t)$ **13.** $6y = t^3 e^{2t}$ **15.** $y = (4 + 6t + \frac{1}{2} t^3)e^{-t}$ **17.** $5y = 3e^{-4t} + 2e^t$

19. $i = 0.6 + 2.4 e^{-100\,t}$ **21.** $i = 2.4 e^{-200\,t} - 2.4\, e^{-250\,t}$

Chapter 6 Review, Pages 211–212

1. Homogeneous; order 2   **2.** Nonhomogeneous; order 2   **3.** Nonhomogeneous; order 1   **4.** Homogeneous; order 3

5. $y = k_1 e^{-5x} + k_2 e^x$ **6.** $y = k_1 e^{3x} + k_2 e^{2x}$ **7.** $y = k_1 + k_2 e^{6x}$ **8.** $y = k_1 e^{(3/2)x} + k_2 e^{-x}$ **9.** $y = k_1 e^{3x} + k_2 xe^{3x}$

10. $y = k_1 e^{-5x} + k_2 xe^{-5x}$ **11.** $y = k_1 e^x + k_2 xe^x$ **12.** $y = k_1 e^{(1/3)x} + k_2 xe^{(1/3)x}$ **13.** $y = k_1 \sin 4x + k_2 \cos 4x$

14. $y = k_1 \sin \frac{5}{2}x + k_2 \cos \frac{5}{2}x$ **15.** $y = e^x(k_1 \sin \sqrt{2}\,x + k_2 \cos \sqrt{2}\,x)$ **16.** $y = e^{3x/2}\left(k_1 \sin \dfrac{\sqrt{23}}{2}x + k_2 \cos \dfrac{\sqrt{23}}{2}x\right)$

17. $y = k_1 e^x + k_2 e^{-2x} - \frac{1}{4} - \frac{1}{2}x$ **18.** $y = k_1 e^{3x} + k_2 xe^{3x} + \frac{1}{4}e^x$ **19.** $y = k_1 \sin 2x + k_2 \cos 2x + \frac{1}{3}\cos x$

20. $y = e^x(k_1 \sin \sqrt{2}\,x + k_2 \cos \sqrt{2}\,x) + 2e^{2x}$ **21.** $y = 4e^{2x} + 2e^{-4x}$ **22.** $y = 1 + 2e^{3x}$ **23.** $y = 3xe^{2x}$

24. $y = 8e^{-3x}(1 + 3x)$ **25.** $y = -2\sin 2x + \cos 2x$ **26.** $y = e^{4x}(\sin 3x + 2\cos 3x)$ **27.** $2y = e^x - 2e^x + 3$

28. $y = \sin 2x + 2\cos 2x + \frac{1}{3}\sin x$ **29.** $x = \frac{1}{2}\cos 4\sqrt{6}\,t$ **30.** $x = k_1 e^{(-32 + 8\sqrt{13})t} + k_2 e^{(-32 - 8\sqrt{13})t}$

31. $i = e^{-100t}(k_1 \sin 200t + k_2 \cos 200t)$ **32.** $i = k_1 e^{(-1000 + 500\sqrt{3})t} + k_2 e^{(-1000 - 500\sqrt{3})t}$ **33.** $\dfrac{1}{s-6}$

34. $\dfrac{s+2}{(s+2)^2 + 9}$ **35.** $\dfrac{6}{s^4} + \dfrac{s}{s^2 + 1}$ **36.** $\dfrac{3}{s^2} - \dfrac{1}{s-5}$ **37.** t **38.** $\frac{3}{2}(e^{2t} - 1)$ **39.** $2(e^{4t} - e^{3t})$

40. $\sin 3t$ **41.** $y = 2e^{(5/4)t}$ **42.** $y = 3\cos 3t$ **43.** $y = \frac{2}{5}(1 - e^{-5t})$ **44.** $y = \dfrac{t^2 e^{-2t}}{2}$

Subject Index